Here's a book to enjoy
before Your vacation so
You will find more than
Patpong, Harry's Bar and
Rome Club in Silom Road.
Have a nice one !!!
Bangkok 31 MAR 83
Klas-Göran R. Wass

© Apa Productions (HK) Ltd. 1982
All rights reserved.
First published 1977.

ISBN 9971-925-14-1 English edition, softcover.
ISBN 9971-941-54-6 English edition, hardcover.
ISBN 9971-941-35-X German edition, softcover.
ISBN 9971-941-36-8 French edition, softcover.

Library of Congress Catalog Card No. 79-113381

Printed in Singapore by Koon Wah Printing (Pte) Ltd.

thailand

Created and photographed by Hans Hoefer
Edited by Charles Levine
Compiled by
William Warren
Star Black
Robert Burrows
Jerry Dillon
Nancy Grace
Frank Green
John Stirling
Tony Wheeler
Marcus Brooke

This edition updated by
David Devoss

Published by Apa Productions (HK) Ltd.
Fourth edition January 1982

"I travel not to go anywhere, but to go," said Robert Louis Stevenson. "I travel for travel's sake. The great affair is to move." Well, yes, RLS has a point, nowhere more keenly established than in his *Travels with a Donkey*. But even Stevenson succumbed to the lure of a place — in his case, Samoa — and stayed; the great affair was also to sit, as though in a warm bath, and soak up deeply felt, pleasurable experiences.

Thailand put the same temptations, the same conundrum, in the path of the Apa Productions team in 1973: travel a lot, stay a lot, or both? The answer was "both", for to do justice to a country of such physical and cultural variety there could be no either/or.

Not that total immersion was any stranger to the originators of the Insight Guides series. *Bali* (1970), *Singapore* (1971) and *Malaysia* (1972) had all involved intensive travel, and intensive "soaking". The difference, this time, was the enormity of the challenge: a country the size of France (but nowhere near so compact, with a long tadpole's tail running south past Burma to Peninsular Malaysia) to be explored in every direction; a financial undertaking with only faith in the book's potential as collateral (earlier Insight Guides had been co-published or sponsored); and an awareness that much of Thailand was then completely off the beaten track in terms of tourist facilities and infrastructure.

The original team consisted of Hans Hoefer and Star Black, fresh from publishing triumphs in Bali, Singapore and Malaysia, and William Warren, a long-time American resident in Bangkok. While Warren honed his acute observations on the "City of Angels" and the complexities of Thai culture and lifestyle, Hoefer and Black made four long sorties into the country's hinterland, south, northwest, east and northeast, covering more than 30,000 kilometres on highways, roads and back-of-beyond tracks.

"We gambled on one major assumption," says Hoefer, "and that was that the sort of traveler or visitor we were writing and photographing for would be interested in moving around, in seeing as many parts and aspects of Thailand as possible in a given time. We knew it wouldn't be enough just to concentrate on well-trodden routes through Bangkok and places like Ayuthaya and Pattaya. We also wanted to dispel the myth that the Thailand depicted in *The King and I,* inaccurate as it was, was representative of Thailand as a whole. In early 1973, when we started work on the book, only a tiny fraction of visitors even went north to Chiang Mai. That's like going to Egypt and not seeing the pyramids!"

The intrepid trio gathered masses of facts, impressions and experiences. Notes piled on notes. But even this was not enough. More writers with first-hand knowledge of Thailand were brought in — Marcus Brooke, Robert Burrows, Jerry Dillon, Nancy Grace, Frank Green, John Stirling, Tony Wheeler — and under the eagle eye of editor Charles Levine *Thailand* took shape.

Several new features, then new to Insight Guides, were introduced and are still used. Each geographical region opens with a touring

Hoefer

Black

map on which recommended places of interest are numbered; these numbers appear again in the margins for cross-reference to the corresponding descriptive text. Location names in Thai script are also given to help travelers in areas where English is not spoken. In the margins are small maps of Thailand with a dot indicating the place covered by the text on that page. Captions, as far as possible, say where each photograph was taken, while the index-glossary is designed to make it easier to understand and locate the subjects written about and illustrated.

A certain audacity is needed in any attempt to summarise the allure and impact of a country in little more than three hundred pages. Hans Hoefer came adequately prepared for such a task. Born in southern Germany, Hoefer travelled extensively in Spain, Turkey, Jordan and Iran while gathering a handful of diplomas in printing, book production, design and photography at Krefeld, where he was subjected to the stern disciplines of the Bauhaus tradition. Arriving in Bali in 1967, he painted for a year before embarking on a project that was to change his life — the seminal *Guide to Bali,* first published in 1970 and the forerunner of the now internationally acclaimed Insight Guides, a series that has expanded since his sojourns in Bali, Singapore and Malaysia to include *Thailand, Java* (1974), the *Philippines* (1980) and *Hawaii* (1980), *Korea* and *Hong Kong* (1981) and *Nepal*, *Florida* and *Mexico*, scheduled for publication in 1982. Most books in the series have been translated into French and German, and some have also been published in Dutch and Japanese; *Bali* alone has sold more than 250,000 copies.

California-born Star Black received degrees in art and English literature from Wellesley before going to live in Bangkok, traveling extensively in Southeast Asia, and writing the first three Insight Guides. She has since returned to the United States, where she now works as a freelance photographer in New

Levine   DeVoss

York. She recently took the photographs for a book, *Texas Boots*, published by Penquin-Viking.

William Warren, one of the most knowledgeable *farang* (foreigners) resident in Bangkok, is a freelance writer and journalist. A regular contributor to Asia-oriented publications, Warren's books include *The Legendary American* and *The House on the Klong*, dealing with the life and art collections of Jim Thompson, the man who took Thai silk from village looms to the international marketplace.

Editor Charles Levine, who coordinated the efforts of *Thailand's* many contributors, worked with the Peace Corps in India for two years before settling in Bali (where he married a Balinese dancer) and subsequently working in Singapore as senior editor with McGraw-Hill and, later, Apa Productions. His expertise with the blue pencil helped mould the textual character of many Insight Guides.

This latest edition of *Thailand* was updated for us by David DeVoss, 34, the Bangkok bureau chief for *Time Magazine*. DeVoss' first assignment in Asia came in 1972 when he joined *Time's* Saigon bureau.

Later that year he was hit by mortar shrapnel while trying to enter the besieged town of An Loc with South Vietnamese marines. He spent four months in hospital during which time four operations were performed to remove metal and bone fragments.

Returning to Vietnam in March 1973, DeVoss covered the final withdrawal of American troops before taking up a new assignment in Los Angeles.

In 1977 DeVoss moved to Hong Kong from which he covered all of Southeast Asia. During the late Seventies he reported *Time* cover stories on China's invasion of Vietnam, the war between Vietnam and Kampuchea and the Khmer refugee exodus into Thailand.

During an 18 month period between 1979 and the middle of 1980, DeVoss made seven trips into Afghanistan. He was one of the first western correspondents to reach Kabul following the Soviet occupation. His final journey was with Islamic "mujaheddin" fighting in Kunar Province.

In January 1981 DeVoss moved to Bangkok, a city that he had visited nearly 50 times over the past three years. Though he continues to travel extensively throughout the region, his principle responsibility is Thailand.

Sincere thanks are also due to other individuals and organisations who contributed to the realisation of *Thailand*: the Tourism Authority of Thailand (formerly TOT, the Tourist Organisation of Thailand), the Montien Hotel, the Thai Consulate in Singapore, General E. Black, Per Bang-Jensen, James Stanton and Henry Aronson, and the many unsung people who made this book possible.

"For us, offering a guide is like showing a friend around," remarked two of our authors in 1972. That feeling has grown with time. *Thailand*, like other Insight Guides, has been produced with painstaking care to make it a worthy companion and aid for the traveler, photographer, student and stay-at-home reader.

Apa Productions

CONTENTS

Travel Formalities, When You
Arrive, Courtesy and Custom,
Festivals and Fairs, Shopping
Tips, Recommended Reading,
Thai Foods, A Thai Menu, The
Thai Language, Useful Expres-
sions, Hotels, Banks, Airlines,
Embassies

There are 13 maps and plans of the
major cities and regions of Thailand
included in the text. The 6 area maps,
outlined in red on this page, open each
travel section, to assist the reader in
gaining an overview of where to go and
what to see in the major geographical
regions. And throughout each travel
section, a small outline map of the
country appears in the margin, showing
which places are covered in the text on
each page.

THE THAI ADVENTURE

Background

Thailand's perhaps most celebrated landmark, pictured on hundreds of travel posters, rises high above the bank of the Chao Phya River across from Bangkok. From a distance, the towering central spire of Wat Arun, the Temple of Dawn, seems solidly coated with some strange glittering substance flashing like a gigantic jewel in the tropical sunlight. When examined closely, the imposing structure turns out to consist of countless bits of colored porcelain cunningly set in a vast mosaic.

A similar discovery lies in store for anyone who wants to get more than a distant, superficial glimpse of Thailand itself. Though unified culturally and politically, to a degree rare among the countries of Southeast Asia, Thailand nevertheless proves on closer acquaintance to be a kingdom of surprising diversity; and you are constantly being surprised by it the longer you stay.

For too long, perhaps, writers have emphasized the prettier, more picturesque Thailand, to the exclusion of almost everything else, and have been unable to resist such tempting labels as "The Land of Smiles." The description may be justified to the extent that Thais are remarkably friendly and more apt to smile than scowl on most occasions, sometimes even on solemn ones; but it is also misleading because it suggests that Thailand is an otherworldly Shangri-la where beaming faces flit charmingly in and out of the original stage set for *The King and I.* Such a preconception proves inadequate during one's initial encounter with Bangkok, where the fantastic temples and palaces of legend coexist with supermarkets, flyovers, luxury hotels, and air-conditioned shopping centers filled with every conceivable modern want.

Lying inland from the apex of the Gulf of Thailand, Bangkok — the country's international gateway, seat of government and monarchy, and booming metropolis — can also seduce the unwary into thinking that its highly westernized surface is an accurate reflection of the entire nation; yet Thailand is still basically a country of villages and towns following traditional ways; a full 80 percent of the population is engaged in agriculture. Tradition still exerts a powerful influence, even in the clamorous streets of the capital.

Diversity and a wide range of contrasts also characterize Thailand's geography. Within an area of 514,000 square kilometers — which makes the country roughly the size of France, or the states of California and New York combined — the landscape includes tropical rain forests, agriculturally rich plains, and forest-clad Himalayan hills. All these types of topography lie just 5° to 21° north of the equator, in the center of the geographical jigsaw puzzle of Southeast Asia.

THAILAND'S NEIGHBORS

Facts at a Glance

Area: 514,000 square kilometers
Population: About 46 million
Government: Constitutional Monarchy
Capital: Bangkok (5 million)
Peoples: Thai 80%, Chinese 10%,
  Malay 4%, Lao, Burmese, Vietnamese, Indian, others 6%
Religions: Buddhism 94%, Islam 4%,
  Confucianism 1½%, Christianity ½%

Highest Point: Doi Inthanon (2,596 meters)
Currency: Baht (23 baht = 1 US$)
Electricity: 220 volts AC

A closer look at Thailand's geography reveals a country that is richly endowed with natural resources. Under the canopies of its southern rain forests, a wide variety of flora and fauna abound: iridescent kingfisher, parakeet, pheasant, blue-tailed broadbill, flying squirrel and lizard, gibbon, dozens of species of snake, hundreds of species of butterfly, and nearly a thousand varieties of orchid. A cornucopia of fruits grows as well, wild in the jungles, or tended carefully on small family holdings and in larger plantations: nearly thirty varieties of banana and plantain, coconut, durian, orange, lime, custard apple, mango, papaya, breadfruit, jackfruit, mangosteen, rambutan, litchi, and *lamyai*.

In the North, Himalayan fold mountains crown the country at an average of 1,700 meters. In the teak forests covering their lower slopes, elephants move felled logs down the steep terrain to mountain streams, where they are lashed together into rafts and floated downriver to mills.

In the Central Plains from May to September, monsoon rains transform the landscape into a vast hydroponic basin, which nourishes an endless sea of rice, the country's staple and number one export. Through this region flows the Chao Phya River, carrying produce and people south to Bangkok, washing rich sediment down from the northern hills, and during the monsoon season pouring more water onto the rain-flooded rice fields. Though only about 300 kilometers long, the Chao Phya is Thailand's Mississippi, her Nile.

Across this landscape live Thailand's population of about 46.4 million people. Along with the ethnic Thais, who make up around 80 percent of the population, there are significant groups of Chinese (about 10 percent), Malays (about 4 percent), Lao, Mons, Khmers, Indians, and Burmese — reflecting this country's long and turbulent history at the crossroads of Southeast Asia.

Historical Sketch

Genial, hospitable, and tolerant though they may be, and gifted with a native charm that makes most visitors recall their stay with nostalgia, Thais have also fiercely defended their country's independence for more than 800 years. They can boast the distinction of being the only country in Southeast Asia never to have been a European colony. Nor have they yet been divided by civil war, as tumultuous as Thai politics can be. Their shrewdness at international diplomacy has won them the admiration of far more powerful nations, and they have proved themselves adept at absorbing outside influences without losing their essential national identity. All this requires something more than mere smiles and charm. To understand that "something more," it is necessary to have some knowledge of Thai history, for as in any country, the present has been largely shaped by past events.

Thailand today: shaped by the distant, legendary past

The beginnings are shrouded in legend and conjecture, but most authorities believe that the Thais as a race originated in China, probably in the province of Szechuan, and appeared on the Indo-Chinese peninsula around the first century A.D. They migrated over the centuries not only toward more fertile lands, but also away from their oppressive Chinese overlords — hence, perhaps, that powerful love of independence which is such an outstanding modern characteristic.

Thais were not the first people to appear in what later became their homeland. Thousands of years before, in prehistory, peoples whose

Bangkok's spectacular Weekend Market (previous pages) offers a colorful microcosm of Thai life and products, with a cross section of the city's population meeting to shop.

story is still being unraveled inhabited the caves of Kanchanaburi, near Burma, and the plateau around the present-day northeastern city of Udorn Thani. The discoveries in the latter region, particularly those in a tiny

Recent discoveries in Ban Chiang and a review of ancient history

village called Ban Chiang, have attracted scholars from all over the world. In what appears to have been a vast burial ground, handsomely decorated earthenware jars have been found, as well as sophisticated bronze objects that in the opinion of some archaeologists may even predate similar objects from the "Fertile Crescent" between the Tigris and Euphrates rivers. If so, the diggings at Ban Chiang will overturn many of the traditional theories regarding the origin of man.

People of Indian origin also came before the Thais, around the 3rd century B.C., and established a somewhat mysterious kingdom called Suvarabhumi. The enormous pagoda *(chedi)* in Nakhon Pathom, the largest in Thailand, was built over a smaller one believed to date from this little-known kingdom; and various objects showing a strong Indian influence have been found in the vicinity. More importantly, in terms of the development of Thai culture, it was to Suvarabhumi that the Indian Emperor Asoka (274-236 B.C.) sent missionaries to plant the seed of Buddhism, which later grew and spread throughout most of the peninsula.

Nor did the Thais come alone. Two other culturally important groups, the Mons and the Khmers, arrived on the scene to set up civilizations of their own. Mon influence is strong on the earliest Buddhist art of the country, known as Davaravati (originating in the 6th to 11th centuries), and through the Mons Buddhism took firm root in Thailand — several centuries before the majority

The earliest Thais appeared around the first century A.D. Before that, though, remarkably sophisticated prehistoric people inhabited the Northeast.

The brief but brilliant Kingdom of Sukhothai in the North marked the real beginning of the Thais as an independent nation.

of ethnic Thais had arrived from southern China. The Khmers, besides building Angkor as the most magnificent reminder of their own empire, played a significant role in the evolution of Thai art and architecture. At one time, the Khmers ruled a large part of what is today Thailand, and ruins of their temples can be found in many parts of the country; the best example, perhaps, is the recently restored temple at Pimai, near the city of Nakhon Ratchasima (Korat), which was once linked by a road to Angkor itself.

Thai settlers in their independent kingdoms of the North

The Thais first settled in the North, around Chiang Mai and Chiang Saen, forming themselves into principalities, some of which later became independent kingdoms embracing most of the area. The city of Chiang Mai was the capital of one of these kingdoms; and long after the main group of Thais moved farther down the peninsula to establish more powerful states, it continued to be ruled more or less autonomously, keeping a distinctive culture of its own.

Even today, for all the leveling influence of education and the mass media, you still notice a strong difference when you go from Bangkok to the North. The architecture is different, the temples having a decidedly Burmese flavor, and so are the dialect, the food, and the customs of the people. Even the girls are different, or so the vast majority of Thai men are convinced: with their creamy skin, soft voices, and gentle manner, the beauties of North Thailand are regular choices for calendar adornment and movie stardom.

The real beginning of the modern Thai nation was the brief but brilliant kingdom of Sukhothai, founded in 1238 not far from the modern city of Phitsanulok, in the

north-central part of the country. Sukhothai lasted less than 200 years, and only a collection of impressive ruins of its capital city remains today, but its influence on subsequent Thai history, both direct and indirect, was immense.

Camelot-like Sukhothai: the first Thai nation

It was in Sukhothai that the first really Thai style of architecture began to develop, moving away from the limitations of stone, the main building material of the neighboring Khmer empire, to start to create those great, soaring, multi-tiered rooftops — expressing joy and a sense of fancy as much as power and religious solemnity — that were later to become so characteristic of the country. The Sukhothai style of the Buddha image, with its enigmatic, elegant smile and elongated, flowing body, is still regarded by most Thais as being supreme in beauty among all the national styles. King Ramkamhaeng the Great, the ruler responsible for Sukhothai's glory — who occupies in Thai history a near-legendary place not unlike that of King Arthur, as Sukhothai itself shimmers with Camelot-like radiance — devised the first Thai alphabet and made Hinayana Buddhism the dominant religion. He brought potters from China to instruct people in the art of porcelain making. He also established the close, paternal relationship between king and people that characterizes the Thai monarchy down to the present day. It is said that Ramkamhaeng placed a bell outside his palace gate, and any citizen with a grievance had only to ring it to gain a royal audience.

Thailand abounds in idyllic tropical scenery, like this tranquil valley near Mae Hong Son (following pages), in the far North. Once remote, it is now easily accessible to visitors by road or regular local flights.

One of the most often-heard quotations in Thailand, which comes from an inscription found on a stone in the ruins of Sukhothai, gives an idea of why that vanished kingdom occupies such a high place in the national history: "This Sukhothai is good. In the water there are fish; in the fields there is rice. The king does not levy a rate on his people . . . Who wants to trade in elephants, trades. Who wants to trade in horses, trades. Who wants to trade in gold and silver, trades. The faces of the people shine bright."

Upon the death of Ramkamhaeng the Great, Sukhothai's decline

Sukhothai declined after the death of Ramkamhaeng, and in the later 14th century it became a vassal state of Ayuthaya, a rising, dynamic young kingdom to the south which was founded in 1350. Built on an island formed by the confluence of three rivers — one of them the Chao Phya, which flows past Bangkok to the Gulf of Thailand — Ayuthaya ruled for four centuries and achieved a splendor that was reported with awe by the first visitors from Europe, who reached the country during this period.

What is left of Ayuthaya today lies about two hours drive north of Bangkok. Going about its spacious ruins, seeing here a crumbled *chedi,* there a fragment of a Buddha image, it is difficult to believe that at its peak, in the second half of the 17th century, it was the largest and most magnificient city in the region, with a population greater than that of London at the same time. It had nearly 400 temples, in which Thai art and architecture reached their full flowering, glittering with gold and multi-colored tiles and mosaics; down its 55 kilometers of waterways moved the stately royal barges, carved in the shapes of fabulous animals, along with thousands of humbler craft; 47 kilometers of paved roads accommodated ornate palanquins carrying noblemen and massive war elephants with their jeweled harnesses; and 19 cannon fortresses made it seem — erroneously, as it turned out — as impregnable as it was impressive.

Ayuthaya: temples, canals, highways, heroes and heroines

The history of Ayuthaya teems with heroic deeds and colorful characters, forming an important part of the folklore of the country. There was 16th-century Naresuan the Great, a favorite of Thai history students, who was taken captive by the Burmese during one of the many wars between the two kingdoms and who, according to legend, won his freedom after a Thai-style boxing match with the crown prince of Burma. Naresuan returned to lead his people to victory over the enemy. There was a queen who rode into battle with her husband and, seeing that his war elephant was about to be attacked, drew the enemy to her own mount and gave her life to save his. And there was an enigmatic but remarkable foreigner named Constantine Phaulkon, a Greek, who first came to the East as a sharpwitted, ambitious cabin boy on an English trading ship and whose career would make a first-rate historical novel. After a series of adventures he arrived at the court of King Narai, ruler of Ayuthaya, where he rose with meteoric swiftness to a position of power and influence only just below the king himself. His fall was even more rapid: in 1688, following the death of the king at his summer palace near Lop Buri, antiforeign elements gained control, arrested Phaulkon on a charge of having conspired with the French to betray the country's independence and beheaded him.

After a series of weak kings, Ayuthaya fell to an invading Burmese army in 1767. They proceeded not

Thai art and architecture reached its highest peak in the magnificent capital of Ayuthaya, destroyed by Burmese invaders in 1767.

Soon after Ayuthaya, the Thai nation had a new capital, this time at Bangkok, watched over by the legendary and much-revered Emerald Buddha.

merely to loot the city, but to burn its temples and palaces and destroy the vast artistic treasure and nearly all the country's written historical

Burmese utter destruction of Ayuthaya, and the daring Thai soldier, Taksin

records, an act of vandalism that still profoundly shocks the Thais. (Even today, hardly a ploughing season passes in the old capital without uncovering some relic of this wholesale destruction.) Abandoned, the city slowly sank into the tropical vegetation for more than a hundred years; only in recent decades has a determined effort been made toward restoration, and at present the Fine Arts Department has an ambitious plan to re-dig the old canals and reassemble as many of the palaces and temples as possible.

The loss of Ayuthaya was a staggering defeat, one the Thais have never forgotten; yet within a few years an enterprising soldier named Taksin succeeded in driving the Burmese out of the kingdom and setting himself up as king in a new capital downriver at Thonburi, across from a prosperous little trading town called Bangkok.

Taksin's reign lasted only ten years, at the end of which he went insane and was executed in the manner prescribed for royalty — being placed in a velvet sack and beaten to death with a sandalwood club. His successor was King Rama I, a former military commander, who founded the Chakri dynasty which still sits on the Thai throne today; all members of the dynasty are given the title Rama, the present monarch being Rama IX.

A new capital at Bangkok for the new Chakri dynasty

The decision to establish a new capital at Bangkok was made partly for defensive reasons (it was thought that the Burmese knew the approaches to Thonburi too well), and partly because the first Chakri king wanted to have a new setting for his dynasty. Renaming the place with a long, resounding string of titles that begins with Krung Thep ("City of Angels") — the name used by Thais in their own language, though the older name of Bangkok has persisted with foreigners and mapmakers — Rama I deliberately set about re-creating the old Ayuthaya capital, still fresh in memory, even to the extent of enlarging and extending an old canal to join the bends of the Chao Phya River to produce an artificial island like the one in Ayuthaya. The original Grand Palace of Bangkok, of which only a small part remains today, was a replica of the one in Ayuthaya, and so was the new royal temple located in the palace compound — and called, in Bangkok, Wat Phra Keo in honor of the small but almost legendary Emerald Buddha, which Rama I had brought back from a military campaign in Laos in 1778 and to which he dedicated his new city.

The legendary Emerald Buddha enthroned at the heart of the kingdom

The little image of the Emerald Buddha — actually made from a kind of jasper — was discovered in North Thailand, near Chiang Mai, in the 15th century; after staying in several temples in the North it went to Laos, where it was kept first in Luang Prabang and then in Vientiane, until Rama I by force of arms brought it back to its homeland. Today, set high on a lofty seat, its jeweled robes changed seasonally by the king, the Emerald Buddha presides over a temple of incomparable splendor — indeed, over the whole kingdom, for it is by far the most revered of all the countless Buddha images in Thailand. So great is its power that anyone swearing upon it when making a statement would never dare tell a lie, and in parliamentary debates oppo-

nents often use this in challenging one another's word.

Today, amidst the traffic and the shopping centers, the broad Western avenues and the international hotels, what Bangkok must have looked like even fifty years ago, much less in the early days of the first Chakri kings, lies mostly beyond our imagination.

Early Bangkok: graceful rooftops, Venetian canals, dazzling royalty

A city of graceful Thai rooftops, of houseboats moored along Venetian canals, interspersed with sparkling temples and exalted by dazzling royal processions, early Bangkok vanished almost as completely as the ancient capital of Ayuthaya — the one swallowed by the 20th century as relentlessly as the other by the jungle. Yet traces remain: in some of the older areas of Bangkok, or along some of the few remaining waterways that have not been transformed into highways, you can find odd places where it takes no effort of the imagination to guess what it might have been to an adventurous European visiting Thailand in the mid-18th century.

The courtyard of the Temple of the Emerald Buddha is such a place, preferably visited in the late afternoon just before the lights are switched on, when the glazed tiles catch the fading sun, and a faint river breeze nudges the bronze temple bells. Or along one of the narrow streets that converge on the square of the Giant Swing, lined with low, fading Chinese shops, spilling treasures out onto the sidewalks. Or drifting in a boat along one of the *klongs* in less progressive Thonburi,

With Cambodia now lost to tourists, Thailand is the only country in Southeast Asia where one can see great Khmer-style ruins, such as these ancient mellow stones (previous pages) at Muang Tham, near the border.

where things are not quite so rushed and where clusters of the old houseboats float among pungent durian orchards.

Progressive Rama IV ironically portrayed as the despot of the *King and I*

The Thai ruler best known to a large Western audience (with the exception of the present well-traveled king and his beautiful queen) is probably Rama IV, or King Mongkut, though not many would recognize him by those names. Nor, perhaps, by the following, accurate description: a farsighted, imaginative monarch who came to the throne in 1851 after more than twenty years as a reformist Buddhist monk and who, voluntarily, even eagerly, opened the doors of his kingdom to new ideas in science, education, and historical research.

It is one of the numerous sad ironies of history that this altogether exceptional ruler should be famous not because of his achievements, but because of a fanciful book of memoirs written by a middle-aged English widow with a vivid imagination and a need for ready cash.

The lady in question, of course, was Anna Leonowens, and her original book was entitled *An English Governess in the Court of Siam,* subsequently adapted by an American writer, Margaret Landon, into *Anna and the King of Siam*, and finally, most spectacularly, into *The King and I* — gaining in sales but losing in veracity with each new version.

The idea of a prim Victorian Christian lady singlehandedly modernizing an oriental despot is obviously one that appeals to many people. The truth is more mundane, as it usually is. Anna did indeed come to teach the royal children, including the crown prince, who later became King Chulalongkorn; but she seldom saw the king because of the vastly complex royal protocol that sur-

Vestiges of early Bangkok still survive, along with fanciful legends like the one perpetuated in the popular but highly fanciful *King and I.*

rounded him in those days, and in any case, he had acquired his modern ideas long before she made her short appearance on the scene, mostly from books and from foreign missionaries he had befriended while a monk. According to contemporary accounts, Anna spent most of her time with the ladies of the British community, worried about dangers that did not exist, and suffered from acute homesickness. Back in England later, she took advantage of the then current vogue for memoirs of exotic places and stitched one together, partly from memory, partly from wishful thinking (plus imagination), and partly from an old book that dealt with events in Burma not Siam.

Thailand on the road to modernization under Chulalongkorn

King Chulalongkorn, once the little boy Anna tutored, sat on the throne for forty-two years, longer than any other king in Thai history; by the time of his death in 1910, the country had seen tremendous changes. He abolished slavery, reorganized and modernized the various government ministries, built railways to open remote parts of country, and embarked on a program of public education that resulted, after his death, in the first university, named after him. The first Thai king to travel abroad, he also sent many of his sons to study in European universities, and they in turn brought back more progressive ideas. During his reign Thailand lost parts of its territory — to the French, areas that are now in Kampuchea and Laos, and to the British several southern provinces — but escaped absorption into any of the European colonial empires. For all these achievements, Chulalongkorn is the most honored of all past kings; the anniversary of his death, 23 October, is a national holiday on which hundreds of students and government officials

lay wreaths at his statue in front of the old Parliament building.

The end of absolutism, the inauguration of experimental democracy

The absolute monarchy, which had ruled Thailand since the kingdom of Sukhothai, came to an end in 1932, when King Rama VII agreed to serve under a constitutional government. This king, however, abdicated a few years later, not because he opposed the constitution — he and his immediate predecessors had, in fact, been preparing the nation for democratic government — but because he thought some of the new leaders were misusing their powers; and young Prince Ananda, elder brother of the present king, was appointed as the ruler.

At the beginning of World War II, Thailand (or Siam, as it was then called) declared war against the Allies in an effort to prevent the country from being occupied by Japan, whose troops were using it for their attack on British Malaya. The then Thai ambassador to Washington, M.R. Seni Pramoj (pronounced "Pramot") refused to deliver the declaration on the grounds that it did not represent the will of the people, and this technicality smoothed the way for the country's early acceptance into the United Nations. Thailand emerged from the war economically intact, but severely shaken by internal political problems.

In the years since the war, the country's internal politics have not always been stable, nor has it been able to remain aloof from the upheavals in the world around it. There have been a number of constitutions since the first, plus 14 coups d'etat. In October 1973 students led a revolution in which, for the first time, widespread bloodshed in the streets of Bangkok accompanied the change in government. In late 1976, after further student demonstrations, the

military returned to power in an attempt to put an end to political instability. As a member of the defunct Southeast Asian Treaty Organization (SEATO), Thailand inevitably was involved in the wars that raged in the neighboring countries of Laos, Vietnam, and Cambodia. Today, in the wake of the withdrawals of United States troops from the area, Thailand tries to steer a more neutral course, seeking internal and regional stability and prosperity.

Politics, however, at least the democratic variety, grows as a frail flower in Thailand, having been allowed to bloom only intermittently since the 1932 revolution that ended the absolute monarchy and, supposedly, inaugurated constitutional government. Few democratically elected governments have survived for more than a few years since World War II, but the pattern is changing and politics as a profession slowly is attracting talented young Thais. Through it all, however, certain fundamental aspects of Thai life and character have remained essentially unchanged. Perhaps most significantly, the Thai people have kept their ancient reverence for their king who, whether absolute or not, is still a living symbol of all that binds them together. Thais have also kept their religious faith, which still pervades the national life from king to commoner and influences conduct in countless subtle ways that outsiders can never hope to comprehend. And they have kept their strong love of independence, that sense of nationhood which led them out of China, beginning two thousand years ago, and which has kept them united through many dangerous times.

All over Thailand, the traditional and the modern coexist in rare harmony, with the Buddhist religion continuing to exert a powerful and stabilizing influence in everyday life.

Portraits of Contemporaries

Even a cursory glance at Thai history, such as the one presented on the previous pages, belies any simplified view of the country and the people. In the following pages we try to capture the more ineffable quality of the character of the Thai nation through a series of portraits of Thai contemporaries.

Whether it is a young monk out and about modern Bangkok in the gentle light of dawn carrying an alms bowl; a chic Thai businesswoman closing a deal with her more traditional compatriot wearing a silk *pasin* (full-length wraparound); or King Bhumibol rushing back by helicopter to an upcountry summer palace after a royal visit to a nearby village school — Thailand sparkles with remarkable individuals.

The King: A symbol from the distant past; a man vital to the present

His Majesty the King is to preside over a royal ceremony at Wat Phra Keo, the Temple of the Emerald Buddha. The crowd has begun to gather hours before the scheduled royal appearance, representing every walk of Thai life — elderly country women with cropped hair and betel-stained lips; farmers in blue homespun cotton; students in neatly pressed uniforms; society ladies in Thai silk dresses; office workers from nearby government buildings; and children brought by their parents to see their ruler. A few moments before the appointed time, a perceptible thrill runs through the crowd.

It is not the first time most of them have seen the king, for within his kingdom he is perhaps one of the most visible rulers in the world — constantly opening fairs, presiding over ceremonies, handing out diplomas, dropping out of the sky in a

The monarchy plays a vital role in Thai life; here the King is shown at the investiture of the Crown Prince.

helicopter — yet the same sense of reverence and excitement grips his subjects every time he appears. Swords clank, the honor guard snaps to attention, the crowd draws its breath — and today through the ornately carved doors that separate Wat Phra Keo from the compound of the Grand Palace steps a slim man in an immaculate white uniform, followed by a woman of breath-taking beauty in a shimmering traditional Thai-style dress. Their majesties, King Bhumibol and Queen Sirikit, have arrived.

The king of Thailand is both a symbol and a man. Born in the distant past in fabled Sukhothai, the symbol has endured through wars and revolutions, the fall of dynasties and the smashing of traditions and governments, both dictatorial and democratic, and through times of tribulation and prosperity. While the idea of kingship has faded in most other countries to that of a figurehead, in Thailand it remains the most powerful unifying force in the country, respected by all groups. Pictures of the king and queen hang in almost every house in the nation; and at the conclusion of every movie, no Thai in the audience would think of leaving the theater before standing at attention for a portrait of the king that is flashed on the screen while the national anthem is being played. The one thing the tolerant Thais will not forgive is any remark disrespectful of the monarchy.

The man himself is as extraordinary as the symbol. He was born in Cambridge, Massachusetts in 1927, where his father Prince Mahidol of Songkhla was studying medicine at Harvard University. His father, a son of King Rama V, was later regarded as the father of modern medicine in Thailand. At Prince Bhumibol's birth there seemed little chance of his ever becoming king. Between him and the throne, according to the laws of succession laid down by Rama V, stood any children the ruling Rama VII

might have, Bhumibol's own father, and his elder brother Prince Ananda. But Rama VII had no children, and Prince Mahidol died in 1929. On King Rama VII's abdication, Ananda, still a young student in Switzerland, became king, though he did not return to his kingdom until after the war. In 1947, he was killed under mysterious circumstances in the Grand Palace and his younger brother, Prince Bhumibol, ascended the throne as the ninth ruler of the Chakri dynasty.

Over the thirty years since his coronation, King Bhumibol has proved himself a worthy successor to his celebrated ancestors. With his beautiful Queen Sirikit, he has traveled to every part of the country and played an active role in solving many of its problems. The spacious grounds of Chitralada Palace where he lives — the old Grand Palace is used now only for ceremonial occasions and state receptions — include experimental rice fields and a dairy farm where the king, at his own expense, tests methods to improve the country's agriculture. He also supports an extensive program of artificial rain making for the drought-plagued Northeast, as well as schemes for improving the lot of the northern hilltribes. In addition to all this, he and the queen take part in the innumerable royal ceremonies that punctuate the year — the seasonal robing of the Emerald Buddha, the various Buddhist holy days, the opening of Parliament, the Armed Forces Day parade, to name only a few — plus the handing out of diplomas at the universities and countless royally sponsored weddings and cremations. If the Thais revere their king traditionally as a symbol, they have also come to feel a similar respect for the present ruler as a man, a fact which makes

On October 23, the anniversary of King Chulalongkorn's death, Thais pay homage to the revered king's memory at his equestrian statue in Bangkok.

the Thai monarchy stronger now than at any period since King Bhumibol's grandfather, Chulalongkorn (Rama V).

Buddhism: A total way of being

A young Buddhist monk walks with grave dignity along a city street in the pale light of early morning, a saffron-colored cloth satchel over one arm, a brass alms bowl in the other. The total number of monks in Thailand varies from season to season, swelling during the rainy season, the traditional time for a young man to enter the priesthood for a period that may range from two weeks to six months. While in the temple, he listens to sermons based on the Buddha's teachings, studies the Tripitaka *or Three Baskets (the teaching of Buddha in Pali), practices meditation, and learns the virtues of an ascetic life free of material possessions. Like the regular priests, he goes out at dawn to receive his morning meal from the devout almsgivers who thereby earn merit.*

A Buddhist monk, according to one authority, "must not only abstain from stealing, lying and idle talk, taking life, indulgence in sex, intoxicants, luxuries and frivolous amusements; he must also obey no less than 227 rules that govern all the minutiae of daily conduct and manners. He can have no possessions except the yellow robe, the alms bowl, and a few personal necessaries." He eats only two meals a day, the first early in the morning and the second before noon.

For all its spartan life, however a Buddhist *wat* (or "temple") in Thailand is by no means isolated from the "real" world. Most *wats* have schools

The spirit of Buddhism is omnipresent in Thailand, most obviously in the thousands of temples throughout the kingdom. This serene image is in Wat Prasingh, one of the numerous temples in the city of Chiang Mai.

of some sort attached to them — sometimes the only school in the village — and except during the period of Buddhist Lent, monks are free to travel from one temple to another at will. Moreover, the *wats* are open to anyone who wishes to retire to them. Monks also play an important part in many of the rituals of daily life, such as the blessing of a new building, a birthday, or a funeral.

To people outside, the *wat* and its priests offer an important opportunity for merit making, which ensures them of greater rewards after death. This is of special importance to women, for though an order of nuns once existed in Thailand (and now and then you still see survivors of it wearing white robes), it was discontinued some time ago, and the only way a woman can attain spiritual advancement is through earning merit; for this reason, an unusual number of the people attending the sabbath-day sermons are females, usually older ones. Besides giving food to the monks, the most popular way of earning merit is to make some needed repairs on the temple or, even better, replacing an old and derelict building with a new one.

The great majority — about 94 percent — of the Thai people are devout Buddhists, but religious tolerance is (and always has been) extended to most of the world's other religions. In Bangkok alone there are over a hundred mosques, reflecting the powerful presence of Islam in the provinces of the South bordering on Malaysia.

"Thai religion is no fire and brimstone affair from the pulpit," writes Valentine Chu in *Thailand Today*. "It is rather a way of being and looking at the world — philosophical, mystical, sometimes baffling to the Westerner — that permeates every part of one's existence." And it is a way of being that is remarkably alive today.

The basic form of Buddhism practiced in Thailand is Hinayana,

also called the Buddhism of the Lesser Vehicle, which originally came from India. This is the same form practiced in neighboring Burma, but even a casual visitor to temples in both places will quickly perceive many differences between them; for as they have done with most outside influences — Khmer temple decorations and Chinese food, for instance — the Thais over the centuries have evolved a Buddhism of their own, suited to the Thai temperament. As a philosophy — as distinct from a religion — Buddhism has played a profound role in shaping the Thai character, particularly their reactions to events. The Buddhist concept of earthly impermanence, its idea of the absurdity of trying to establish certainties in an ever fluid existence, has done much to create that relaxed, carefree charm that is one of the most appealing characteristics of the country. Tension, ulcers, nervous breakdowns, and the like are not unknown in Thailand, at least not in places like Bangkok; but that they are remarkably uncommon is in no small way due to the influence of Buddhism.

Spirits: A commonplace belief

An old woman, kneeling reverently before a small spirit house, clasps her hands in the prayerlike gesture called the wai. *Before the house she has placed burning incense sticks and a wreath of sweetly scented jasmine: these, she hopes, will persuade the spirit to look fondly on her and grant her wish — to win a lottery, perhaps, or get a grandson, or maybe just have good luck in general. Though the Thais are mostly Buddhist, other, older beliefs — in*

Tattoos are regarded as an effective means of warding off evil spirits, especially in rural parts of Thailand. This friendly fisherman from Chon Buri, shows off the Ramakien hero, Hanuman.

spirits, in astrology, in good and bad omens — also figure importantly in their lives.

Nearly every Thai male, and a large number of women as well, carries some sort of amulet, usually on a chain around his neck. Some wear as many as half a dozen charms, to protect them from all sorts of hazards, such as automobile accidents, gunfire, snakebite, and almost any other disaster one can think of. In the provinces, tattoos are regarded as effective in warding off evil. According to official Thai chronicles, the first Thai embassy to France, to the court of Louis XIV, amazed the king by telling him they possessed a magic charm that rendered them immune to bullets. A demonstration was arranged, and when the French squad fired, the chronicles continue, their bullets fell harmlessly to the ground without reaching their target.

Astrologers today are consulted regularly in Thailand to learn the most auspicious time for weddings, important journeys, moving into a new house, and even the promulgation of a constitution. Auspicious wedding dates seem to come in groups, and sometimes for three or four nights running, every available hall and hotel reception room in Bangkok is booked for nuptial banquets.

Many of the Thai's non-Buddhist beliefs are Brahman in origin, and even today Brahman priests — coming from the approximately four thousand Brahman families in the country — have an important place in Thai religious life and officiate at a number of major ceremonies. One of the most popular and impressive of these, the Plowing Ceremony, takes place every May on the Pramane Ground across from Bangkok's Temple of the Emerald Buddha. To inaugurate the first rice planting of the year, a team of sacred oxen draws a gilded plow, seeds are symbolically sown (and afterwards eagerly collected by farmers to bring them luck), and the head priest, after complex calculations, makes predictions on the forthcoming rainfall and the bounty of the next harvest. The Thai wedding ceremony, too, is almost entirely Brahman; and so are many of the rites attending a funeral.

The Thai word for spirit is *phi* and the variety of *phis* is immense, particularly in the countryside, outnumbering, so it is believed, the human population manyfold. One, a seductive female *phi*, is believed to reside in a certain kind of banana and to torment young men who come near. Another bothersome one takes possession of her victims and forces them to remove their clothes in public. (For some reason, the most destructive spirits all seem to be female.)

Stroll through the residential areas of any town in Thailand, including sophisticated Bangkok, and you will notice that in nearly every compound there is a miniature house, generally set on a post in a site selected after complex astrological consideration. In ordinary residences the small doll-like house may be a simple wooden structure that resembles a Thai dwelling; in grander establishments, hotels, and office buildings, it may be an elaborate mini-temple, made of cement and painted and gilded. In either case, the abode of the resident spirits of the compound, who have it in their power to favor or plague the human inhabitants, is regularly adorned with placative offerings of food, fresh flowers, and incense sticks. If calamity or ill luck befalls the compound, it may be necessary to call in an expert (frequently a Buddhist priest) who will consult the spirit to determine what is wrong.

One of the most famous spirit houses in Bangkok is in the compound of the Erawan Hotel, at the corner of Rajadamri and Ploenchit Roads. This shrine, honoring the Hindu god Shiva, was erected by the owners during the construction of the hotel, after several workers had been injured in a mysterious accidents; but the shrine soon acquired a widespread reputation for bringing good fortune to outsiders as well. As a result, believers asking for special favors nowadays so crowd the shrine that the hotel has built a special courtyard around it, and policemen are on hand on especially busy days.

A less well-known shrine in the capital, but highly regarded by its followers, is accessible only through a narrow, unmarked gate in a fashionable residential neighborhood. Its offerings consist entirely of phalluses, ranging from small to gargantuan, sculpted from wood, wax, stone, or cement with scrupulous fidelity to life.

To the average Thai, there is nothing inconsistent about the intermingling of such practices and beliefs with Buddhism. Their broad, easygoing tolerance makes it possible for them to accept, or at least to absorb, all such beliefs.

The Thai Woman: Gracefully balancing tradition and modernity

A Thai businesswomen, small, soft-spoken, gentle-mannered is the antithesis of the Western "career woman." According to an old Thai proverb, "A woman is the hind legs of the elephant," and Thai tradition requires that she honor and obey her husband, deferring to him in all matters, large and small. As if to ensure that she does so, Thai law forbids her to get a divorce, or dispose of property, without his consent.

During the drafting of the 1974 constitution a proposal that for the first time equality between men and women be clearly spelled out (made

Traditionally, the Thai woman has been regarded as "the hind legs of the elephant." Today, though, many of them are as up-to-date as their Western sisters and the old submissive stereotype is fast becoming the exception.

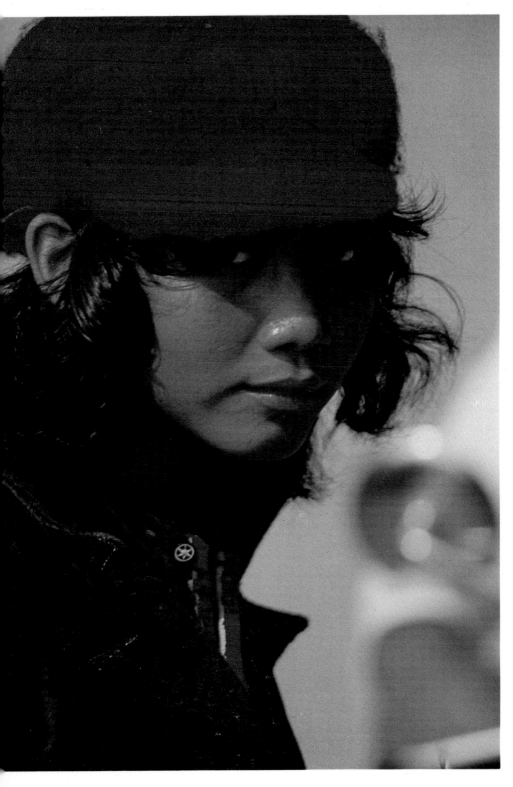

by the sole woman member of the drafting committee) was soundly defeated. From all this it would appear that the women of Thailand are sorely oppressed, and that a fertile field exists for proponents of Women's Lib. In truth, however, this is yet another example of how Thai appearances can be misleading; with a few activist exceptions, Thai women would be amazed at the suggestion that they are downtrodden, for they know just how much real power they have.

Without losing a bit of their feminity, almost without having to raise their voices, they have managed to prove that whatever their role in helping the elephant to move, it is at least as significant as that of the male's, and possibly more so; if they wanted to, they could cite another proverb: "All men are children, who must be cared for by their mothers."

The idea that the Asian woman is thoroughly subjugated and downtrodden probably had its origin in the old days of polygamy, when Western visitors were shocked by the seeming complacency with which the various wives accepted their relegated position within the family. But even then — in Thailand, at any rate — things were not quite what they seemed. The first wife often played an important part in the selection of the younger ones, and she usually got a number of more tangible rewards for being deprived of her husband's full attentions. In Thai family life today, it is the woman rather than the man who is more apt to be the dominant one, who handles the family finances and makes important decisions, although many Thai men scarcely know it.

If you rent a house in Thailand, you will probably pay your monthly check to a woman, no matter whose name might be on the title deed to the property; and if you move in business circles, especially in Bangkok, you will sooner or later have dealings with one of the famous "lady tycoons" who have been written about with wonder

by several American magazines. The oldest and largest bus company in Bangkok is operated by a woman, and so is the largest fleet of ferry boats that ply the Chao Phya River; so, also, are at least three of the largest hotels in the capital. Whether she sits behind a desk actively directing a business operation, or she sits at home and "helps" her husband, the Thai woman exercises a power that is no less real for being unwritten into the law of the land. Indeed, some of them would prefer that it remains that way. "I don't understand what all the fuss is about," one lady owner of a big Bangkok jewelry shop said during the drafting of the constitution. "It's better to keep things the way they've always been. If it's all put down in black and white men might start thinking about it and then they would lose face. Let them keep their little proverbs; it doesn't do any harm."

The Civil Service: Once the main vocation for the well-educated

A civil servant. You will see him (or her) whenever you go into any government office, or into any public school or university, for teachers in Thailand are civil servants, too, and come under the same regulations as employees of the Internal Revenue Department. The civil service also includes the employees of the various government monopolies and business enterprises like the state railways, the lottery, the tobacco monopoly, and the telephone organization. Altogether they number in the hundreds of thousands, after farmers perhaps the largest single work force in the country — a massive, often cumbersome bureaucracy that administers the kingdom out of Bangkok.

Restful spots like this square near Wat Suthat still exist in Bangkok, only a a short walk from the government buildings of the Thai bureaucracy.

Civil service pay-scales are much lower than those of business and industry (a university lecturer with a Ph.D from abroad, for example, gets less than US$300 a month), but there is never a shortage of applications for even the lowest positions. One reason for this is that government service offers great security; civil servants are almost never fired, except in cases of blatant dishonesty or corruption. Another, more important, reason is that government service carries a high degree of social prestige. The Thais do not use "civil servant" when translating the Thai term into English; it comes out "government official," a lofty designation that covers everyone from the prime minister down to the lowly clerk earning a few hundred baht a month for doing anonymous paper work in some vast Kafkaesque office. Dating from the days of King Chulalongkorn's broad reform of the government administration in the latter part of the 19th century, acceptance into the civil service has been looked upon as an honor, a dependable way of earning respect from those outside in society at large. For young women in particular it was one of the few socially acceptable ways of earning a living, for business was regarded as unsuitable for any young woman from a good family.

There is not much doubt that this is another aspect of Thai life that is in the process of changing. The traditional Thai attitude that business was an activity best left to outsiders, such as the Chinese and Indian newcomers, is fast dying out, if it is not dead already; and the cost of living along with expanded job opportunities are sending many who in the past would have become civil servants into advertising and airline offices, trading companies, or in the case of teachers, into one of the private schools that offer better salaries than the government. It would certainly be inaccurate to say that being a "government official" has lost its appeal for the mass of Thais, but it is no longer the main avenue open to the well-educated and the ambitious.

The Military: A sprawling organization, active in all sectors of the country

The Thai soldier, like the civil servant, belongs to a rather sprawling, complex organization, which is often misunderstood by visitors who compare it to armies back home. In many ways, of course, it is the same, in that it has the job of defending the country: and Thai conscriptees serving their obligatory two-year terms before returning to civilian life fill most of the lower ranks. At the same time, however, the Thai army — more so than either the navy or the air force (though the same applies to them to a lesser degree) — is far more intimately involved in the business and government of the country than would be the case in most places in Western Europe or the United States.

High-ranking military officers sit on the boards of banks, own hotels, take part in business — at the same time as they actively pursue a military career. This has mainly resulted from army rule of the country almost continuously since the 1932 coup ending the absolute monarchy. However, one must not get the wrong impression that civilian influence and position were achieved purely by the use of force by military men otherwise unqualified. In certain cases, no doubt, this has happened; but not nearly as often as outsiders might think. Actually, the military in Thailand, as in several other developing nations, has evolved — whether by accident or design — into a career not unlike that of the civil service, and is one of the few careers in which a bright but poor

The military, exemplified by this bemedaled guard of honor, offers a popular career to bright but poor young men who want to get ahead; the army is an integral part of Thai society.

young man can achieve advancement on merit. The military establishment is now such an integral part of Thai society that is difficult to imagine life without it.

Rural life: The backbone of the country

A phu yai ban, or Thai village headman, middle-aged usually, or older (experience and stability are counted as important qualities in a leader), must have a sharp perception of all the nuances of village life. Far more important to the villagers than the more modern government-appointed district officers, the head-man is the backbone of Thai rural society. Selected by his fellow villag-ers in an open election, the phu yai ban has a large role in village affairs: to speak for the village when negotia-tions are necessary with the outside world; to settle disputes of various kinds; to organize cooperative village undertakings; to listen; to under-stand. Most Thai villages, even those ly-ing a relatively short distance from large towns and cities, are remarkably insular; some have no electricity, and for many in the dry Northeast, the nearest fresh water may be an hour's walk away. Their concerns, like those of most insular people, are mainly inward and personal. When university students from Bangkok embarked on an ambitious "political education" plan in the countryside before the 1975 elections, some of them were surprised to discover that many villagers were totally uninterested in what was going on in Bangkok, and a number had no news of events in the capital or the country at large. An elderly couple from a village in the South, brought on

Farmers, like these taking a lunchbreak at harvest time near Phrae in North-Central Thailand, are still the backbone of the national life.

their first visit to the capital by their son who had made good in the big city, found only one thing that really im-pressed them in the noisy, confusing place: the electrically operated auto-matic doors of a department store. But even this turned out to be a some-what droll discovery, for when they returned to their village and told people about the doors, no one be-lieved them; one old villager had a good laugh at their story.

The land and the crops it pro-duces; the vagaries of weather; the local temple and the opportunities it offers for earning merit as well as the special pleasures of its fairs and cer-emonies; the strange spirits that lie everywhere in wait for the unwary; the love affairs and small scandals that provide occasional diversion from everyday cares; illness and death — these are the immediate concerns of rural life, as they have been from time immemorial. When one of the vil-lagers, generally one of the young men, leaves the village to try his luck in the city, his family views his depar-ture with a mixture of hope and sad-ness: hope because he may find a good job, in which case he will cer-tainly send money home each month; sadness because they know that a young man who leaves his village rarely ever comes back except to visit, and when he does he has changed beyond all recognition.

But the village and the *phu yai ban* will go on, as they always have; and as long as they last, so will the country.

Hilltribes: Seminomadic peoples living in the misty hills of the North

Wearing an enormous turban, a costume of heavy, shiny black mate-rial, and a large quantity of silver jewelry that flashes in the sun, a tribeswoman of the H'mong (popu-larly called the Meo), down from the hills for a look at the market of Chiang Mai, the nearest city to her

tiny hamlet, is an exotic, even a bizarre, sight in this otherwise wholly Thai marketplace. But no one pays her much attention; in the last decade the hilltribes have become a common sight in the cities of the North.

Approximately twenty distinct tribes of seminomadic peoples live in the mountains along the Burmese and Laotian borders of the North, and the tribes range from large, relatively sophisticated groups like the H'mong to tiny groups like the elusive Phi Thong Luang ("Spirits of the Yellow Leaves"), whose very existence was in doubt until an expedition tracked them down some years ago. Culturally, the tribes are of interest because their relative isolation has enabled them to retain almost unchanged customs and traditions that go back centuries. To the Thai government, they are a matter of concern because of their agricultural methods, which tend to deplete the land; their reliance on illegal opium as their chief cash crop; and their uncertain political loyalties.

For a long time, the main contact between the hilltribes and the outside world was the missionaries, mostly American, who elected to go and work among them, learning their languages and often living as far as five days' walk from the nearest civilization. As the government became more aware of the problems, actual and potential, presented by the tribes, it began to take more definite official steps; and now a sizeable tribal development program is underway. The king takes a personal interest in developing new crops for the tribespeople to grow — among them coffee, tea, and fruit trees — and the Border Patrol Police are establishing schools, while keeping the opium-rich

A girl of the Akha tribe, one of the several exotic hilltribes who inhabit Thailand's wild northern mountains. Basically nomadic, they are now being assimilated into the national life through novel programs.

area under surveillance. Moreover, the distinctive handicrafts of the tribes — encouraged first by the missionaries and now by Queen Sirikit's SUPPORT Foundation — are beginning to find popularity not only in Bangkok but also abroad, providing the hilltribes with another source of income.

The Chinese: Thailand's largest minority group excelling in trade and commerce

A Chinese storekeeper, sitting behind the counter of his miscellaneous-goods shop in one of the long, narrow, two- or three-story rows of shop houses that can be found in every town in Thailand. He lives with his family — a large family, usually — upstairs over the shop. Every day of the year he opens for business except for a short break at Chinese New Year, when the iron bars are drawn across the doors for two or three days and the family enjoys feasting, visiting ancestral graves, and the rare luxury of doing nothing.

Like every country in Southeast Asia, Thailand has had Chinese merchants since the earliest days of commerce. When King Rama I decided on Bangkok as his new capital, the site on which he wanted to build the Grand Palace was occupied by Chinese shops; he moved them a kilometer or so down the riverbank, where they settled and formed the nucleus of what is today Yaowaraj, the Chinese center of the capital. Throughout the 19th century and through the first half of the 20th, immigrants from China continued to pour into the country; only with the coming of the communist regime to mainland China did the flow turn into a trickle and finally stop altogether. As in other Asian countries these immigrants gravitated naturally toward trade — agriculture and government administration being already in the hands of the Thais. They opened banks, pawnshops, export-import

firms, and the innumerable little variety shops and restaurants that you find in even the smallest hamlet.

One thing, however, has long distinguished the Thai Chinese from their counterparts in most of the other countries in the region: they have been assimilated to a remarkable degree into the life of their adopted land. In part this has been due to deliberate government policy: all children, Chinese or otherwise, are required to learn the Thai language in primary school (Chinese language was not even taught at the university level until a few years ago), and the Chinese were encouraged, sometimes pressured, into taking Thai names if they wanted a passport, a government scholarship, or some other official document. Mostly, though, the lack of religious barriers, as exist in places like Malaysia and Indonesia, has encouraged Chinese and Thais to intermarry freely, so that today especially in the cities, it would be difficult to point with assurance to anyone and say that he or she were "pure" Thai. King Taksin who avenged Ayuthaya and established his capital at Thonburi had a Chinese mother; and most of the prominent Thai families have a Chinese branch somewhere on their genealogical tree.

The most outstanding result of this has been that the Thai Chinese have never really lived in an exclusive, separate world as they do elsewhere; even places like Yaowaraj, where the atmosphere is as Chinese as Hong Kong, have never been ghettoes, and the various Chinese associations are charitable rather than cultural in purpose. There is no deep-rooted anti-Chinese bias in Thailand, nor have there been any of the serious racial conflicts that have marred the

As this typical newsstand suggests, Thailand has a thriving communications industry, with dozens of daily newspapers and hundreds of magazines. There is also a large audience for popular novels on various subjects.

recent histories of neighboring countries. Only among the older generation will you find many people who think and speak of themselves specifically as "Chinese." The younger generation thinks of itself as Thai, if it considers such racial matters at all.

Literature: A testing ground for change

A popular novelist, a thin, rather intense woman in her early forties, the author of a half dozen successful romances, most of which have been adapted to the movies or television. All of her novels first appeared serially in a woman's magazine, and all appealed primarily to a female audience. A typical plot concerns a wellborn young girl who falls in love with a poor boy and is forbidden to marry him by her family; true love finally triumphs (after many chapters and many obstacles) as the boy at last convinces her parents of his sterling character.

Classical Thai literature, which mainly consists of the *Ramakien* (the Thai version of the Sanskrit epic *Ramayana*), folk tales in verse, and court poetry, is studied by university students, who also read some Thai translations of Western classics *(The Merchant of Venice* was translated by King Rama VI); but the general reading public prefers escapist, sentimental stories generally written by and for women. There are, however, a few exceptions to this rule, as well as some indications that an audience may exist for novels on more serious contemporary subjects. One of the exceptions is provided by M.R. Kukrit Pramoj, a versatile figure who has been a classical dancer, a movie star (he was in *The Ugly American)*, a newspaper editor, and a politician, and has written popular novels dealing with court life *(Four Reigns)* and with the struggle between Buddhism and communism *(Red Bamboo)*. Also several of the newer novelists have found a wide readership, especially

among students, for books about current social problems. In *Letters from Thailand,* a writer who uses the pseudonym of Botan, discusses the relationship between the Thai and the Chinese in Thailand and makes some sharp criticisms of both races. In *A Man Called Karn,* which won a SEATO prize and became a successful Thai movie, Suwanee Sukonta tells the story of an idealistic doctor who goes to work in the provinces and is defeated in the end by corrupt officials. Khamsing Srinawk, author of *The Politician and Other Stories,* is undoubtedly one of the best, if not the best, contemporary short-story writers in Thailand. The popularity of these and other similar works of literature in recent years has pointed out new directions to Thai writers and may lead to a literature that reflects the reality as opposed to the daydreams of the country.

The Movies: A kaleidoscope of Thai myth and legend

A Thai movie star, like movie stars everywhere, represents an ideal, a dream, of beauty rather than the reality commonly seen. She has pale, flawless skin and an artfully made-up face; she speaks in a soft, almost childlike voice, often hardly more than a whisper; her clothes are the latest fashion, and her jewels look expensive; she manages, somehow, to suggest purity and the promise of sex at the same time. She can be seen usually smiling demurely throughout the kingdom on calendars and on gigantic advertising billboards. At any given time she is making an average of ten movies simultaneously, playing more or less the same role in all of them.

Few foreign visitors go to see a Thai movie during their stay. This is

Mammoth movie billboards like this one are a common sight in Thailand, achieving what some foreign experts consider a unique form of pop art.

understandable in view of the language barrier, but it is also unfortunate, for popular arts like the movies reveal much about the contemporary culture and tastes of their country. There are five major movie studios in Thailand, all of them in Bangkok, and they produce several hundred films a year; though they have a larger audience in the capital than one might think considering the number of Western films being shown there, their greatest popularity is in the provinces, where the average price of a ticket is only five to ten baht and movies are the major entertainment.

Until fairly recently, most Thai movies were silent 16 mm films and the sound was provided by narrators — often a *single* narrator — who stood near the screen and spoke all the parts, or else recorded them on tape for distribution with the movie; as the narrators frequently had strong personalities of their own, people paid as much to hear them as to see the stars. In the last seven or eight years, however, more and more Thai movies have been made in 35 mm with sound track: producers have adopted the more sophisticated moviemaking techniques of the West; and a few directors have even experimented with departures from the tried-and-true story formulas of the past. But only a few, for the Thai-film audience knows what it wants.

To begin with, it wants familiar faces, the same stars over and over again, playing predictable roles. The two leading superstars of the present, Naowarat and Sorapong (their last names are rarely used, the first being sufficient to identify them) have been superstars for many years; they make twenty to thirty movies a year, usually together. Audiences also want the same stories, with only slight variations. The Cinderella theme is highly popular; poor girl (or boy) meets bright boy (or girl), encounters many difficulties along the way, finally gets him (or her) at the end when all the misunderstandings are cleared away.

Another popular story is the poor boy from the country who comes to the wicked city, is subjected to all sorts of temptations (usually sexual), finally settles for the virtuous girl who has loved him all along. Ghost stories, the gorier the better, are also favorites with Thai movie-goers. No matter how sad the theme, Thai audiences also insist on comic relief, and there are several slapstick comedians who are as much in demand as the superstars; and a good deal of singing and folk dancing is also considered a powerful asset. Finally, they want their money's worth in length — two and a half hours is common for a Thai film, and many go for three or more.

Whether they go to Thai or Western films, Thais have similar tastes; a foreign movie that is too "talky" or slow moving will have a short run, while comedies, musicals, and cowboy films attract large crowds. The two most popular western movies ever shown in Thailand have been *The Sound of Music* and *The Deer Hunter*.

Traditional Dance: The classical epitome

A group of students of Thai classical dance solemnly practice the complicated movements essential to this ancient form of theater. Most of them are girls, for traditionally the masked khon dances were performed only by women in the inner court of the Royal Palace where no men were allowed, although nowadays young men also take part, especially in such athletic roles as Hanuman, the white monkey god. The students training in the school are also mostly young, for after a certain age it is difficult to train the body to do some of the contortions by which a dancer is judged; the fingers, for example, must be able to bend gracefully backward almost to the wrist.

In a *khon* performance, masks, heavy makeup, and elaborate jeweled costumes and headdress subordinate and hide the individual personality of the dancer; to purists, it is a cardinal sin to smile or otherwise indicate the human being behind the role. Every gesture is highly stylized, immediately recognizable to a connoisseur though often not to an outsider; and a full-length performance can last for as long as eight hours.

The *khon* has never been an art form for the masses. Born in the royal palaces, and for many centuries only performed there, the *khon* was created for the pleasure of the king. It lives today in Thailand largely through the efforts of the Fine Arts Department, which has a school for training dancers and sponsors occasional performances at the National Theater in Bangkok. The excerpts presented at certain tourist restaurants are, like the Thai food served, but pale imitations of the originals, but worth seeing if only for the costumes.

Two more popular dance forms with the general Thai public are *lakhon*, which uses no masks and in which the movements are somewhat less stylized; and the *likay*, which might be described as a burlesque form of the classical dance, relying heavily on pitfalls and bawdy lyrics. A prominent feature of almost every provincial Thai fair, *likay* occupies a place roughly analogous to popular folk singing in the West. In the early part of the evening, low comedy fills the stage, but once the children have been put safely to bed, sex comes to the fore in a flurry of puns and double entendres which can keep the show going and the audiences wide awake until the wee hours of the morning.

The spectacular costumes and angular yet sinuous movements of the Thai classical dance are still a prominent part of the national culture; once only for royalty, the dances are now performed at the National Theater.

BANGKOK AND SURROUNDINGS

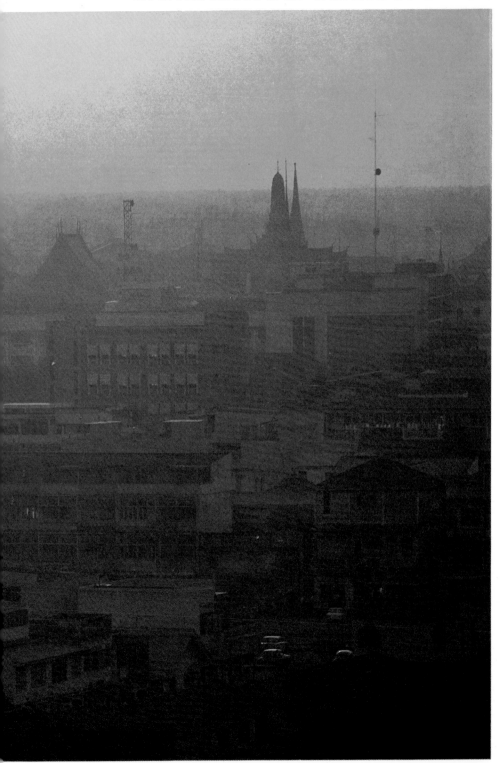

A City of Many Faces

Some cities are easy: after only a few days you have a clear sense of their design, their personality, and you do not hesitate to set out boldly on explorations. Others are less accesible: they sprawl they are confusing, and they seem to have not one but a dozen personalities, often contrary. Almost every visitor without hesitation would put Bangkok in the second category. For this metropolis of over five million appears at first glance to be a bewildering conglomeration of new and old, East and West, serenity and chaos, the exotic and the commonplace — all thrown together haphazardly into a gigantic urban stew following no apparent recipe. Lying roughly midway between Taipei and New Delhi, Bangkok for several decades has also been at the hub of airline routes through South Asia, adding to its vitality.

You can stand at one moment in a hushed temple courtyard, lulled by the rhythmic chanting of priests and the silvery tinkle of bells, and at the next, risk life and limb crossing a street down which hurtles some of the most lethal traffic in Asia. You can start out with the most up-to-date city map and find yourself on streets that do not exist (at least on the map) — not little, unimportant streets either, but major thoroughfares, lined with shops that look as if they have been there for years.

Bangkok is not an orderly city. It never really has been during the present century, not even in what old

The spires of the Grand Palace glow in the evening light (previous pages), giving Bangkok an air of tranquillity that is belied by its sometimes chaotic traffic, which the policeman on the right tries to direct.

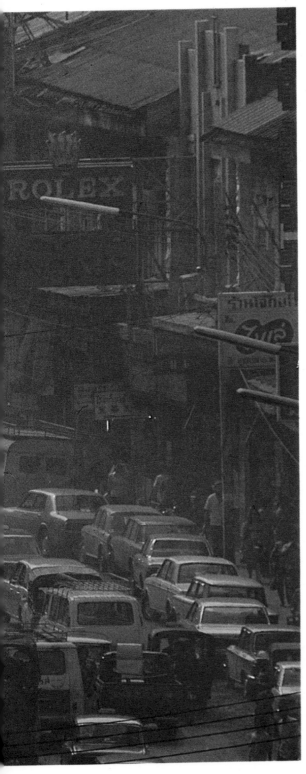

timers nostalgically look back on as "the good old days," by which they mean twenty-odd years ago when there were as many pedicabs as automobiles, when many of today's avenues were narrow lanes bordered by *klong*s however smelly, and when going across town did not assume the proportions of a major expedition. Life may have been more leisurely in those days, but even so Bangkok was a city that had developed more by whim and historical vicissitude than by design, here spilling over into rice fields, there leaving almost untouched a scene from the 19th century. And even then the "center" of Bangkok depended on who you were — government official or Chinese businessman, military or civilian, tourist or resident, rich or poor.

The biggest, most disorderly building boom in Bangkok's history started in the late 1950s, and a large part of what strikes the eye most forcibly today has appeared since then: the lofty office buildings, the air-conditioned supermarkets and shopping centers, nearly all the broad streets, movie theaters, and international hotels, the endless blocks of row shops following what one critic called the "egg-crate principle of design." Before the boom the now fashionable residential streets on either side of Sukhumvit Road were mostly agricultural; you could go by boat along Rama IV Road from where the Dusit Thani Hotel now stands to the river, and the newly built Erawan Hotel was regarded as rather inconveniently located on the city's outskirts.

After the boom, it seemed to some, a whole new Bangkok had emerged; and yet there were large areas around the old Grand Palace, in the Chinese district, and across the

A typical scene along crowded Yaowaraj Road, the heart of Bangkok's teeming Chinese district; except for the traffic, it still looks today very much as it did fifty years ago.

river in Thonburi (now included in the Greater Bangkok Metropolitan Area) that were hardly touched by the building fever, and still looked almost exactly as they did fifty years ago.

Today about one out of every ten Thais lives in Bangkok. About 90 percent of all the automobiles in the country are registered there. The metropolitan area is more than forty times larger than Chiang Mai, Thailand's second city. At least 65-percent of Bangkok's population is of Chinese descent. The population has grown five-fold since World War II. About 80 percent of the country's university students study there, and the monarchy has reigned there for 200 years.

To many lovers of Bangkok, it is precisely its vital, changing, clashing, unpredictable nature that gives the city its special flavor. Quite apart from its celebrated tourist attractions, you are constantly being confronted, and sometimes amused, by unexpected sights: a narrow *klong* of soothing tranquillity, meandering in the shadow of a 400-room, supermodern hotel; a leafy tropical garden with full-sized trees and an elegant little Chinese pagoda on the roof of an otherwise commonplace row shop; a slightly derelict but still noble Victorian palace, with turrets and gingerbread, behind a cinema; a barbershop whimsically called the Darling and a restaurant the Puberty; an old woman calmly stringing ropes of jasmine blossoms on a busy sidewalk; a mammoth standing Buddha, three storys high, inadvertently glimpsed between two glass-and-cement office blocks; an apartment house built entirely in circles; a little Greek temple in the grounds of a hospital once the palace of a crown prince; a short-time hotel called the Bungalow Home Fun; a group of street urchins moving like ballet

Draped in a monk's robes and honored with offerings of flowers, this figure adorns the famous Wat Phra Keo.

dancers as they kick a rattan ball from one to another with the side of their feet; a vast movie poster in which a smiling woman's entrails spill down the side of a building; thousands of migratory swallows roosting unperturbed over one of the noisiest streets in the city; Thai classical dancers in the sunlight, on a velvet green lawn at a tea party. All in Bangkok.

* * *

As a possibly helpful clue to getting your bearings in the sprawl of present-day Bangkok, think of it as being roughly (very roughly) divided up as given below.

1. *Early Royal Bangkok*: The area around the Grand Palace, including Wat Phra Keo, Wat Po, Sanam Luang, Wat Suthat, Wat Rajabopitr, the Giant Swing.

2. *Later Royal Bangkok:* Chitralada Palace (the residence of the present king), the Marble Temple, Parliament, Dusit Zoo.

3. *Military Bangkok:* Actually a part of No. 2, the military having taken over many of the palaces and government offices built during the latter part of Rama V's reign in the Dusit area.

4. *Chinese Bangkok:* Yaowaraj Road and surrounding districts.

5. *Old Tourist Bangkok*: New Road, the Oriental Hotel, lower Suriwong and Silom Roads.

6. *New Tourist Bangkok*: Upper Silom and Suriwong Roads, around the Dusit Thani Hotel; Rajprasong, around the Erawan and President Hotels.

7. *New Residential Bangkok*: The streets leading off both sides of Sukhumvit Road, all the way to Prakanong and beyond.

8. *Even Newer Residential Bangkok:* Vast middle- and upper-income housing estates on the New Petchburi Road and on the superhighway leading north from the city.

9. *Principal Thai Markets*: Pratunam, Bangrak, Thevet, Klong Toey, to mention some of the largest.

Key to Touring Bangkok

1. Lakmuang
2. Grand Palace
3. Wat Phra Keo
4. Sanam Luang (Pramane Ground)
5. Royal Hotel
6. National Museum
7. Thammasat University
8. National Library
9. Silapakorn University (Fine Arts)
10. Wat Mahathat
11. National Theatre & Nattasin
12. Wat Po
13. Wat Rajabopitr
14. Giant Swing & Wat Suthat
15. Chalerm Thai Theater
16. Golden Mount & Wat Sakhet
17. Wat Rachanada & Amulet Market
18. National Assembly
19. Khao Din (Dusit) Zoo
20. Chitralada Palace
21. Amporn Gardens
22. Royal Turf Club
23. Wat Benchamabopit or Marble Temple
24. Chinatown, Heart of
25. Pahurat Cloth Market
26. Nakorn Kasem or Thieves Market
27. Wat Trimitr (Golden Buddha)
28. Hindu Temple
29. Bangkrak Market
30. Siam Center
31. Siam Square
32. Wat Pathum Wan
33. Royal Bangkok Sports Club
34. Chulalongkorn University
35. Erawan Shrine
36. Rajprasong (Gaysorn) Area
37. Pratunam Market
38. Snake Farm & Pasteur Institute
39. Suan Pakkard Palace
40. Flower Market
41. Jim Thompson's House
42. National Stadium
43. Wat Arun
44. Royal Barges
45. Lumpini Stadium
46. Lumpini Park

Boat Tours   Hotel   Embassy

Map not drawn to scale,

The Inner City

Look at any map of Bangkok. Locate the Grand Palace, Wat Phra Keo (Temple of the Emerald Buddha), and the broad expanse called Sanam Luang (Pramane Ground). In this vicinity, where the Chao Phya River arches dramatically, a narrow *klong* (canal) connects the sides of the oxbow, setting off an area roughly the shape of a mango. Surrounded by the waters of the river and the canal, this man-made island was the original Bangkok, its "inner city," as it were; and it is here that any exploration of Bangkok should start.

In this relatively small area in the heart of Bangkok you will find most of the sights that every visitor must include in his or her itinerary —those sights that really look like the pictures you remember from your schoolbooks and the scenes that linger from the film *The King and I*. If you approach this area from Democracy Monument on Rajadamnern Avenue (King Rama V's version of the Champs Élysées), the tree-rimmed expanse of Sanam Luang will appear ahead, and there flashing in the sunlight rises Wat Phra Keo, a sight guaranteed to stir even the most jaded traveler.

A good place to start your tour of the inner city is at the official heart of Bangkok — for contrary to what many people think of the sprawling metropolis, it does have one: a small shrine not far from the Ministry of Defense across the entrance to Wat Phra Keo. In this shrine stands **Lakmuang**, a stone pillar placed there by Rama I at the beginning of his reign as the foundation stone of his new capital. Distances within the city are measured from this stone. Sheltered by a graceful, little temple-like building, Lakmuang is believed to have the power to grant many wishes, especially a winning ticket in the National Lottery or fertility to a childless

The numbers in the margin in this section refer to the map on pages 60-61

1..Lakmuang
ศาลเจ้าหลักเมือง

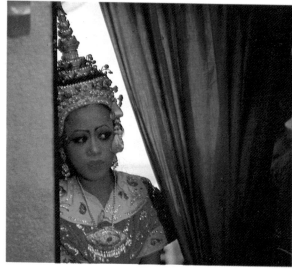

The Lakmuang Shrine, containing an ancient stone pillar placed there by King Rama I, is the official heart of Bangkok. Offerings of fragrant flowers and incense adorn the shrine (left), while in an adjoining room (right) a dancer awaits her performance, commissioned by a supplicant whose wishes have been granted. Not far away from the shrine, the fabled spires of the Grand Palace and Wat Phra Keo (facing page) gracefully pierce the sky.

couple. Floral offerings are always piled high around the pillar, and the air of the shrine is potent with the smell of incense. In an adjoining room a performance of Thai classical dance and music, by either amateurs or professionals, is usually under way, hired by supplicants whose wishes have been granted by the spirit of Lakmuang. The best times to visit the shrine are in the late afternoon, on holidays, and especially on the day before the drawing of the lottery.

2 The Grand Palace
พระบรมมหาราชวัง

The grounds of the **Grand Palace,** open to visitors daily (a certain decorum in dress is demanded), occupy part of a larger compound which also includes the Temple of the Emerald Buddha, used as the royal chapel. Here too is the Royal Collection of Weapons and the Coin Pavilion.

Chakri Maha Prasad
พระที่นั่งจักรีมหาปราสาท

The palace compound right away introduces the visitor to Thailand's characteristic blend of temporal and spiritual elements.

Surrounded by high, crenellated walls and entered by the huge Piman Jayasri double gate, the Grand Palace was originally built by the first king of Bangkok in 1782; almost every subsequent king of the present Chakri dynasty has added to it, so that today the buildings of the Grand Palace present a melange of architectural styles ranging from Thai to Victorian. After the palace murder of King Ananda in 1946, his brother, the present King Bhumibol, moved to the more modern and comfortable Chitralada Palace; and the Grand Palace nowadays is used only for state banquets, presentation of ambassadorial credentials, and other royal ceremonies.

The royal residence of the Grand Palace, called the **Chakri Maha Prasad** — of which visitors are allowed to see only the reception rooms — was constructed during King Rama V's reign (1868-1910) to commemorate the hundredth anniversary of the Chakri dynasty. It is an impressive mixture of Thai and Western architecture — the roof being pure Thai, and the lower part of the building, designed by a British architect, being what might be called "Imperial Victorian." The top floor, under the tall central spire, contains a golden urn with ashes of the Chakri kings. The large reception rooms are decorated with pictures of past kings, busts of foreign royalty (most of whom Rama V met on his trips abroad), and a quantity of mostly European objets d'art. In the center of the building is the magnificent Chakri Throne Room, where the king receives foreign ambassadors on a niello throne under a nine-tiered white umbrella made originally for King Chulalongkorn.

The hall to the right (west) of the Chakri Maha Prasad is the **Dusit Maha Prasad,** built by Rama I in 1789. This is a splendid example of classic Thai architecture, with a four-tiered roof from which rises an elegant nine-tiered spire. The balcony on the north wing contains a throne once used by the king for outdoor receptions; the last occasion was when Rama VI received the oath of loyalty from his court after his coronation in 1911. Just outside the Dusit Maha Prasad is a beautiful little pavilion called the **Arporn Phimok Prasad,** "Disrobing Pavilion," built to the height of the king's palanquin, from which he alighted to take off his ceremonial hat and gown before proceeding to the audience hall. This graceful structure — the most exquisite pavilion in Thailand — was reproduced by Rama V at Bang Pa-In, his summer palace just south of Ayuthaya; and a replica of it was exhibited at the 1958 World Fair in Brussels.

To the left of the Chakri Maha

Dusit Maha Prasad
พระที่นั่งดุสิตมหาปราสาท

Arporn Phimok Prasad
พระที่นั่งอาภรณ์พิโมกข์ปราสาท

Gold-plated street lamps (above) add a touch of old-world Western elegance to the outside of the Chakri throne room of the Grand Palace. In the outer courtyard of the palace (facing page) a Thai family strolls across the spacious green lawn; the gate in the walls leads to the adjoining Temple of the Emerald Buddha, the Royal Chapel and also the most famous of all Thailand's innumerable Buddhist temples among Thais as well as foreign visitors.

Prasad is a door leading to the **Forbidden Quarters,** an area where the king's many wives used to live. The king himself was the only man ever allowed to enter the door which led to the harem's lovely garden of cool fountains, pavilions, and carefully pruned trees. Even today this inner section is closed to all visitors, except for once a year when the king throws a garden party on his birthday for diplomats and government officials. North of the women's quarters lies **Borompiman Hall,** built in a Western style of King Chulalongkorn as a residence for the then crown prince who later became Rama VI; it was in this building that the young King Ananda was killed.

The **Amarin Vinichai Hall,** just beyond the doorway leading to the former harem, is another of the palace's few remaining original buildings, having been built by Rama I. The splendidly painted audience hall is used for coronations, and the king also uses it for some special ceremonies such as presenting medals to government officials. During these ceremonies, the throne is at first concealed by two curtains, called *Phra Visud* in Thai; the king takes his seat unseen by those in the hall; then a fanfare sounds, the curtains part dramatically, and the king appears adorned in fabulous regalia.

Wat Phra Keo, Temple of the Emerald Buddha, adjoins the Grand Palace and serves as the Royal Temple where the king performs his various religious duties. Beyond any doubt, it ranks among the world's great spectacles: a dazzling, dizzying collection of gilded spires and pavilions and mythological gods both awesome and delightful. It is what most foreigners expect to see when they come to Thailand, and it is the single most powerful image visitors take away when they leave. The temple compound is open to the public free on Sundays and Buddhist holidays; on other days there is an admission charge: 20 baht for farangs (foreigners) and 5 baht for Thais.

For a full appreciation, Wat Phra Keo really deserves at least two visits. The first should be on one of the nonpublic days, when admission is charged; the compound is relatively uncrowded, and you can wander about at leisure inspecting its serene treasures. The second visit, however, should be on a public day, for only then can you witness the vital role the temple and its celebrated image play in the life of the Thai people. Then ardent worshipers who fill the sanctuary prostrate themselves on the marble floor before the golden altar; the air is alive with the noise of the supplicants, yet heavy with the smell of floral offerings and burning joss sticks. Bathed in a strange light, high on its pedestal, the small image looks serenely down from the focal point of all eyes as well as prayers. Only on days like this can you sense the power and the role the Emerald Buddha has had through the long years of Thai history.

Wat Phra Keo was originally built by King Rama I in 1782, in imitation of the Royal Temple of the Grand Palace in Ayuthaya, to house the celebrated Phra Keo, or Emerald Buddha. No one knows the precise origin of this small 75-cm-high image, the most sacred in all Thailand, but some experts believe it to be of northern workmanship.

Today, in its blue-tiled sanctuary, the Emerald Buddha sits atop a gilded altar 11 meters high, almost lost in the swirls of smoke from joss sticks burned on days the temple is open to the public. Poised above the image is a nine-tiered umbrella, and on either side are crystal balls representing the sun and the moon. Three

The Emerald Buddha glows mysteriously (above), while a Chinese stone guardian keeps watch outside. The Royal Pantheon (opposite), open once a year, honors the Chakri dynasty, which still sits on Thailand's throne.

times a year, at the beginning of each new season, the king changes the Emerald Buddha's robes, donning it with a golden diamond-studded tunic for the hot season; a gilded robe flecked with blue for the rainy season; and a robe of enamel-coated solid gold from head to toe for the cool season.

A spectacular collection of structures crowds the compound of Wat Phra Keo: buildings, pavilions, *chedis* (pointed spires), *prangs* (rounded spires), and mythological gods and goddesses, most of which are gilded or encrusted with bits of porcelain or glass. A full listing of all the things to be seen would require another book, so we shall mention just a few of the highlights.

The walls of the cloister that surround the entire temple are painted with murals telling the story of the *Ramakien,* the Thai version of the *Ramayana* epic of Indian origin. The murals were originally painted during the reign of Rama III (1824-1850), but had to be restored by his two successors. In 1932, there was a more drastic restoration, during which many Western influences crept into the classic Thai style. The Fine Arts Department recently finished work on yet another restoration of the paintings, this time trying to achieve the original style. As you walk around the cloister the story starts on the left.

You will see that the *Ramakien* regales in epic battles, intrigues, and occasional scenes of low comedy, the most colorful character being the white monkey-god Hanuman, who is also a favourite in Thai classical dance performances. Marble slabs set in pillars in front of the paintings are inscribed with Thai poems describing each episode of the story.

On a broad, raised marble terrace — higher than the rest of the compound because it was built on the ruins of some earlier buildings that were destroyed by fire during the reign of Rama I — are the Royal Pantheon, the library (Mondop), and a golden stupa erected by Rama IV. The **Royal Pantheon** contains life-size statues of the kings of the present dynasty and is open to the public only once a year, on Chakri Day, 6 April. In front of it stand many marvelous gilded statues of mythological creatures, including the charming half-bird, half-woman *kinaree*. Behind the Pantheon is the library, surrounded by monuments commemorating the sacred white elephants, symbol of royal power, that were found in the kingdom during the reigns of the first five Chakri kings. Nearby is a large, detailed model of the famous Khmer temple of Angkor Wat, built by Rama IV to show his people what the temple looked like, during a period when it was located on Thai territory.

Wat Po is the popular name for Wat Phra Jetupon, the oldest and largest temple in Bangkok, which covers nearly 8 hectares. Located just south of the Grand Palace, it is divided into two sections, one containing the living quarters of the monks and the other the various religious buildings. The two parts are separated by the narrow Jetupon Road, down which, according to Thai legend, King Rama 1 marched on his way back from Cambodia to Thonburi on 6 April 1782, the day he officially founded the Chakri dynasty.

There are sixteen gates in the huge, massive walls of Wat Po, but only two of them, both on Jetupon Road, are open to the public. The temple compound is so large, yet so crammed with buildings, pavilions, statues, and enclosed gardens, that it tends to overpower many visitors who fail to give it the attention it deserves. The first temple building on this

12. Wat Po
วัดโพธิ์ (เชตุพนวิมลมังคลาร

Royal Pantheon
ปราสาทพระเทพบิดร,

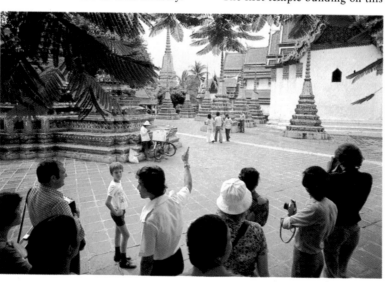

Visitors entering the courtyard of Wat Po (above), Bangkok's oldest and largest temple, are guided through a maze of fascinating buildings and objects. Known as "Thailand's first university," the temple was filled by early kings with varied items aimed at the general edification of the people. It also contains some superlative examples of Thai art adorning the temple buildings, like the delicate ceramic mosaic pictured on the facing page.

site was built as long ago as the 16th century, but the place did not begin to achieve real importance until the establishment of Bangkok as the capital. Wat Po was a particular favorite of the first four Bangkok kings, all of whom added to its treasures; the four large *chedis* to the west of the main chapel are memorials to them, the earliest being the green-mosaic *chedi* built by Rama I, and the latest being the blue one built by Rama IV in the mid-19th century. All round the cloisters leading to the chapel are a total of ninety-one other *chedis* — seventy-one small ones and twenty larger ones; the small ones contain the ashes of various royal descendants, while the larger ones hold relics of the Buddha.

The vast quantity and variety of things to be seen at Wat Po are more meaningful if you bear in mind that the early kings regarded the temple as a primary source of public educa-

tion — it is sometimes called "Thailand's first university." Objects were placed in the compound as a way of letting people acquire knowledge, not necessarily connected with Buddhism. The contorted figures on a little artificial mound just inside the main entrance, for example, illustrate methods of massage and meditation practiced by hermits. There are twenty small hills around the compound displaying stone specimens from different parts of Thailand for anyone's geological education. In most of the buildings are inscriptions or murals giving information on such diverse subjects as military defense, astrology, morality, literature, and archaeology. On the walls of a small open pavilion, which you pass on your way to the Reclining Buddha, are plaques that prescribe treatments for different ailments. The modern building to the left houses the headquarters of the traditional-medicine

Pramane Ground

practitioners of Bangkok, and in the late afternoon (around 4:00 to 6:00 p.m.) each day people still flock for treatment by the old methods.

For most tourists the big attraction of the temple is the gigantic **Reclining Buddha,** the largest in Thailand, 46 meters long and 15 meters high and entirely covered with gold leaf. The soles of the feet, 15½ meters high, are marvelously inlaid with mother-of-pearl designs depicting the 108 auspicious signs of the Buddha. The inlaid feet are all the more fascinating, because to Buddhists and Hindus alike the lowest part of the anatomy would ordinarily represent what is spiritually least exalted. Make a point of looking closely at what remains of the mural paintings in the rather cramped and dimly lighted building that houses this great image; though in a bad state of repair, the murals rank among the finest traditional Thai paintings to be seen in Bangkok and show many fascinating vignettes of daily Thai life. In the courtyard outside the Reclining Buddha are stalls selling souvenirs, including stone-rubbings made from the reliefs depicting scenes from the *Ramakien* epic on the balustrades of the main chapel.

The huge, top-hatted stone figures (which supposedly represent Europeans) that guard the gates of Wat Po and the delightful little stone animals and pagodas all over the compound came to Thailand as ballast on the royal rice boats returning from trade with China.

One of the most beautiful, smaller buildings in the temple, near the four big *chedis,* is the library, entirely covered with pale bits of broken porcelain. Near it lies a walled Chinese garden that once contained crocodiles.

Fiery chili peppers (right) are an essential ingredient in Thai cooking. These and a thousand other local products are on sale at the fabulous Weekend Market (opposite), which attracts throngs of people.

Between Wat Phra Keo and the beginning of Rajadamnern Avenue is a large oval expanse known alternatively as the **Sanam Luang** (Royal Field) and the **Pramane Ground** (Royal Cremation Ground). Traditionally, this space was used for royal cremations and such ceremonies as the annual plowing Ceremony in May which marks the start of the riceplanting season. The last king to be cremated there was Rama VIII, brother of the present ruler. In a significant departure from tradition, the bodies of those killed in the 1973 revolution were given a royally sponsored cremation in the field.

Mostly, however, it is used for less solemn purposes and, for the Thais, it is a favorite place to go *paitio* (take a leisurely stroll) in the late afternoon. During the week there are bicycles for rent, and sports teams play soccer in the central field. From around mid-February through April,

4. Sanam Luang
สนามหลวง

Reclining Buddha
พระไสยาสน์

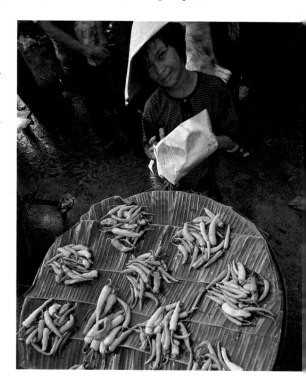

when a dependable breeze springs up every afternoon to break the day's heat, the big attraction is kite-fighting, which starts about 4:30 p.m. when the many government offices in the vicinity close for the day. Watching a Thai kite-fight is one of the most pleasant ways of ending a day. A row of temporary restaurants springs up along the Thammasat University side of the field (so that the afternoon sun declines behind you), and spectators can lounge comfortably in reclining chairs with a beer and a wide choice of Thai snacks. Many of the restaurants have musical shows that go on into the evening. Although there are always a lot of children flying fanciful little kites in the shape of snakes and bats and dragons, the fights themselves are very much an adult affair: various business companies and governmental departments sponsor teams; there is an elaborate system of scoring; and

at the end of the season prizes are awarded.

Two kinds of kites oppose each other in a match — the *chula*, or "male" kite, sometimes as long as 2 meters and requiring a team of ten or more to fly it; and the *pukpao*, "female," smaller and faster, flown by a single player. In a match, the field is divided in half, with *chula*'s territory located at the Wat Phra Keo end and the *pukpao*'s at the other. The object of the fight is for the big kites to cross the boundary, snare one of the small ones, and bring it successfully to earth in *chula* territory. Since the greatest amount of skill is required to maneuver the *chulas*, most of the action is at that end of the field.

The Sanam Luang is most noted for its **Weekend Market,** held every Saturday and Sunday except when the field is reserved for a special activity like the New Year's celebra-

Weekend Market
ตลาดนัดสุดสัปดาห์

tion. There is nothing in Bangkok that quite compares to the Weekend Market, and for anyone whose visit includes a weekend it is a must. Early morning or late afternoon is the best time as far as comfort goes, but there are tamarind trees for shade around the perimeter, most of the stalls have canvas awnings, and there are plenty of refreshment stands to help you beat the heat.

The market follows the same general arrangement every weekend. If you stand facing the market at the bridge that crosses Klong Lawd to Rajadamnern Avenue, on your left is the plant section. Here on both sides of the *klong* you can see a dazzling variety of the wild and hybrid orchids grown in Thailand, along with all sorts of other garden plants and supplies; the stalls nearest the bridge specialize in jungle plants brought from as far away as Chiang Mai. Across the street is the secondhand book section, the only part of the market that is open all week. The nearest side of the big field (toward Rajadamnern Avenue and the Royal Hotel) is devoted to foods, the far side (toward Napralan and Naprathat Roads) to cloth, clothing, and household goods. The central part of the field, perhaps the most fascinating of all, contains pets (look for the baby pythons); Thai handicrafts (musical instruments are a good buy); antiques (mostly fake but a few genuine discoveries lie in store); semiprecious gems; herbal medicines; and such miscellaneous treats as cobra-mongoose fights staged to boost the sales of patent medicines. Bargaining is definitely the rule at the Sanam Luang as nothing has a fixed price, but Thais claim that the prices on the whole are cheaper than in other markets. If you get tired, have an iced coffee (*o-liang*) or some chilled coconut juice (*nam maprao*).

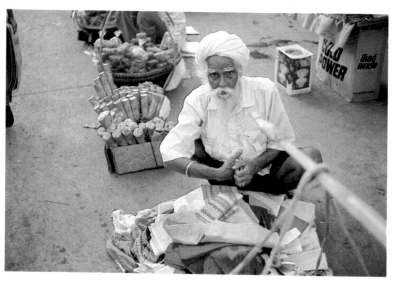

Goods of all kinds are available at the Weekend Market, including the rich silk sarongs being sold by the Sikh merchant (above) from a portable shop. Along a gallery in Wat Mahathat, just across from the market, a row of gilded and berobed Buddha images (opposite) gaze serenely down in timeless contemplation; this temple is an important center of Buddhist instruction, specializing in meditation, and dates from the reign of the first Bangkok king.

Across from Sanam Luang, on the way from Wat Phra Keo to the National Museum, you first pass buildings belonging to **Silapakorn University**, the University of Fine Arts, located on Naprathat Road diagonally opposite the Grand Palace, where students are trained in painting, sculpture, archaeology, and architecture. The older part of this university was a former palace, and despite many modern additions there are still attractive shady courtyards where students can relax between classes. Frequent art exhibitions are held here, and there is a small but interesting archaeological museum. Next door is the pink-colored **National Library** and, in the same compound, **Wat Mahathat, Temple of the Great Relic**. Built during the reign of Rama I, it is an important Buddhist teaching institution, specializing in meditation. During his long period in the priesthood before

becoming king, Rama IV was abbot of this temple.

In the large area between the *wat* and the National Museum stands **Thammasat University**, founded just before World War II and now one of Thailand's leading educational institutions, especially in law and economics. The students of Thammasat tend to be less conservative than those of the older Chulalongkorn University; many leaders of the 1973 revolution came from Thammasat. In late 1976, there were further student demonstrations at Thammasat, which were violently suppressed, followed by a military takeover of the faltering government. Except for one quaint, rather Victorian administration building, there is little of architectural interest to be seen in Thammasat, but those who would like to sample Thai student attitudes will usually find a student willing to chat over a cup of coffee or a soft drink.

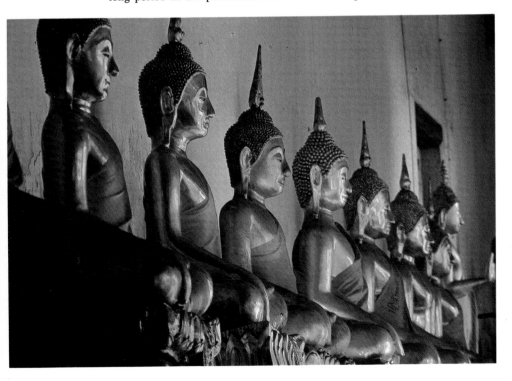

The **National Museum**, possibly the largest in Southeast Asia, located next to Thammasat University on Naprathat Road, consists of a group of older buildings, on either side of which two new wings were added in 1966. It is open everyday, except Monday and Friday, from 9:00 a.m. until noon, and from 1:00 until 4:00 p.m.; admission is free on Saturday and Sunday, and a few baht on other days. On Tuesday, Wednesday, and Thursday mornings at 9:30 a.m., there is a special English-language tour of the museum, starting from the entry pavilion at the main gate and lasting about two hours.

Besides housing a vast treasure of antiquities, the museum has an interesting history of its own. The oldest buildings in the compound date from 1782 and were built as the palace of the second king, a sort of deputy ruler — a feature of the Thai monarchy in the early Bangkok period. Originally, the palace included a large park that went all the way to Wat Mahathat and covered the northern half of the present Pramane Grounds as well; however, the office of the second king was abolished during the reign of Rama V, who handed the buildings over to be used as a museum.

The first building to the left of the entrance is the **Sivamokkha Biman Hall**, which was originally an opensided audience hall. It now houses the prehistoric art collection, in particular the bronzes and handsome painted earthenware jars found in Ban Chiang in Northeast Thailand which are arousing much interest in the international world of archaeology. Also near the entrance is the **Buddhaisawan Chapel**, built by the second king as his private place of worship. It contains some well-preserved murals, depicting the life of the Buddha, and the famous *Phra*

6. National Museum
พิพิธภัณฑ์สถานแห่งชาติ

Sivamokkha Biman Ha
พระที่นั่งศิวโมกข์พิมาน

Buddhaisawan Chapel
ตำหนักพุทธไธศวรรย์

National Museum in Brief

For the museum visitor in a hurry, the following are the main periods of Thai art, with a brief description of the principal characteristics of their statues or images, and the rooms where they are displayed.

Davaravati (6th-11th centuries): Mon in appearance, with broad, usually smiling faces and tight curls, often showing Indian influence especially in the robes and the slightly curved bodies of standing figures. In rooms 32 and 33 you will find Davaravati figures in terra-cotta, Buddha images, and lively groups of dancers and musicians.

Srivichaya (8th-13th centuries): Contemporaneous with Davaravati but from areas farther south and strongly influenced by Javanese art. Bronzes are in room 35.

Lop Buri or *Khmer* (11th-14th centuries): Similar, sometimes identical, in style to the art of Cambodia, with many stone and bronze figures of Hindu deities as well as Buddha images. Figures look strong and masculine. Rooms 29 and 31.

Chiang Saen (12th-20th centuries): From North Thailand; rather plump, somewhat Chinese-looking faces and curled hair. Room 41.

Sukhothai (13th-15th centuries): The first purely Thai style and still regarded as the most original; images displaying long, flowing, idealized bodies and faces with enigmatic smiling expressions. Many of the features are based on descriptions in Sanskrit poetry of gods and heroes. Be sure to see the famous black bronze of the walking Buddha. Rooms 42 and 43.

Ayuthaya (15th-18th centuries): A mixture of styles with graceful but stylized figures, the lavish decoration reflecting the wealth and power of the kingdom. Rooms 44 and 45.

Bangkok or *Ratanakosin* (late 18th century to present): Round, rather sweet faces and elaborate Thai costumes; more decorative than figures of earlier periods; unfortunately not well represented.

The National Museum is housed partly in an old royal palace (below) and contains a comprehensive collection of Thai art.

Buddha Sihing, a bronze Sukhothai-style image greatly revered by the Thais. Another interesting building in the museum compound, behind the prehistoric-art pavilion, the **Tamnak Daeng**, or Red House, was the residence of an elder sister of King Rama I and was formerly located in the grounds of the Grand Palace; it has a fascinating collection of furniture used by early royalty.

The finely proportioned old palace of the second king, which formerly housed the museum's entire collection, now is limited to ethnological exhibits of elephant howdahs, ceramics, palanquins, royal furnishings, weapons, and similar objects. The Buddhist art collection, in the new wings on either side, includes exhibits from most Asian countries, but the greatest attraction, naturally, is the Thai collection, ranging from Davaravati, the earliest period, up through Ratanakosin (Bangkok) art.

Brochures and pamphlets available at the entrance will help you understand the evolution of the various artistic styles.

If you turn left when you come out of the museum gate, you will see the **National Theater**, a huge building in a not entirely happy mixture of Thai and Western architecture. This is where performances of Thai classical dance are presented on certain occasions; check inside (or in the newspapers) to find out if one is scheduled during your stay, for they are full-length performances worth seeing. If not, you can visit the dancing school run by the Department of Fine Arts, called **Nattasin**, behind the National Theater in one of the old buildings of the second king's palace. Here students, mostly children, are trained in the complex gestures and steps of the *khon*, the masked dance dramas once performed only for the king and his court.

Other Bangkok Temples and Sights

One of the most attractive small temples in Bangkok, an architectural curiosity visited by relatively few tourists, is **Wat Rajabopitr**, located near the Ministry of the Interior off Klong Lawd. You can easily recognize it by its distinctive doors, carved in relief with jaunty-looking soldiers wearing European-type uniforms. Built by King Chulalongkorn in 1863, the temple reflects the king's interest in Western art and in blending it with traditional Thai forms. The most prominent feature of Wat Rajabopitr is the tall, gilded *chedi*, covering a round vaulted room that contains a stone Buddha image seated on a *naga*, or sacred serpent, from Lop Buri. The lower part of the *chedi*, the circular cloister around it, and the outside of the *bot* (chapel) are completely covered with decorative pieces of colored Chinese porcelain, a delicate mixture of blue, yellow, red, and green, which con-

tributes greatly to the unique charm of this little temple. The doors and windows of the *bot* are inlaid with mother-of-pearl in designs depicting various honors bestowed by the king. In a recess beside one of the doors is a bas-relief of a god named Khio Kang, "the one with long teeth," who is supposed to guard this sanctuary. Four chapels, connected to the central gallery by small porticos, further enlarge the size of this colorful temple.

Wat Rajabopitr was built before King Chulalongkorn made his first trip to Europe, but even so, his strong interest in the West is apparent inside the vaulted *bot*, which appears Italian Gothic in inspiration and, to one observer, suggestive of "a rather ornate drawing room." The king was to carry this interest in mixing the native and the foreign even further when forty years later he built Wat Benchamabopit.

13. Wat Rajabopitr
วัดราชบพิตร (สถิตมหาสีมาราม)

Bamrung Muang Road, beside the Ministry of the Interior (just north beyond Wat Rajabopitr and east of Wat Phra Keo) leads into the Square of the **Giant Swing**, *Sao Ching Cha* in Thai. Take a stroll down Bamrung Muang Road, for both sides are lined with old shops selling nothing but a variety of religious objects for temples or home shrines. The Swing itself consists of two gigantic red poles in the center of the square, joined at the top by a carved beam. The Swinging Ceremony, now no longer held, was a popular Brahman ritual held in honor of the Brahman god, Phra Isuan, who was believed to visit the earth for ten days every January.

Wat Suthat, facing the Giant Swing, was started under the first Bangkok king and finished during the reign of its third (1824-1851). It is noted for its outstanding and enormous *bot* (chapel), said to be the tallest in Bangkok, and for its equally large *viharn* (hall for keeping sacred objects), surrounded by a gallery of gilded Buddha images. The principal Buddha image, called the *Phra Buddha Chakyamuni*, was cast in the 14th century and was originally in a temple at Sukhothai; impressed by its size and beauty, Rama I brought it down to Bangkok by river. The interior building that houses this image contains some monumental, finely carved doors, partly commissioned by Rama II, who, it is said, ordered the instruments used to be thrown into the river so that no one would be able to duplicate the fine carving. There are also excellent murals in the *bot* dating from the reign of Rama III which are in a better state of preservation than those in most Thai temples. Bronze horses and stone pagodas grace the lower courtyard. The *wat* is normally entered by Ti Thong (Dinso) Road.

Pigeons soar into the sky from the courtyard of Wat Rajabopitr (opposite); feeding them is regarded as a way of earning merit by those who go to the temple. The Giant Swing (above, left) is a relic of old Bangkok that survives in the modern city, where a unique Brahman ceremony used to be held with teams swinging a full 180-degree arc. A dramatic bronze horse (above, right) raises its head silently against the brooding evening sky in the lower courtyard of Wat Suthat.

At the point where Rajadamnern Avenue crosses Klong Banglampoe, just outside the remains of what was once Bangkok's city wall, stand **Wat Sakhet** and the **Golden Mount**, one of the city's most imposing sights and for many years its highest point. Ayuthaya had had a great artificial hill, and King Rama III decided to reproduce it in Bangkok. Because of Bangkok's soft earth, however, he was never able to raise it to the desired height, and it was not until the reign of Chulalongkorn (Rama V) that the mount was completed — 78 meters high, the top level reached by a circular stairway of 318 steps. A gilded *chedi* at the top contains relics of the Buddha given to Rama V by Lord Curzon, the then Viceroy of India. The climb is fairly exhausting, especially on a hot day, but the view from the top spans all of Bangkok which lies supinely at its feet.

Wat Sakhet, at the bottom of the Mount, was originally built during the Ayuthaya period, when it was called Wat Sakae; according to legend, Rama I stopped here and ceremonially washed himself on the way back to Thonburi to be crowned, and the name of the temple was later changed to Sakhet, which means "the washing of hair." It also became noted, rather grimly, for cremations. By custom, the Pramane Ground could be used only for cremations of kings and other royalty; commoners had to be taken outside the city walls for the ceremony, and since Wat Sakhet stood just outside one of the main gates, it was a handy place.

Every November, Wat Sakhet and the Golden Mount are the scene of one of Bangkok's prettiest fairs. Food stalls and stage shows by the dozens are set up in the grounds; the mount is bathed in colored lights; and the devout make their way in candlelight processions to the top.

16. Wat Sakhet
วัดสระเกษ (มหาวรวิหาร)

16. Golden Mount
ภูเขาทอง

The man-made Golden Mount (above) was for years the highest point in Bangkok, and it still offers a panoramic view of the city. The Amulet Market (opposite) is where Thais go to buy the small votive plaques, often made of pressed terra cotta, that a large part of the population wear as a means of protection from a wide range of ills. Usually Buddha images, the amulets vary in price from a few baht to thousands, depending on their protective powers.

Even if the fair is not going on, the restaurants along the *klong* are pleasant places to relax in the late afternoon.

Across the street from the Golden Mount, behind the Chalerm Thai movie theater which is on Rajadamnern Avenue, and just a short way down Mahachai Road, hides **Wat Rachanada**, worth a visit because of its **Amulet Market.** This market used to be located in Wat Mahathat, near the National Museum, but was moved about a year ago. Thais are staunch believers in the protective powers of amulets, which they usually wear around the neck on a gold or silver chain, and great care is taken in the selection of precisely the right amulet. The majority of charms are Buddha images, often in pressed terra-cotta plaques covered in plastic, but there are likenesses of many other gods and goddesses who are supposed to have protective powers.

A ten-eyed deity, for example, protects not only from the front, but from the back and both sides as well. There are amulets that attract women to men, while others that act vice versa, and amulets that ward off bullets, or protect you from harm in car and airplane accidents. Some, believed to be especially powerful, sell for thousands of baht, and according to those who buy them, are worth the investment. The Thai methods of selecting an amulet are somewhat mysterious to an outsider, having, it would seem, little to do with either the charm's age or its visual beauty. Also, a visitor should keep in mind that the primary purpose of wearing an amulet, however far removed from Buddhism, is religious rather than decorative. Around the amulet stalls, gold- and silversmiths sell chains for the amulets and a variety of other charms and Buddha images for home shrines.

After crossing the *klong* near the Golden Mount, Rajadamnern Avenue turns into a pleasant, tree-lined boulevard, that leads straight into the square in front of the old **National Assembly**. The square is dominated by an equestrian statue of King Chulalongkorn who had so much to do with the construction of this part of Bangkok. On the anniversary of his death, 23 October, the square is crowded with students and government officials who lay wreaths at the statue in his honor. The area is also used for the trooping of the colors on the king's birthday and on armed forces day. To the left lies **Amporn Gardens**, a spacious park with fountains and trees, the setting for many royal social functions and fairs, among them the annual Red Cross Fair in January. Straight ahead across the square stands the imposing National Assembly, of white marble with a huge cupola in neoclassical style, built in 1907 by King Chulalongkorn as his Throne Hall. Special permission is required to go inside the building, which is decorated with huge murals depicting famous events in Thai history. Until 1974, the building was used for meetings of the Assembly during periods of democratic government; now a new and more modern building, not far away, is used for this purpose.

18. National Assembly
รัฐสภา

The streets around the National Assembly, a district called **Dusit**, are among the few remaining in Bangkok that have been relatively untouched by the building boom of the past decade. Tall trees shade the sidewalks; the *klongs* are relatively clean; high, pleasantly faded walls enclose military barracks; and, here and there, reposes a lovely old palace, an echo of the days when many royal princes lived here, in what was then looked upon as the suburbs, far from the pomp and cere-

21. Amporn Gardens
สวนอัมพร

The investiture of Crown Prince Vajiralongkorn several years ago took place at the former National Assembly (above) amid splendor and traditions that go far back to the earliest days of the Thai monarchy. Massive lions made of Italian marble (opposite) overlook the broad courtyard of Wat Benchamabopit, popularly known as the Marble Temple, which was built during the reign of King Chulalongkorn and which contains many unique architectural features.

mony of the old city. If you turn into Sri Ayuthaya and continue for a short distance, you will come to one of the city's most beautiful temples, Wat Benchamabopit.

* * *

The newest of the royal temples in Bangkok, **Wat Benchamabopit**, the **Marble Temple**, was started by King Chulalongkorn in 1901 and finished ten years later, just after his death; the name means "Temple of the Fifth King." It is also one of the most unusual, for the architect, a half-brother of the king, made a number of departures from traditional style. The most obvious of these are the Carrara marble used on the main buildings; the enclosed courtyard; and the curved, yellow Chinese tiles of the roof. Two gigantic marble lions, or *singha*, guard the entrance to the *bot*. The marble courtyard has a Renaissance quality about it, with clouds of pigeons that

descend to eat bread thrown by visitors. Try to be there in the early morning or in the evening when the monks come to chant in the *bot*. In a gallery around the courtyard are fifty-one Buddha images, slightly larger than life-size, in a variety of different styles and attitudes. All the periods of Thai Buddhist art are represented, as well as art from China, India, Japan, and Tibet. Some of the images are originals of the period; others were recast and enlarged from smaller images to achieve a uniform size. The principal Buddha image is a replica of a famous one in Phitsanulok called *Phra Buddha Chinaraj*.

Through the rear entrance of the courtyard is a huge Bodhi tree, seventy-odd years old; it was brought as a seedling from a tree in South Thailand that came from Buddha Gaya in India, the Buddha's birthplace. A canal filled with large turtles (released there by people wishing to

23. Wat Benchamabopit
วัดเบญจมบพิตร (ราชวรวิหาร)

earn merit) separates the religious buildings from the monks' quarters where the present king spent his monkhood shortly after his coronation. Towards the front of the monks' section is a group of buildings called the **Royal Ordination Pavilions**, well worth seeing if you can find the man who has the key (not always an easy task). These buildings were originally located inside the compound of the Grand Palace.

* * *

Farther down Sri Ayuthaya Road stands **Chitralada Palace,** the residence of the king. Not much can be seen from the road except for a group of traditional Thai-style buildings used for entertaining, and the king's experimental dairy farm. The area between the Palace and the National Assembly is occupied by **Khao Din Zoo,** also popularly known as **Dusit Zoo.** The main entrance is on Rajawiti Road. *Khao Din* means "Mountain of Earth," and the place is so called because its central topographical feature is a man-made hill affording a view of the whole park. This is one of the most popular places in Bangkok for family outings, especially on weekends. Gibbons swing from the trees, there is a monkey show, and you can ride on an elephant. To meet the Thai demand for frequent snacks, there are many restaurants and food stalls. There is even a lake where young lovers can rent a rowboat. This is also the place where the royal white elephants are kept in a fancy enclosure all their own. By tradition, every white elephant found in Thailand belongs to the king, and after complicated and detailed examination to attest its whiteness, it is brought to Khao Din, where it receives lavish attention and special food; in the old days, the power of a

Dusit
ดุสิต

Royal Ordination Pavilion

20. Chitralada Palace
พระราชวังสวนจิตรลดา

19. Khao Din (Dusit) Zoo
สวนสัตว์ดุสิต (เขาดิน)

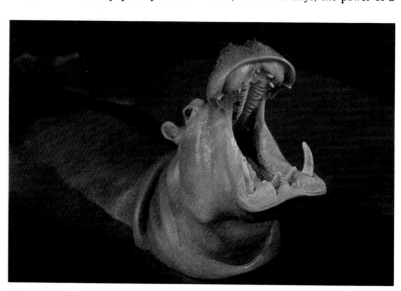

This hungry hippopotamus (above) is but one of the hundreds of animals on display at Dusit Zoo, a spacious park that is a popular place for city dwellers on weekends; the royal white elephants are also at the zoo in a special enclosure all their own. The narrow, twisting lanes of Bangkok's Chinatown offer an endless variety of surprising sights to a stroller, like the advertisements for a happy dentist and an expert palmist on the opposite page.

king was measured in part by the number of white elephants he possessed. Actually, as you will see, the elephants are not white at all, but albinos of pinkish hue, though in an odd way they do seem rather more regal than ordinary run-of-the-mill elephants!

The zoo also houses a fine collection of birds in a huge aviary on the "Mountain of Earth," and a large variety of other animals such as giraffes, kangaroos, crocodiles, quaint little mouse-deer (native to Thailand), and even bears, for whom blocks of ice are thoughtfully provided. The zoo is open from 7:00 a.m. until 6.00 p.m. everyday. Admission is only several baht.

* * *

The **Chinatown** of Bangkok is a large and rather ill-defined area, on either side of two large streets, Charoen Krung (New Road) and Yaowaraj, with Suapa (Rajawong) Road

found somewhat in the middle of the area. By day, these crowded, boisterous streets reach a noise level impressive even by Bangkok standards, though a certain degree of relief can be attained by turning off into one of the narrow, twisting lanes that teem with shops doing a brisk business selling everything imaginable, from motorcycles to birds' nests, Chinese paper lanterns, and ancient remedies of the Celestial Kingdom. Some of Bangkok's leading banks and commercial firms still have their headquarters in this district, reminders of the days when nearly all trade was in the hands of Chinese, Thailand's largest minority and a third of Bangkok's population; but most have now opened branch offices elsewhere.

Yaowaraj is famous for its gold shops — hundreds of them, one after another, looking exactly alike and for the most part selling articles at

24. Yaowaraj
ย่านเยาวราช (ไชน่าทาวน์)

almost the same prices since the price of gold is fixed by the government. People from all over Bangkok come here to invest their money in gold chains which are, rather confusingly for a tourist, sold by the baht — referring in this case to a weight and not the coin. If they prosper, the customers come back and exchange the first chain for a heavier one; if they encounter difficulties, Yaowaraj also has a large number of convenient pawn shops. At night, Yaowaraj quiets down a bit, but another phenomenon replaces the action on the street — thousands of small, migratory birds come to roost on the telephone wires and power lines above the street.

Another part of Chinatown that attracts people from all over is **Pahurat,** the cloth section. (It can be reached by walking west on narrow Soi Wanit, located just below and parallel to Yaowaraj Road, and going past Chakrawat and Chakraphet Roads, beyond the King's Theater.) Despite the location, a large proportion of the shop owners here are turbaned Sikhs from India. Fabric prices, especially of imported goods from Japan and Europe, are generally much cheaper than in other parts of the city.

In the heart of Yaowaraj, as Chinatown is called for short — also not far from the King's and Queen's Theaters — is an area of narrow, claustrophobic old streets known as **Nakorn Kasem,** the **Thieves Market** in many guidebooks. This is something of a misnomer, since it happens to be an eminently respectable district on the whole, with no more than its fair share of thieves in the legal sense of the word. The majority of its small shops sell such emphatically unromantic articles as toilets, water pumps, and lighting fixtures; but its lure for tourists is its close to two

26. Nakorn Kasem
เวิ้งนครเกษม

25. Pahurat Market
ตลาดผ้าพาหุรัด

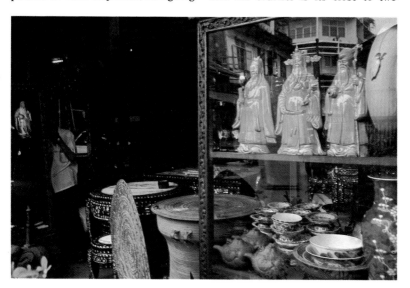

Chinatown's Thieves' Market (above) contains a fascinating collection of goods for sale, including antique porcelains and Laotian war drums as well as ordinary water pumps. Wat Trimitr's immense Golden Buddha (opposite) is made of $5\frac{1}{2}$ tonnes of solid gold; disguised for centuries by a drab stucco covering, the priceless statue was only discovered by accident when the outer covering cracked as the image was being moved to a new location.

dozen antique shops that spill out treasures along the sidewalks. There was a time, not too many years ago, when every antique lover in search of a bargain was obliged to go to Nakorn Kasem, and many a treasure was uncovered in its dusty, dimly lighted shops. To a large extent, that has now changed; many old Nakorn Kasem dealers have struck it rich and opened flashy, new air-conditioned shops over on the other side of Bangkok in the tourist centers; but there are still things to be discovered by the buyer with a sharp eye and a gift for tough bargaining (as a general rule, every price can be talked down at least 20 percent). The best bargains are in Chinese items — porcelains, furniture inlaid with mother-of-pearl, rosewood screens, snuff bottles. Besides antiques, shops sell new but charming (and cheap) brass and copper oil lanterns and bell-shaped temple lighting fixtures.

Just east of the point where Yaowaraj Road meets Charoen Krung Road (not far from Hua Lampong Railway Station) is **Wat Trimitr,** worth visiting to see its famous **Golden Buddha,** found by accident when a construction company was extending the port of Bangkok. Entirely covered in stucco when it was discovered, the figure was moved to a temporary shelter at Wat Trimitr while a building was constructed to house it. On the night before it was scheduled to be moved by crane to the new building, torrential rain soaked the stucco covering, and during the move the image was accidentally dropped into soft mud — the stucco cracked, revealing the pure gold beneath. When the covering was removed, the whole Sukhothai image, 3 meters high and weighing about 5½ tonnes, was discovered to be made of gold. Experts believe it was probably originally in an Ayuthaya temple and cov-

Experts believe the Golden Buddha was camouflaged to keep the invading Burmese from finding it in early Ayuthaya.

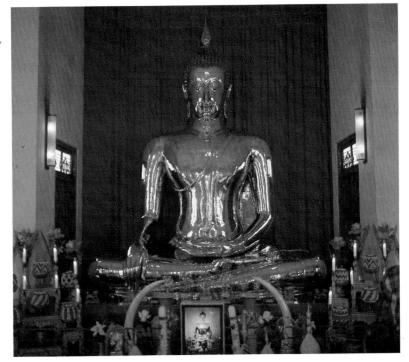

ered with the stucco to conceal its value from the invading Burmese in the 18th century; the ruse worked so well that it remained hidden from the Thais as well for nearly 200 years.

*　*　*

New Road (Charoen Krung) one of the oldest roads in Bangkok in fact, used to be the center of the tourist and *farang* ("foreigner") shops, but a decade or so ago, this aspect of the city began to shift over to the Rajprasong-Ploenchit area. Now the most significant landmarks left are the G.P.O., the Portuguese, Finnish, and French Embassies, the Oriental Hotel (down Oriental Lane which passes the Monaco Consulate and leads to the river), and the **Bangrak Market,** one of the city's busiest. To reach the latter walk south down New Road past Oriental Lane and you will see on your right between the road and the river, dozens of stalls selling mountains of fresh fruits and vegetables, along with other food. People come here from all over Bangkok in the belief that the produce is fresher and cheaper, because it comes by boat straight from the farms and orchards upriver. The variety of fruit is bound to stagger anyone from a temperate country. Bananas come in more than ten kinds (the small firm ones are best for cooking), and huge, sweet pineapples and papayas are only a few bant each. A tropical grape, developed at the agriculture university, is now available all year round in both red and green varieties. However, the two fruits most prized by the Thais are mangoes and durians, both of which appear on the market only in the hot season. If the only mangoes you have ever eaten are the Caribbean or Mexican varieties, you are in for a treat, for the pale Thai mangoes have an infinitely more delicate flavor. The Thais eat them green in a salad or dipped in sugar; or

Charoen Krung
ถนนเจริญกรุง

29. Bangkrak Market
ตลาดบางรัก

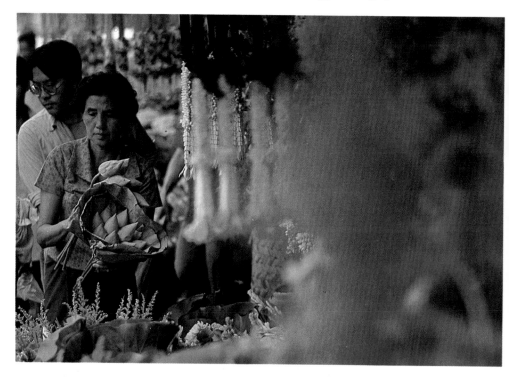

Modern Bangkok

ripe as a sweet along with glutinous (sticky) rice and coconut milk. Durian is a large, spiky, pungent prehistoric-looking fruit that you either like or loathe; nobody seems neutral about it. If you have a taste for it, be prepared to pay anywhere from 20 baht for one of the ordinary to several hundred for a superior *kanyao* ("long stem"), the most prized of all. If you are having your first durian, it might be helpful to remember that a very ripe fruit at room temperature tastes much stronger than a chilled one just ripening.

Located a few blocks farther south on New Road, **Wat Yannawa** has the unusual shape of an ark.

Besides the many temples and traditional sights, new tourist Bangkok invites exploration and shopping.

To the left (west) of the picturesque Siam Intercontinental Hotel on Rama I Road stands **Siam Center,** an airconditioned shopping center with four levels of shops catering to tourists. Behind it is the residence of the king's mother and an office building housing the Princess Mother's Charities. On the second floor of the small building (enter from Phya Thai Road) is a store selling northern hill-tribe handicrafts — fine pieces of embroidery, homespun cloth, basketwork, sling bags; prices here are cheaper than in most of the tourist-oriented shops selling the same things, and the money goes to the welfare of the tribes.

To the right (east) of the Siam Intercontinental Hotel, just beyond a primary school, stands **Wat Pathum Wan,** also called "The Lotus Temple," because of the great number of lotuses and water lilies blooming in the large pond behind it. The *bot* contains some attractive murals done

Only a short stroll from the Oriental Hotel, Bangrak Market (left) is noted for its fresh fruits, flowers and vegetables that are brought along the nearby Chao Phya River from neighboring farms and orchards.

during the period of Rama V (1868-1910). However, the temple itself was built by Rama IV and was part of a large park which also included a palace where the king came in the summer to escape the heat of the Grand Palace — this part of Bangkok then being "in the country." The palace is gone now, but despite ominous rumors of "development" — in Bangkok always meaning a new shopping center or hotel — much of the park still remains, its ponds and islands and large trees something of an anachronism in this busy commercial area. A peculiar distinction of Wat Pathum Wan is that it is the most popular temple in Bangkok among taxi drivers for having their vehicles blessed against accidents.

The large shopping area across from the Siam Intercontinental, extending from Phya Thai Road to Henri Dunant Road, is called **Siam Square.** This is a highly popular place with Thais, since it has three large movie theaters — the Siam, Lido, Scala — plus dozens of relatively inexpensive Thai and Chinese restaurants and coffee shops. There are also some good bookshops (the D.K. Bookshop has a wide range of paperbacks), antique shops, men's and women's tailors specializing in mod fashions, and the British Council, a striking example of modern architecture in red, white, and blue.

Along Henri Dunant Road (still called by Thais by its old name of Sanam Ma, "Race Course Road") are found two important old Bangkok institutions. On the left, walking south away from Siam Square, you come upon the **Royal Bangkok Sports Club,** a multinational private club with sports facilities — golf course, swimming pool, tennis courts — and racing on Saturdays during all but the rainiest months. The club is closed to nonmembers, but the racing is open to the public through separate entrances. You get your money's worth: the program commences at noon and consists of fifteen races.

Across the road from the Sports Club stand the spectacular templelike buildings of the Faculty of Arts of **Chulalongkorn University**, the country's oldest and most prestigious institution of higher learning. The campus extends from Henri Dunant to Phya Thai Road and has fourteen faculties. Built in a mixture of Thai and Western styles, with spacious yellow-roofed pavilions, an open gallery, and an assembly hall, the university was founded by King Rama VI (1911-1925) and named for his father, King Chulalongkorn.

* * *

The intersection at the government-owned Erawan Hotel (where Rama I becomes Ploenchit Road), called **Rajprasong** after the sidestreet by that name, is one of the most fashionable shopping areas in the city. (The area is alternatively called **Gaysorn**, after the other popular shopping sidestreet just off Rajadamri Avenue.) The **Erawan Shrine** at the corner is busy every night, since Shiva, the Hindu god it honors, is said to have powers to grant all sorts of wishes, from a male child to a winning lottery ticket (the nights before the lottery drawing are the busiest of all). Believers offer jasmine garlands, incense sticks, and carved wooden elephants to please the spirit, and if their wishes are granted they often sponsor performances of Thai classical dance in gratitude.

If you cross the street from the shrine and walk a short distance north up Rajadamri Avenue you will come to perhaps the most popular of all the new shopping centers in Bangkok, **Rajadamri Arcade**. Thai teenagers by the hundreds crowd its air-conditioned corridors, window-shopping and showing off their best clothes. The coffee shop in the basement is one of the best in Bangkok for low-priced, good European and Chinese food. At the back of the arcade is the Japanese-owned **Daimaru Department Store**, which has just about everything you would find in any similar store in Europe or the United States. (Another good department store, **Central**, the newest and largest in Bangkok, is up Ploenchit Road, east from the Erawan near Soi Chidlom, just before you get to the British Embassy. An almost identical branch of the Central Department Store is at 306 Silom Road, a few blocks west of the Narai Hotel.)

Walk on farther north from the Rajadamri Arcade and you will come to **Pratunam** on the left, a favorite shopping place for many Thais. *Pratunam* means "Water Door," referring to the lock at the bridge to prevent **Klong Saen Sap** on the right (east) from being flooded by the one on the left (west) which leads to the Chao Phya River. Under the bridge there are shops selling straw goods,

and you can hire a boat here to make the trip up Klong Saen Sap, one of the few really busy *klong*s left in Bangkok. The noodle shops of Pratunam Market are popular late at night after the bars and movie theaters close; everybody from royalty to taxi drivers comes to have a snack before going home.

* * *

South of the shopping areas along Rama I Road, at the corner of Henri Dunant and Rama VI Roads, stands the **Pasteur Institute**, part of the Thai Red Cross and open everyday except Sunday. Locals (as may the visitor) come here to have cholera, smallpox and typhoid inoculations, as well as rabies treatment, for moderate fees; but it has become a tourist attraction because of the **Snake Farm** behind the main administration building. Here, under huge, shady rain trees (also called monkeypods), three large, deep pits contain hun-

The Erawan Shrine (opposite) honors a Hindu deity and is one of the most popular of Bangkok's innumerable shrines; piles of sweet-smelling jasmine wreaths are offered by those in search of favors. Lethal snakes (above) are milked every Thursday at the Pasteur Institute; the pale yellow venom is injected into horses to produce serum which is subsequently sent all over the country to treat those bitten by cobras, vipers, and banded kraits.

dreds of poisonous snakes used in the production of anti-snakebite serum, mostly sent to the provinces where cases of snakebite are common in the rice fields. The principal species kept at the farm are king cobras (some of them 3 to 4 meters long), ordinary cobras, banded kraits, and Russell vipers. A different kind of serum is produced from each, and it is essential to know what kind of snake has bitten you, since krait serum, for example, is not effective against cobra bite, and vice versa. Every Thursday morning, around 10 o'clock, the snakes are "milked" by a pair of workers, who go into the pits, as if they were going into a coffee shop, and nonchalantly pick up suitable snakes. Though it may give you a case of the gooseflesh, viewing the handling of such legendary serpents can be a rewarding, eye-opening experience. One worker inserts a glass plate under the fangs of the selected snake while the other holds its neck and presses the venom sacs just behind the eyes, whereupon a pale, yellowish liquid is deposited on the glass. "By nature snakes are not aggressive and will attack human beings only under provocation," reads a bulletin produced by the Snake Farm. And although nature intended the venom for animals the snake can eat, and the men are skilled at their job, accidents have been known to happen. A few years ago an ill-tempered king cobra — not as potent as a banded krait, but more dangerous because of the amount of venom it can produce — bit a worker who was cleaning the pit. The man *was* saved by prompt treatment. After the men have extracted the venom, it is injected into horses kept for the purpose in a stable near the pits. The horses are periodically bled and tested for potency, and when the desired antibodies have been developed in the horse-blood, the serum is separated and freeze-dried for shipment to the provinces and to a number of surrounding countries with similar venomous snakes.

For plant lovers, especially from temperate lands, visiting a tropical country can be a dream come true. **Tropical gardens** virtually know no seasons, and countries like Thailand are perennially abloom.

Unfortunately for those who like to look at other people's gardens, however, Bangkok tends to be a city of high walls, many of them studded with intimidating bits of broken glass, so a drive through a residential area is not very rewarding. Bangkok has no botanical garden per se (the closest thing being the agricultural college, Kasetsart University, on the city's edge off Route 1 near Don Muang Airport), but a number of flower markets and private estates open to the public amply present the country's floral riches. One famous private garden that is open to the public is at **Suan Pakkard Palace** on Sri Ayuthaya Road (just east of the intersection with Phaya Thai Road), the splendid residence of Princess Chumbhot of Nagara Svarg, one of Thailand's leading gardeners and art collectors. Actually, the beautifully landscaped grounds (*suan* means "garden") containing numerous plants the princess brought from all over the world as well as from the Thai jungle, are only part of the reason for visiting Suan Pakkard, for it has a great diversity of other treasures. Five old, traditional Thai houses overlooking the garden contain a large collection, made all the more charming by its presentation without the stuffiness of a museum, of Buddha images, Khmer statues, old paintings, porcelain, musical instruments, and the regalia of the late Prince Chumbhot. At the back of the garden stands an exquisite little lacquer pavilion, which Prince Chumbhot discovered in a temple

39. Suan Pakkard Pala
วัง งมผักกาด

In the manicured gardens of Suan Pakkard Palace, maintained by Princess Chumbot, sits an exquisitely decorated lacquer pavilion, originally found in a temple near Ayuthaya.

near Ayuthaya, brought in pieces to Bangkok, and had carefully restored. The pavilion's black, gold panels are considered masterpieces of Thai decorative art. In various other buildings at Suan Pakkard are found collections of seashells, mineral crystals, and painted pottery and bronze objects from the prehistoric burial ground at Ban Chiang in Northeast Thailand. The palace is open every day except Sundays and admission is 30 baht.

Plant lovers who fail to be in Bangkok on one of the days of the Weekend Market at the Sanam Luang can visit the permanent **Flower Market in Thevet** (or Theves) district where many of the plant dealers have stalls during the week. (Tell the taxi driver you want to go to *talat dokmai Thevet.)* On a pretty street that runs down to the river and is shaded by flamboyant trees (a showy relative of the poinciana), about fifty plant shops spill out onto the road selling all the ornamentals used in Bangkok gardens. Across Klong Krung Kasem that runs behind the shops is the principal coconut market of Bangkok, where the barges from plantations come to unload their produce; note the large, handsome, cone-shaped baskets which are used only for loading and measuring coconuts. The arched bridge across the *klong* in the middle of the flower market is a good place for picture taking.

The flower that comes closest to being Thailand's national flower, expressing through its multicolored petal, leaf, and stem much of the character of the land, is the **Orchid**. Nearly a thousand species grow native to the country, and the home cultivation of hybrid varieties has long been a popular hobby. Just about every Thai house you see, even in a slum, has at least one pot of orchids, hanging somewhere. In the past decade,

Tame pelicans and sea gulls have the run of Suan Pakkard's carefully trimmed green lawns.

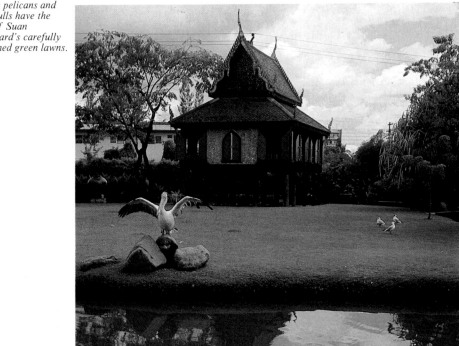

orchid growing has turned into a booming commercial enterprise. Today hardly a plane leaves Bangkok for Europe that does not carry a cargo of cut flowers or whole plants destined for German or French florists or cultivators.

Orchid lovers can visit one of the numerous nurseries where orchids are grown commercially for export. The majority of these are over in Thonburi or along the superhighway leading to the airport, where the air and water are fresher and cleaner, but nurseries can be found scattered throughout the city. Most have no objection to visitors coming to look about, though it is usually a good idea to have a Thai along to help interpret questions. Some of the larger nurseries are Phairot's Orchids (376 Satupradit Road, Yanawa); T. Orchids (30/71 Suthisanvinichai Road); Napa Orchid (9 Soi Santisuk); and CY Orchid (458/1 Sukhumvit).

The **Siam Society** on Soi 21 (Soi Asoke), off Sukhumvit Road, is a royally sponsored group founded in 1904 to promote studies in the history, botany, zoology, anthropology, and linguistics of Thailand. The society publishes a scholarly journal containing articles by experts on those subjects, and also special books on specific subjects like the orchids of Thailand, Thai customs, and gardening; copies of these are on sale at the society's headquarters, and there is an excellent reference library for anyone doing research on Thailand.

Any visitor interested in the culture of North Thailand should go to see the Kamthieng House in the Siam Society compound. This lovely old house, which is approximately 120 years old, was the ancestral home of a prominent family in Chiang Mai, one of whom donated it to the society. With the help of a grant from the Asia Foundation, it was dismantled,

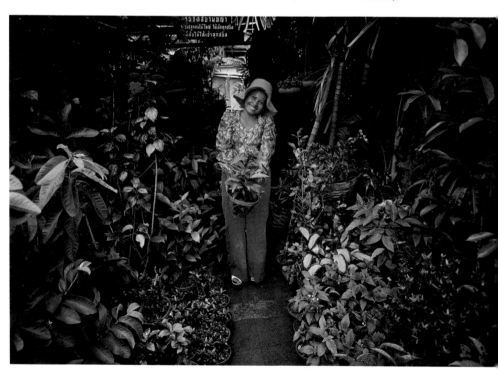

brought to Bangkok, and carefully reassembled in a garden composed mostly of traditional Thai plants. It was decided to use it as an ethnological museum devoted to the folk art and other aspects of northern culture, a needed addition to Bangkok since the National Museum has no such collection. Among the things on display are various everyday objects of farmers and fishermen, fine wood carvings from temples and houses in the North, lacquerware, and hilltribe costumes. Notice in particular the beautifully carved teak lintels from traditional domestic houses, which are fast vanishing in the North. These were placed over the doorway leading to the inner main room of the house and are called in northern dialect *ham yon*, meaning "sacred testicles" — so named because the inner room was believed to contain not only the ancestral spirits of the family but also the virility of the present inhabitants.

1. Jim Thompson's
บ้านทรงไทยของ จิม ทอมป์สัน

When an old northern house is dismantled, or when a new owner moves in, the *ham yon* are often symbolically castrated by beating them severely to destroy the powerful magic accumulated in them under the old owner. A guide to the Kamthieng House and the collection in it is available in the library of the society. The society also intermittently organizes excellent tours around the country, which the visitor on a longer stay may be able to join.

* * *

On Klong Maha Nag at the end of Soi Kasemsong II, across from the National Stadium on Rama I Road, stands **Jim Thompson's House**, open daily except weekends from 9 a.m. to 5 p.m. This is the Thai-style house — or, to be more precise, a collection of seven Thai-style houses joined together — built by the remarkable american who came to Thailand at the end of World War II

Plant lovers are in store for a treat in Thailand, where lush tropical gardens are perennially in bloom. One of the dealers at the Thevet flower market (opposite) shows off a friendly smile as well as a specimen. Jim Thompson's House (above) was the home of the American who revived the Thai silk industry after World War II; assembled from seven teak Thai-style houses, it contains an extensive collection of beautifully displayed Asian antiquities.

and started the Thai silk industry. In 1967, while on a visit to the Cameron Highlands in Peninsular Malaysia, Thompson mysteriously disappeared; despite an extensive search, no trace at all has ever been found of him.

Besides his contribution to the silk business, Thompson will also be remembered for his fabulous collection of Asian Art and the house in which he displayed it and which his heirs have decided to keep as he left it. "Not only have you beautiful things," Somerset Maugham once wrote Thompson after dining with him, "but what is more rare, you have displayed them beautifully." Scattered about the lovely teak-paneled rooms of the house are hundreds of pieces of Chinese blue-and-white Ming export ware; splendid Cambodian stone figures; the largest public collection of Bencharong ("five colors"), a multi-colored porcelain made in China for export only to Thailand; wooden Burmese statues; rare 17th-century Thai stone Buddha images; a dining table once used for card games by King Rama V; and such oddities as a charming little "mouse palace," an ornately carved cage for keeping white mice as pets. The garden around the house is a luxuriant tropical mini-jungle, and looking across the *klong* from the terrace, you can see the houses of some of Thompson's first silk weavers, with brilliant ropes of silk thread hanging out to dry in the sun. There are volunteer guides to explain the collection to visitors, and admission is 20 baht, which goes to a favorite charity of Thompson, the local School for the Blind. (The Thai-style houses you pass on your way to the house, incidentally, are not part of the Thompson estate; they were built by the daughter of one of his weavers as rental houses.) The Thompson Silk Company is on Suriwongse Road.

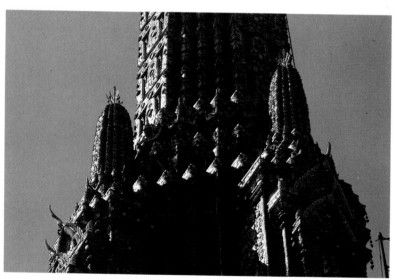

Seventy-nine-meters tall, the spire of Wat Arun (above), encrusted with a glittering mosaic of broken bits of glass and ceramic, looms loftily above the Chao Phya River. The tower was raised on the site of an older one during the reign of King Rama II. The temple compound also contains many other outstanding artistic treasures, like the delicate gold-and-black lacquered doors (opposite) depicting armed but smiling soldiers.

Across the River

Wat Arun, Temple of Dawn, is located across from Bangkok in the sister city of Thonburi, and is most interesting and easily reached by water-taxi from any of the landing stages along the river. (The closest ferrying point is at Tha Tien, just on the opposite bank, where boats leave very frequently in the morning.) An older temple, called Wat Chaeng, was on this site when King Taksin established his capital at Thonburi, and he used it as the royal *wat*, the palace being located nearby. King Rama II of Bangkok, in the early years of the 19th century, decided to enlarge the temple and raise the height of the central tower from 15 to its present 79 meters, making it one of the tallest religious structures in the country. Because of the soft earth, this engineering feat took years to carry out and was finally completed during the reign of his successor. The great *prang* (rounded spire) is completely

covered with pieces of multicolored Chinese porcelain embedded in cement. The builders ran out of porcelain for this large edifice, compelling Rama III to call upon his subjects to contribute any broken crockery they could find to complete the decoration; he was rewarded with thousands of pieces. You can climb about halfway up the tower by one of four steep staircases and get a fine view of the temple compound and the river — though anyone suffering from vertigo should think twice before doing so.

Some good murals cover the inside of the *bot*, guarded by two giant masked gods. There is a large amount of the charming statuary similar to that found in Wat Po, and many lovely pavilions.

A visit to Wat Arun can be combined with one to the **Royal Barges**, also on the Thonburi side on Klong Bangkok Noi, farther north up the river. (Look on the map for the Thonburi Railway Station which sits near the mouth of the *klong*.) These splendidly carved boats were used by the king when he made his royal *kathin* at the end of the rainy season, bringing robes and gifts from the Grand Palace to the monks of Wat Arun. The king sat high on a throne in the largest barge in a procession of dozens, while brilliantly costumed oarsmen chanted as they moved upriver. Discontinued in 1967, this spectacle is being revived for the Chakri Dynasty's Bicentennial celebration. The Royal Thai Navy has lavished over US$440,000 restoring the barges with special attention going to *Sri Supannahong,* the oldest and most richly carved. Nearly 43 meters long, it requires a crew of fifty-four oarsmen, two steermen, two officers, one flagman, one rhythm keeper, and one singer who chants to the cadence of the oars. Two seventiered umbrellas are placed, one in front of and the other behind, the golden pavilion that shelters the king. The gilded bird's head that forms the prow of the barge represents a *hansa*, or sacred swan.

Waterways

While on the Thonburi side, a trip to the **Floating Market** on Klong Dao Kanong will provide a glimpse of the still-active waterborne life of Thailand. Bangkok was once dubbed the Venice of the East, so numerous and important were its canals and rivers, which crisscrossed the entire area to form an extensive transportation network. In fact, up until the last century there were probably fewer roads than waterways in the area. Lying at sea level and flood-prone a good part of the year, Bangkok and the surrounding plain lent themselves naturally to water travel.

Though many *klong*s, especially in Bangkok, have been filled in to make way for the motorcar, thus diminishing considerably in recent years of progress the area's waterborne life, a lot of it still goes on, both on the main artery of the Chao Phya and on the extant canals.

Long-time foreign residents of Bangkok may advise you against going to the Floating Market in Thonburi, the early-morning attraction that, after the numerous temples, probably remains Thailand's most celebrated spectacle. Old hands will tell you that it is not what it used to be, that it has become something of a tourist trap. And in a way they are right: in the twenty-odd years since the market was discovered by the tour agencies, it has certainly lost a good deal of its original innocence; and the Thais who bring things to sell there have not remained immune to the lure of the yen, the mark, and the dollar. (It would be a miracle indeed were the reverse true.) All the same, remember that the old-timers are speaking from the experience of having watched the change; visitors seeing it for the first time are nearly always delighted and count it among the highlights of their stay, the commercialism notwithstanding.

Floating Market
ตลาดน้ำ

Endlessly interesting traffic moves along the Chao Phya River flowing through the heart of Bangkok.

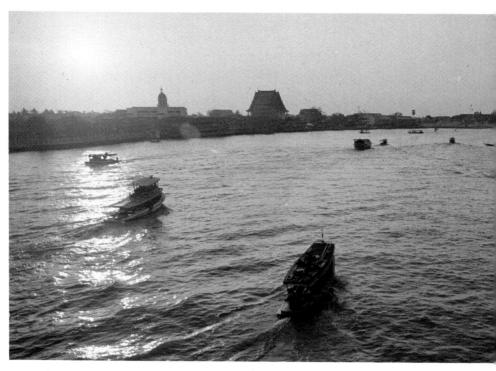

The easiest way to see the market is to take one of the tours which leave daily from the landing near the Oriental Hotel down Oriental Avenue, off Charoen Krung (New Road); these usually go to the Floating Market first and, on the way back, stop for a look at the Royal Barges and Wat Arun. The tour starts early in the morning, around 7:00 a.m., and usually finishes around 11:00 a.m. If you want to go on your own, you can arrange to hire a private boat at the same place, or at one of the other landing stages along the river, but this is likely to turn out to be more expensive unless you have a Thai friend along to haggle over the price of the outing.

To reach the Floating Market from the Oriental landing, the boat goes south down the Chao Phya River to the Krungthep Bridge, then turns right (west) into Klong Dao Kanong, which leads through smaller *klong*s and eventually to the center of the

market on Klong Dan, near Wat Sai. An early start is essential because the market reaches its peak of activity about 7:30 a.m. An hour later, it is merely another Thonburi *klong*, though with rather more souvenir shops than others. If you get there in time, however, you see hundreds of boats, loaded with fruits, vegetables, dried fish, rice, and other produce, paddled by pretty girls wearing broadbrimmed lampshade hats and looking as if they had been carefully selected for eager tourists to photograph. Other boats sell ready-to-eat foods: the inevitable noodles, of course; fried bananas; fresh coconut milk; and little custardlike sweets wrapped in banana leaf. The market presents a colorful and exotic scene; and even if there are almost as many tourist boats as vendors' on some mornings, it is still not the sort of sight you will see anywhere else in the world.

Concerned over criticism about the growing commercialization of the Thonburi Floating Market, the Tourist Organization of Thailand (T.O.T.) encourages visitors to go to another water market outside of Bangkok on a *klong* called **Damnern Saduak**, in Ratchaburi Province, about an hour's drive to the southwest of the city. This is now being scheduled by many tours as part of the trip to the great *chedi* in Nakhon Pathom and the Bridge on the River Kwai in Kanchanaburi. Aside from being far less crowded with tourists than the Thonburi Floating Market, the one at Damnern Saduak has the added advantage of lasting until around 10:00 a.m.; it is especially famous for its fruits which come from surrounding orchards, particularly large, succulent grapefruitlike pomelos, called *sam-o* in Thai. (The route to this market leaves Bangkok across the Memorial Bridge, follows Route 4 to Nakhon Pathom, and 25 km farther turns left on Route 325 for Damnern Saduak, which is on the road to Samut Songkram.)

Damnern Saduak
ดำเนินสะดวก (ตลาดน้ำ)

Klong Dao Kanong
คลองดาวคะนอง

There are other more customary **water tours** which set out on the Chao Phya and on *klong*s in Thonburi, like Bangkok Yai and Bangkok Noi, which remain much as they were fifty years ago. Without traffic lights and smoggy jams to hang you up, the boats breeze past Thai-style houses, orchards, and temples along the river banks. Seen from the river, which has played such an important part in its history, the Bangkok area takes on a completely different aspect. From a new and dramatic angle, you see such fine old European buildings as the French and Portuguese Embassies just up from the Oriental Hotel, faded old shop buildings, gaudily decorated Chinese temples, the Royal Landing Stage with its Thai-style pavilion, and the spires of the Grand Palace and Wat Phra Keo. The river life itself presents an endlessly interesting spectacle: huge rice and sand barges, so heavily loaded that the prow is almost level with the water, with families cheerfully cooking meals on deck; ferry boats packed with commuters, going back and forth between Bangkok and Thonburi; ships belonging to the Royal Thai Navy; and innumerable other craft of all shapes and sizes.

The same rules apply to taking a motorboat on the main river as on a *klong*. The small sleek boats are called *hang yao*, and they usually rent by the hour, unless you take the regular water-taxis that go up and down the *klong*s on fairly regular routes and are not for charter. The price for chartering your own "long tail" should be around 40 baht an hour, but this can depend on a number of factors; in any case, be sure to settle on a price before you set off. If you are intrepid and want to try the regular commuters' boats on the main river, ask for the *rua rew*, or fast boats, as the public launches are re-

Klong Saen Sap
คลองแสนแสบ

ferred to. All the regular taxis and public launches are extremely inexpensive.

On the Chao Phya, you can also take larger, more comfortable (and more expensive) boats which are especially hired to tourists; these are fine for traveling on the river itself, but a *hang yao* is better for exploring the narrower, shallower *klongs*. The Oriental landing is the most common place to hire a large boat — most of the boatmen here speak some English and are accustomed to taking tourists — but you could also get on at the landing near Silapakorn University if you happen to be in the Grand Palace end of town.

The Supatra Company Ltd (254 Arun Amarin Road Thonburi), have daily river cruises for parties of fifteen to twenty-five people (on a single-deck boat) or thirty to forty (on a double-decker). You can pick your own destination or choose from set cruises to standard attractions like Wat Arun or into the countryside.

The Oriental Hotel owns a luxury ship — the Oriental Queen — which sails up the river daily, except Mondays, to Ayuthaya, passengers returning by air-conditioned bus; or you can travel up by bus and return by river, in either case ending the trip at 5:00 p.m. The price per person is several hundred baht, including lunch. (The adventuresome traveler can try the inexpensive commuter's water route to Ayuthaya: from Tha Tien ferry point near Wat Po, take a *rua kao*, or white boat, to Baan Phan, and then transfer to a *hang yao* for the trip downriver.) On Wednesday evenings the Oriental Queen becomes the Jazz Riverboat and cruises on the river

from 8:00 until 11:00 p.m.; the fare includes dinner and dancing. And a young American has done up a rice barge that he calls the Tassaneeya Nava for sunset cruises and a Thai dinner; book through travel agencies or at leading hotels.

One of the most scenic klongs for exploring residential Bangkok is **klong Saen Sap**, a lotus-choked waterway than runs from Bangkapi east to the rice fields beyond. One of the early Bangkok kings supposedly had this canal dug in order to sail war boats all the way to the gulf and thence to Cambodia. Other excellent places in Bangkok to pick up motor-boats are at the Ekamai Bridge on Soi 63 off Sukhumvit and at Prakanong Klong Tan Bridge on Soi 71 off Sukhumvit. If you go from Pratunam to Bangkapi, you will see more Western-style houses than Thai ones, but it does pass a number of picturesque Muslim settlements. If you take a boat out of the center of town at Soi 63 or Soi 71 and head southerly toward Prakanong and beyond, you soon enter real countryside where good-sized villages live entirely on waterborne commerce. Boats make available a vast range of goods: hot dishes served up from a floating restaurant; the daily newspaper; a piece of cloth for a new dress. Once along certain *klongs* in Bangkok — and perhaps still today in other places — floating prostitutes, known as "water babies," housed in little curtained boats paddled by discreet boatmen, plied their age-old trade. The people who live on the *klongs* not only use them for shopping and traveling, but also for bathing and washing — but not, as many visitors seem to think, for drinking; for that, there are boats which supply fresh water in large earthenware jars.

Other interesting boat trips may be made north to Rangsit, famous for its noodles; south to the Port of Bangkok; and to the *wats* both north and south along the Chao Phya. For more details consult the T.O.T.

Bangkok's surviving waterways still offer one of the best ways to see the traditional life of the city. A long-tail motorboat (opposite) races through one of the narrow canals that lead out into the countryside.

Thai Boxing

A Thai boxing ring *looks* like one anywhere else in the world, but what goes on inside is uniquely Thai: a mixture of ballet, gymnastics, and mayhem in which just about anything goes short of biting. The difference is apparent as soon as the fighters enter the arena; they wear the familiar gloves and boxing trunks, but also a colored cord around their head and biceps (usually containing a lucky amulet), often a jasmine wreath around their neck, and they are barefoot. Before the fight starts they go through an odd, slow-motion little dance, designed to show off their talents in a stylized form. To an outsider, the dances may look pretty much the same, but in fact each boxing camp has its own distinctive version and connoisseurs can tell immediately which camp a fighter comes from. A four-piece orchestra composed of a Java pipe, cymbals, and a pair of long drums accompa-

nies the dance and also the fight itself, following the action and stepping up the tempo as the blows fly and the excitement rises.

Thai boxing originated in the Ayuthaya period when it was transformed from a self-defensive art into a spectator sport. A curious combination of balletic grace and murderous ferocity, accompanied and whipped up by the music, makes it a thrilling sport to watch. "Wrestling, judo, throwing, butting, biting, spitting, and kicking your opponent while he is down" are forbidden by the rules; but a fighter can use his feet, elbows, legs, knees, and shoulders — almost every part of his body. The bare feet are the favored means of attack, and the art aptly has been dubbed eight-arm pugilism. You do not have to watch a fight long before you realize that diminutive size is no measure of a Thai boxer's capacity to inflict injury. A well-delivered kick (often to

Thai-style boxing combines ballet, gymnastics, and more than a little mayhem; anything goes, short of biting.

the groin) can floor an opponent; it is an open secret in martial arts' circles that a good Thai boxer is virtually unstoppable.

Until about forty years ago, Thai boxers did not wear gloves but bound their hands with hemp, in which ground glass was sometimes put for added effect. It was also the custom for the fight to go on for as long as both fighters could stand up. Now there are five rounds of fixed three-minute duration, no ground glass, and if one fighter appears to be injured the referee stops the bout. Thai boxing can be seen in Bangkok at **Rajadamnern Stadium** (Rajadamnern Avenue), starting around 5:00 p.m. on Monday, Wednesday, Thursday, and Sunday and at **Lumpini Stadium** (Rama IV Road) on Tuesday, Wednesday, Friday, and Saturday. Two Thai fighters have held the World Flyweight Championship, and as a result Western-style boxing now

rivals the older Thai-style; programs in Bangkok's boxing stadiums now usually include both styles. Fans also avidly follow championship matches abroad, and if you happen to be in the capital when an international bout appears over TV, you will find almost all the streets deserted and crowds huddled around every set.

Although programs at the Bangkok stadiums start around 5:00 p.m., the main fight of Thai boxing takes place around 7:00 p.m. Ringside seats cost about 100 baht, but you can sit in the bleachers for less than half that. If you sit in the cheaper seats — in Bangkok often separated by wire mesh from the expensive ringside seats, to protect the better-paying (and presumably more sedate) customers from the masses who hurtle bottles when angered by a referee's decision — you will also get an introduction to another aspect of Thailand: a strong love of gambling.

Rajadamnern Stadium
สนามมวยราชดำเนิน

45. Lumpini Stadium
สนามมวยลุมพินี

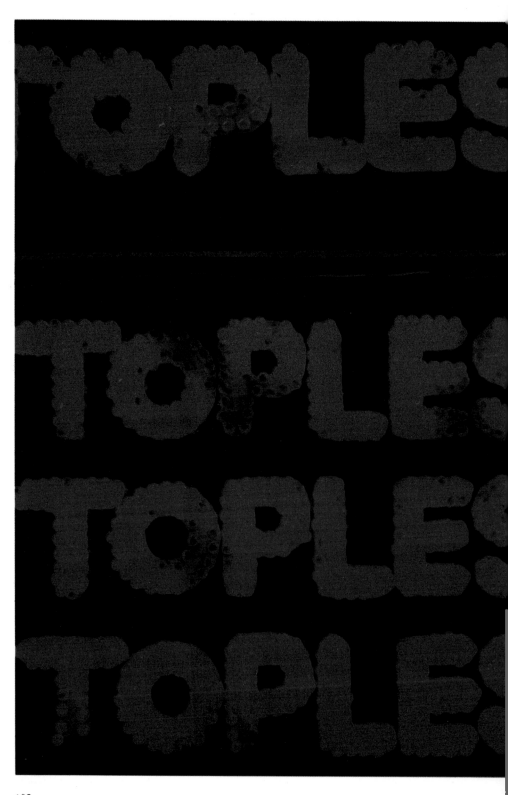

Bangkok at Night

When night falls, a different Bangkok emerges. **Bangkok at night** has many faces, offering just about any form of amusement you could want somewhere in the city. Some areas are transformed into an unbroken neon forest of bars and nightclubs, with touts hawking their attractions at each doorway; restaurants, movie theaters, and massage parlors are jammed, especially on weekends; and almost any taxi driver you encounter in the vicinity of a big hotel is prepared to offer, sometimes on a card printed in several languages, a mind-boggling menu of vices catering to every imaginable taste, and not couched in innuendoes either.

While no part of the city's night life could be described as strictly *farang*, meaning that Thai patrons rarely go there, certain areas do have a predominantly European clientele. Foremost among these is **Patpong**, a short, privately owned street that runs between Silom and Suriwong Roads a short walk from the Dusit Thani Hotel. Twenty years ago Patpong boasted only one or two rather sedate nightclubs and a couple of good restaurants; now it is nearly all night spots from one end to the other, and to accommodate the overflow there is Patpong II running parallel to it. The Patpong places change name, ownership, and decor with bewildering frequency, so that printed guides become obsolete almost before the ink dries, but at any given time they run the gamut from raunchy to reasonably refined. Most of them have some gimmick to attract customers: topless go-go dancing, old movies, dart-throwing contests, and "special shows" that are occasionally raided by police (who do not, however, arrest

Patpong Road, a center of nightlife, offers topless go-go clubs, restaurants, massage parlors, and just about every other kind of evening entertainment, ranging from the raunchy to the reasonably refined.

the customers). Several better massage parlors are located on Patpong II. If you happen to see delectable-looking young ladies loitering around the sidewalks, incidentally, especially between Patpong and the Dusit Thani on Silom, the chances are good that they are not ladies at all but what the Thais called *kra-toeys,* or transvestites, some of whom could fool even a sober expert.

In the years when Bangkok was the leading rest and recreation center for the American military in Vietnam, a similar stretch of night life sprang up along the New Petchburi Road, starting roughly around the intersection of Soi Asoke (Soi 21) and generally referred to as **The Strip**. There were clubs with names like The San Francisco and Jack's American Star Bar, featuring soul food and country music, and massage palaces that looked like a cross between a bowling alley and a mansion. There were also innumerable "short time" hotels, almost as much a feature of Bangkok's evening world (and afternoon, too) as the massage parlors; they were discreet, motel-like establishments where you could drive your car straight into a garage adjoining the room, and a curtain came down immediately to conceal it. Thousands of such places are all over Bangkok, catering to every pocketbook, and many are full from mid-morning until late in the evening. The ones in the Sukhumvit-New Petchburi Road areas are among the fanciest; one has mirrors on the ceilings as well as on the walls, and a control board over the bed with push buttons for lights, music, air conditioning, and *sanuk* (if you press *sanuk* the bed begins to undulate slowly). With the passing of the American soldiers, a good deal of the ethnic life has gone out of The Strip, but most of the bars and massage parlors are still there, the customers now being mostly Thai. Latterly, the New Petchburi Road has become better known for its large outdoor restaurants specializing in sea-

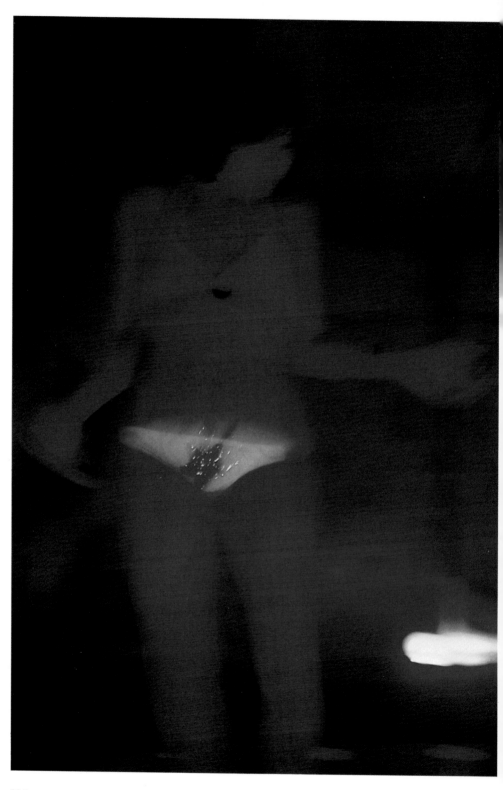

food and for a couple of huge establishments where you dine in private rooms and are hand-fed by scantily clad waitresses.

For those whose night tastes run to the really basic, there is another strip of bars at **Klong Toey**, Bangkok's port area, just before the customs gate that leads to the docks. Patronized mostly by the crews of ships, these have an atmosphere reminiscent of the Shanghai dives of bad old movies. They are not recommended for the squeamish, for couples, or for anyone too arthritic to dodge a beer bottle during one of the melèes that occasionally break out.

When Thais go out in the evening they tend to do so in large, masculine groups, leaving wives and girl friends at home. (The wives are not left entirely uneducated, however; on Rajadamnern Avenue, there are a number of "day clubs" — indistinguishable from nightclubs except that they are open at lunchtime — and you often see parties of respectable-looking matrons having lunch in them.) Generally, eight or ten male friends from work or school will go to a Thai or Chinese restaurant after which, fortified by several bottles of *mekong*, they will pass a few hours in a night club or a massage parlor; the evening will end, almost always, with a late-night snack at a noodle shop or in one of the large markets — Pratunam is a favorite gathering spot. Or they might spend the evening bowling, a sport that has achieved great popularity in the last decade all over the country. The younger, better-heeled, more westernized set enjoy going to the clubs in the large hotels — usually *with* their girl friends — and dancing until closing time.

When night falls, Bangkok shows a different face. The go-go girl on the left is one of the thousands to be found in bars scattered all over the city, catering to every taste and to every pocketbook.

Whether the **massage parlor** originated in Bangkok, as some local enthusiasts claim, or whether they have merely reached their apotheosis here is a question best left for scholarly debate. Certainly they have been a feature of the city for as long as twenty years, and they now number in the hundreds, from rather suspicious-looking establishments in dark, narrow streets to glass-and-marble palaces that the sybaritic Romans might have envied. And they *do* really offer massages, either pure and simple or with such local embellishments as the method called, for reasons totally mysterious, B-course, in which the massuese does the job with her entire body as well as her hands. In the larger massage parlors, the girls are on display behind a one-way glass show window and customers select the one they want by her number, rather as you would select a fish from the tank in a seafood restaurant. You then proceed to a comfortable private room that contains a massage table and a bath tub with hot water; refreshments such as beer and soft drinks can be ordered. The usual length of a massage is an hour and prices vary from around 100 baht to several hundred, depending on the grandeur of the establishment; the girl gets part of the fee, but a tip is expected — small in the case of a simple massage, more if it has been accompanied by what are euphemistically referred to as "special services." To clear up one persistent misunderstanding: massage parlors are not brothels, and massage girls are not per se prostitutes. The price you pay for a massage in most places entitles you to precisely that and no more. Whatever arrangements you may make with your masseuse are strictly between you and her. On the other hand, the popularity of massage parlors with Thais as well as *farang*s, can scarcely be credited solely to a passion for bodily health or greater cleanliness.

Bangkok is the hub of Thailand, not merely for commerce and government but also for tourism. Though today more and more visitors venture upcountry into the far provinces, the great majority still do their sightseeing in the city itself or within a radius of a hundred kilometers. For this reason many of the major newer attractions, like the Ancient City, the Rose Garden, and the Crocodile Farm, have been located within easy driving distance of the capital, adding to the Bangkok area's standard and traditional sights such as Bang Pa-in and the ruins of Ayuthaya which lie on the southern rim of Thailand's Central Plains. The most popular resorts on the East Coast of the Gulf of Thailand are also conveniently reached from Bangkok for a weekend outing. Excellent highways now lead out of Bangkok in all directions, and a trip that used to take three or four hours — to Ayuthaya, for example —

can now be made in just over an hour, thus enabling a visitor with a limited amount of time to see a lot in a couple of days. In the following eighteen odd pages we cover the main attractions near Bangkok — each of which can be visited in a day's round trip from the capital. The places of interest are covered in a counterclockwise spiral, starting southeast of the city.

* * *

The **CROCODILE FARM** is located in Samut Prakarn Province, near the river-mouth town of Pak Nam, half an hour's drive (30 km) southeast of Bangkok on the old Sukhumvit Highway (Route 3). A brochure describes it as "a happy marriage between wildlife conservation and commercial enterprise," and while the crocodiles that get turned into ladies' handbags might argue about the first part, no one can deny the second. Starting twenty-five years ago with a capital of 10,000 baht

1. Crocodile Farm
ฟาร์มจระเข้

TOURING BANGKOK SURROUNDINGS

Map not drawn to scale

2. Ancient City
เมืองโบราณ

The numbers in the
margin in this section
refer to the map on
page 96.

US$5,000), the owner has three farms (two others in the Northeast) worth some 100 million baht (US$5 million). At present the Samut Prakarn farm has about 20,000 crocodiles including both fresh- and salt-water Thai varieties, as well as some South American caimans and Nile River crocodiles. The highlight of a visit to the farm is a show in which handlers go into a pond teeming with crocodiles and toss them about rather roughly; a few overly sensitive visitors may feel that this is adding insult to injury, considering what lies in store for the beasts at the end of their show business career, but most find it exciting. After the crocodiles are skinned, incidentally, their meat is sold to various restaurants in Samut Prakarn and Bangkok, where diners claim it tastes like frog. Besides crocodiles, the farm also has other zoological amusements. There are two elephants for those who want to ride

them; some charming gibbons (now on Thailand's protected species list); a collection of poisonous snakes; and a small zoo that contains lions, tigers, a tame python, a huge black bear, and an elephant that has been taught to do a somewhat ungainly dance to a Thai folk song. Children love it.

Also in Samut Prakarn, a few kilometers from the Crocodile Farm, is an attraction called the **ANCIENT CITY** which bills itself, maybe correctly, as "the world's largest outdoor museum." The brainchild of a Bangkok millionaire with a passion for Thai art and history, it took around three years to construct in what used to be open rice fields, the whole thing being roughly the shape of a map of Thailand and covering some 80 hectares. There are scale replicas (some full size, others one-third the size of the original) of famous monuments and temples from all parts of the kingdom, some of them recon-

Man and beast put on a hair-raising show at the Crocodile Farm *(left)*. The Ancient City contains a monumental re-creation of Thai ruins and temples, and a collection of art, including this standing Buddha image *(above)*.

Northeast of Bangkok

structions of buildings that no longer exist, like the Grand Palace and Royal Chapel of Ayuthaya, and some copies of real places like the huge temple of Khao Phra Viharn on the Thai-Cambodian border, which was awarded to Cambodia by the World Court some years ago after a long dispute over its ownership. Experts from the National Museum worked as consultants on the reproductions to ensure accuracy of historical detail. At present there are more than sixty constructions, covering fifteen centuries of Thai history, and more are planned. In addition to the monuments, the Ancient City also has a model Thai village, in which you can see artisans at work on various native handicrafts, such as lacquerware, ceramics, and paper umbrellas; its own version of the Floating Market, picturesquely staged for photographers; assorted shops for buying souvenirs; and a Thai restaurant. The king of Thailand has visited the place several times to bring royal visitors, among the first of whom, in 1972, were Queen Elizabeth and Prince Philip on their state visit to the country. On Rajadamnern Avenue, facing the Democracy Monument, is a booking office for bus trips to Ancient City; air-conditioned buses make the 33-km trip twice daily.

* * *

Located near enough to Bangkok for a comfortably paced day's trip, the eastern province of **NAKHON NAYOK** features waterfalls, a pretty park, and picturesque temples. The most scenic route to this province lies along Road 305, which branches off Route 1 north of Bangkok, runs northeast along the canal to Ongkharak, and then goes on above rice fields and small rivers to Nakhon Nayok town, a total of about 140 km from the capital. From the town, Road 33 goes northwest and then, within a few kilometers, another road leads off to the right towards two waterfalls and Wang Takrai Park. After 11 km you reach an intersection: straight ahead takes you to **SALIKA WATERFALL.** Near the parking lot are pleasant outdoor restaurants and stalls selling fruits and drinks. The waterfall itself is impressive around the end of the rainy season (September to November).

Turning left at the intersection takes you to **WANG TAKRAI PARK.** On the way stop at the **Temple of Chao Pau Khun Dan,** named after one of King Naresuan's advisers whose spirit is believed to protect the area. Prince Chumbhot (of Suan Pakkard Palace in Bangkok) established the 80-hectare **Wang Takrai Park** in the 1950s; a statue of him now stands on the opposite bank of the small river flowing through the park. Prin-

3. Nakhon Nayok
นครนายก (จังหวัด. ตัวเมือง)

4. Salika Waterfall
น้ำตกสาลิกา

5. Wang Takrai Park
วังตะไกร้

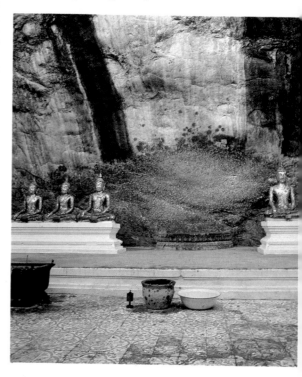

Gold leaf adorns the sacred rock of the Temple of Chao Pau Khun Dan (right). In the countryside near Bangkok (opposite) a boy enjoys a ride on a companionable albino buffalo.

cess Chumbhot, wife of the founder, has carefully managed the planting of many varieties of flowers and trees, including some imported species. Cultivated gardens among tall trees line both banks of the main stream that flows through the 2-km-long park. Bungalows are also for rent in this picturesque botanical garden.

Before driving back to Bangkok, visitors can have a meal at the park restaurant. On the way out at the park entrance, the road on the left crosses a river and continues 5 km to **NANG RONG WATERFALL**, an inviting three-part cascade situated in a steep valley, where open-air restaurants and fruit stalls await visitors.

* * *

KHAO YAI NATIONAL PARK, the nearest hill resort to Bangkok, lying 205 km north of the capital, covers 2,000 sq km in four provinces. The government has provided this

cool retreat with bungalows, motels, restaurants, an 18-hole golf course, and many nature trails and roads. You can drive to Khao Yai ("Big Mountain") in about three to four hours directly from Bangkok by taking Route 1 north towards Saraburi. Near Saraburi, about 107 km from the capital, the Friendship Highway (Route 2) heads northeast and about 58 km from Saraburi, Dhanarajata Road goes another 24 km to the foot of the park. At that point the road begins to climb and twist among the hills for 16 km until it reaches **Nong Khing Village** atop one of Khao Yai's peaks. At Nong Khing dine at the Khao Yai Restaurant and check out the accommodations for overnight stays: sixteen two-bedroom and four three-bedroom luxury bungalows with bathrooms, sitting rooms, and servants' quarters; fourteen one-bedroom and four two-bedroom motel units; and cheapest of all for

North of Bangkok

large groups, the tourist houses that sleep up to ten people each. (You can book rooms through the T.O.T.)

Khao Yai's highest peaks lie east in the Korat sector: Khao Lam is 1,328 meters high and Khao Kheo 1,270 meters. Evergreen and deciduous trees, the latter dropping many of their leaves during the arid hot season, palms, and bamboo provide ample greenery throughout the park. At night temperatures may drop to below 15°C, depending on the season. Monkeys, gibbons, and langurs are commonly seen in the trees. Wild, but not considered dangerous, elephants, bears, gaurs, tigers, boars, and deer also roam the huge, protected reserve. After dark you can "hunt" for deer with flashlights.

From Nong Khing hike over the many trails to Orchid and Hew Suwat Waterfalls. If you camp in the park, notify officials as to where you want to camp and take mosquito nets.

A city greater than the London or Paris of its time, early European residents were forced to admit — but in 1767 the Burmese beseiged and so utterly destroyed **AYUTHAYA** that it was never rebuilt. Today, located 85 km north of Bangkok, its ruins stand as a fascinating link with Thailand's past.

Ayuthaya's site had been carefully chosen to make it defensible. Built at the junction of three rivers, it was necessary only to cut a canal across the loop of the Chao Phya to convert Ayuthaya into an island. In the four centuries following its foundation in 1350, a great mass of temples and palaces, linked by canals, was erected on and around the man-made island. Its glittering opulence which astonished foreign visitors enticed the Burmese to savagely tear it apart in search of booty.

Today Ayuthaya is a bustling country town sprawled along the

8. Ayuthaya
อยุธยา (ตัวเมือง)

Lakeside bungalows (above), maintained by the Tourist Organization of Thailand, rim the edge of a peaceful lake in Khao Yai National Park, which covers 2,000 square kilometers in four provinces. The park contains kilometers of scenic walking trails where nature lovers can see a variety of native animals and plant life; an 18-hole golf course and a motel are also available. For most of the year the weather is cool, making it a popular retreat.

main street from the **Pridi Damrong Bridge** to a little beyond the **Chandrakasem Palace.** The majority of Ayuthaya's visitors cover the town in a day trip from Bangkok. Should you feel Ayuthaya's long history requires more time to absorb, there is a single motel and a pair of Chinese hotels across from the Chandrakasem Palace. The hotels are clean but spartan, and inexpensive. Open-air food stalls in the market area can look after the inner self in delicious fashion; or for a more romantic meal Ayuthaya can boast not one, but two, floating restaurants. Berthed slightly up- or downstream from the Pridi Damrong Bridge, the restaurants serve excellent sour hot beef, and you can eat while watching the waters rustle by.

The obvious way to arrive at a waterborne city is by boat and there are frequent river connections with Ayuthaya from Bang Pa-in. The fare is only 8 baht for the 40-minute trip,

and a pleasant way to travel is by road to Bang Pa-in and thence by water. Alternatively, convenient bus and train services run from Bangkok, both taking one and a half hours. The excellent road from Bangkok will whisk you to Ayuthaya in about 90 minutes once you have extricated yourself from Bangkok's eternal traffic jams. It is also possible to travel all the way to Ayuthaya by riverboat, and tours can be arranged in Bangkok (see "Bangkok Water Tours").

Once in Ayuthaya a circular river tour in a long-tailed boat can be easily arranged on the landing stage close to Chandrakasem Palace. This is the best introduction to the ruined city and the only way to reach some of the more isolated sites on the mainland side of the river. A boat hired for about an hour should not cost more than 40 to 50 baht.

As you start out on your boat tour, close to the junction of the Nam

AYUTHAYA

1. Pridi Damrong Bridge
2. Chandrakasem Palace
3. Wat Raj Burana
4. Wat Mahathat
5. Wat Dhamik Raj
6. Wang Luang (Royal Palace)
7. Wat Phra Sri Samphet
8. Viharn Phra Mongkol Bopit·
9. Wat Phra Ram
10. Wat Na Phra Meru
11. Wat Lokaya Sutha
12. Queen Suriyothai Memorial
13. Wat Suwan Dararam
14. Chao Phya National Museum
15. Wat Phanan Choeng
16. Wat Buddhaisawan
17. St. Joseph's Cathedral
18. Wat Chai Wattanaram
19. Wat Konthi Thong
20. Phom Phet Fortress
21. Phu Kao Thong
22. Wat Yai Chai Mongkol

Pasak and Chao Phya Rivers you pass the imposing **Wat Phanan Choeng.** Founded twenty-six years prior to Ayuthaya, it houses a huge seated Buddha, so tightly crowded against the roof that he appears to be holding it up. Wat Phanan Choeng was a favorite of the Chinese traders of Ayuthaya who would pray there before setting out on long voyages — it still has an unmistakably Chinese atmosphere.

Ayuthaya was at one time surrounded by walls with stout fortifications. Only portions remain, one of the best examples of which is at **Phom Phet,** across the river from Wat Phanan Choeng.

Upstream from Wat Phanan Choeng, the recently restored **Wat Buddhaisawan** stands serenely on the riverbank. Farther upstream, the restored Catholic **Cathedral of St. Joseph** is a reminder of the large European population of the city when it was in its prime. At the bend of the river stands one of Ayuthaya's most eloquently romantic ruins, **Wat Chai Wattanaram.** A Buddha keeps solitary watch, perched on a high pedestal in front of the ruins. The stately *prang* with its surrounding *chedis* and rows of headless Buddhas have an almost lost-city feeling in their jungly, overgrown isolation. They make a fine contrast to the restored **Memorial to Queen Suriyothai** on the city-side of the river. The valiant Ayuthaya queen, dressed as a man, astride an elephant accompanied her king to battle and gave her own life to save his.

The junction of the Chao Phya and Lop Buri Rivers marks the section of the Chao Phya that was bypassed. Over the centuries the river has become narrower and shallower, so much so that it looks more like an artificial canal. Children splash in the water or paddle by adeptly in small boats; gaggles of geese drift imperiously across the murky water. Lines of saffron robes hanging out to dry mark the site of a riverside monastery; even the ubiquitous spirit houses stand semisubmerged. The riverside seems to virtually throb with activity as the boat passes under the last few bridges and arrives back at the landing stage near Chandrakasem Palace.

Chandrakasem Palace was known as the Palace of the Front, and was originally constructed outside the city walls. Built close to the junction of the old rivers and the new bypass, it had an important, defensive function — it was built by King Naresuan, the first ruler of Ayuthaya, to gain control over their northern rival, Chiang Mai. The Burmese burnt and destroyed the palace but King Mongkut later rebuilt it. It now houses a small museum. The palace looks out onto the noisiest part of town, where a continuous stream of vehicles passes by, including what must be the least silenced motor *samlors* in all of Thailand.

The old royal palace, **Wang Luang,** was completely leveled by the Burmese. The bricks were later removed to Bangkok to rebuild the capital, so now only scattered foundations among the trees mark the palace site. Close by stands the royal temple of **Wat Phra Sri Sanphet,** enclosed within the area of Wang Luang rather like the Temple of the Emerald Buddha stands within the Grand Palace compound in Bangkok. The gold-leafed Buddha, *Phra Sri Sanphet,* that gave the *wat* its name, was irreparably damaged by the Burmese. Today the three central *chedis* of the *wat* have been restored and stand in regal contrast to the surrounding ruins.

For centuries after Ayuthaya's fall, a huge bronze Buddha sat unsheltered near Wat Phra Sri Sanphet. His flame of knowledge and one of his arms had been broken by the collapsing roof of his temple. Twenty

Waterborne commerce and travel once dominated the rich, flat plains around Ayuthaya. Typical Thai river barges, filled to the brim, are towed upriver in long processions.

Wat Phanan Choeng
วัดพนัญเชิง

Wat Buddhaisawan
วัดพุทไธศวรรย์

St. Joseph's Cathedral
วัดคริสต์ของ เซนต์ โยเซฟ

Wang Luang
วังหลวง

Wat Chai Wattanaram
วัดชัย วัฒนาราม

Wat Phra Sri Sanphet
วัดพระศรีสรรเพชญ

Queen Suriyothai Memorial
อนุสาวรีย์สมเด็จพระศรีสุริโยไท

years ago **Viharn Phra Mongkol Bopitr** was built around the restored statue. With a large car park, and rows of souvenir stalls facing it, this is an often-used starting point for Ayuthaya tours. Apart from the cluster of souvenir shops and postcard emporiums, a line of antique specialists can also be found close by. They sell all sorts and sizes of "genuine" antique Buddhas.

In the same area is **Wat Phra Ram,** one of the older temples, begun in 1369 by the son of Ayuthaya's founder; in later years it was completely restored twice. Elephant gates still stand at intervals around the old walls, and the central terrace is dominated by a crumbling *prang* to which cling a gallery of stucco *nagas, garudas* (mythical sun-birds), and statues of the Buddha. Wat Phra Ram's *prang* shimmers, reflected in the pool, Beung Phra Ram, that almost surrounds the temple. Once a marshy

swamp the pool was dug out to provide fill for the temple sites.

Two of Ayuthaya's finest temples stand side by side across the lake from Wat Phra Ram. Built by the seventh king of Ayuthaya as a memorial to his brothers, **Wat Raj Burana** contained many fine images and items of royal jewelry which were discovered during a 1958 restoration. The two *chedis* at the crossroads contain the ashes of the royal brothers, Princes Ai and Yo. Across the road, **Wat Mahathat** has little remaining apart from the base of its huge *prang.* Originally built to a height of 46 meters, it later collapsed; undeterred the people of Ayuthaya rebuilt it 4 meters higher.

Why is it that ruins are always so much more appealing than restorations? **Wat Dhamik Raj** is an excellent example of this. Around a precariously leaning *chedi,* rows of lions growl defiance at the encroaching

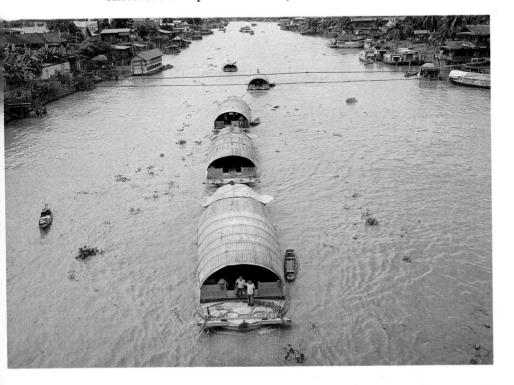

vegetation; but it is too late — already some of the statues lie shattered and greenery sprouts from the heads of others. Beside the *chedi*, the high walls and columns of the *wat* reverently enclose a solid mass of plant life.

Wat Suwan Dararam was built towards the close of the Ayuthaya period and has been beautifully restored and preserved. The walls of the *bot* have foundations that dip in the center, typical of the architecture of that time. Delicately carved columns support the roof, and the inside walls are decorated with brilliantly hued frescoes. Still used as a temple today, the *wat* has a seemingly magical effect in the early evening as the monks chant their devotions.

Across the river from the old palace stands another restored building, **Wat Na Phra Meru.** Here a small *viharn* houses a stone Davaravati Buddha, seated in the "European

manner" in contrast to the yoga position of Ayuthaya Buddhas. Found in the ruins of Wat Mahathat, the statue is believed to have originally come from Nakhon Pathom. The *bot* contains an Ayuthaya-style seated Buddha on the altar.

A winding road from Queen Suriyothai's *chedi* leads to **Wat Lokaya Sutha.** Little remains here, apart from a massive reclining Buddha, calmly contemplating the view, freed from the claustrophobic walls which once encompassed him. A scattering of food stalls stand close by, their owners gazing back with equal equanimity.

A path runs down to the river close to the bridge leading to Wat Na Phra Meru. The precarious pathway of planks and boards snakes its way along and across the river, rising in the middle just enough for a boat to sneak underneath. On the other bank the bouncing planks lead right into a

Wat Suwan Dararam
วัดสุวรรณดาราราม

Wat Lokaya Sutha
วัดโลกยะสุธา

Wat Na Phra Meru
วัด ณ พระเมรุ

The ruins of Ayuthaya have an evocative, haunting quality, recalling the splendors of the old capital, destroyed by Burmese invaders in the 18th century. At Wat Raj Burana (above and opposite), once one of the city's largest and grandest temples, one sees shattered Buddha images and the lonely remains of a once-noble doorway framing a memory of past glory. The ancient city contains kilometers of such relics, which are carefully preserved today.

Wat Yai Chai Mongkol
วัดใหญ่ชัยมงคล

monastery, its temple gong hung in a riverside tower. A robed monk will show you through to the back door from where you can walk across to the secluded ruins of **Wat Konthi Thong.**

Many more relics can be seen in Ayuthaya's fine **Chao Phya Museum** and still more outside the city. At the roundabout on the Bangkok road is a crowded sales lot, selling spirit houses to suit every type of dwelling — from a small hut to a large mansion. A left turn takes you to **Wat Yai Chai Mongkol** with its huge *chedi*. In single-handed combat on elephant-back, King Naresuan slew the crown prince of Burma in 1592. The *chedi* was built to match the Phu Kao Thong Pagoda just north of Ayuthaya in celebration of the victory. Contemporary Buddha statues line the courtyard and make a pleasant contrast to the venerable *chedi*.

North of Ayuthaya the **Phu Kao Thong Temple,** better known as the **Golden Mount Chedi,** towers incongruously over the flat countryside — its upper terraces commanding a pastoral view of the rice paddies. Built by the Burmese after their earlier and less destructive conquest in 1569, it was later remodeled by the Siamese in their own style. To mark 2,500 years of Buddhism, a 2,500 gram gold ball was mounted on top of the *chedi* spire in 1956.

Going in the opposite direction to the Golden Mount, the road runs to the only **Elephant Kraal** left in Thailand. This kraal is a reminder of the days when elephants were not only caught and trained to work in the jungles, but were also an essential requisite for a strong army. Standing at the edge of the huge pit, one can still imagine the thunder of the mighty beasts that helped raise Ayuthaya to its peak, but could not stay its downfall from a great kingdom to a mere country town.

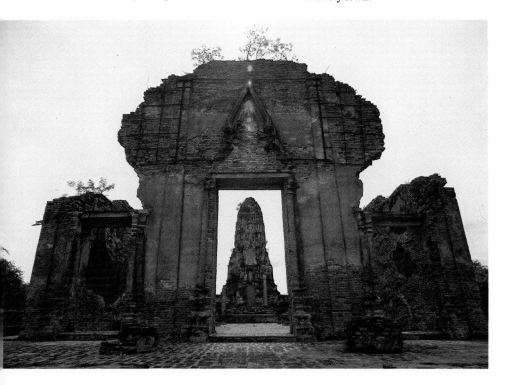

BANG PA-IN, a charming collection of palaces and pavilions once used by the kings of Thailand as a summer retreat, lies a short distance downriver from the ruins of Ayuthaya; it can be reached by water on a tour boat like the Oriental Queen or by road in about an hour from Bangkok. The rulers of Ayuthaya used Bang Pa-in in the hot season as long ago as the 17th century, but the buildings one sees today date from the late 19th- and early 20th-century reigns of Rama V and Rama VI, who used to come up from Bangkok. A pretty palace on a lake in a mixture of Italian and Victorian styles, built by Rama V, is closed to the public; but visitors can see an ornate Chinese-style palace in which the king stayed during visits. A Thai style pavilion called the **Aisawan Tippaya Asna** in the middle of the lake as one enters the grounds, is regarded as one of the finest examples of Thai architecture.

The former summer capital of Siam, **LOP BURI** lies 155 km north of Bangkok. You can drive to Lop Buri from Bangkok in less than four hours. The journey through the fertile rice bowl of Thailand is a pleasant one. Just 10 km north of Ayuthaya, the hills of the Korat plateau appear on the horizon — the first break in the flatness of the Central Plains.

Artifacts of the Neolithic and Bronze Ages have been found in quantity in Lop Buri, testifying to the great antiquity of the city. In the Davaravati period (6th to 11th centuries) it was a major town. At the height of the power of the kings of Angkor (11th and 12th centuries), it was a provincial capital of the Khmer empire. Then came the Thais, who put their imprint on most of the old buildings which now survive.

Tentative contacts with Dutch and Portuguese explorers came in the 16th century, but it was not until the mid

9. Bang Pa-in
วังบางปะอิน

10. Lop Buri
ลพบุรี (ตัวเมือง, จังหวัด)

Aisawan Tippaya
พระที่นั่งไอควารย์ทิพยอาสน์

The summer palace of Bang Pa-in (above) is a charming collection of palaces and pavilions in a variety of architectural styles. Among them is an elegant little pavilion, the most photographed structure in all the country, which seems to float on shimmering surface of the lake. Boldly sculptured faces (opposite) stare from a corner of Prang Sam Yod, part of a Khmer-style temple in Lop Buri, once a provincial capital of the Khmer empire.

1700's that Ayuthaya became a bustling international city with missionaries from Italy and Spain and traders from Britain, Indonesia and China. Some French architects even ventured as far as Lop Buri, where King Narai retreated each summer to escape Ayuthaya's humidity.

However, Narai was one of the most luckless kings of the Ayuthaya dynasty. The last scenes of his life were played out in Lop Buri in the **Suttha Sawan Pavilion.** In May 1688, as he lay mortally ill in this pavilion, his Minister of Defense, Phra Phetracha, seized the throne. According to one tradition, the dying king was attended by only ten royal pages who remained loyal to him. Realizing that the rebels might never allow them to leave the palace alive, the king called in a Buddhist abbot to ordain the pages as monks, so that the saffron robe of Buddhism would guarantee their safety. In return, he

offered the Suttha Sawan Pavilion to the monkhood as a temple. The truth of this tradition is attested by the actions of a later king, Mongkut, when he came to reoccupy the Lop Buri palace in the 19th century — he had to offer other lands to the Buddhist authorities in exchange for the palace and its grounds.

The grounds of the **Lop Buri Palace** (Narai Raja Niwes Palace) are enclosed by massive walls which still dominate the center of the modern town. The inner side of the walls flanking the gates are honeycombed with hundreds of leaf-shaped niches meant to contain small lamps fed by coconut oil. In the heyday of the palace, they were lighted on state and religious occasions.

Of King Narai's buildings, the only one which has substantially survived is the **Dusit Maha Prasat Hall.** This was built for the audience granted by the king in 1685 to Che-

Lop Buri Palace
วังลพบุรี (นารายณ์ราชนิเวศน์)

Suttha Sawa Pavilion
ตำหนักสุทธาสวรรค์

Dusit Maha Prasat Hall
พระที่นั่งดุสิตมหาปราสาท

valier de Chaumont, ambassador of Louis XIV. It is recorded that the walls of the front structure were panelled with mirrors given by the French king. Holes for the mirrors can still be seen.

Another surviving building of the Narai period is the **Chantra Paisan Pavilion** also in the palace grounds. Now part of the Fine Arts Museum, it was the first structure built by King Narai, and was later restored by King Mongkut. The wooden decorations of the roof are not in good proportions, somewhat spoiling the overall effect, but the classic Ayuthaya-period curve of the base is good. The sagging line of the multiple roofs is also classical and designed for elegance.

Adjoining the Chantra Paisan Pavilion is the **Phiman Mongkut Pavilion** — a three-storied mansion in the colonial style built in the mid-19th century by King Mongkut. The immensely thick walls and high ceilings show how the summer heat was averted most effectively before air conditioning arrived. The mansion, small but full of character, and also part of the Fine Arts Museum, displays a mixed bag of bronzes, Chinese and Sukhothai porcelain, coins, Buddhist fans, and shadow-play puppets. Yet some of the pieces, particularly the Ayuthaya bronze heads and Benchurong porcelain, are extremely fine. On the top floor are displayed some of King Mongkut's personal effects. They reveal the character of this remarkable man who, though Siam's "Lord of Life," led a Spartan existence.

Other buildings in the palace complex which should be visited are the eight bijou houses behind the museum. In King Mongkut's time they accommodated the court ladies, their children, and servants. One of the buildings has now been converted into a **Farmer's Museum**, which displays the traditional implements of Thai agriculture.

King Narai had a Greek adviser, Constantine Phaulkon, whom the king ennobled with the title of *Chao Phya Vichayane* ("Noble Victorious Lord"). Though not officially the foreign minister, it was Phaulkon who managed Siam's relations with the European powers. However, his ambition also led him to meddle in domestic matters, making him most unpopular with the Buddhist clergy and also with officials of King Narai's government. When the king lay on his death bed, his minister of defense seized power and had Phaulkon beheaded.

The remains of a grand palace in Lop Buri said to have belonged to Phaulkon rival those of the royal palace. Located just north of Narai's palace, and now overgrown with weeds, the buildings show traces of European influence — straight-sided walls and pedimental decorations over Western-style windows. The estate is now kept locked to prevent vandalism, and also possibly to hide from visitors the shocking neglect of the ruins. Hopefully, restoration work will be undertaken before it is too late.

Of particular interest in Lop Buri are two important relics of the Khmer (Cambodian) and pre-Khmer periods. One, located just west of the railroad and north of the town's main road, is a 13th-century laterite-block shrine with three spires which give it its Thai name of **Phra Prang Sam Yod** ("Sacred Three Spires"). Restored in 1926 by the Fine Arts Department, the stone carvings on the towers and the door columns are particularly fine. The second is the Hindu Spire (**Prang Khaek** in Thai) in the center of the town — also of great antiquity. A group of three laterite spires, it was probably built during the 11th century and restored by King Narai in the 17th century.

A slow-motion ride on an elephant is one of the offerings at the Rose Garden, a newer tourist attraction for people who want a quick survey of Thai life all in one place.

Chantra Paisan Pavilio
หลับพลา จันทรไพศาล

Phiman Mongkut Pavi
หลับพลาพิมานมงกุฎ

Phra Prang Sam Yod
พระปรางค์สามยอด

Prang Khaek
ปรางค์แขก

Farmers Museum
พิพิธภัณฑ์เกษตรกร

West of Bangkok

Located on the bucolic Tachin River, less than an hour's drive west from Bangkok, the **ROSE GARDEN** is the brainchild of a former lord mayor of the capital. The garden, known as *Suan Sam Phran* in Thai, lies 32 km west of the capital on Route 4, the road to famous Nakhon Pathom. It covers a large area of well landscaped gardens — yes, there are roses, and healthy ones, too — and includes a modern hotel with convention rooms, traditional Thai-style houses for rent by the night, several first-rate restaurants, a swimming pool, a golf course, a bowling alley, facilities for boating and waterskiing on the river, and a model Thai village where each afternoon a cultural show is performed for tourists. To a discerning traveler, it might sound a bit calculated and "cute," but somehow it is not; the whole thing is done with such good taste, the gardens are so beautiful,

and the quality of the food served so high, that many jaded tourists who come with reluctance leave with praise.

A display that might catch your interest at the cultural show because of its novelty to Westerners is the sport of *takraw*. In fact, you may come across it in Bangkok: a group of boys or men, standing in a circle casually keeping a rattan ball aloft by knocking it from one to another using any part of the body except the hands. *Takraw* might be called the national sport; certainly it is the national pastime, for men of all ages spend their leisure playing *takraw*. There are semiprofessional *takraw* teams, too, who put on performances at various fairs and parties. If you are in Bangkok during the kite-fighting season, you can see the teams in action at the Rajadamnern Avenue end of Sanam Luang every weekday afternoon. Using the sides of the feet is the preferred method of keeping the ball aloft, but a real star also uses his elbows, head, and shoulders, making the whole thing look as effortless as a great dancer going through his paces.

A visit to the Rose Garden can be arranged in Bangkok through the Rose Garden booking office, 264/4 Siam Square.

Just 54 km west of Bangkok beyond the Rose Garden on Route 4 is the town of **NAKHON PATHOM**. As you drive toward Nakhon Pathom, a colossal landmark seems to rise above the town and tower over the surrounding countryside. Standing 127 meters high, **Phra Pathom Chedi** is the tallest Buddhist monument in the world.

The original Phra Pathom Chedi was small and was built more than a thousand years ago during the Mon empire when culture flourished in the Nakhon Pathom area. In 1057, King Anurdha of Burma besieged the town, leaving it in ruins for the next hundred years. It was not until King Mongkut had visited the old *chedi* and was impressed by its significance as the oldest Buddhist monument in Thailand, that restoration of the temple began in 1853. However, the original structure was found to be in such a state of collapse that repair proved impossible, and a new *chedi* was built to cover the old one. This too collapsed in a rainstorm, and eventually the present building was completed by King Chulalongkorn.

Set in a huge square park, the massive *chedi* rests upon a circular terrace dotted with examples of trees connected with the Buddha's life. In November each year, a gay fair in the temple grounds attracts crowds from far and near.

In the days of canal travel, a royal visit to Nakhon Pathom was more than a day's journey, and so it is

12. Nakhon Pathom
นครปฐม (ตัวเมือง, จังหวัด)

Phra Pathom Chedi
พระปฐมเจดีย์

The tallest Buddhist monument in the world (above) towers like a cathedral over Nakhon Pathom. Each November a country fair (right) lights up the spire. Samut Sakhon (far right) is a typical Thai seaport.

not surprising that various palaces and residences were built there. **Sanam Chand Palace** has a fine *sala* (formerly a meeting pavilion) — now used for government offices — and a building in a most unusual Thai interpretation of English Tudor architecture, used appropriately as a setting for Shakespearean drama. In front of this building stands a statue of Yaleh, the pet dog of King Rama VI. The fierce dog, unpopular with the court, was poisoned by the king's attendants. Even as a statue, Yaleh looks insufferable.

A good way to approach the port of **SAMUT SAKHON**, for a view of Thailand's coastal life, is by the branch railway connecting it with Thonburi, Bangkok's sister city. The line, called the Mae Klong Railway, runs at a loss, but has been reprieved from extinction because of its usefulness to the population of the three provinces west of Bangkok. For a few baht, you can take the "express" which leaves approximately every hour, from Wong Wien Yai station in Thonburi. The express train moves at a leisurely pace. The 40-minute journey passes first through the suburbs, then through thriving vegetable gardens, groves of coconut and areca palms, and rice fields.

A busy fishing port, Samut Sakhon (also called Mahachai) lies at the meeting of the Tachin River, the Mahachai Canal, and the Gulf of Thailand. The main landing stage on the riverbank has a clock tower and a restaurant which, as might be expected, serves excellent seafood, including grilled crab with vegetables. Nearby at the main **Fish Market** fishermen unload hauls of fish, crabs, squids, and prawns from their boats.

At the fish market pier, you can hire a boat with an outboard engine for a 40-baht round trip to Samut Sakhon's principal temple, **Wat**

13. Samut Sakhon
สมุทรสาคร (ตัวเมือง, จังหวัด)

Chom Long, at the mouth of the Tachin River. Most of the buildings are modern except for an old *viharn* immediately to the right of the temple's river landing. The *viharn* dates back about a century. The extensive grounds overlooking the water are charmingly laid out with shrubs and flowering trees. There is also a bronze statue of King Chulalongkorn commemorating his visit to the temple. His homburg hat does not in the least detract from his immense dignity.

* * *

An odd-looking railway bridge crosses the Meklang River a few kilometers from **KANCHANABURI**. The bridge leaves the bank over a series of elliptical spans; in the center of the river the spans become awkwardly rectangular, without apparent reason, and then revert to their elliptical way before disappearing into the forest on the other side. Crossing over the bridge flows a constant stream of

pedestrians taking vegetables home from the market or just out for a walk. Occasionally a motorcycle buzzes across the bridge skirting between the railway tracks. When the river's other name is mentioned, the mystery behind the strange pattern of spans becomes clear. The Meklang River, also known as the Kwai Yai, is spanned by the infamous **Bridge on the River Kwai**. And we soon learn that towards the end of World War II the central spans were knocked out by Allied bombers and later rebuilt with those incongruous angular replacements.

Kanchanaburi town, in the province of the same name, is about 122 km northwest of Bangkok, past Nakhon Pathom, and not far from the Thai border with Burma. It was from here that the Japanese put to work Allied prisoners of war to construct 415 km of rail leading to the Three Pagodas Pass at the Burmese

Wat Chom Long
วัดชมล่อง

15. River Kwai Bridge
สะพานข้ามแม่น้ำแคว

14. Kanachanaburi
กาญจนบุรี (ตัวเมือง, จังหวัด)

Lashed together into rafts (above), newly cut bamboo poles float downstream to market. Though peaceful-looking today, the waterway is spanned by the infamous Bridge on the River Kwai, built by Allied prisoners during World War II. Mute testimony to their suffering is offered by the Kanchanaburi Allied Cemetery (opposite) where 6,982 of those who labored on the notorious "Death Railway" lie buried in neatly labeled graves near the river.

border. It is estimated that 100,000 oppressed laborers as well as 16,000 Allied prisoners of war lost their lives due to beatings, starvation, disease, and exhaustion when constructing the railroad. In Kanchanaburi, endless rows of war graves mark the resting places of 6,982 of those Allied soldiers.

Although the Bridge on the River Kwai probably owes much of its fame to the novel by Pierre Boulle and later to the film, it is worth a visit from an historical point of view. It can be reached by boat or *samlor* from Kanchanaburi. The Kanchanaburi Tourist Bureau, located on the main street of Kanchanaburi opposite the Allied War Cemetery, can arrange tours to the bridge and surroundings. A combined boat landing and restaurant is moored near the bridge and provides an excellent vantage point to watch for the occasional train to cross. The pedestrian path over the bridge is not as unsafe as it looks — niches between the spans provide an escape in case of an unexpected train. A steam locomotive used shortly after the war is displayed beside the tiny Kwai Bridge station platform, along with an ingenious Japanese supply truck that could run on road or rails.

The entire railway was bought by the Thai government from the Allies for fifty million baht. It was a "pig in a poke" purchase, as the British had already dismantled several kilometers of track at the Burmese border, and the whole line was in need of considerable repair. The prisoners had done their utmost to make the worst possible job of constructing the railway. Quite apart from frequent bombings, the wooden supports were often rotting even before they were put in place.

Shortly before the end of the war, British bombers from Ceylon succeeded in destroying the fourth, fifth, and sixth spans of the bridge. As war reparations, the Japanese replaced these three spans by two larger ones — the "Made in Japan" signs on the newer girders strike an ironic note. Today, the quiet little railway runs peacefully from nowhere to nowhere.

There was one fortunate outcome during construction of the railway: a Dutch prisoner of war discovered what he thought to be evidence of Neolithic remains nearby. However, not until 1961 did a Thai-Danish archaeological search party confirm the find and open a whole new page of Thai prehistory. A small museum close to the original excavations has many of the finds on exhibition, including a skeleton from one of the burial sites. The bulk of the finds from this first Neolithic site to be found in this part of Southeast Asia is on display in the National Museum in Bangkok. Sugar cane has long over-

grown the archaeological site, but university students still manage to conduct diggings from time to time. The dusty little town of Ban Keo near the site, and a couple of kilometers walk from the small museum, lies 30 km north of Kanchanaburi and can be reached by bus or train from the provincial town.

Long before it assumed its strategic role in the last war. Kanchanaburi had been a continual battlefield between the warring Siamese and Burmese, and evidence of old battlements can still be seen. North of Ban Keo, before the station of Wang Po, are the ruins of the Khmer town of **MUANG SING**, City of the Lion.

The Kanchanaburi area is bountifully blessed with caves and waterfalls, and if you have the time, you will find the **ERAWAN FALLS**, or "Elephant Falls," about 67km north of Kanchanaburi and a magnificent sight. The tranquil setting of these

Muang Sing
เมืองสิงห์

Erawan Falls
น้ำตกเอราวัณ

124

An old locomotive chugs across the River Kwai Bridge, which inspired the famous novel.

falls creates one of the most beautiful spots in Thailand.

Alternatively, you could catch the train from Kanchanaburi west to Nam Tok, the railway terminal, where you can stay overnight. Near Nam Tok, are the **KAO PANG FALLS** where the water trips down over a series of limestone steps. From here you can take a three-hour boat ride to the **SAI YOK FALLS** where the water plunges directly into the river. On the way to Sai Yok, the river passes the **CAVE OF THAM KUNG** with its impressive stalactites and stalagmites. It would take several days further travel by river and a long trek on foot to reach the aged pagodas that mark the Three Pagodas Pass and the border with Burma.

About 80 km from the famous Bridge over the River Kwai, there is a sixty-unit lodge, constructed by a Bangkok travel agency (Diethelm Travel, 544 Ploenchit Road). The **River Kwai Village**, as it is called, is sited on the bank of the river and is surrounded by low, jungle-clad hills.

Made up of five longhouses, the sixty air-conditioned rooms have Thai-style decor in which local laterite stone, teak, and bamboo are used to good effect. The lodge also has an air-conditioned restaurant with a terrace overlooking the river, a treetop bar, and a pool fed by a waterfall.

As a base for travel in the Kanchanaburi area, the River Kwai Village organizes trips to nearby caves, waterfalls, Karen and Mon villages, and raft-dwelling communities. The hotel also operates a daily coach service to and from Bangkok.

Another tourist development on the river are plans for an organized raft trip up to the Kwai River Farm, which consists of cottages and barges on the Little Kwai, a branch of the larger River Kwai.

TOURING THE CENTRAL PLAINS

The Heartland

A cluster of simple, thatched-roof farmhouses, almost hidden amid tall, graceful plumes of bamboo swaying lazily in the breeze: like a small island in the vast, acid-green sea that stretches for seemingly endless kilometers in all directions, broken only by similar islands of darker green or, occasionally, by the swooping orange roof and glittering gilt of a Buddhist temple that flashes out of the sea like an improbable jewel. This rippling expanse is the traditional source of Thailand's wealth, the intricately diked and dependably watered rice fields that have fed its people for more than 700 years, that still produce the kingdom's number one export to less fortunate neighboring countries. These are the Central Plains, the fertile heart of the country toward which the early Thais steadily, inevitably migrated from the mountains of the North and the jungles of the South, coming here to found their greatest cities.

If you drive across the Central Plains toward the end of the dry season in May, the fields are alive with blue-shirted, straw-hatted farmers and broad-backed water buffaloes, turning the cracked and arid earth. A month or so later, when the rains have come, water flickers in the shallow paddies, and the young rice plants are of a vivid green that almost hurts the eye with its intensity. In late October the rains cease with dramatic suddenness. The grain turns golden, and it is harvest time; the people reappear from the little hidden hamlets, from the temples where they have been passing the wet months as monks, from the city where they have been doing seasonal work; for it is upon the harvest that their lives depend, upon which to a very real extent the whole

The colossal seated Buddha at Wat Si Chum meditates stolidly on the ruins of Sukhothai (previous pages). Here was founded the first truly Thai nation, built on the prosperity and stability of the Central Plains.

country depends. And so to the fields come just about all the able-bodied members of every farming family. Later, when the crop is in, there is time for festivals, for relaxation; and the air over the Central Plains is hazy for hundreds of kilometers with smoke from burning fields, as the earth is prepared for another cycle of cultivation. So it has been for ages; so it will continue to be, despite governments and politics and the rise and fall of cities.

Several major rivers water this fertile heartland, most notably the broad Chao Phya which flows like an artery from the North all the way to the Gulf of Thailand, just below Bangkok, feeding the paddies through an incredibly complex network of streams and man-made canals. Thai history has moved down these rivers, through these rich fields, and its remains are scattered about like an archaeological scrapbook: the Angkor-style towers of Lop Buri, where the Khmers once ruled to reap the bounty of the Plains; the sprawling ruins farther south near Bangkok of once great Ayuthaya — precariously leaning pagodas and the shells of palaces, half-submerged beneath the rampant vegetation that always lies in wait to take over when man turns his back (see "Bangkok Surroundings"). The smog-enshrouded immensity of Bangkok, latest of the capitals to be built on the prosperity of the Central Plains, shimmers on the horizon, half-threat, half-dream, tantalizingly near, yet in many ways as remote from the life of the farmers' fields as the moon.

Broad superhighways such as National Route 1 now slice through the fields carrying flashy cars, roaring trucks, and air-conditioned tour buses to all parts of the country. Jumbo jets scream overhead, fluttering the rice stalks, on their way to and from Bangkok's Don Muang Airport. And even within the fields themselves the wail of the transistor radio, that harbinger of the modern world, sometimes breaks the traditional silence.

Yet for all these 20th-century intrusions, there is a strong sense of timelessness about this part of Thailand, for fundamentally it has changed remarkably little over the centuries. The cities like Bangkok, and the larger towns with their mass-produced row shops, have the look of temporary aberrations, huddling along the highways as if for reassurance of their reality. Outside them, though, the Central Plains is still basically a region of small, self-contained little hamlets, each with its carefully ordered way of life revolving around family, fields, and temple, more than a little wary of city folk with their strange ways. These hamlets are simple, but they are not, in terms of Thai life, poor. In the mountainous North and the often-parched Northeast, farming can be a perilous, unpredictable occupation and land can often slip into the hands of the moneylenders. In the Central Plains, on the other hand, nature has always been generous; land tends to stay in the same family for generations; and such inequities of distribution as there may be have never loomed large among the country's problems. There is a feeling of solidity, of continuity, about the plain wooden houses, set high on sturdy poles above the family's domestic animals: the pigs, chickens, and water buffalo. Not as many of the young people of this region decide in despair to leave the land and seek their fortunes in the capital, and the elders are inclined to be conservative in both political and social matters. Though chemical fertilizers and mechanized equipment could double the crop yield, farmers prefer their traditional methods, reasoning that if one crop is sufficient to feed their family and yield a small profit why worry with double cropping. Though a noted inventor

In the country's rice bowl, transplanting the rice seedlings into the muddy fields is a communal affair, with time for levity and enjoyment.

in Bangkok is reportedly working to perfect something called a "mechanical buffalo" to do the work of ploughing the paddies, the news does not greatly excite the hamlet dwellers; they still place their trust in the slow, patient animal whose broad back can seat several small children and whose dependable strength has turned their fields for countless generations. Many more young Central Plains farmers returning from progressive agricultural schools today are questioning the old methods, and to ask whether this rich earth will be forever adequate to feed a population that has grown from 17.5 million just after world war II to about 46.5 million today, not to mention having enough left over for export.

The hamlets of the Central Plains reveal Thai life at its purest, least diluted by the outside cultures of neighboring countries and the Western world. To begin with, more than in any other part of the country you still see houses in the classic style of Thai architecture, the plain but elegant domestic equivalent of the magnificent temples that reached their full flowering at Ayuthaya: the panelled walls slanting slightly inward to achieve an oddly graceful effect and the steep roof seeming to strain toward the sky. The faces of the people, too, are less likely to show the imprint of the Chinese and the Lao, the Burmese and the Malay, all the races that have intermingled with the Thai in the cities and in the border regions. In the hamlets, with their extended families, their communal approach to farming, their reliance on the village temple as a source of social as well as spiritual sustenance, their deeply rooted sense of independence, the strongest, most enduring aspects of the Thai character can be seen more clearly than anywhere else.

Another cheerful farmer works in rice fields soon to sprout into a "vast, acid-green sea" of plants.

Entering the Plains

The numbers in the margin in this section refer to the map on page 128.

Wat Chomkiri Nagaproth
วัดจอมคีรีนาคพรต

2. Bung Borapet
บึงบรเพ็ด

1. Nakhon Sawan
นครสวรรค์ (ตัวเมือง, จังหวัด)

3. Kamphang Phet
กำแพงเพชร (ตัวเมือง, จังหวัด)

Phom Seti
ป้อมเศรษฐี

Reaching one's destination in the Central Plains, as in most other parts of Thailand, is generally quick and comfortable. The main cities in the center are linked with the capital by road, rail, and air. Of these three modes, the most recently developed is travel by coach. A number of "super-bus" companies now offer rapid trips by air-conditioned coaches to most major destinations in Thailand. The standard of service on these vehicles is generally excellent. Snacks of the airline type are served by stewardesses, and soothing music is played on a tape deck. A Coach Tour Association of Thailand has been formed with eighteen members. Among them, Grand Tour, Pat Tour, Siam Coach, and Tour Royale cater particularly for foreign passengers.

The State Railway takes the traveler at a more leisurely pace through the Central Plains on a line slightly to the east of Route 1. The railway passes through Ayuthaya, Nakhon Sawan, Phitsanulok, and Uttaradit on its way to Chiang Mai. On the Northern Express, air-conditioned first class sleepers are available, as well as couchettes in the first and second class. A restaurant car serves excellent Thai food and European breakfasts. Thai Airways Co. provides frequent service to the Central Plains and North, its main destinations in the Central Plains being Phitsanulok and Uttaradit.

* * *

NAKHON SAWAN has always been an important commercial entrepôt because of its location at the meeting of roads and rivers connecting North and Central Thailand. The Ping, Yom, and Nan Rivers, which flow through the northern highlands, meet above Nakhon Sawan. Under its

Centuries of weathering have removed the stucco covering of this laterite image of the Buddha in the old fortified town of Kamphang Phet. revealing the serene elegance underneath.

old name of Paknam Po, the town played a vital role in the teak trade, for it was here that the great teak rafts, which had sometimes been traveling for two or three years from the northern forests, were broken up into smaller rafts for floating down to Bangkok on the Chao Phya River. Teak rafts may still be seen on the river above Nakhon Sawan, but they are not as numerous as they were in the heyday of Thailand's teak trade.

There are few traces of Nakhon Sawan's past in the modern commercial town. The most notable shrine is outside the town, across the bridge over the Chao Phya River. Here on a small hill stands **Wat Chomkiri Nagaproth**. The main structure dates from the Sukhothai period, but the Buddha image, seated on a throne supported by demons, is of the Ayuthaya period. Behind the main shrine is a massive, finely adorned bronze bell, about one hundred years old, supported on modern brick pillars.

A favorite outing for those living in and around Nakhon Sawan is a trip to **BUNG BORAPET**, the seasonal lake located 2 km to the east. This lowlying area acts as a catchment during the rainy season. At the height of the monsoon in September and October, the lake covers an area of some 120 sq km. The best time to visit the lake is on a moonlit night in the cool season when you can picnic on the island in the middle of the waters.

* * *

The "new" city of **KAMPHANG PHET** lies 3 km off Route 1, on the east bank of the Ping River about 120 km northwest of Nakhon Sawan. This city was built by King Li Thai (1347-1368) of the Sukhothai dynasty to replace the older town of Chakangrao on the opposite bank. Both served as garrison towns for Sukhothai. On the right-hand side of the approach road to Kamphang Phet are the remains of a laterite fort, **Phom Seti**, built to defend the first and older city. Farther along the road is the well-restored *chedi* of **Wat Ched Klang Tung**, also a relic of the fomer city of Chakangrao.

Crossing a bridge over the Ping, you come to the modern town. A short distance from the center, with its numerous rice and noodle eating-houses, is the well-designed **Provincial Museum** containing one of the finest bronzes of Siva in Thailand. This life-sized image was cast on the orders of the governor of Kamphang Phet in the first quarter of the 16th century. Early in the reign of King Chulalongkorn (1868-1910), a German visitor to the town saw the image and decided to remove its head and two hands. The governor at the time, too afraid to arrest a *farang* (foreigner), quickly sent word to Bangkok that the priceless fragments were on their way there by boat. Officials in Bangkok detained the German, who declared that he was going to give the fragments to the Berlin Museum.

King Chulalongkorn (whose skilful diplomacy saved Thailand from much more serious threats from the West) found a way to placate the German as well as keep the cultural treasures for his country. He promised to send an exact copy of the whole Siva image to Germany, so the fragments could remain in Thailand. And so it was done. The copy of the bronze is still in Berlin, while the head and hands of the image in the Kamphang Phet museum have been skilfully restored. Other exhibits in the museum include pre-Sukhothai bronzes, stucco Buddha heads from monuments in the neighborhood, and some fine ceramics.

For a tour of the fortifications and temples, a car or coach is necessary since they are a considerable distance from the modern town. A visit to **King Li Thai's fortifications** reveals why the town was called Kamphang Phet or "Diamond Wall"

Wat Chedi Klang
วัดเจดีย์กลาง

Museum
พิพิธภัณฑ์

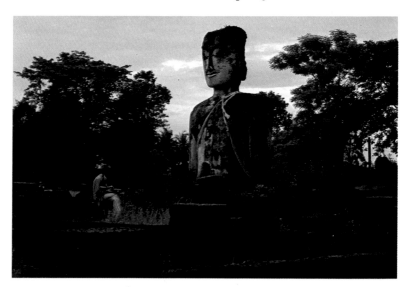

Old Kamphang Phet dates from the 14th-century Sukhothai dynasty, the first true Thai kingdom. This fragment of a massive Buddha image (above) sits in evocative solitude among the tumbled stones of its vanished temple. Numerous other remains of buildings and statues, like the fallen Buddha head on the right, lie scattered about the luxuriant undergrowth covering much of the old site, mute relics of the rise and fall of past kingdoms.

— the massive ramparts of earth topped by laterite rise about 6 meters above the outer moat, now overgrown with water hyacinths.

The chief monuments of Kamphang Phet lie northwest of the walled city. The monks who built them were a forest-dwelling sect, strongly influenced by teachers from Sri Lanka. Their temples, constructed solidly of laterite, show Sri Lankan influence. However, most of them underwent changes during heavy restoration in the Ayuthaya period. The familiar themes of Buddhist architecture are repeated in the ordination halls, *viharn*s, and *chedi*s of these temples. Two temples are of special interest and should be visited even on a rapid tour.

Wat Phra Si Iriyaboth derives its name from Buddha images which are depicted in four postures (*si* meaning "four," and *iriyaboth,* "postures") on the central square *mondop* (sanc-

tuary). The standing image is largely intact, with the original stucco coating on its head and lower part of the body. This is an impressive and unaltered example of Sukhothai sculpture. Unfortunately the other images (in the sitting, walking, and sleeping postures) are in very poor condition. The whole temple stands on a platform encircled by the original laterite railing and walls.

The other temple, **Wat Chang Rob**, or Shrine of the Elephants, consists of the base of a great laterite stupa surrounded by elephant caryatids — a theme borrowed from Sri Lanka. The row of elephants on the south side is almost complete, but several are missing on the other flanks of the stupa. Unfortunately, the spire of the great monument has vanished, but the ruins of a crypt on the upper level of the stupa can still be inspected. The pillars of the former *viharn* also remain.

Sukhothai
ทัย (ตัวเมือง, จังหวัด)

n Prasat
อนปราสาท

mkamhaeng
โธกัณฑ์สถานแห่งชาติรามคำแหง

at Mahathat
มหาธาตุ

Magical Center of Old Siam

As you head towards the ancient city of **SUKHOTHAI** northeast of Kamphang Phet, you pass through "new" Sukhothai, a dreary and dusty collection of shop houses. About 12 km farther on, the road enters the city limits of old Sukhothai through the **Kamphang-hak ("Broken Wall")** **Gate.** The remains of the massive walls reveal that the Maginot Line concept was not new: the capital was protected by no less than three rows of earthen ramparts and two moats which enclosed the inner city.

A short distance from Kamphang-hak Gate is the **Ramkamhaeng National Museum,** a good starting point for a tour of the enclave. The museum contains a fine collection of Sukhothai sculpture, ceramics, and other artifacts, and also has exhibits from other periods. The entrance hall is dominated by an impressive bronze image of the walking Buddha. This style of image is regarded as the finest sculptural innovation of the Sukhothai period (1230-1440?) — there had been earlier essays in high and low relief, but the Sukhothai sculptors were the first to create walking Buddha images in the round.

In this period, the Thais adopted Theravada Buddhism and invited monastic help from Sri Lanka. But Hindu influence remained strong as is revealed by the two bronze images of Hindu gods which flank the walking Buddha in the museum. The one on the right, with the combined attributes of Vishnu and Siva, is specially fine. Also worth noting is a stone torso of an *Apsara*, or divinity, in the Khmer style. (Look behind the statue; in spite of ugly iron struts, you can still see the superb detail of its costume.)

Farmers take a lunch break, just as their ancestors did more than 600 years ago, near the statue of the walking Buddha at Wat Chetuphon in Sukhothai. This image is regarded as one of the finest of its type.

An important object proudly displayed on the mezzanine floor is a copy of the famous stone inscription of King Ramkamhaeng — the original and most prized exhibit of the National Museum in Bangkok. It was at the **Non Prasat (Palace Mound)** — now merely a slightly raised terrace of earth and brick — that the famous stone inscription was found. In 1833, then Crown Prince Mongkut discovered the stone which had been inscribed in the year 1292. On it, King Ramkamhaeng had recorded his conquests in surrounding kingdoms, and also the fact that in 1283 he devised the Siamese alphabet, an achievement which has outlasted most of his conquests. Once situated on the Non Prasat was the stone throne of King Ramkamhaeng, and although there is little to be seen now apart from the walled terrace, this was the numinous center of old Siam. Alexander Griswold notes: "The political significance of the throne can scarcely be exaggerated, for the king sat on it when he discussed affairs of state . . . and when he received his vassals who came to do homage." The stone throne, called the *Manangasila*, is now in the Temple of the Emerald Buddha in Bangkok.

Within the walls of Sukhothai are the ruins of some twenty *wats* and monasteries, the greatest of them being **Wat Mahathat.** It is not definitely known who founded this shrine, "the magical and spiritual center of the kingdom" (A. Griswold), but it is reasonable to assume that it was King Sri Indraditya (1220?-1250), the first king of the Sukhothai dynasty. Wat Mahathat owes its present form to a remodeling completed by King Lo Thai around 1345. The original design — as the Fine Arts Department discovered a few years ago when making some repairs — was a quincunx of laterite towers standing on a laterite platform. The four axial towers, which can still be seen, are of the Khmer style but with stucco decorations added by King Lo Thai. The central tower is now hidden in the basement of Lo Thai's "lotus bud" tower. The axial towers were linked to the central tower by laterite buttresses which are still visible. The principal Buddha image, cast in bronze by King Li Thai (1347-1368) is now in Bangkok at Wat Suthat. The stucco frieze of walking monks around the base of the main tower is unusual.

Of the twenty other shrines within the walls, and the seventy odd in the neighborhood, many repeat familiar architectural themes. The following short list, drawn up with the help of Professor Prince Subhadradis Diskul, an authority on the history and art of Sukhothai, indicates the monuments of special interest (for more detailed information, a guide to Sukhothai, published in English by the Fine Arts Department, is available at the museum.)

Wat Sri Sawai, southwest of Wat Mahathat, was originally a Hindu shrine which contained an image of Siva. Triple towers remain, built in a modified Khmer style; and the stucco decoration, added to the towers in the 15th century, showing mythical birds and divinities, is particularly fine.

Wat Sra Sri, on the way to the southern gate of the city has a spire (*chedi*) of the Sri Lankan type. The ordination hall (*bot*) lies on an island to the east of the spire. The ruins of the main shrine consist of six rows of columns, which lead up to a well-restored seated Buddha image. Achille Clarac comments: "The detail, balance, and harmony of the proportions and decoration of Wat Sra Sri, and the beauty of the area where it stands, bear witness to the unusual and refined aesthetic sense of the architects of the Sukhothai period."

Located immediately north of Wat Mahathat, **Wat Chana Songgram** and **Wat Trakuan** have particularly fine Sri Lankan-style *chedi*s,

Wat Sra Sri
วัดสระศรี

Wat Chana Songgram
วัดชนะสงคราม
Wat Trakuan
วัดตระกวน
Wat Sri Sawai
วัดศรีไสว

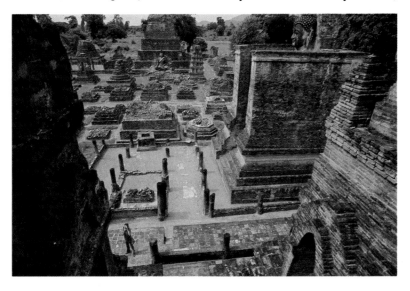

Sukhothai, dating from the 14th century, was the capital of the first Thai nation. Wat Mahathat (above), "the magical and spiritual center of the kingdom," was built partly in the style of the Khmers, whose powerful kingdoms preceded those of the Thais. Around the base of the temple's main tower is a stucco frieze of walking monks (right) that indicates the high degree of artistry that characterized this short-lived but influential city.

of which only the lower parts still stand. Wat Trakuan has revealed many bronze images of the Chiang Saen period, which pre-dates Sukhothai.

Leaving the walled city by the northern San Luang, or "Royal Shrine," gate and traveling about a kilometer, you arrive at the important shrine of **Wat Phra Phai Luang**. It originally consisted of three laterite towers covered with stucco, probably built in the late 12th century when Sukhothai was still part of the Khmer empire. This shrine might have been the original center of Sukhothai, since Wat Mahathat is of a later period. A fragmentary seated stone Buddha image, accurately dated to 1191 in the reign of the Khmer King Jayavarman VII, was found here and is now in the grounds of the town's Ramkamhaeng Museum. During restoration by the Fine Arts Department in the mid-1960s, a large stucco im-

age of the Buddha in the central tower collapsed, disclosing numerous smaller images inside. Some date these images to the second half of the 13th century.

To the east of the main shrine lies a pyramidal brick stupa. Originally it contained seated Buddha images in stucco on each story, dating from the late 13th century. Later the niches were covered over with bricks, which were removed during a restoration started in 1953. When heads of the stucco Buddha images appeared on the antique market in Bangkok, it was realized that the stupa was being pillaged. A team from the Fine Arts Department was despatched to the site, but most of the damage had already been done. Those heads (facially of the Chiang Saen style) which have not left the country are in private collections in Thailand or in the reserves of the National Museum in Bangkok.

Beyond Wat Phra Phai Luang is **Wat Si Chum**, which has one of the largest seated Buddha images in the kingdom. The *mondop*, or enclosing shrine, was built in the second half of the 14th century, but the image itself, called *Phra Achana*, or "The Venerable," is believed to be the one mentioned in King Ramkamhaeng's inscription. There is a stairway within the walls of the *mondop* which leads to a space behind the head of the image. The ceiling of the stairway is made up of more than fifty carved slate slabs illustrating scenes from Buddhist folklore. Their function is to turn the ritual climbing of the stairs into a symbolic ascent to Buddhahood.

South of the walled city is another group of shrines and monasteries. One of the most interesting is **Wat Chetupon**, where the protecting wall of the *viharn* is made of slate slabs shaped in imitation of wood. The gates are also formed of huge slabs of slate which was mined in the nearby hills. On a small scale, they resemble the megaliths of England's Stonehenge. The bridges across the moat which surrounds the temple are also made of stone slabs. On the central tower of Wat Chetupon are Buddha images in the standing, reclining, walking, and sitting postures. The walking Buddha here is regarded as one of the finest of its type.

"To the west of the city of Sukhothai," says King Ramkamhaeng's inscription, "is a forested area where the king has made offerings . . . In the forest is a large, tall, and beautiful *viharn* which contains an 18 cubit image of the standing Buddha." This is now identified as **Wat Saphan Hin**, "Monastery of the Stone Bridge." It is so called because it is approached by a stairway of large stone slabs. The image is situated on the crest of a low hill and can be seen at a considerable

Wat Si Chum
วัดศรีชุม

Wat Saphan Hin
วัดสะพานหิน

Wat Chetupon
วัดเชตุพน

Vendors near Sukhothai's ruins sell amulets and semiprecious stones (above, left), tokens of the spiritual power radiating from the kingdom. Decorated sherds (above, right) lie at the site of an ancient kiln in which potters from China produced the distinctive Sawankhalok stoneware, exported all over Southeast Asia. In Sukhothai's twin city (right) of Si Satchanalai rise the impressive stucco-covered walls of Wat Chedi Chet Thaew.

Wat Pa Mamuang
วัดผะมาเมือง

Wat Chang Lom
วัดช้างล้อม

5. Si Satchanalai
ศรีสัชนาลัย (ตัวเมือง, อำเภอ)

distance. It is 12½ meters high, with its hand raised in the attitude of "giving protection." This is almost certainly the image described by King Ramkamhaeng.

Many other monuments are to be found in this western area. They were probably built by monks from Sri Lanka who preferred to locate their monasteries in the forest. Another monument worth visiting, near the road not far from the western gate of Sukhothai, is **Wat Pa Mamuang**, "Shrine of the Mango Grove," where King Li Thai installed a famous monk of the Theravada sect in 1361. Still standing are the foundations of the shrine and the ruins of the main *chedi*.

* * *

About 55 km north of the modern town of Sukothai along a new concrete highway lies the old city of **SI**

SATCHANALAI. Founded at the same time as Sukhothai in the middle of the 13th century, it served as the seat of the viceroys of Sukhothai and was always mentioned as the twin city of the capital.

To reach the walled city, cross over the newly constructed bridge or hire a sampan, the only way until recently to get across the river.

The first and most important monument to visit in Si Satchanalai is **Wat Chang Lom**. There can be little doubt that this is the "Elephant-girdled Shrine" described in King Ramkamhaeng's stone inscription. The great king records that he started to build it in 1285 to house some exceptionally holy relics of the Lord Buddha, and that it was finished six years later. It is the only surviving stupa which can be attributed with virtual certainty to King Ramkamhaeng. Built of laterite and stucco, it is a large bell-shaped spire of the Sri

Lankan type standing on a two-story, square basement. The upper tier contains niches for Buddha images, now mostly empty, while the lower level has thirty-nine elephant caryatids, built of laterite blocks. Enough of them remain to give a good idea of the original design.

South of the Elephant Shrine are the ruins of **Wat Chedi Chet Thaew,** which include seven rows of stupas, believed to contain the ashes of the viceroys of Si Satchanalai. One of the stupas has a stucco image of the Buddha sheltered by the Naga (divine serpent), which is in unusually good repair.

Farther south still, and close to the massive walls of the city, are the remains of **Wat Nang Phy,** "Temple of the Queen." This is worth visiting, if only for the fine stucco decoration on one of the external walls. Dating probably from the 16th century, this stucco work has some affinities with

European baroque.

Other temples worth visiting include **Wat Khao Phanom Pleung** and **Wat Khao Suwan Kiri,** set on two scenic hills linked by a walkway. **Wat Prasi Ratana Mahathat,** one of the most beautiful temples, lies 2 km southeast of the old city and must be reached by a ferry. In Si Satchanalai it is possible to buy genuine antique Sawankhalok ceramics.

* * *

PHITSANULOK, a city famous in Thailand for 500 years, now has only a few survivals from its past, because of a disastrous fire 16 years ago which razed most of the old town. The new city is a rather dull collection of recently built shop houses. However, nothing can detract from its superb location, spanning the Nan River with its quays shaded by flowering trees, and its houseboats moored beside the steep banks of the river. Phitsanulok also boasts a first-class

Wat Chedi Chet Thae
วัดเจดีย์เจ็ดแถว

6. Phitsanulok
พิษณุโลก

Wat Nang Phy
วัดนางพี

Intricate floral patterns (above, left) adorn the walls of Wat Chedi Chet Thaew at Si Satchanalai. The sanctity of a seated Buddha (above, right) is guarded by the seven heads of a divine serpent, or naga, at Wat Prasit Ratana Mahathat, also at Si Satchanalai. A young boy enjoys his ride on a merry-go-round (right) at a country fair near Phitsanulok, one of the contemporary scenes that bring to life the ancient ruins one sees in the Thai countryside.

144

hotel, the Amarin Nakorn, which is air conditioned and offers Western-style cuisine.

The great fire fortunately spared **Wat Mahathat**, the principal shrine in Phitsanulok. It is still a focus of piety, as it has been for several centuries. *Phra Buddha Chinaraj*, the image in the main *bot*, is venerated all over Thailand. Regrettably, this has given rise to a busy traffic in religious objects and souvenirs. The much-revered image is seated, has a round face in the Sukhothai style, a rather corpulent body, and fingers of equal length. There were two other bronze images of the same style in Wat Mahathat, but they were taken to Wat Bovornives in Bangkok.

The *bot* which enshrines the *Phra Buddha Chinaraj* gives the visitor an idea of the ancient style of Thai religious architecture. The three-tiered room of the *bot* sweeps down steeply to low side walls, focusing attention on the gleaming image at the end of the nave.

On either side of the image are two wooden pulpits of superb late-Ayuthaya workmanship. The large one on the left is meant for a chapter of monks chanting the Buddhist texts in ancient Pali, while the smaller pulpit on the other side accommodates one monk who translates the chanting into Thai (since few of the congregation would understand Pali). Before leaving the *bot,* note the main doors from the late 18th century inlaid with mother-of-pearl.

The *prang* (spire) in the center of the temple complex was rebuilt in the Khmer style by King Borom Trai Lokanat. The cloisters surrounding the *prang* are well worth visiting since they contain Buddha images of various periods, some of them of great artistic value. There is also a repository of objects including rare Thai and Chinese ceramics.

TOURING THE NORTH

A Region with a Character All Its Own

Another group of simple houses, but different in architecture, and in atmosphere, than those we saw on the Central Plains. Different in setting, too: this village is even more remote than the farming hamlets of the Central Plains; its surrounding ocean consists not of rice fields, but of rocky hills and mist-covered mountains, a wild and almost roadless terrain where distances are measured in walking hours rather than in kilometers. In these jungled mountains, secret, sketchily-mapped, and all but inaccessible to outsiders, live unusual people: Meo tribesmen who wear vast black turbans and clanking silver jewelry; Yao tribespeople who wear finely worked embroidery and speak a language that until recently only a handful of foreign missionaries could interpret; and several almost legendary small nomadic groups, like the Phi Thong Luang, "Spirits of the Yellow Leaves," whom some thought to exist only in myth until an expedition came across their jungle hiding place and confronted them with the modern world. Here, also, in lost valleys where fields of forbidden poppies grow, begins a complex trail of illicit activity that ends on the streets of many major Western cities. The poppies and the opium by-product were outlawed in Thailand more than twenty years ago, but the problem is not that simple: it is hard for the authorities to adequately patrol this wild terrain, but easy for offenders to slip back and forth across the borders with Burma and Laos, which form the notorious "Golden Triangle" mentioned in so many narcotics news stories. Recent efforts, however, are meeting with growing success. From his winter palace on Doi Suthep, overlooking the northern capital of Chiang Mai, the king personally directs an ambitious crop-substitution program aimed at the hillpeople who traditionally derived their main income from the poppy plant. Missionaries and organizations, such as the royally sponsored Hill Tribe Founda-

tion, are finding markets for the fine handicrafts of the tribespeople. And members of the elite Border Patrol Police are dropping by helicopter into the remote mountain villages not only to enforce the law but to set up schools and bring modern medicine for the first time. The hilltribes are still an exotic thread on the fringe of Thai life, but gradually they are being woven into the national fabric, venturing to the larger cities in the North, some even to distant Bangkok, breaking through their traditional shell of isolation.

But the North has more to offer than strange hilltribes and jungled wilderness. It is also a place rich in history, with great kingdoms, legendary rulers, and artistic achievement that go back beyond the founding of the first Thai capital at Sukhothai in the 13th century. The celebrated Emerald Buddha, the most venerated of all the images in Thailand, was

In Thailand's North, as in the rest of the kingdom, rice is the staple food. Here a farmer near Mae Sariang, close to the Burmese border, threshes the grain in a huge basket that measures more than two meters across.

found in the North (most experts also believe it was made there) and spent much of its early existence in various northern temples. According to a northern legend, King Mengrai of Chiang Saen, who ruled the North in the 13th century, was so powerful that when he decided to found a new capital, the future Chiang Mai, he was able to call on royal friends from other parts of the country, including Sukhothai, to assist him in the selection of a suitable location. The eminent surveyors knew they had found an auspicious site when they heard of a place where an extraordinary assembly of rare animals had been seen: two white sambar deer (a variety now extinct), two white barking deer, and a white mouse with a family of five. King Mengrai, so the story goes, immediately ordered Chiang Mai to be built on the spot.

The North has been the scene of epic battles, of Burmese invasions, of the rise and fall of independent kingdoms, only distantly related to the ruling cities of the central part of the present-day country. Until the early part of this century, it was accessible from Bangkok only by a complicated river trip or by a journey of several weeks on elephant back. There are still old residents in the capital who remember the great day when the northern railway line was finally opened in the late 1920s, after more than ten years of tunneling and blasting through the mountains. It is not surprising, then, that the region has retained a distinct flavor all its own, one still so strong that tourists from other parts of Thailand come here almost as if to another country, marveling at the profusion and beauty of the temples with their splendid teak carvings and intricate Burmese-

Fabulous, almost medieval costumes are daily dress to the exotic hilltribes who inhabit the wild mountains of Thailand's North. The life-style of this Meo woman is changing, but she retains much of her distinctive culture.

inspired decorations (there are more than a hundred in moderate-sized Chiang Mai alone); the splendor of the wild orchids that grow so profusely in the hills; the gentle good manners of the people (among whose hospitable habits it is to place a basin of cool water outside their gates for the benefit of thirsty passing strangers); the fabled good looks of the girls; and the novelty of having to bundle up in a sweater in the cool season. Ancient handicrafts which have either succumbed to the machine or which never even existed in other regions still thrive here: delicate lacquerware, thin silver bowls pounded into complex designs over wooden molds, supple handwoven cottons and shimmering silk, expertly carved teak, paper umbrellas painted in bold designs, and fine celadon stoneware.

Nor is the culture of the North something that has been artificially preserved for the pleasure of the tourists, who have flocked to the North and turned it into Thailand's leading provincial attraction. In fact, for all their gracious manners, the northerners have a perceptible sense of superiority toward the aggressive newcomers of Bangkok and are quite firm in their ideas of what they will and will not accept in the interests of "development." At the height of the Vietnam War, for instance, when Thailand was a major rest and recreation spot for American servicemen, some profit-minded operators in the capital got the idea of turning Chiang Mai into a hillstation for pleasures. The Chiang Mai city fathers politely turned down the offer; if the soldiers wanted to enjoy northern culture as it was, they replied, they were welcome to come, but if they were after the kind of things Bangkok specialized in they would be far happier there. End of discussion.

Mae Hong Son market. An elderly woman of Burmese origin thoughtfully puffs on an old-style cheroot as she goes about her business.

Along with its manners, handicrafts, and relative serenity, the North has also kept its love of festivals, which are observed with greater frequency and enthusiasm than anywhere else in Thailand. A visitor who comes in the winter months — that is, between October and the end of January — is almost certain to come across some kind of celebration, ranging from the famous Loy Krathong water festival, when Chiang Mai hotels are booked for months in advance, to localized affairs, like the bringing in of the garlic crop in Lamphun, when one of the local beauties is chosen "Miss Garlic."

The North is also a region of great natural wealth and scenic beauty. Vast hardwood forests cover much of it, the working of which still requires the services of trained elephants, which drag the huge logs downhill to the banks of rivers, to be floated down to mills below. Mines for minerals such as wolfram have been sunk in the mountains, producing booming new industries. In the high-altitude fields grow tobacco, coffee, tea, strawberries, garlic, and a delectable fruit called *lamyai*, whose annual harvest is, inevitably, the occasion for a festival. Experimental crops being tested on Doi Inthanon, Thailand's highest mountain, include apples, peaches, plums, and other temperate fruits. The production of cut flowers is another new industry, and in the winter season the florist shops of Bangkok are filled with unfamiliar gladiolus, snapdragons, carnations and other blossoms which, like so many things in the North, seem strange and special.

Getting to the North is now much easier than in the days of travel by boat and elephant. Thai Airways'

Near Mae Sariang, a Karen tribeswoman trudges through the burnt stumps of a former forest cleared by the nomadic hilltribe. Efforts are being made to get the tribes to replace their traditional opium with other crops.

domestic service offers at least five flights daily from Bangkok to the North. These include at least two direct flights to Chiang Mai every day, and other flights with touchdowns in the provincial capitals of Lampang, Phrae, Phitsanulok, and Chiang Rai.

Several trains and many buses leave Bangkok daily for northern destinations. The best train, the Daily Express, departs Bangkok in the late afternoon, stops at Ayuthaya, Lop Buri, Nakhon Sawan, Phichit, Phitsanulok, Uttaradit, Den Chai, Lampang, and Lamphun, and arrives in Chiang Mai early the next morning. Reservations for seats and sleepers should be made well in advance during school holidays and especially around the mid-April Songkran or winter Loy Krathong festival when hotels in Chiang Mai are full.

If the express train is fully booked, one can still travel comfortably and inexpensively to the North by air-conditioned buses. Every day, three buses leave Bangkok's northern terminal on Phaholyothin Road for an express ride to Chiang Mai. The first bus pulls out at the invigorating hour of 5:25 a.m. Eight non-air-conditioned but quite modern and breezy buses also make the 700-km trip in about nine hours (compared with fifteen hours by train). From the northern terminal one can also go by bus to Chiang Rai, Lampang, Bhumibol Dam (Tak), and Sukhothai.

For travelers with cars, Route 1 leaves the Central Plains around Kamphang Phet, passes the northern gateway province of Tak, and follows the Wang River north-northeast to Lampang. From Lampang you can branch off on the all-weather road to Chiang Mai or continue on Route 1 to Chiang Rai. You should try to make several sidetrips on the North's scenic secondary roads. Occasional reports of insurgent activities along roads in the North should not necessarily deter your explorations. Most of these incidents occur in very remote areas and involve soldiers, government officials, or road construction crews, but not travelers.

Try to visit the North during the cool season (late November to February) when the days are usually bright and sunny but not too hot, and the nights cool enough for sweaters and jackets. Blue skies and clear air allow for good photography, and the evening chill makes you appreciate the warming effect of Chiang Mai's *kow tom* (hot rice porridge with egg and meat).

Travel beyond the North into Burma is not yet legally possible as the Burmese government does not issue visas for overland entry from Thailand. For years travelers have been allowed to cross the Mekong River from Chiang Khong over to Ban Houei Sai in Laos. Now, with relations between the two countries uncertain, you should first check with the Laotian Embassy in Bangkok.

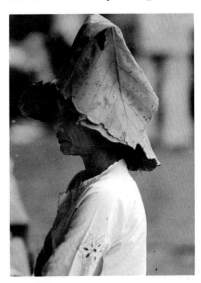

A hunter armed with an old flintlock (left) goes in search of birds near the town of Hot. Leaves serve a variety of purposes in Thailand, from thatching a house to serving as an emergency hat (above) in a downpour.

Gateway to the North

One of the first interesting places to explore in the North provides a touch of Burma: the town of **MAE SOT** near the Burmese border just west of Tak. Tak itself, the gateway to the North, has little of interest, but can be the point of departure for trips to Mae Sot and the Bhumibol Dam.

Although truck drivers make offerings at the spirit house below Phawoh Mountain for a safe passage, as you approach Mae Sot, Road 105 sweeps through forests into a peaceful valley dotted with miniature farmhouses, white *chedis*, and ornate Burmese-style temples.

A confusion of short streets, sidewalk stalls, bicycles, and pedestrian shoppers: Mae Sot thrives as a backwoods trading post. The town even boasts a short airstrip. Shops advertize their wares in Thai, Chinese, Burmese, and English. At the Siam Hotel one finds dramatic (if tasteless) wood carvings for sale.

From Mae Sot a 5-km drive takes you to the Burmese border. On the way an ornate Burmese temple can be visited. This temple has a rectangular roof with red shingles and silverwork piled heavenward into a tower. Within the sanctuary are four Buddha images, one of which has gold jewelry spilling out from its earlobes. After seeing this temple you can drive to the Moei River which forms the border with Burma and the point at which the Pan Asian Highway may someday enter Thailand, linking Southeast Asia with Europe by road.

On the way to Tak from Mae Sot, if time allows, stop at the *nikhorn*, or "settlement," for Lisu, Lahu, and Meo hilltribes on Doi Mussu. About 12 km outside of Tak lies Luang Larn National Park where waterfalls hide behind bamboo groves. Road 105 soon rejoins Route 1 going north to Tak.

1. Mae Sot
    เเม่สอด (อำเภอ, ตัวเมือง

The numbers in the margin in this sectiion refer to the map on page 148.

This scenic winding road (above, left) leads to the bustling little town of Mae Sot, on the border of Burma; one day it may form part of Asia's great Route 1 which will take overland travelers all the way from Istanbul to Singapore. Shy Karen girls (above, right), members of one of the hilltribes who live in the surrounding hills, come down to hawk fruits and vegetables beside the road and get a look at the outside world passing by.

TAK was a prosperous riverine junction for goods coming from Chiang Mai to Bangkok before the era of the highway; but today travelers enter Tak not by ferrying sampans, but along a small road that weaves through tiny manicured gardens and around a pond near the provincial offices. A broad, drab esplanade separates the market and the old wooden houses from the Ping River, so as to prevent too much flooding from the notorious Ping floods in the rainy season.

Tak is a peaceful place, offering few sights other than the river at sunset and two temples in the northern part of town. These are **Wat Phrae** and **Wat Sibunruang**, the latter of which has a gold-topped *chedi* and contains *Phra Buddhamon,* an early Sukhothai image. For an overnight stay in Tak, choose from several inexpensive hotels: Tawee Sak, Tak, Charoen Suk, and the air-conditioned Bhumibhol.

Off Route 1, about 20 km past Tak on the left, lies the village of **BAN TAK**. Tiny and undisturbed, Ban Tak stretches precariously over the Ping River. Houses on stilts and a rickety bamboo footbridge look down upon children swimming eagerly against the current of the Ping. At sunset the Ping turns silver, and boatmen drift like silhouettes in a shadow-play across the reflected light.

BHUMIBOL DAM (also called Yanhee Dam), lies north of Ban Tak about 29 km on a turnoff on the left off Route 1. With permission, you can drive across the 154-meter-high cement arch to view the reservoir which stretches more than 100 km northwest to Hot District, not far from Chiang Mai. This huge dam generates enough power to help light Bangkok and thirty-seven of Thailand's seventy-two provinces. The

With the water level controlled by the huge Bhumibol Dam (above), the catchment area near Ban Tak is calm and shallow enough to allow a bamboo footbridge (left) to span the waters.

Bhumibol Guest House complex consists of nine facilities, two of them air-conditioned. House 100, with both air conditioning and reasonable charges, has twenty-six rooms. Below the Bhumibol Dam lies a mini-city of workers' quarters, a school, the Energy Authority offices, a restaurant, and a swimming pier. The area surrounding the dam has resort potential, but to date, the only tourist incursion is an 18-hole golf course.

About 63 km beyond the Bhumibol Dam turnoff, Road 106 crosses Route 1 at **THOEN**. Although Thoen can be passed rapidly, it does cherish a small claim to fame as the home of lucky stones. Each *pohng kham* contains a variety of colors and internal "scenes." Some pieces are clear and have strange, crystalline formations inside — resembling wisps of blue hair, jungle moss, or even a city skyline.

From Thoen to Lampang, Route 1 undulates over teak-covered hills and a mountain pass sprinkled with spirit houses before dipping into the broad, cattle-grazing Yom River Valley of Lampang. About 18 km south of Lampang, Route 1 crosses the road to **KO KHA**. By turning left, passing the town, crossing the Wang River, and bearing left for 1 km, you will reach the elegant old temple, **Wat Lampang Luang**. Cherished by scholars for its antiquity and delicate artwork, the temple compound is all that remains of a fortressed city that flourished more than a millennium ago; it is believed to have been founded by a Lop Buri princess, Chama Dewi, who bore two sons: one became king of Lampang, the other king of Lamphun. The *wat*, entirely rebuilt in the 16th century, wove a golden pattern through the history of the North's ruling families. About 200 years ago, Burmese invaders occupied the temple. According to legend, Thai at-

6. Ko Kha
เกาะคา (ตัวเมือง, อำเภอ)

Wat Lampang Luang
วัดลำปางหลวง

5. Thoen
เถิน (ตัวเมือง, อำเภอ)

tackers sneaked through a drain to surprise and overwhelm their enemy. A hole in the balustrade is said to have been caused by the cannon-shot that killed a Burmese general.

The temple's museum features lacquered bookcases, wooden *tong* emblems that hang from poles like stiff flags, and many jeweled Buddhas. Most revered is a small "Emerald Buddha" believed to have been carved from the same jasper stone as its famous counterpart in Bangkok. Some eaves have been carted off to antique collections, but the wooden facade of the *viharn* remains a fine example of northern carving. A bronze Lop Buri Buddha sits in the dark interior.

About 18 km past Ko Kha, Route 1 enters the provincial capital of **LAMPANG**. Half the size of Chiang Mai and far less developed, Lampang epitomizes the bucolic peacefulness of North Thailand. In no other Thai city do horse-drawn carriages continue to resist the march of taxis. The graceful old railway station takes the viewer several decades back in time.

Two Burmese-style temples in the town are worth visiting. Seven chapels, one for each day of the week, stand at the base of the *chedi* in **Wat Pha Sang**, on the left bank of the Wang River. On the right bank, **Wat Phra Keo Don Tau** presents a lovely fusion of Burmese and local architecture. In the 18th-century chapel, columns soar to great heights; the ceilings are a kaleidoscope of inlaid enamel, mother-of-pearl, and cut glass. For an overnight stay, Lampang has several modern hotels: the Siam, Sri Sangar, Lampang, and Asia Lampang. North of town stand the twenty chalky spires of **Wat Chedi Sao Phra** set in the rice fields. Approximately 100 km farther north of Lampang lies Chiang Mai.

The countryside temple of Lampang Luang (far left), one of Thailand's oldest, is adorned with intricate decorations (above). Village musicians (left) perform at the ordination ceremony of a new monk.

Chiang Mai: Flower of the North

The cacophonous whine of thousands of motor cycles and *thuk-thuks* (three-wheeled, motorized pickups) hammers at the eardrums; countless souvenir shops, their wares spilling onto the streets, make a complementary visual assault. Only a few years ago a small, relaxed place, the town today has an overlay of tinsel modernity which, fortunately, fails to completely hide the real **CHIANG MAI**. Situated 710 km north of Bangkok in a valley 305 meters above sea level, Chiang Mai makes a pleasant dry-season escape from the sticky humidity of the capital. The second largest city of Thailand, with an amazing array of handicrafts, impressive mountain scenery, historical temples, and colorful hilltribes, still greets visitors with a graceful *wai*, making comfortable friends out of those who arrive as strangers.

On the green mass of nearby Doi Suthep, which rises like a backdrop

to the town, Wat Prathat appears with crystalline clarity through the chill morning air, which in December could almost be described as cold. At breakfast-time a minibus (perhaps by the moat) is already filling with a group of hardy travelers setting off for a three-day jungle walk from Fang, 150 km to the north. The murky moat beside the food stalls offers little hope of fish, but two young undaunted boys dangle lines in the water. An elderly monk, who as you realizes that this is Chiang Mai's best breakfasting spot, returns the courtesy of his meal with a blessing for the kneeling waitresses. Another day begins in Chiang Mai.

Getting around Chiang Mai is a breeze; buses charge a standard one baht for any journey in town. Some follow such circuitous routes that your baht buys a complete town tour. *Thuk-thuks* should not cost more than two or four baht for most rides;

8. Chiang Mai
เชียงใหม่ (ตัวเมือง, จังหวัด

Shops & Markets	① Wat Chiang Man	④ Wat Jet Yod	⑦ Wat Suan Dork
Hotels	② Wat Phra Singh	⑤ Wat Koo Tao	⑧ Wat Chedovan
Bus Terminal	③ Wat Chedi Luang	⑥ Wat Saen Fang	⑨ Wat Duang Di

ool, leisurely
hiang Mai
mbines small-city
arm with a
ultitude of
scinating things
see and do.

Wat Chiang Man
วัดเชียงแมน

just hail one going your way. Pedal *samlor*s provide a more leisurely way of seeing Chiang Mai; or hire a push bicycle and pedal yourself. The tour agents around the eastern moat gate do a thriving business renting push bicycles and motorcycles. The Tourist Organization of Thailand has a branch in Chiang Mai at 135 Praisanee Road for further tips on enjoying your stay.

Chiang Mai's history is as old as that of the Thais themselves. In the 13th century, when Thais were fleeing en masse from southern China, King Mengrai ruled a Thai Kingdom around Chiang Rai. When Kublai Khan sacked Pagan in 1287, Mengrai formed a life-long alliance with the kings of Sukhothai. With his southern boundaries secure, Mengrai captured the old Mon Kingdom at Haripoonchai in 1292, and thereafter founded his new capital at Chiang Mai in 1298.

Chiang Mai, with its moat and walls, was at first a great city, repelling invaders and overshadowing both the Mons and Khmers to the east. But less than a century after its founding, Chiang Mai's relations with Ayuthaya became strained. For the next 400 years its southern borders were unsafe and hostile. Ayuthaya crushed in the 16th century an invasion by Chiang Mai, and from 1550 to 1650 Chiang Mai's power began to wane. The Burmese invaded in the early 18th century. Fighting continued until 1775, and although the Burmese were finally defeated, the inhabitants of Chiang Mai were so dazed and exhausted from centuries of warfare that they drifted away, leaving Chiang Mai deserted until 1796, when it came under the sway of Siam. The present moat in Chiang Mai dates from soon after the reestablishment of the city, but only the patch of coal at the southeast corner is original; all the other fragments of the wall and gates are reconstructions.

The low rays of the morning sun

brilliantly illumine the *bot* of **Wat Chiang Man**. Behind it the *chedi* is supported by rows of fine elephant buttresses. In this the oldest temple in Chiang Mai, built by Mengrai who resided there during the construction of the city, two ancient and much venerated Buddha images are kept in the abbot's quarters. The images can be seen on request. One is a crystal Buddha (*Phra Sae Tang Tamani*), a small image brought by Mengrai to Chiang Mai from Lamphun where it was said to have been for 600 years. Apart from a short sojourn in Ayuthaya, the image has remained in Chiang Mai ever since, and each 1 April it is ceremoniously paraded through the town. The other sacred image is a stone Buddha (*Phra Sila*) in bas-relief, believed to have originated in India around the 8th century. These two statues apparently have the power to bring rain.

In Chiang Mai's most important

"The second largest city of Thailand still greets visitors with the graceful gesture of the wai, *making comfortable friends out of those who arrive as strangers." A statue at Wat Prasingh (above) extends a welcome.*

temple, **Wat Prasingh**, founded in 1345, the spacious grounds seem to shut out the bustle of traffic on the main road in town which runs right up to it. The *wat* contains a collection of buildings, including a fine library. The small chapel behind the ancient *chedi* shelters the main Buddha image which has a long and undoubtedly much embroidered history. Claimed to be more than 1,500 years old and to have originated in Sri Lanka, it is said to have arrived in Siam during the Sukhothai period and eventually to have found its way to Chiang Mai. As the statue is in the Sukhothai style, and as there are similar images in Bangkok and Nakhon Si Thammarat, it is hard to say how much truth there is in the story: any one of the "copies" could be the original. What is certain is that the head of the Chiang Mai image was stolen in 1922, and that the present head is a replica.

The crumbling base of a huge *chedi* is visible to the southeast of Wat Prasingh. In 1545 a violent earthquake shook Chiang Mai, toppling the 90-meter-high, 500-year-old pagoda of **Wat Chedi Luang**. This monstrous *chedi* was never repaired. For eighty-four years the restless Emerald Buddha was housed in this *wat*; King Mengrai is romantically said to have been killed nearby by a bolt of lightning. Close to the entrance to the *wat* stands a tall gum tree: should it fall, legend insists, Chiang Mai will suffer a great misfortune. The "spirit of the city," a town boundary post, is sheltered in a small building near the fateful gum.

Located outside the city walls, **Wat Jet Yod** suffered damage from a more mortal cause. Begun in 1453 its square *chedi* has, as the name describes, seven spires. Having been built in imitation of a temple in the Burmese capital of Pagan did not stop the

Wat Prasingh
วัดพระสิงห์

Wat Chedi Luang
วัดเจดีย์หลวง

Wat Jet Yod
วัดเจ็ดยอด

Strikingly carved gilded doors (above, left) lead into a building at Chiang Mai's most important temple, Wat Prasingh. The city has many other attractive temples, such as Wat Duang Di (above, right), where the main spire is inlaid with colored mirrors, and framed by a parasol and stylized guardian lions. Slender chedis containing the ashes of Chiang Mai's royal family rise gracefully in the compound of Wat Suan Dok (right).

Burmese from severely damaging it during one of their periodic invasions in 1566.

Chiang Mai proper has still more temples worthy of a visit. **Wat Koo Tao**, hidden away behind the bus station, has a strange bulbous *chedi*, like a pile of diminishing spheres. **Wat Saen Fang**, with its unusual monastery, is reached by a narrow lane guarded by long *naga*s. The mass of small *chedi*s at **Wat Suan Dok** contain the ashes of Chiang Mai's royal family, and the huge central *chedi* is said to hold no less than eight relics of Lord Buddha. **Wat Chedovan**, close to the east gate, has three tiled *chedi*s and a menagerie of mythical animals which almost come alive in the slanting rays of the morning sun.

A hairpin switchback ride climbs 12 km uphill to Chiang Mai's best-known temple. Seven-headed *naga*s snarl menacingly at visitors, their ceramic tails undulating up the 290 steps leading to **Wat Prathat (Doi Suthep)**. From this hilltop lookout at 1,000 meters, Thailand's northern metropolis appears like a toy below.

The sidetrip to Doi Suthep and its gilded temple can make an interesting morning excursion from Chiang Mai. The road to the mountain sanctuary leaves the old city at its northwest corner and crosses the plain studded with rice fields. (Transportation can be arranged at the White Elephant Gate.) After passing a large hospital, the road comes to the fairly new **Chiang Mai University**, officially opened in 1965 on its 200-hectare campus. A little farther on, an arboretum cultivates many of North Thailand's species of trees. About 7 km from town, where the road turns to begin its climb of Doi Suthep, is the entrance to the **Chiang Mai Zoo**. Started as the private collection of Mr. Harold Young and his son, the popular zoo was donated to

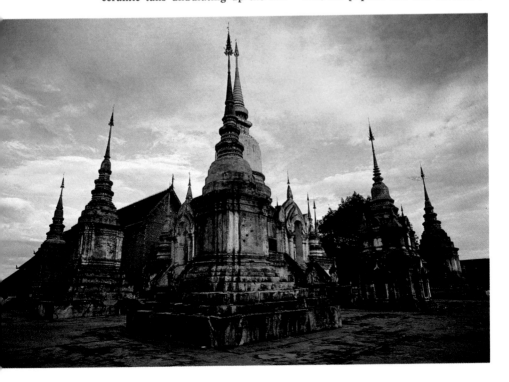

the town; it houses most of the regions wild animals.

After beginning its ascent, the road passes the statue of the monk Krupan Srivichai, who in 1934 began construction on the first road to the temple to make it more accessible to pilgrims. The completed road reaches the foot of the temple, where cars must be left. The temple on the summit is reached by the staircase of 290 steps flanked by *naga* balustrades. The two sanctuaries, the temple, and the cloister were built in the 16th century. Since then, the buildings have been maintained through gifts from pilgrims.

The outside pediment between the two doors leading to the cloister has been heavily restored, but inside the two sanctuaries are sumptuously decorated facades with murals depicting Buddhist tales. There are also Buddha images in the Sukhothai and the Chiang Saen styles. The 24-meter-high *chedi* is surrounded by gilded bronze parasols and covered with engraved gold tiles.

From the parking area of Wat Prathat, a road continues to ascend for about 5 km to **Bhubing Palace**, the summer palace of King Bhumibol. Situated at an elevation of about 1,300 meters, the palace grounds are completely furnished with audience halls, guest houses, dining rooms, kitchens, and official suites to carry on the royal affairs at this remote hilltop retreat. On weekends and holidays, when the royal family is absent, the public may visit the grounds and its well-tended gardens aflame with roses, orchids, hibiscus, and double-headed bougainvilleas; but the buildings cannot be entered.

About 400 meters before the palace entrance, a track goes 2 km to a crossroads, and from there the left branch leads to a **Meo village**. The first 2 km can be covered by jeep, but

Bhubing Palace
ตำหนักภูพิงค์ราชนิเวศน์

Meo Village
หมู่บ้านแม้ว

the remainder must be done on foot; although the track descends steeply, it takes only about 10 minutes to cover. On the way one passes smiling tribesmen carrying fresh game they have shot, or perhaps a few tribeswomen heading home. The Meo village consists of several huts perched all along the hillside; the people are extremely friendly and eager to talk and ask questions. Grubby faced children in bright red and black costumes wave happily at you; each seems to carry around their neck half their weight in jewelry. These people are members of one of the hilltribes that adds so much color to North Thailand. A nomadic people, groups of whom are also found in neighboring Burma and Laos, the Meo once depended on opium cultivation for their livelihood. While the government began persuading them to turn to less harmful crops, it discovered in the process

that the tribes are a major tourist attraction. The Meo women, small and active, wear heavy dark-blue skirts embroidered with bands of red and white. Because of its relative accessibility, this village receives far more visitors than most other tribal villages. For those who lack the time to go deeper into Thailand, this Meo village offers a typical example of hilltribe life; the disadvantage, however, results from their exposure to tourists, which has made them pecuniary-minded, and they now insist on payment for being photographed. This, however, is unusual in Thailand. Most tour operators, such as Diethelm, can arrange excursions to more untouched, less frequented hilltribe villages. Outings can include roughing it on three-day treks into the surrounding Himalayan foothills.

Another place to see the hilltribes is at the **Old Chiang Mai Cultural Center** south of town. Here,

Old Chiang Mai
Cultural Center
ศูนย์วัฒนธรรมดั้งเดิมเชียงใหม่

In evening light people pay homage at the famous sanctuary atop Doi Suthep (far left). The young girl (left) and the old man puffing a cigarette through a water pipe (above) live in the Meo village nearby.

Handicrafts

every night, while sitting cross-legged on the floor, you can indulge in a northern Thai style banquet *(kantoke)* and watch and listen to traditional Thai dances and songs. This is followed by an excellent genuine hill-tribes show during which you can chance to see the costumes and the dances of the seven tribes in the area (Meo, Red and White Karen, Lisu, Lahu, Yao, and Akha). The Center also contains representative houses which have been built and which are occupied by the several tribes. Although the setting is obviously artificial, it is nonetheless worthwhile.

Elephants are still used in the forests around Chiang Mai. Just off the main road, 58 km to the north, an enterprising lumber camp owner puts on a **daily elephant work show.** Arrive early to see the huge beasts having a morning scrub in the river before getting down to a few hours of hard log hauling.

What would anyone do with a half-life-size wooden elephant? There must be a good answer, for every other Chiang Mai handicrafts shop seems to have one. Chiang Mai's range of carvings is enormous; elephants from matchbox size up to those big ones are available. Visit Chiang Mai Carving on Rat Chiang Saen Road where 200 youngsters spend their mornings chiseling teak elephants, dolls, and furniture. All the carvers learn their skills at home, since the company cannot afford taking risks on a novice. Only one designer draws the patterns for the carvers. Buyers should patronize such established carving shops since much of the teak hawked on the street is green and cracks within a few months. Teak salad bowls or trays are equally plentiful, if you want something smallish and utilitarian.

Each of Chiang Mai's other prolific crafts seems to have its own

Elephant Show
การแสดงของช้าง

section of the city; but a good place to get a glimpse of the entire range of crafted goods that awaits the shopper is along **Tapae Road** near the eastern gate, where shops sell everything. In one stop you can buy lacquerware, silk, cotton, clothes, and jewelry. One of the more popular of these all-purpose centers is Hudson Enterprises, run by a very English gentleman, Roy Hudson, who was active in Southeast Asia during the war and eventually settled in Chiang Mai to become the resident expert on everything in North Thailand. In the evening, Tapae Road and nearby Chang Kian Road become shopping malls, rivaling London's Carnaby Street, as vendors lay out their wares in front of the tour coaches preparing to return to Bangkok.

After you have whetted your appetite for further exploring the treasures of Thailand's handicraft capital, you can investigate each craft more closely. Near the south gate is the **silversmiths' street, Wualai Road**, where all manner of jewelry and silver objects are crafted. The shops may look modern, but in the back rooms barechested, muscular smiths pound away at silver muscles propped on iron pegs. They hammer out intricate patterns of hilltribe-inspired designs, as well as scenes from the familiar *Ramayana* epic and stories of the Buddha's many incarnations. A number of Chiang Mai shops also sell, besides the work of city artisans, the less refined silverwork of the hilltribes. Most tribes prefer silver to paper for money; the women usually wear their wealth in heavy chunky necklaces and earrings.

Just beyond the silver shops, farther out on the road to Chom Thong,

You can look an elephant in the eye at the pachyderm's training school north of Chiang Mai. Elephants are still used in the teak forests of the North, where the terrain is rugged and the loads are mammoth.

the traditional **lacquerware industry** still flourishes. Village artisans first shape bamboo strips into a framework. Over this frame, layers of lacquer must be applied, dried, and then polished with a special ash and clay compound. The artisans laboriously build up layer upon layer of lacquer to make a beautiful black and gold tray, plate, or bowl, or a brightly colored orange, green, and yellow container. The similarity to the lacquerware of Burma results from the cultural intermingling that has taken place in this area for centuries. Much of the antique lacquerware found on the market, in fact, comes from Burma.

Chiang Mai's **umbrella-making and silk-weaving areas** are centered east of the city, over the river and past the ungainly Railway Hotel. Except for the rice fields, the drive presents an almost European vignette with an old, tree-lined road, orchards, and distant mountains. After 9 km a left turn enters the one-street village of **Bor Sang**, where freshly dyed paper umbrellas dry in front of every other house, providing a visual feast for passersby. The homes double as shops selling handbags and brocaded shirts in addition to the cheerful-looking umbrellas which they manufacture in a true cottage industry.

Umbrella production begins with a cane stem carefully cut and trimmed by young men deft with their cleavers. Young girls form bamboo strips into frames, over which translucent paper locally made from a special tree is meticulously pasted. Some of the painters seem less careful, chatting or glancing over at the TV next door, as they sketch zigzags and rose patterns with a two-toned brush onto the translucent umbrellas.

Three kilometers beyond the turnoff to Bor Sang, silk and cotton weaving on traditional Thai looms occupies many women in the district town of **San Kamphaeng**. Here North Thailand's best-known craft is on display in shops that are a panoply of

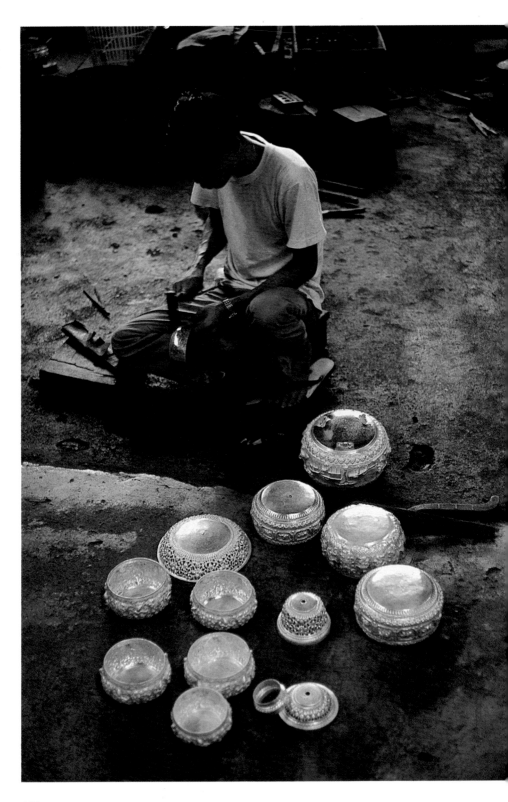

shiny colors, orchestrated by the steady rattle of the hand looms in adjoining rooms. Apart from small modern additions, such as a piece of wire, or a nail, the looms have changed little in the past fifty years or more. Young girls frequently do the weaving, as a friend or a suitor lingers nearby. With concentration, a weaver can produce about 6 meters of finished cloth per day. Only young eyes can function for long in the scant light that pierces the latticework of the bamboo walls which enclose the dirt-floored weaving area. Like the cloth shops in Pa Sang (see below), San Kamphaeng's stores are also full of former or hopeful beauty contestants.

Just east of San Kamphaeng one can stroll through the ruins of a pottery-making center where, 300 years ago, Chinese craftsmen fired a distinctive regional pottery called Sawankhalok pottery, the modern recreation of which is called **Thai celadon.** Clay and feldspar found in this area are particularly good for pottery making and give it its distinctive characteristics. Nowadays, such stoneware is again made at the Thai Celadon Factory on the Fang Road (several kilometers north of Chiang Mai) and at the Chiang Mai Sankalok Factory (in Chiang Mai). Tours of the former are conducted every day except on Monday. Here one can watch workers in faded blue shirts turn bowls, inscribe intricate designs on them, and then fire them to give the characteristic cracked look to the deep green or brown glazing. A small showroom offers a selection of pieces for sale.

A short drive about 13 km beyond San Kamphaeng takes you to Doi Saket where the lotus pond named Nong Bua is a favorite weekend retreat from Chiang Mai for *paitio.* An excellent new highway now continues from Doi Saket to Chiang Rai. This more than halves the driving time between Chiang Mai and Chiang Rai.

For the impecunious, **Pa Sang** 36 km south of Chiang Mai, specializes in less fine but equally eye-appealing **Thai cotton.** In an area reputed to have the most beautiful girls in Thailand, this village claims to have the prettiest of the lot. Local tailors will turn your silk or cotton purchases into clothes; ready-made shirts, blouses, and dresses can be picked up at bargain-basement prices in Chiang Mai or in the surrounding villages.

Not everything is sparkling new; Chiang Mai is also a treasure trove for the **antique hunter.** Those little metal weights in the shape of elephants and birds on sale in many shops are opium measures. Unhappily the plethora of antiques available in Chiang Mai is indicative of the economic misfortunes of neighboring Burma. Many of the antiques on sale here are smuggled from Burma to be exchanged on the black market for consumer goods.

Chiang Mai is the center of handicrafts in Thailand. A silversmith (left) hammers out paper-thin bowls covered with delicate designs; in the village of Bor Sang (above), paper umbrellas dry in the sun.

Be careful on the streets of Chiang Mai on 13 April and for several days thereafter, for a sudden deluge of water can fall on you despite clear blue skies. The reason behind the unexpected local downpour is Songkran, the Thai new year. Coming at the hottest part of the dry season, Songkran is celebrated especially enthusiastically in Chiang Mai when the weather is hottest and driest. How better to celebrate a dry season festival than by throwing water on everybody and anybody?

Chiang Mai's other important festival is a far more peaceful affair. On a full moon night in late October or early November the river sparkles with thousands of tiny lights. Countless candles float downstream borne across the water by tiny boats called *krathong*s. The festival is Loy Krathong and the effect is particularly bewitching in this northern capital.

Chiang Mai has a wide variety of hotels, ranging from the luxurious Rincome, Suriwongse, and the Chiang Inn where doubles cost several hundred baht, down to the old-fashioned Station Hotel and the friendly guest houses where a pleasant room with bathroom is only 40 to 60 baht. Popular guest houses are Poung Keo (called "PK") and Saitum near the east moat, or the favorite of the budget traveler, Je T'aime, in a quiet setting across the river from the town center. Several new hotels are in the works; by the late 1970s Chiang Mai will certainly be a buyer's market for hotel rooms.

At night a busy band of food stalls by the old east gate to the city provide a long menu of some of the cheapest and tastiest food in Thailand. Darets restaurant has a tempting array of fruits to be fed through their blender for delicious iced drinks, and their watermelon and orange combination has to be tasted to be believed. Here too is the Thai-German dairy stall where the results of a successful attempt to introduce dairy produce to Thailand are sold. They always have a crowd of people in the morning, breakfasting on the best bacon and eggs in Southeast Asia.

Confusingly two of Chiang Mai's most popular eating places have the same name. If you glance back at those frenetic food stalls the one with the biggest crowds is Pat's. Perhaps it is due to their energetic waitresses who, if they see you heading towards another stall, will blithely rush out to steer you in the right direction, even taking your order at another stall then asking you to transfer. On the other side of the moat and a hundred or so meters north stands the other Pat's. This one is Pat's Tavern Grill and is a popular restaurant for those in need of western nourishment or a well stocked bar.

If you want some authenticity in your northern eating, then opt for Aroon Rai and its flanking restaurants on the other side of the moat for real northern Thai cuisine at very reasonable prices. But make sure a glass of water is at hand: such food can be fiery.

At the Rincome Hotel or at Old Chiang Mai one can enjoy a traditional *kantoke* dinner. Sitting on the floor around a low table, (from which the name comes) guests are served a variety of curries with the northern staple, glutinous rice, and exotic dances are performed while you dine.

Beware lest you are overtaken by the fate that befell Thomas Samuel who, at the start of the 17th century, was one of the first Westerners to visit the City of Flowers. His employers, the East India Company, ordered him several times to leave the city but Samuel had fallen in love with Chiang Mai, was taken prisoner when the Burmese invaded in 1615 and died in Burma.

A sienna sunset softens the lines on one of the most venerable temples in North Thailand, Wat Haripoonchai, in Lamphun. The oldest building is the gold-topped chedi, the base of which dates from the ninth century.

Chiang Mai has hotels and restaurants to suit the needs and taste of all kinds of travelers.

172

Sidetrip to Lamphun

Several interesting sidetrips may be made from Chiang Mai. These include excursions to Lamphun, Mae Hong Son and Doi Inthanon, Fang, and the Chiang Rai area.

* * *

The road to **LAMPHUN,** situated 26 km south of Chiang Mai, leaves Chiang Mai across the Nawarat Bridge and then turns to follow the Ping River. About 4 km from the bridge, a turn on the right at the Shell station leads to a dirt road and a small diversion. The dirt road passes the five-tiered *chedi* of the Burmese-style Wat Chedi Liem, then goes by Wat Pa Peu on the right and finally arrives after 4 km at the gates of the **McKean Leprosarium.** There, several hundred lepers and their dependents receive treatment and care in a park-like setting on a secluded peninsula framed by the Ping and one of its tributaries. Visitors need not fear contagion.

Lamphun itself is famed for two old *wats*, attractive women, and young and fecund *lamyai* fruit trees. Located on the right bank of the Kuang River, a tributary of the Ping, the provincial town was once situated on the main road to Chiang Mai; but now a new highway bypasses Lamphun, which is perhaps a blessing in disguise, because the town has managed to preserve a mellow upcountry atmosphere, appropriate to its historical significance. Lamphun was once the seat of the Haripoonchai kingdom. On the site of the original palace now stands Wat Prathat Haripoonchai, on the left side of Lamphun's main street.

You should enter **Wat Prathat Haripoonchai** through its riverside entrance, because the temple faces that way. Large statues of lions guard its main entrances, overlooking the waters of the Kuang. Inside the large compound, monks study in a large

Buddhist school, set among the monuments and buildings which date as far back as the late 9th century. This makes the *wat* one of the most venerable in North Thailand. The base of the 50-meter-high gold-topped *chedi* in the center of the courtyard is the oldest structure in the temple. Ten centuries younger, but still respectably old, the gilded-roofed library stands to the left of a *sala* that shelters one of the largest bronze gongs in the world. The *sala* was restored in 1915 after damage by fire. The somewhat disorganized temple museum contains a representative sampling of several styles of old Buddhist art, including a rare silver Buddha head. Another small building close by is garishly illustrated with frescoes showing the good getting their reward and the bad their just deserts.

A kilometer west of Lamphun's old moat, stands **Wat Kukut,** also known as **Wat Chama Devi**, which has uninteresting buildings, but a pair of unusual *chedi*s. The larger *chedi* consists of five tiers, each of which contains three niches, each holding a Buddha statue — making an impressive display of fifteen Buddha images on each side, or sixty Buddhas in all gazing from their ancient domicile. This *chedi* is thought to have been built by Chama Devi, the fabled princess of Lop Buri and queen of Lamphun.

Before leaving Lamphun province, fruit lovers and horticulturists may visit **TONKHAM** village to see the "10,000-baht *lamyai* tree" which annually nets its owner that handsome sum through the sale of its fruit and seeds.

The trip to Lamphun can also be combined with a visit to **PA SANG,** about 12 km southwest of Lamphun on Road 106, which is the center for cotton weaving around Chiang Mai.

A young monk (above, center), taking a stroll with two companions, is unknowingly on his way to appearing on our cover. Many Thai men become novitiates at an early age, and almost all of them become monks for a short period of time sometime in their life to study Buddhist scriptures. Frothy Mae Klang Waterfall (right), in Doi Inthanon Park, is one of the numerous picturesque cascades in the North; paths in the park lead up to panoramic views.

Sidetrip to Hot and Mae Hong Son

From Chiang Mai, Thai Airways several times weekly offers a bumpy, 40-minute flight over cloud-covered hills to **MAE HONG SON.** By land, a bus leaves Chiang Mai Gate daily at around 7:00 a.m. for the 11-hour, 368-km horseshoe journey, which passes through Hot and Mae Sariang, then goes north through jungle, past the Shan settlement of Khun Yuam, to arrive at Mae Hong Son by dusk. However, you are more flexible in a car, and if time does not allow you to make the full trip to Mae Hong Son, you can drive down to Hot and back in a leisurely half-day.

By road, the excursion to Mae Hong Son heads south from Chiang Mai on Road 108, and just before the 57-km-stone turns right and goes 10 km to the entrance of **DOI IN-THANON NATIONAL PARK,** named after its prime attraction, Doi Inthanon, the highest mountain in the country at 2,596 meters. Girls rush out to sell bead necklaces, and cold beer is served in small shops on the river's edge below **MAE KLANG WATERFALL.** From the shops you walk up 20 meters to see this powerful cataract and its loud fusion of muddy brown water and white spray. Clearly marked footpaths branch up the rocky hills; one leads around a corner of boulders to a full view of the wider falls, **PAKAU NA,** which slides over its broad, craggy slopes for 120 meters like a liquid highway. Another path weaves up to nearby Doi Hua Chang which provides helicopter views of the broad farmlands south of Chiang Mai. On the leafy dome of Hua Chang plants quiver in the humid heat. The peak of Doi Inthanon hides behind a curtain of clouds 25 km away; you can glimpse sections of the new road which climbs to the signal station on its summit.

DOI INTHANON is a limestone knob in the long geological range that

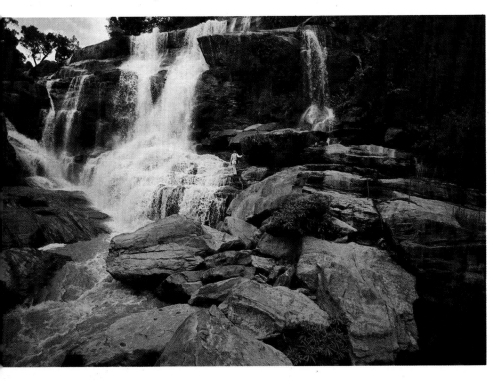

stretches southeast from Yunan in southern China and resurfaces as far south as Irian Jaya. But Doi Inthanon, Thailand's tallest peak, is a mere foothill in this southern extension of the Himalayan range. The trumpeting of work-elephants still echoes from the slopes of Inthanon, where Karen and Meo tribesmen dwell in isolated villages. They have been slowly moving out, as the mountain is now a national reserve.

By making prior arrangements with park authorities in Chiang Mai, you can take a three- to five-day hike on foot or by pony up the mountain. Simple campsites along the route are maintained by the Wildlife Association, affording simple accommodation for trekkers. During the climb you can observe rare birds and enjoy nature under a broad canopy of trees. Rather than a barren peak, the summit is lightly forested, complete with picnic tables.

At the 58-km-stone on Road 108, which is about 1 km south of the park turnoff, lies the town of **CHOM THONG.** The town's distinction rests with elegant **Wat Phra Thai Si Chom Thong,** where glints of subdued light accentuate an unusually beautiful collection of bronze Buddhas. The monastery creaks with old age, as the slumping boughs of its courtyard trees do. The Burmese-style *chedi* dates from 1451, and the sanctuary itself was built only fifty years later. The broad stairway leading to a facade of wood carvings is actually the back entrance.

A large *prang,* carved deeply with a profusion of floral patterns entwined with birds and *naga* serpents, dominates this temple compound. Four standing Buddhas, clothed like celestial kings, flank the *prang.* Although much of the decoration in the temple reflects the Burmese penchant for elaboration, the

North Thailand is rich in teak, and the temples of the region are usually adorned with intricately carved and gilded pieces of wood. Wat Phra Thai Si Chom Thong (above) is noted for its elegance, as well as for its collection of bronze Buddha images. The temple's Burmese-style chedi dates from the mid-15th century, and the sanctuary is only a little less ancient. Splendid woodcarvings and Burmese decorations abound in the compound.

central Buddha image with its protective *naga* seems extremely Thai, and resembles the famed image at Wat Prasingh in Chiang Mai. On either side of the *prang* stand enshrined collections of miniature gold and silver Buddha images, some bejeweled and metallic, others carved of crystal.

Continuing south on Road 108, you will see many northern touches: rambling, stylized elephants carved on the back of bullock carts; *lamyai* trees and green bean-patches; giant plaited baskets which farmers use to thresh harvested rice; and shady, thatched-roof *sala*s dotting the rice fields.

HOT, lying 88 km southwest of Chiang Mai on Road 108, seems like the preview of a new town yet to come. Hot once lay 15 km farther south at the mouth of the Ping River, until the rising reservoir behind the Bhumibol Dam submerged its site. Shop houses, hotels, and restaurants were constructed hastily in this new town.

Farther south on Road 1012 lies the **site of ancient Hot.** Cracked, rain-washed *chedi*s dot the landscape like dignified relics from the time when Hot was part of the early kindgoms of the North. Excavations at these sites have unearthed gold jewelry, amulets, and lively stucco carvings, now on display in the Chiang Mai Museum.

Road 1012 goes on to **WANG LUNG** a tiny village that earns its keep by selling dried fish caught in the catchment area created by Bhumibol Dam. Karen people have settled much of this area. Their necks hidden by a profusion of black beads, and their bodices covered with thick, colored patchwork, Karen tribeswomen walk into the tiny town to buy provisions.

You can hire a boat at Wang Lung for an hour's ride among the bamboo- and reed-covered islands at

*aren girls at Hot
corate their daily
ess with black-bead
cklaces and novel
acelets made of
hite shirt buttons.*

the estuary of the Mae Ping and out onto the vast expanse of water at the upper end of the reservoir. Reflections of ruined *chedis* and strangely eroded cliffs enliven remote mountain scenes; but unless you speak Thai you will need a guide.

From Hot, Road 108 strikes out west across the Chaem River, following its right bank toward Mae Sariang. About 17 km from Hot, the road passes **OB LUANG GORGE,** called Thailand's version of the Grand Canyon, though it could be considered so only in miniature. Stop at the *sala* for a look into the deep, ragged incision in rock, cut over the ages by the river.

After the gorge, the road continues to wriggle like a belly dancer. Butterflies and plumed blossoms brighten the way. Lovers of hot springs should turn left 4 km after the gorge and drive another 5 km to reach a lonely sulfur spring with a

small campsite. Chances are nobody will be there.

The drive to the Mae Sariang district seat is more exciting than the town itself. The road goes like a roller coaster over the mountains. Not even motorbikes can reach the small leaf-and-bamboo huts tucked away in these hills. Most of the villages in the area belong to the Skaw Karen, one of the largest groups of hillpeople in Thailand, who have settled all the way down the Thai-Burmese frontier as far south as Chumphon. In the moist valleys they plant wet rice on steep terraces. The nomadic Karen burn away the forest to make clearings to plant new crops. This slash-and-burn technique has scarred the mountainsides and caused extensive erosion. On the slopes, black tree stumps stand out like whiskers on a green background of rice sprouts. In places the road skirts around high banks of red earth. Fresh mounds of

16. Ob Luang Gorge
ขอดออบหลวง

Incised in rock over the ages, Ob Luang Gorge (above, left) has been perhaps optimistically dubbed Thailand's Grand Canyon. On past, the road to Mae Sariang traverses hilly terrain, hugging the slopes, and affords tranquil views of Karen villages (above, right). Giant stone lions (facing page) flank a forgotten stairway leading up to the hilltop temple of Doi Kong Mou, above the remote and serene little town of Mae Hong Son.

178

mud on the asphalt show that land-slides are not uncommon, because the banks cannot always hold back the runoff. The solution to this problem is the pinetree. Though it is not the tree one associates with tropical Thai-land, the pine is well suited for re-building the soil. Its roots form an extensive earth-holding network un-derground, and its seeds do not burn. Before reaching the highest point on the road (at about 1,130 meters) on the way to Mae Sariang, you pass the Thai-Danish Reforestation Camp which resembles a tropical Christmas tree farm.

Hemmed in by mountains, **MAE SARIANG** lies 103 km west of Hot at the bend where Road 108 curves north. Only a Burmese-style temple and Karen handicraft shops distin-guish this small district seat and border trading post.

Road 108 continues north on a rough track from Mae Sariang

through mountain scenery that is among the most breathtaking in Thailand, reaching **MAE HONG SON** 171 km later. Mae Hong Son fits into Thailand like the overlooked last piece of a jigsaw puzzle. Secluded by jungle ridges and framed on the north and west by the Shan states of Burma, the province peacefully bene-fits from years of relative neglect by the outside world. This is the place for seekers of old-world serenity. The presence of Karen, Meo, Lawa, Shan, Lisu, Lahu, and Burmese, all of whom easily outnumber the ethnic Thais, adds intrigue to the ill-kept secret that Mae Hong Son lies on bor-der smuggling routes.

The town bustles only in the early morning. By 7:30 a.m., when half the market is deserted, sellers busily pack their bunches of long beans, dried fish, chips of fried pig skin, cabbages, carrot-size chilies, cheroot tobacco, and betel nut. By

8:00 a.m. the market has emptied. Over the town's small buildings loom the deep-green mountains, which are separated by hidden valley hollows. Some of the peaks are usually obscured by heavy clouds or dark gray curtains of falling rain.

A commanding view of the town of Mae Hong Son and the surrounding countryside is afforded from Doi Kongmou which lies about 250 meters above the habitation. At night, the *chedis* of **Wat Prathat Doi Kongmou** atop the hill light up like timid beacons of civilization in this remote corner of Thailand.

To return overland to Chiang Mai, you must retrace your steps on Road 108 via Mae Sariang and Hot. There will eventually be a shorter route on a surfaced road through Pai to Mae Taeng 40 km north of Chiang Mai. A Thai Airways flight can also return you to Chiang Mai, completing this northern excursion.

To reach the border outpost of **FANG** take Road 107 north from Chiang Mai (beginning at the Elephant Gate), past the Thai Celadon Factory and continuing on to Mae Rim, 13 km from Chiang Mai. Left from Mae Rim is the drive to **MAE SA WATERFALL.** At the nearby royal *sala* the Thai government occasionally stages performances of working elephants in preparation for visits by the royal family and their guests.

Road 107 continues north through rice fields and small villages. Up ahead on the right one can see the outline of Chiang Dao Mountain. Slowly, the road leaves flat farmland, enters the Mae Ping Gorge, then follows the river's right bank through scenic countryside. About 60 km from Chiang Mai on Road 107, a dirt road branches left and goes to **DOI CHIANG DAO,** which is at an elevation of 2,186 meters. You need a jeep or a scrambler motorcycle to negoti-

21. Fang
ฝาง

19. Mae Sa Waterfall
น้ำตกแม่สา

20. Doi Chiang Dao
ดอยเชียงดาว

Non-Thai peoples, such as this woman and child (above, left) from a rare hilltribe subgroup, outnumber the ethnic Thais in Mae Hong Son, adding to the distinctive charm of the place. Fractured light (above, right) filters through a hole in the grotto roof of Chiang Dao cave, north of Chiang Mai. Visitors can take local transportation (opposite) for a breathtaking boat trip through the rapids on the river between Chiang Rai and Tha Thon.

20. Chiang Dao Cave
ถ้ำเชียงดาว

ate this 9-km-long track which emerges at a lookout spot 1,000 meters up on the mountainside. From the government station there, officials trek out to assist hilltribes living on the slopes of Doi Chiang Dao and the neighboring mountains. At the nearby nursery, horticulturists experiment with new strains of tea that someday may be cultivated throughout the region. The government's agricultural aid on Doi Chiang Dao is aimed at eradicating opium cultivation.

Farther north on Road 107 is the town of Chiang Dao, located 72 km from Chiang Mai; at the end of town a dirt road leads off to the left going 6 km to **CHIANG DAO CAVE.** Buddha statues and a small white *chedi* with many spires grace the cave site.

After visiting the cave, the drive goes on to **FANG,** located 152 km from Chiang Mai. The district around Fang combines the elements of the Wild West with the mysteries of the East. During the 1950s the district witnessed a "black-gold rush," following a minor discovery of crude oil; but production never matched expectation. Now the only get-rich-quick gamble is illegal, dangerous, and reprehensible: smuggling opium. Located on the Burmese border adjacent to the infamous Golden Triangle, Fang is a natural conduit for opium. To help seal off an otherwise hopelessly porous border, the government allowed remnants of Chiang Kai-shek's Kuomintang Army to settle in Fang and act as an auxiliary border patrol. The Hunanese-speaking soldiers fled China in the late 1940s.

Dressed in distinctively embroidered clothing, Yao hilltribes also live in the mountains around Fang. The women wear black hats decorated with red or magenta woolen balls, while babies carried on their mothers' backs sport little embroidered caps. Young girls may spend an entire year embroidering large pants-panels for their weddings. To appreciate the meaning and cultural context of this handicraft, read Jacqueline Butler's *Yao Embroidery*.

The government has worked extensively with the Yao, promoting crops as substitutes for the more lucrative opium. One Yao headman of a fifteen-house village proudly listed his new produce: potatoes, corn, garlic, chickens, and pigs. His eyes widened as he happily described the size of the breeding pig presented to the village by the king. About 8 km northeast of Fang is an agricultural station near the hot springs of Baw Nam Rawn.

From Fang a rough road leads north 24 km to **THA THON** on the Burmese border, where you can rent a boat for a five- to six-hour exciting journey down the Mae Kok River to Chiang Rai.

After visiting Fang, you may want to continue exploring the far northern crown of Thailand, tucked between Burma and Laos — the area which is called the Golden Triangle. As the crow flies, **CHIANG RAI** lies only 65-odd km to the east of Fang; but at present Road 1001, which wriggles east from below Fang through Mae Suai toward Chiang Rai, is unsurfaced and in poor condition. This means that a sidetrip to Chiang Rai begins in Chiang Mai, the focal point for the North.

Chiang Rai is linked to Chiang Mai by air; each day Thai Airways flies from Bangkok to Chiang Rai, with a stopover at Chiang Mai. Otherwise, the standard way to Chiang Rai is via Route 1, which continues north from Lampang.

Route 1 twists around and over mountains on its way to **NGAO** 81 km northeast of Lampang. At the highest point in the road, below twin

22. Tha Thon
ท่าทอน

23. Ngao
งาว (ตัวเมือง, อำเภอ)

On the road from Lampang to Ngao: spirit houses cluster at the highest point in the road (right); a recess at the FIO elephant school (above); finally, limestone formations in Tham Pha Thai cave (facing page).

rocky peaks, drivers stop, or if in a hurry just blow their horns or *wai,* to pay respects to the *phi*s believed to inhabit the pass. Scores of spirit houses, some simple like farmers' houses, others as elaborate as the Marble Temple, cluster along the roadside.

Teak saplings line Route 1 between Lampang and Ngao, thanks to the Forest Industry Organization (FIO). The FIO also runs an elephant training school about 54 km from Lampang, 1½ km west of the highway behind Pang-la village. Visitors can watch the mahouts put their young pachyderms through mounting, marching, and log-dragging drills until noon. If made to train beyond noon, the elephants stamp their feet in protest until they are allowed to lumber off to their stalls for a snack of sugar cane.

About 19 km before the district town of Ngao, a left turn leads in less than 1 km to a small grove of teak trees and a refreshment stand that mark the entrance to **THAM PHA THAI** probably the most interesting cave in Thailand. The climb up to the cave covers 283 concrete steps, some broken by roots or rocks, past the monks' quarters, to the huge arched entrance to the grotto. In front of the entrance stands a white *chedi*; a gilded Buddha image inside sits near the sunlit edge. Most striking, though, is the colossal stalagmite rising like a white explosion from a sea of limestone. Often a young novice monk will lead visitors down into the cave and point out bizarre limestone formations which, with a little imagination, can resemble a throne, a rabbit, or a turtle. Slithering green snakes wrap themselves around electric wires or coil up in crevices. The novice guide explains that these snakes are protected and have never bitten anyone. The 400-

meter walk into the cave ends at a small mound of bat guano. Light streaks down from a jagged opening in the cave roof, projecting the silhouettes of flying bats onto the cavern walls.

About 12 km before Ngao, on the left of Route 1, Burmese-style **Wat Chong Kram** exudes charm in the face of alarming decrepitude. The ceiling is gradually becoming more crooked as its supporting pillars sink into the mud; as one guidebook has advised, "See it before it falls down!"

Route 1 continues through Ngao and then goes 49 km farther to **PHAYAO,** a district town lying on the eastern shore of a shallow lake at the foot of a 1,700-meter-high mountain. Although quite small and outwardly undistinguished, Phayao holds interest for archaeologists, as the town was rebuilt in the 11th century on a more ancient deserted site. Judging from the remains of a moat

and eight city gates which enclose an area measuring about 2 km square, scholars believe the older site may predate the Bronze Age. Between the lake and the road, as you leave Phayao, sits **Wat Si Khom Kham,** considered by scholars the most important temple in the area for its 400-year-old, 16-meter-high Buddha image inside a *viharn.* Local legend claims that a *naga* king in disguise gave a young couple gold for sculpting this large image.

From Phayao Route 1 continues north 94 km to the provincial capital of **CHIANG RAI,** located in Thailand's northernmost province, at an elevation of about 580 meters. Although linked to Bangkok 940 km away by daily Thai Airways flights, and strategically important because of its location near the borders with Burma and Laos, Chiang Rai has taken the slow path to commercial development. King Mengrai, who

Wat Si Khom Kham
วัดศรีโคมคำ

Wat Chong Kram
วัดช่องคราม

25. Chiang Rai
เชียงราย (ตัวเมือง, จังหวัด)
24. Phayao
พะเยา (ตัวเมือง, อำเภอ)

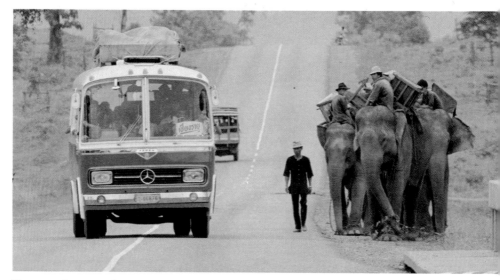

Upcountry buses go almost everywhere (above), sometimes at hair-raising speeds, passing such rural sights as this pack of elephants slowly commuting to work. A closeup of Yao embroidery (right) shows the intricate and colorful patterns which the hilltribe women excel in making to decorate their clothes. Tribal embroidery is now being used by many high-fashion designers in Bangkok boutiques and makes an excellent souvenir of the North.

6. Mae Chan
แม่จัน (ตัวเมือง, อำเภอ)

Wat Prasingh
วัดพระสิงห์

Wat Phra Keo
วัดพระแก้ว

also established Chiang Mai as a walled city, founded Chiang Rai in 1262. Legend claims that the king decided to conquer regions south of his seat of empire located at Chiang Saen after his favorite elephant ran away in a southerly direction. The search for the elephant led to the banks of the Kok River, where the king decided to build Chiang Rai. A statue of King Mengrai now stands north of Chiang Rai along the road to Mae Chan.

Two temples in Chiang Rai are of interest: Wat Prasing and Wat Phra Keo. Both share the distinction of having once sheltered famous images. The *chedi* and *viharn* at **Wat Prasingh,** where legend holds that an important Theravada image was located, have been restored too many times to allow accurate dating, but documents suggest the 15th century or earlier. **Wat Phra Keo,** situated behind Wat Prasingh, is believed to

have been the original residence of the Emerald Buddha which is now in Bangkok at the royal temple of the same name. To the west of Wat Phra Keo rises Ngam Muang Hill. Inside the *wat* atop the hill, a reliquary is believed to contain the bones of King Mengrai, placed there by one of his sons.

From Chiang Rai, Road 110 goes 29 km north to **MAE CHAN.** (Check on road conditions.) Formerly a center for silverwork, the tiny district town now serves as a trading post for Akha and Yao hillpeople who sell their goods and buy manufactured items. You can still view some silver and other tribal handicrafts at the shops of Lao Tzan, a Yao merchant, and Lao Taa, who is half Lisu and half Haw Chinese (like the Kuomintang soldiers).

More about Hilltribes

About 2km beyond Mae Chan, a dirt road on the left off Road 110 leads through a valley noted for its fragrant rice, and then ascends to Doi Thong (or "The Flag Mountain"). From the Mae Kam community development station on the mountain, government officials go out to assist local hillpeople in agricultural and village projects. The trail leading from the Mae Kam center continues on to Ko Saen Chai, an **Akha village.** Considered to be among the least sophisticated of the hilltribes, the Akha nevertheless seem to have beaten the West in one trend: Akha women were wearing miniskirts long before they became fashionable elsewhere. The Akha, who inhabit Thailand only in Chiang Rai province, build characteristic wooden swings and hold swinging ceremonies around their New Year to bring good luck and to enhance the fertility of the soil. Akha women embroider their black shirts and hats with bright cloth beads and silver ornaments.

Chiang Rai province hosts, besides the Akha, other hilltribe groups: the Yao, the Blue and White Meo, Lisu, Lahu, Lahu Shi, and Skaw and P'wo Karen. Each main group speaks its own language, and follows animist customs (based on a belief in spirits) as well as adhering to other more recently adopted religious beliefs. Most of the tribes came to Thailand from China via Burma and Laos within the last 100 years. The Meo are probably the best known of these hillpeoples, partly due to the proximity of several Meo villages to Chiang Mai, and also because of the tribal insurgency in the 1960s known as the Meo War.

Basically shy and clannish, the hillpeople tend to settle at specific altitudes, some building villages only above 1,000 meters. Although members of some tribes have embraced

Akha village
หมู่บ้านชาวเขาอาข่า

At Mae Kam community development center, the government assists the hilltribe people living nearby. Among them are an Akha boy (above), a Yao girl with her little brother (right), and Lisu girls (facing page).

ahu
ฦาหู

aren
ะเหรี่ยง

ao
เย้า

Meo
แม้ว

isu
ลีซู (หรือ ลีซอ)

Islam, Buddhism, or Christianity in response to missionary work, most retain strong animist convictions. They protect their homes and villages with altars, fertility symbols, totems, and objects of sympathetic magic (including model airplanes), to ward off evil spirits.

About 70,000 **Karen** in Thailand live in Mae Hong Son, Chiang Mai, Chiang Rai, and Lamphun. They are of Tibeto-Burman stock. Many are Christians and have beliefs bearing some resemblance to early Christianity, leading to speculation about their origin and antiquity which remains a mystery. The Karen are endogamous and matrilineal.

Nearly 20,000 **Lisu,** also of Tibeto-Burman origin, live in North Thailand going as far south as Tak, where one group lives near a Black Lahu tribe. Different hilltribes often live peacefully in close proximity. The Lisu come originally from the upper reaches of the Salween River. The Lisu are patrilineal and have strong animist beliefs; each village has a folk healer and exorcist *(tongpa)*. Along with the Meo, the Lisu have been major opium cultivators.

The **Lahu** are famed for their hunting skills. Some groups reportedly recognize a "man-god" who must qualify himself through physical and magical feats. **Yao** villages celebrate the Chinese lunar new year by slaughtering a pig, drinking great quantities of rice wine, and making merry for days. The **Meo** practice a courting ritual in which boys and girls standing in separate lines throw balls to each other to "break the ice."

Gradually all the tribes are assimilating Thai culture through trade contacts and education in *nikhorn* ("settlement") schools built by the government. The sale of their crafts has improved the economies of many

Apex of the
Golden Triangle

of the tribes. Organizations like the Thai Hill-Crafts Foundation (with offices in Bangkok and Chiang Rai) and the Border Patrol Police have found domestic and foreign markets for the colorful and distinctive tribal crafts. Many shops in Bangkok and other cities sell hilltribe jewelry, embroidery, shoulder bags, and weaving.

From Mae Chan Road 101 continues 34 km due north to **MAE SAI** at the northernmost point in Thailand. Mae Sai and Chiang Saen lie at the apex of the Golden Triangle. This district on the frontier does a thriving business selling a variety of goods, especially shoes, to Burmese who cross the border on shopping sprees. Many Thais from Chiang Rai *pai-tio* in Mae Sai and browse over smuggled items from Laos and Burma. Supplies of liquor and cigarettes from Laos have dwindled, although gems still arrive from Burma.

On returning south toward Mae Chan, a swing northeast on Road 1010 goes to the ancient capital of **CHIANG SAEN.** Scholars believe the town was founded around the end of the 13th century and strongly fortified about 100 years later. The Burmese captured it in the 16th century, but the first king of the Chakri dynasty later recaptured it. Fearing history would repeat itself with another Burmese invasion, however, Rama I ordered the town destroyed. Chiang Saen remained deserted until the reign of Rama V, and in 1957 the town became a district seat. Chiang Saen's lovely setting on the Mekong River strongly enhances the charm of its old temples. Just west of the town stands **Wat Pa Sak,** whose name derives from the use of 300 teak *(sak)* trunks for the original enclosure. The temple's foundation was laid in 1295 during the reign of King Ramkamhaeng. Earlier Srivichaya and Dava-

28. Chiang Saen
เชียงแสน (ตัวเมือง, อำเภอ

27. Mae Sai
แม่สาย (ตัวเมือง, อำเภอ

Wat Pa Sak
วัดป่าสัก

This merchant in Mae Chan (above, left) still sells handsome silver bracelets by weight, in the traditional way; the far north offers a multitude of bargains in fine handicrafts and Thai and Burmese antiques. In a pond near the ancient city of Chiang Saen (above, right), local fishermen employ a small-scale version of the same poled nets used traditionally along the distant shores of the Gulf of Thailand to the south.

ravati influences, along with the predominant Sukhothai style, are evident in the *that* ("reliquary"), the clothing of the deities, and in the stucco walking Buddhas. Located about 1 km west of the town gate, **Wat Prathat Chom Kitti** occupies a hill commanding a good view of Chiang Saen. Local chronicles suggest that the old *that* with a leaning top was first built around the 10th century and subsequently restored at least twice. Below this temple lies a ruined *chedi* in **Wat Chom Chang.** From there a staircase leads farther downhill toward town. Close to the western gate of town stand **Wat Chedi Luang** and a branch of the National Museum. The 60-meter-tall 13th-century *chedi* stands out in style as well as size; its bricks rise from an octagonal base to a bell-shaped top. In the grounds of the museum one can see a good assortment of bronze Buddhas and other Chiang Saen art.

The most scenic return trip from Chiang Saen to Chiang Rai is via water in a long-tail boat down the Mekong River as far as **CHIANG KHONG,** a three-hour trip after the rainy season when the river is high. Be sure to check on security conditions before setting out. The river follows an approximately S-shaped path, first flowing southeast to the mouth of the Kok River, then curving north between beautiful mountains, then finally south again for 20 thrilling kilometers down deep narrow sections, through rapids and eddies beneath steep, jungled mountainsides. At Chiang Khong, the river widens slightly. Set on left-bank hills, the Laotian town of **BAN HOUEI SAI** lies opposite the Chiang Khong district seat. Laotian government officials still work in fortifications built by the French who named the town Fort Carnot. If relations between Thailand and Laos are cordial

A Buddha image (left) in the small museum at Chiang Saen displays the style of that period: Chinese features and curled hair. The ghostly ramparts of a French citadel (above) guard Ban Houei Sai in Laos.

Excursion through the Nan Valley

and you have the proper travel documents, take a ferry across the river to Ban Houei Sai (after checking with Immigration in Chiang Khong on what this will entail for your Thai visa). From Ban Houei Sai there used to be daily flights to the beautiful Laotian royal capital at Luang Prabang, with connections onward to Vientiane. Check with a travel agent on the possibility of flying through Laos to Northeast Thailand. The town of Ban Houei Sai offers few sights; hilltribe people come to the market and to the hospital founded there by Tom Dooley, which is now run by the Pathet Lao government.

From Chiang Khong Road 1021 goes to Thoeng; Road 1020 then returns to the provincial capital of Chiang Rai.

From Chiang Rai, one can continue eastward across North Thailand toward **NAN**. One must follow Route 1 cross-country from the provincial capital south through Phayao and on to Ngao, where road 103 branches southwest to the Song and Rong Kwang districts of Phrae province. Phrae province, which was once notorious for its hired gunmen, is now better known for its tobacco plantations. At Rong Kwang, Road 101 heads northeast 96 km to Nan. Taxis travel this route taking passengers who disembarked from the train in Den Chai for Phrae and Nan. Nan is now linked by air with Chiang Mai about five times a week on a shuttle that touches down at Phitsanulok.

Road 101 winds through sparsely settled hills and teak reserves. You may see some elephants dragging logs alongside the road. The government, through reforestation, is trying to reduce dependence on teak imports, but the trees take long to grow. Beyond Sa District, 24 km before Nan, the road begins to parallel the Nan River flowing southward a few kilo-

31. Nan
น่าน (ตัวเมือง, จังหวัด)

meters to the east. The fertile Nan valley supports rice and corn. The provincial capital, seat of an independent kingdom until this century, lies on the right bank of the river.

Nan's town walls were rebuilt in 1857 to replace the original walls destroyed in a severe flood forty years earlier. The walls are roughly circular, indicating Mon influence in the late 14th century, when the town was established. The first recorded settlement of Nan province dates back to 1282 when Khun Fong, brother of the founder of Vientiane, set up a court in Wora Nakhon, 70 km north of the present provincial capital. Nan's inaccessibility helped it remain relatively free, although it did fall occasionally under the sway of Chiang Mai, the Burmese (for 200 years), and other powers — until 1931 when the province came fully under the control of Bangkok. The presence of Thai Army soldiers in Nan indicates that

there are security problems in the remote districts. Nan town, though, is safe. The Thevarat Hotel has air-conditioned rooms although Nan is usually cool. Around 5:00 a.m. the main market begins to bustle; look for rattan products, famous Nan tangerines, and crafts sold by Yao women. Just south of the *sala klang* government offices stands the town's most interesting temple, **Wat Phumin,** built in 1596 and extensively restored in the 19th century. The carved doors are nearly comparable to the famous doors of the *viharn* of Bangkok's Wat Suthat (now kept in the National Museum). Although the *wat's* murals were inexpertly restored, they tell an interesting story of the kingdom, with scenes depicting the arrival of foreigners, and even some bawdy comic portrayals. Inside the unusual cross-shaped hall are four gilded stucco images facing the cardinal directions.

The isolated but rice-rich Nan valley (left) was once the center of an early independent kingdom; not until 1931 did the Bangkok government gain full control of the province. Nan boasts many venerable temples, such as Wat Phumin (above), which is perhaps the most famous in the area. Inside the temple, murals tell stories of the ancient kingdom, including the arrival of foreigners and even a few bawdy portrayals thrown in for comic relief.

The "Elephant-Supported Temple" or **Wat Chang Kham** is located in what was the center of the old walled city, now opposite the provincial administrative offices. Actually, it is an old *chedi* supported by elephant buttresses, seven elephants per side under the second tier of the base. A Nan prince built the *viharn* in 1547. Two walking and one standing Buddha images in front of the main altar are good examples of the Sukhothai style. An inscription dated 1547 records the installation of the *viharn*'s principal image in that year. On the reverse side is a prophecy about the fifth (future) Buddha, Sri Ariyametteya Bodhisattva.

Two life-size Sukhothai Buddhas, dated 1427, reside in **Wat Phya Phu**. One bears an inscription telling that it was cast in the fourth lunar month of that year. The total of five similar images at both *wats* was chosen to ensure that the then prince would be reborn as a man in the lifetime of the future fifth Buddha, and also to attest that Buddhism would last 5,000 years.

Wat Suan Tan, the only temple in the North with a *prang* (rounded ornate spire), also features an interesting 500-year-old bronze seated Buddha in its *viharn*. In 1450, the conquering King Tiloka of Chiang Mai gave the people of Nan seven days to collect enough metal for a new image, then he set a 100-day deadline for refugee Sukhothai artists to fashion it. The image is called *Phra Khao Thong Thip*.

Across the river from Wat Suan Tan, 3 km southeast of town on a small hill, sits **Wat Chae Haeng**. There, during the fourth lunar month, Nan residents hold a boisterous fair, complete with fireworks. The temple's name, meaning "to soak the parched," refers to an incident in the life of Buddha which the pious believe

Wat Chang Kham
วัดช้างค้ำ

Wat Suan Tan
วัดสวนตาล

Wat Chae Haeng
วัดแช่แห้ง

Wat Phya Phu
วัดหญ้าภู้

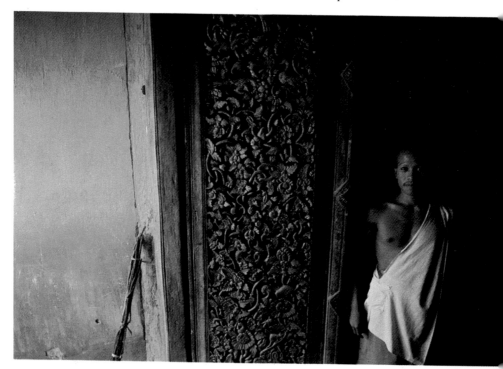

predicted that this spot would shelter relics.

Southwest of town, down a dirt track off Road 101, **Wat Khao Noi** affords a good view of Nan from a small mountain. A golden parasol tops the old Chiang Saen *chedi* there. This temple hosts an annual fair in the sixth lunar month.

Those who are not deterred by the sight of passing military convoys filled with weapon-toting troops can venture 60 km north of Nan town to to the district of **PHUA.** There, missionaries and civil servants, including a district officer with a price on his head, attend to the needs of several thousand people from the hilltribes and other ethnic minorities living in resettlement camps. The government has relocated these people to isolate them from insurgents, but life in the Phua valley does not particularly suit hillpeople.

A more scenic and relaxed side-

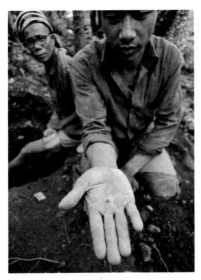

A monk poses pensively beside the beautifully carved doors of Wat Phumin in Nan (left). Hardly a stone has been left unturned or a hill unexplored in the gem country just southwest of Phrae (above).

trip goes south from Nan on Road 101 to Sa, then on the dirt road due south to Na Noi. A few kilometers beyond Na Noi lies **SAO DIN CANYON,** a small but striking arrangement of wind-carved rock, used as a film setting in many Thai movies. From the canyon, return to Road 101, pass the junction with Road 103 at Rong Kwang and drive 31 km to **PHRAE.** There, located on Road 1022 about 8 km east of town is **Wat Prathat Cho Mae,** on a small hill surrounded by orchards. The high-ceilinged *viharn* and parts of the courtyard were recently renovated.

From Phrae Road 101 follows the Yom River. Around Sung Men you may see hundreds of people digging and panning for gems, when news or rumors of new finds send them scurrying in search of instant wealth. About 10 km beyond Sung Men lies Den Chai. From there the shortest way to Uttaradit, the next provincial town, is by train. By car you have to take Road 101 to Si Satchanalai, then turn east on Road 102 for a total of just over 130 km to reach Uttaradit.

Most of the buildings in **UTTARADIT** seem new, and they are. A fire in 1967 burned most of the city to the ground. From Uttaradit town, which lies between the rail line and the Nan River, you can travel east 55 km to **SIRIKIT DAM,** named after the queen. Completed in 1973, the dam generates power and provides great amounts of sorely needed water during the dry season to farms around Uttaradit. Below the dam, near Pak Pat village, stands the tallest teak tree in Thailand.

From Uttaradit one could begin a trip to the Northeast, by going to Sukhothai and taking Road 12 east through Phitsanulok to Lom Sak, then going north on Road 203 to Loei. Or from Sukhothai you can return to Bangkok by continuing down Road 101 to Kamphang Phet, then picking up Route 1 for the rest of the way south to the capital.

Map not drawn to scale

VIETNAM

LAOS

CAMBODIA

Mekong River

Mekong River

Moun River

Ban Aut

Thakhek

SAVANNAKHET

Amnat Charoen

Det Udom

Kantharalak

KHAO
PHRA VIHARN

NAKHON
PHANOM

Nong Han

BAN RENU

THA
RAE

THAT PHANOM

MUKDAHAN

SAKON NAKHON

UBON

SI SAKET

SIKORAPHUM

Khukhan

BAN PLUANG

SURIN

Prasat

MUANG THAM

YASOTHORN

Suwan Naphum

MAHASARAKHAM

KALASIN

ROI ET

LAMPAO
DAM

BAN CHIANG

VIENTIANE

NONG KHAI

UDON THANI

ELEPHANT
CAVE

Chiang Khan

KHON KAEN

Friendship Route 2

Buri Ram

Prakhon
Chai

PRASAT
PHNOM
RUNG

PIMAI

NAKHON
RATCHASIMA

Chok Chai

PAK
TONGCHAI PRASAT

PRASAT
PHRANOMWAN

Chaiyaphum

Mekong River

LOEI

PHU KRADUNG

PHETCHABUN

To
Phitsanulok
and
North
Thailand

Lom Sak

Nam Pasek River

Lam Ta Klong
Dam

Muak Lek

Pak Chong

SARABURI

Khao Yai

Nakhon Nayok

A Problem Area in Transition

Thailand's age-old problem area, the Northeast is now undergoing many changes and the future is brighter.

A Thai village of little romantic appeal: a tired-looking, dusty place where a few scrawny chickens peck in the shade of mean houses; not the sort of place likely to appear on any picture postcard. It is all too characteristic of hundreds of other villages in the Northeast, a region other Thais call *Issan*, and one that has been Thailand's chronic problem area, where nature and neglect have combined for too long to make life hard for the gentle-natured inhabitants. Many of them of Lao extraction, whose ancestors drifted across the great Mekong River which forms the natural border today, they retain the Lao quality of sweet passivity in the face of adversity. Historically, they have had ample opportunity to put the quality to use, for the Northeast has not been an easy place to live. The soil is thin and infertile, producing as much dissatisfaction as crops; there is either not enough rain or too much, and the Mekong can be a terror at flood-time; and because of inadequate transportation few industries chose to settle here. Traditionally, northeasterners have been drawn to the magnet of Bangkok, leaving their poor villages behind to fill the most menial of unskilled jobs in the capital — servants, day-laborers, pedicab drivers.

The basic agricultural products of the Northeast are poor-soil staples like cotton and jute; mulberry trees, too, are grown to feed the worms that spin the silk that travels far away, light years in terms of life in the Northeast, to adorn a beautiful woman in New York or Paris. Small wonder that the Northeast also has a tradition of dissident politicians whose demands for social reform have been louder than those from

Wispy clouds float against a sultry red sky in Thailand's Northeast (previous pages), where about a third of the country's population lives. The soil in the region is thin and infertile, and the life is hard.

most other parts of the country. It is the area that most idealistic younger Thais have in mind these days when they talk about the need for improvements in the national life.

Changes are being made, however, and the future of the Northeast is beginning to look brighter than ever before in recent history. In the late 1950s, the modern Friendship Highway, a joint Thai-American undertaking, for the first time made this region, a high plateau on which about one-third of the country's population live, easily accessible in the rainy season as well as the dry, providing farmers and manufacturers with a way of getting their goods to the all-important markets of Bangkok throughout the year. Former Prime Minister Sarit Thanarat, himself a northeasterner, initiated many projects to help the people; dams to control flooding and to expand irrigation; roads linking remote villages; rural electrification; better medical facilities; and experimental agricultural stations. The establishment of several large American military bases during the Vietnam War, whatever their moral and political shortcomings, at least pumped new and needed money into the region and made boom towns out of once sleepy places like Nakhon Ratchasima (Korat), Ubon, and Udon. A northeastern university has been opened at Khon Kaen to serve the students of the area and introduce new ideas at the local level. A northeastern doctor, Krasae Channawong, a member of the new generation, won the Magsaysay Award (the Asian equivalent of the Nobel Prize) for his pioneering work in rural medicine and birth control in the impoverished village of Muang Phon where he grew up. There is a growing sense of achievement and purpose in Issan, and the day may not be far off when the name is no longer synonymous with poverty and problems.

For reasons that should be plain, the Northeast does not usually figure prominently on anybody's list of travel destinations in Thailand. But even this may be changing, too, thanks to some extraordinary discoveries being made at Ban Chiang concerning the region's distant past that someday could conceivably result in schoolchildren all over the world memorizing details about the place.

The more recent past of Northeast Thailand, covering a millennium, may also lure visitors interested in archaeology. Parts of the region were ruled by the Khmers during their great period at the time they built Angkor Wat, and a number of major Khmer temples still exist on the Thai side of the border. One, Pimai, not far from Nakhon Ratchasima (Korat), the largest city in the Northeast, has been carefully restored by the Department of Fine Arts; dubbed the "Angkor Wat of Thailand," it is already an important tourist attraction. If Angkor itself remains closed to outsiders, the Northeast may be the best available place in Asia to view the remains of this splendid culture.

Nor is the Northeast completely devoid of fine natural scenery that is the equal of anything the North has to offer. Among more adventurous Thai tourists, a popular hot-season undertaking is a trip to Loei Province to climb 1,500-meter Phu Kradung Mountain. The ascent is a mild endurance test, but the rewards are breathtaking views, a parklike plateau forested with pine trees, and a dramatic drop in the temperature. During Thailand's cool season, Loei in general, and Phu Kradung in particular, usually register the lowest temperatures in the kingdom.

The Northeast is a region in the

The jaws of a skeleton unearthed at the burial grounds of Ban Chiang seem to emit a raucous laugh from the past. The discoveries made in this small village indicate that agrarian civilization got its first start here.

midst of transition. The conventional traveler in search of the picturesque and the romantic would probably be best advised to miss it and concentrate on the other areas of Thailand; for those who want to see something of contemporary problems, however, and thus get a more balanced view of the country as a whole, it is an essential part of the itinerary.

* * *

Travel in the Northeast today is generally fast and easy over a terrain that in most places slopes gently from an elevation of 250 meters above sea level in the northwest corner to less than 100 meters in the southeast.

Thai Airways flies from Bangkok to Nakhon Phanom, Udon, Ubon, Khon Kaen, and Loei in the Northeast, and to Vientiane in Laos across the Mekong River from Nong Khai.

Scores of buses depart Bangkok's Northern Terminal on Phaholyothin Road every day for direct trips to most northeastern provincial capitals with many stops along the way. Connections are available up-country for buses to practically any town in the Northeast. It is surprising how many small towns are served by large, modern buses. The inside of a provincial bus may resemble a rolling market, but it gets you there. Even remote villages can be reached by small, converted pickup trucks, "baht buses." For luxury travel, there is air-conditioned bus service to Nakhon Phanom and Surin.

The state railway has two lines to the Northeast beginning in Bangkok and branching at Nakhon Ratchasima (Korat): one goes east to Ubon and the other almost due north

Rice is harvested by hand near Nakhon Phanom, as in most places throughout Thailand and Southeast Asia. The yield each year depends on the vagaries of the monsoon.

Superhighway to the Korat Plateau

The numbers in the margin in this section refer to the map on page 186.

to Nong Khai. Express trains with sleeper provision (book as far as ten days in advance of weekend or holiday travel) leave Bangkok every evening at 6:30 p.m. for Nong Khai and at 7:30 p.m. for Ubon. Each stops at provincial capitals and major district towns enroute. On the eastern line that lies below the Northeast and above the Eastern Gulf Coast, an ordinary train leaves Bangkok every morning at 8:00 a.m. for the Cambodian border town of Aranyaprathet.

* * *

The good roads of the Northeast invite travel by car, which undoubtedly is the best way to see the many out-of-the-way sights of this part of the country. Choose from two basic itineraries. Route 2 begins near Saraburi, north-northeast of Bangkok, and runs through the heart of the Northeast. Also called the *Mitraparb* or "Friendship" Highway, this road passes most of the big provincial capitals and ends at Nong Khai on the Mekong. For a more leisurely trip through rural Issan, take the "Elephant's Ear" route through Surin and Ubon for about four days along the scenic and ethnically interesting periphery of the Northeast.

The Friendship Highway or Route 2, the main road through the Northeast, begins about 105 km from Bangkok, just before the town of Saraburi. About 20 km after the Saraburi turnoff on Route 2, a dirt road on the right leads to an experimental farm run by the Kesetsart Agricultural University of Bangkok and beyond to **PHRA NGAM CAVE ("Beautiful Buddha Image" Cave)** where a Davaravati-era image may be seen. There are many other caves nearby, most of them unexplored.

Another 15 km leads to **MUAK LEK VALLEY**. Once known for malaria, Muak Lek has been transformed from an unhealthy jungle into dairy land that features a small Arboretum Garden Department where roses bloom around a blue

stream and a roadside stand from which the Thai Danish Dairy sells fresh milk products, including yoghurt.

* * *

About 43 km east of Saraburi, a sign points to **Wat Teppitakpunnaram** where a monumental white Buddha sits on a green mountain like an alabaster relic. The countryside in this area belongs to Khao Yai ("Big Mountain") National Park, hidden 40 km to the south (see "Bangkok Surroundings"). Route 2 continues northeast up the Korat Plateau, passing the reservoir of **LAM TA KONG DAM**. Soon the blue lake disappears and scrub brush, typical vegetation of the dry Northeast, begins to dominate the scenery. Past the district town of Pak Chong 62 km from Saraburi, going another 86 km leads to the provincial capital of Korat, now officially called Nakhon Ratchasima.

A warrior (opposite) charges into mock battle on elephant back, at the elephant roundup in Surin. An alabaster Buddha (above), at Wat Teppitakpunnaram, dominates the last hill before the Korat Plateau.

Richest and largest city in the Northeast, **NAKHON RATCHA-SIMA (KORAT)** serves as a trade, communications, and military center for the region. It is also the capital of the most densely populated up-country province in Thailand with over 1½ million people living in the province of Nakhon Ratchasima. Kòrat grew rapidly in the 1960s with the buildup of its Royal Thai Air Force Base where American fighter-bombers operated during the Indo-china War.

Although a busy commercial center, Korat has not forgotten its past. A statue of national heroine Khunying Mo (Tao Suranari) pre-sides over the town square and the whitewashed ramparts of the old city wall. Khunying Mo was the wife of an assistant provincial governor in the early 19th century, when Prince Anu of Vientiane led his army into Korat. After taking the city, the prince threatened to enslave its resi-dents. Khunying Mo rallied the women of Korat who enticed many of the Laotian soldiers to a drunken revelry and then killed them. Shortly thereafter, Prince Anu, who mean-while had gone to attack Saraburi, was thus forced to withdraw to Vien-tiane.

With comfortable hotels such as the Chomsurang, Korat, Sri Pattana, Chompon, and Thai Pokaphan; which have air-conditioned rooms; a big night market; and at least five cinemas with films fresh from Bang-kok, Korat makes a comfortable and convenient base for sidetrips.

To visit an important nearby silk production center, take Road 304 south towards Kabin Buri. After 27 km lies the town of **PAK THONG-CHAI** which produces silk thread for the weaving industry of Bangkok. (Road 304 also provides an alterna-tive return route to Bangkok.)

4. Nakhon Ratchasima นครราชสีมา (ตัวเมือง, จังหวัด)

5. Pak Thongchai ปักธงชัย (ตัวเมือง, อำเภอ

Major Khmer Ruins

7. Prasat Phranomwan
ปราสาทพนมวัน

8. Pimai
พิมาย (ตัวเมือง, อำเภอ)

Korat's main nearby attractions, though, are two sites created nine centuries ago by Khmer architects. Both Prasat Phranomwan and Pimai lie north of Korat off Route 2. A drive north about 14 km from the provincial capital to a dirt road that leads off to the right 4 km takes you to the isolated and peaceful monastery of **PRASAT PHRANOMWAN**. Heavy stone galleries reveal the Khmer penchant for false windows with stone mullions. Romantic zigzags, rather than straight lines, cover the carved stones. An uncommon stillness pervades the place, broken only by the footsteps of resident monks. Unlike the majority of Khmer ruins, this one contains an active temple. Behind its well-preserved vaulted entrance, the original dark sanctuary is filled with many more recent Buddha images of different styles, most of them covered with patches of gold leaf. Full-grown

trees sprout from the oldest chambers. The presence of older monks reminds visitors that donations are needed to help with the upkeep of the site.

Farther north 34 km on Route 2, lies the turnoff on the right that goes about 10 km east to the ruins of **PIMAI**, which along with the elephant roundup at Surin and the cool plateau of Phu Kradung, are the main tourist attractions of the Northeast. A sense of contemporary organization emerges among the awesome *prangs* and galleries of Pimai. Red paint spells danger where an incredibly heavy stone lintel balances precariously. Another sign informs the visitor that an ancient library vanished here. These are the only ruins in Thailand with hours; they close at 4:30 p.m. to prevent plundering.

King Jayavarman VII, last of the great Angkor monarchs, who had his face chiseled in dozens of eerie

Glittering like a silver ribbon, the Friendship Highway (facing page) is playing an important role in opening up the Northeast for development. The region also boasts numerous Khmer ruins that date from the same period as Angkor Wat, such as the standing Buddha image (above, left) at Prasat Phranomwan and Pimai (above, right), both near the city of Korat. The remains of Pimai have become one of the major tourist attractions of the Northeast.

angles on the towers of Angkor Thom, could easily have traveled from his palace along a 240-km road to Pimai, at the western extent of his kingdom. During his reign (A.D. 1181-1201), Pimai prospered within a walled rectangular area 1,000 meters long by 560 meters wide, situated on an artificial island created by linking the Moun River and one of its tributaries by means of a canal. Like the shrines at Angkor, the monuments at Pimai which endure in stone were never inhabited. Shops, pilgrim shelters, libraries, and houses were built of wood and have long since disintegrated.

The old city gate, probably the main entrance to the sanctuary, still stands at the end of the main street in the village of Pimai. Along the street near the Moun River Bridge, the Fine Arts Department maintains an open-air museum displaying some of the more beautifully carved lintels and statues found in the area.

Before leaving the area, see *Sai Ngam*, "Beautiful Banyan Tree," 1km east of the temple on an irrigation reservoir; it has an extraordinary umbrella of dense leaves and roots which local people revere as a shelter for special spirits.

* * *

From Pimai you can continue north on Route 2 to Khon Kaen and beyond directly to the Mekong at Nong Khai. But, for a better look at the rural Northeast, more Khmer temples, and folksy Issan atmosphere, try the "Elephant's Ear" journey roughly running parallel to the Cambodian and Laotian borders.

For the longer route through the region, you return to Korat and from there take Road 24 dipping south and then east at Chok Chai. Farther east about 80 km Road 218 branches north to the town of Buri Ram. Stay on Road 24 for another

. Prasat Phnom Rung
ปราสาทหินพนมรุ้ง

18 km, then at Ban Ta Ko turn right at the sign for Prasat Phnom Rung. Follow the road to Ban Wan, bear left, and soon you reach Khmer hilltop temple ruins.

Three full ponds, essential elements of Khmer monumental architecture, and pretty farmland surround **PRASAT PHNOM RUNG**. Historians believe this temple was an important station between Angkor and Pimai during the 11th and 12th centuries. Several generations must have elapsed during its construction, since several of the stone lintels resemble the early Baphuon style while the *naga*s date from the later Angkor Wat period. A stone inscription in Sanskrit mentions King Suryavarman II who built Angkor Wat.

Although damaged by plunder, the main *prang* of Phnom Rung and its galleries and chapels still reflect the geometric precision of Angkor architecture; there are symmetrical doors and windows and antechapels that face the four cardinal points. The monumental staircase, interrupted by landings, exudes the sense of mass and power typical of Khmer design. Look for the sandstone bas-reliefs of elephants and enthroned Hindu deities.

Monks of the Dharmayuti sect maintain the temple. During the Songkran festival in April, country folk walk in processions up the main staircase.

* * *

Going farther east on Road 24 to Prakhon Chai takes you near another site worth visiting. These second ruins can be reached by going south on Road 2075 about 1 km to a smaller road which branches right (west) near a modern temple. Follow it for 12 km to Ban Chorake, "Village of Crocodiles," then another 1 km to the Khmer temple ruins of Muang Tham.

A reassembled lintel at Pimai (left) reveals skillful carving that shows scenes of the ancient Khmer kingdom and its godlike kings, whose rule once extended over this part of Thailand. Although the splendor has been gone from such ruins for centuries, daily life continues undisturbed in and around them. At Muang Tham (above), villagers and monks from a nearby temple enjoy an outing among the tumbled remains of the once-great civilization.

Other Khmer Temples

MUANG THAM or Lower Temple sits on a mossy lawn like an art historian's daydream. Older than Prasat Phnom Rung, its cornerstones were laid in the 10th century and the temple finished about a hundred years later. Thick jungle surrounded Muang Tham until recently, when a group of families migrated there from Ubon, cleared the area and founded a large village.

At dusk, women fetch water from the lotus-filled ponds and young novices of the monastery wander among the meter-thick walls, perhaps to meditate or to enjoy watching their teenage contemporaries practice Thai boxing in the courtyards.

Five *prangs*, surrounded by galleries, protected by walls, and now shaded by trees, constitute Muang Tham. A beautiful lintel on the ground shows Krishna standing on the head of Kirtimukha and holding

up Mount Govardhana. The central shrines have crumbled, but the temple retains hints of vivid detail. The huge rectangular stone blocks that form the outer walls contain drilled circular holes probably used for stone figures shaped like lotus buds.

Road 24 continues 38 km to the town of Prasat. To see more Khmer art, turn right on Road 214 and go about 4 km south to the Mon-Khmer village of Ban Pluang. A track between the 30- and 31-km-stones (from Surin) branches east 500 meters to **PRASAT BAN PLUANG**, a small temple that features excellent carving. Drive back to Prasat and continue 29 km north on Road 214 to the town of Surin.

* * *

Located on an old Mon-Khmer site, **SURIN** was known primarily for silk raising until the T.O.T. organized an annual elephant roundup

9. Muang Tham
เมืองธรรม

11. Prasat Ban Pluang
ปราสาทบ้านปลวง

10. Surin
สุรินทร์ (ตัวเมือง, จังหวัด

Armies of elephant-borne warriors charge each other thunderously at the annual Elephant Roundup in Surin province, one of Southeast Asia's leading tourist attractions. The lofty Khmer-style sanctuary of Khao Phra Viharn (right) sits impressively atop a mountain just a few hundred meters beyond the Thai border with Cambodia. Hopefully, some day the temple, of great historical and artistic interest, will be open again to visits from Thailand.

Wat Ra Ngeng
วัดระเริง

Si Sa Ket
ศรีสะเกษ

13. Khao Phra Viharn
เขาพระวิหาร

2. Sikoraphum
รีขรภูมิ (ตัวเมือง, อำเภอ)

there in early November. The people of Surin are famed for their skill at training elephants. During the well-publicized roundup, local mahouts put their pachyderms through a variety of acts and demonstrations. Special buses and a train from Bangkok take tourists to the popular event.

A direct rail line connects Surin to the next province in the Northeast which borders on Cambodia, **SI SA KET**. Traveling by car is less direct. When Road 24 is improved as far as Khukhan, you will be able to drive easily from Khukhan on Road 220 all the way into Si Sa Ket town. Otherwise, you must drive north on Road 214 from Surin to Suwanphum, then southeast to Rasi Salai, crossing the Moun River twice in the process, and on to Si Sa Ket. At the start of either roundabout trip to Si Sa Ket, you can detour to **SIKORAPHUM** 31 km northeast of

Surin, via Roads 2077 and 2079, to see **Wat Ra Ngeng**, an 11th-century Khmer temple in a lovely natural setting. Four *prang*s are set at the corners of a square; a fifth graces the center and has beautifully carved pillars and a lintel which frame the door.

The province of Si Sa Ket's former main attraction no longer lies in Thailand. In 1963 the World Court awarded to Cambodia the splendid cliffside temple complex of **KHAO PHRA VIHARN**. If relations between Bangkok and Phnom Penh allow, you may be able to visit Khao Phra Viharn, which can be reached from Si Sa Ket along a 63-km drive southeast to Kantharalak, then straight into the jungle on another 37-km leg to the border.

Khao Phra Viharn stretches almost a kilometer in length. Its awesome stairs alternate between hewn bedrock and imported stones

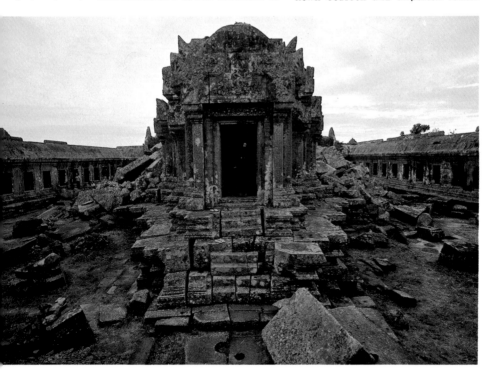

placed there before the days of Angkor Wat. They rise in a succession of layers, each marked by an increasingly large *gopura*, or gate, and end at the topmost sanctuary that honors the god Siva.

To the east of the first *gopura*, a trail descends through the jungle to the Cambodian plains. Before the second *gopura*, a sacred pond cut in the rock was found to contain a 45-kilogram fish that now rests in Phnom Penh's National Museum.

The second *gopura*, shaped like a Greek cross, is superbly carved in the Khmer style of the 11th century. Its lintels show Vishnu in a scene from the Hindu myth of creation. The stairs continue up, in a symbolic ascent to heaven, past another purificatory basin, to the first courtyard with its two palaces and *gopura*, finally up to the second and third courtyards and the main sanctuary.

UBON (sometimes spelled Ubol) lies 680 km east of Bangkok and sports the full name of Ubon Ratchathani, meaning "Royal Town of the Lotus Flower." Its size and opulence contrast strongly with the surrounding countryside. Office buildings, multistory construction sites, and some of the most well-endowed *wat*s in the Northeast rise abruptly behind the banks of the Moun. The river flows eastward, emptying into the Mekong about 100 km downstream from Ubon. Much of the town's growth coincided with the buildup of the Royal Thai Air Force Base during the 1960s when squadrons of American planes flew missions over Indochina from there. The Pathumratana,. Bordin, SiamWatana, and Ubon hotels offer air-conditioned rooms that are welcome in the hot season when the Northeast generally is hotter than the Bangkok area.

14. Ubon
อุบลราชธานี

210

Touring Along the Mekong River

Ubon province was the country's largest in area until its western half was split off and designated Thailand's 72nd province, Yasothorn. Ubon province still has a population well over one million, ranking third in that department after Bangkok and Korat.

* * *

Allow a full day for the trip north from Ubon to Nakhon Phanom. First, drive 76 km on Road 212 to Amnat Charoen. The dry land looks barely arable but somehow produces the rice that turns golden brown in late October and the kenaf that stands in bunches against the farmhouses.

Beyond Amnat Charoen about 2 km on the left side, shine the golden tiles of **Wat Phra Mongkol**. Behind an arbor, about 300 meters off the road the temple shelters a new 4½-meter-high Buddha image.

Continuing north on Road 212 about 88 km takes you to the district town of **MUKDAHAN** on the right bank of the wide and sluggish Mekong River, opposite the Laotian town of Savannakhet. Take the road to the river, turn right, and visit **Wat Sri Nongkran**, a buff-colored temple built by Vietnamese refugees in 1956. The gates present a curious mixture of Thai contours, Vietnamese script, and Chinese-inspired dragons. Farther down the river bank stands the colorful **Wat Jok Keo**. An unsophisticated but vibrant mural enlivens its small *prang*.

From Mukdahan, 55 km north lies **THAT PHANOM**. The road is in good condition, straight and flat. You feel far upcountry, and you are. Traffic consists of an occasional motorcycle. Uncultivated brush interspersed with rice fields rushes by. Black-shirted farmers balance produce-laden baskets from the ends of long poles. You drive close to the

Fanciful folk art decorates many of the temples of the Northeast, such as the relatively new Wat Sri Mongkran (opposite), which was built by Vietnamese refugees in a mixture of styles. The mighty Mekong River (above), one of Asia's great waterways, sweeps around the Northeast of Thailand for about 1,000 kilometers, forming most of its border with Laos. Viewed from Nakhon Phanom, the distant hills of Laos rise hazily above the Mekong River basin.

Mekong River all the way up to the village and temple of That Phanom.

Thousands of pilgrims from Northeast Thailand and Laos used to make an annual pilgrimage to **Wat That Phanom** to worship and make offerings at the base of the spire that was built around the 9th century and restored several times thereafter. But in mid 1975 disaster struck again when the spire collapsed after four days of torrential monsoon rains. But in 1979 the temple was restored again making it well worth a visit for those interested in history or simply seeking a beautiful riverside setting.

For a short and pleasant side-trip into the countryside, 7 km north of That Phanom and 8 km inland is **BAN RENU.** Like several small weaving villages in North Thailand, Ban Renu is famous for pretty girls and cloth. Embroidered shirts, northeastern *ikat* sarongs (in which the material is predyed in patterns), head

rests, and long dresses hang outside a dozen shops on the main street. The people are friendly bargainers. **Wat Prathat Renu,** the village's temple, features an extremely pretty spire covered with finely painted reliefs in bright blues, reds, and yellows as well as in pastels. Portraits of elephant riders, angels, guardians, and foot soldiers convey a vibrant realism that distinguishes such contemporary temple art in the Northeast.

* * *

Farther north about 45 km on Road 212 lies **NAKHON PHANOM.** On a fresh morning in Nakhon Phanom, a chain of powder-gray mountains can be seen behind the little Laotian town of Thakhek across the wide Mekong over 25,000 Vietnamese refugees crossed the river during the 1950s and '60s to settle in this province. Although security precautions complicated their resettlement, many Vietnamese have pros-

Wat Prathat Renu
วัดพระธาตุเรณู

18. Nakhon Phanom
นครพนม (ตัวเมือง, จังหวัด

17. Ban Renu
บ้านเรณู

212

19. Tha Rae
ท่าแร่

20. Sakon Nakhon
สกลนคร (ตัวเมือง, จังหวัด)

pered financially in the town's own markets, and seem to have matched the overseas Chinese in business acumen.

During the Indochina war, American rescue and reconnaissance missions flew from the Royal Thai Air Force Base hidden behind grassy mounds 12 km west of town. NKP, as the Americans dubbed the base, was also a listening post for radio and electronic sensor devices. At that time you could buy at the market an appropriate symbol of such technologically sophisticated activity set in rural Thailand: fried bananas wrapped in discarded computer printouts listing traffic movements on the Ho Chi Minh Trail. But today there is little to see in town. The Srithep, First, Chai Pattana, Winsor, and Nakhon Phanom hotels all offer air-conditioned rooms if you decide to break your tour here.

From Nakhon Phanom, Road 22

goes west about 86 km to Sakon Nakhon town. On the way you pass the village of **THA RAE.** There the largely Catholic population, including many Vietnamese, supports a diocese complete with a seminary.

It is not unusual to see military convoys moving along Road 22. The wild, remote terrain around Sakon Nakhon, particularly in the Phu Phan Mountains, harbors insurgents. Ordinary travelers will probably not notice anything unusual and need not fear hostilities.

* * *

SAKON NAKHON town itself seems totally removed from any hint of nearby guerrilla warfare. Spread out along a low plain that borders Nong Han, Thailand's largest lake, the town enjoys being the only northeastern province with plenty of water. For a delicious Thai meal in town, stop at Som Jai Restaurant for a full selection of curries. The Araya, Som-

Thailand's thousands of temples play an integral role in its daily life. Supplicants at Wat That Phanom (left) receive blessings from the resident monks. Merit-making devotees have richly endowed the temple with elaborate decorations such as carvings, paintings, tiled floors, and gold-leafed statues. The freshly painted spire of Wat Prathat Renu (above) is an example of the intricate art work that distinguishes contemporary Northeastern temples.

Major Archaeological Finds

kaeit, and Charoensuk hotels have air-conditioned rooms.

The ancient Khmers left monuments in Sakon Nakhon although their significance is so minor that only those with keen archaeological interest or vivid imagination should go see them. **Wat Choeng Chum,** in the town center, has a plain laterite *prang* of the 10th century hidden inside a brand-new white *prang.* You literally glimpse antiquity through a crack in the door. Outside of town, on Road 22 heading west for Udon, 3 km past the experimental rice station a sign points to **Wat Narai Cheng Weng,** built by a princess in the 11th century. Today, the survival of the crumbling sandstone *prang* is so precarious it looks as if Dr. Seuss drew its outline. But its carved lintels beautifully exemplify the Khmer Baphuon style. The *wat* supports a large school, so you may receive help from a novice studying English.

From Sakon Nakhon, Road 22 heads west toward Udon. About 110 km from Sakon Nakhon, in the dusty topland of the Northeast, a small sign in Thai points to **BAN CHIANG** located about 5 km north of the highway. The Thai-Lao farm community in Ban Chiang and nearby Pulu Village sits on what may be the most significant archaeological find in Southeast Asia in many years.

At first most archaeologists hesitated to venture broad theories about the Ban Chiang find. But further study, mainly conducted by a team from the University of Pennsylvania has convinced many of the skeptics that an agrarian bronze-making civilization first appeared not in Mesopotamia or China, but in Southeast Asia.

Pending further excavations and analysis, archaeologists, including a team from the University of Pennsylvania, hesitate to venture broad theories about the Ban Chiang finds.

Wat Cheong Chum
วัดเชิงชุม

21 Ban Chiang
บ้านเชียง

Wat Narai Cheng Weng
วัดนารายณ์เชงเวง

The little village of Ban Chiang sits on one of the most significant archaeological finds in Southeast Asia. Distinctive pottery decorated with bold red swirls (above, left) and human skeletons (above, right) have been dated at up to 8,000 years old; bronze objects predate those of the Middle East. At Nong Khai on the southern bank of the Mekong River (opposite), the younger set peddles cheerfully home from school in the late afternoon light.

214

However, further study could possibly determine that an agrarian bronze-making civilization first appeared not in Mesopotamia or China, but in Southeast Asia.

The Thai government has cracked down on the illegal digging and sale of Ban Chiang artifacts, but villagers may approach visitors offering to sell green or dark blue beads, metal bracelets, pottery, and even human bones. Do not buy any of these items; you can be arrested for the unlicensed possession of antiques.

* * *

From Ban Chiang, Road 22 continues 47 km west to **UDON** where you again encounter Route 2 heading north at this point to Nong Khai and south to Khon Kaen. Like Korat and Ubon, Udon has a longer formal name, Udon Thani, and also grew quickly with the influx of American airmen during the 1960s. Ten years ago, the air in Udon was often thick with red dust raised by military trucks bouncing over the town's pothole dirt roads. Now motorcycles and flashy cars zoom over asphalt streets punctuated by increasing numbers of traffic lights. You wonder what will be the long-term cultural effects of so many bars, dance halls, and massage parlors that sprang up during the war.

While in Udon, you should sample some real Issan food. Udon offers several air-conditioned hotels: the Chaiporn, Seri Udon, and Udon. For western food, try the Three Sisters Restaurant.

From Udon, Route 2 runs north 53 km to reach **NONG KHAI** on the southern bank of the Mekong. Many buses and interprovince taxis travel to Nong Khai, some carrying passengers

Sidetrip to Laos

bound for the ferry to Laos. Several police checkpoints interrupt the journey, but the stops are very brief. The express train from Bangkok runs through Udon on the way to Nong Khai; this way to the border is strictly for early risers who do not mind boarding the train around 5:30 a.m. in Udon.

Quiet Nong Khai town has few attractions other than the wide Mekong and a forgettable monument marking the end of the Friendship Highway. In some years, usually during September or October, monsoon rains swell the river, causing it to overflow its bank and damage crops and property in lowlying sections of the province. When the water level drops in the dry season, islands appear in midstream, and on weekends local residents take food, drink, and radios out to *pai-tio* on the sandbars.

Despite some tension between Bangkok and the new Pathet Lao government, the border at Nong Khai has remained open. One night in 1975 some Pathet Lao soldiers fired across the river into Nong Khai town, later claiming they mistook some floating logs for an invasion force. Fortunately there were no injuries.

Nong Khai has two immigration checkpoints. One, located a little upstream from the railroad station, serves people taking vehicles to Laos. The main post lies close to the center of town at the top of a long flight of stairs leading up from the river. Foreigners going from the railroad station to the main immigration checkpoint often have a hard time with the young *samlor* drivers and porters. Make clear immediately whether you want your bags carried.

The ferry from Nong Khai crosses to Tha Deua in Laos. From there you travel about 20 km to Vientiane in taxis that normally take four or five passengers, who split the total fare. This type of taxi should take you to any destination in or near the city.

Vientiane, the city of sandalwood, once was one of the most charming spots in South-east Asia. The pace was slow, the people friendly and the aroma of freshly baked French bread wafted through the markets. Today, wall posters and blaring loudspeakers exhort the support of the people and the allegiance of army and party. People sweep the streets and plant trees, and largely ignore the gilded temples and elderly monks.

The Lao embassy in Bangkok rarely grants a tourist visa. Only citizens of Socialist countries are encouraged to visit, but in truth there is little to see. Foreigners are not allowed outside of Vientiane, and inside the capital most of the shops and restaurants have closed. The Lane Xang (Million Elephants) Hotel still overlooks the placid Mekong and some government cars continue to putter along the broad Lane Xang Avenue, but nearly all the meat has

24. Vientiane
เวียงจันทร์ (ประเทศลาว)

216

disappeared from the morning market and at least one old nightclub now features Soviet propaganda.

Vat Phra Kaew, near the royal palace, doubles as a museum for religious art and features some good carvings and a number of Buddha images.

Vat Phra Kaew
วัดพระแก้ว

Persons with visas should go to the ungainly gray cement **Triumphal Arch** on Lane Xang Avenue and walk around the inside to the top for a good view of the city and river. You may have to ask permission to ascend. Beyond the arch, at the end of the right fork leading from the traffic circle, stands **That Luang,** a revered temple where every November there is a big *boon,* or fair, with displays from many countries, a carnival, and scores of food sellers, including many women hawking fried chicken.

Luang Prabang
หลวงพระบาง

If time allows, fly to the royal capital of **LUANG PRABANG.** You may have to secure police permission first. Many seasoned travelers feel that Luang Prabang has more peaceful charm and beauty than any other city or town in Southeast Asia. Exquisite temples, the confluence of the Mekong and a tributary, cracked brick sidewalks, nearby mountains, and a delightful lack of commercialism make Luang Prabang an unforgettable experience.

* * *

From Vientiane, returning to Tha Deua and crossing the river back to Nong Khai, you can go comfortably down to Bangkok on the night express train that departs at 6:40 p.m. By car you can drive down Route 2 all the way to the capital in about nine hours. Or you can detour west at Udon to see one of Thailand's most breathtaking and unspoiled natural wonders at Phu Kradung, southeast of Loei.

That Luang.

Road 210 runs west of Udon 143 km to the rugged, beautiful province of **LOEI**. What is now the traveler's delight was once the civil servant's nightmare; in the Thai bureaucracy, being assigned to Loei was like going to Siberia, for Loei in the old days was a jungle outpost that meant fever, cold weather, little comfort, and poor security.

Enroute, stop at the **ELEPHANT CAVE** *(Tham Erawan)* about 54 km before Loei and 2 km off the road on the right. Despite its isolation, the monastery there is well organized. Signs in English entreat visitors "Please keep the law of Buddhist brother." A new and life-size statue of Erawan, the triple-headed elephant of Thai mythology, marks the steep stairway and rocky path to the cave's entrance. Prehistoric artifacts have been found here, but all that distinguishes the cave, apart from its size and an occasional cobra

emerging from the rocks, is an elephant's skull. The climb up is rough.

Road 210 continues west to finally reach the town of Loei. A minor agricultural boom has not changed Loei's shy simplicity. Some shop houses display signs of the Siam Cement Co., but thankfully the town has not yet turned concrete as so many other provincial capitals have done. The usually placid Loei River flows through the center of town. At the Thai Udom and the Sahrai Thong, the town's only hotels, you can find inexpensive rooms.

To plunge further into the Loei wilderness, 50 km west on Road 203 takes you to **PHU RUA** ("Boat Mountain"). The road cuts through heavy banks of red laterite, past a sawmill and fields of kenaf and cotton, the latter being the province's big money spinner. About 30 km west of town on the way to Phu Rua, a *sala* refreshment area overlooks chains of

25. Loei
เลย (ตัวเมือง, จังหวัด)

Elephant Cave
ถ้ำช้าง

24. Phu Rua
ภูเรือ (ตัวเมือง, อำเภอ)

218

bluish hills. In December the mountains lie under thick blankets of smoke as farmers burn back the forest. Phu Rua itself is about 1,370 meters high. There is a rough road to the top which affords a view of the surrounding national forest. From Phu Rua hardy travelers can take a spine-jolting bus ride south on Road 203 to Lom Sak, then on to the provincial capitals of Phitsanulok or Phetchabun.

To see the Mekong near where it once again becomes the Thai-Lao border, drive 53 km north of Loei to **CHIANG KHAN.** A boat can be hired for the 4-km ride downstream to the Kuang Kud Ku rapids, worthwhile if only for the sheer sense of being locked in the deeper heart of Southeast Asia.

No experience in the Loei area can match the crisp beauty of **PHU KRADUNG NATIONAL PARK,** the most memorable escape in Northeast Thailand. Phu Kradung came to public attention only 50 years ago during the reign of King Rama VI. Today it is rarely visited on weekdays; students who have endured a 12-hour bus ride from Bangkok come on weekends to savor the invigorating cool, dry air. Some say the mountain's name derives from the mysterious sound of a bell *(kradung)* that supposedly grows louder on holy days. Others believe the name is a corruption of *krating,* the wild bull which used to inhabit the remote plateau until hunters killed them off.

The entrance to Phu Kradung lies about 50 km southeast of Loei on Road 201 that goes to Chum Phae. About 3 km from the entrance you arrive at the park office where you can arrange for porters, store excess equipment, and park your car. Bring along tennis shoes, a wind breaker or

The climb to the top of Phu Kradung in Loei province is arduous, but the cool air, extensive wildlife, and spectacular views in the national park make the effort worthwhile.

sweater, packaged food (only one noodle shop operates on weekends), toilet articles, a camera, and a walking stick, if you are so inclined — for Phra Kradung, a plateau lying between 1,200 and 1,500 meters, beckons the naturalist-at-heart to set out down the trail. The park provides bedding and blankets in cabins that hold up to eleven people. Unless you are a champion hiker, let the porters carry everything up the 5-km trail to the plateau. (You can even hire four porters and a sedan chair for the climb!)

The climb is not easy but well worth the effort. After the fourth kilometer there is a cabin with cold water. Stop here, for the last kilometer is the toughest. Ladders negotiate the steepest boulders; views of the valley mitigate the strain. Once you make it up to the plateau you forget the tiring climb.

Atop Phu Kradung, clear and mostly level paths crisscross the 60-square-kilometer tableland. Rare birds, including hornbills, woodpeckers, and pheasants, may be seen; and even wild elephants and panthers somehow manage to climb up. Most of the fauna is quite shy.

The park's cabins and upper offices are located 3 km from a small radar station and a helicopter pad. Pick up a mimeographed map of trails and set off on nature walks. A good day begins before dawn with a chilly stroll to **Liem Pha Nok Hain** cliff to watch the sunrise. It is a long way down to the jungle where gibbons hoot. Spend part of the day finding the six waterfalls north of the cabins. About an hour before sunset, head for the serene setting of **Liem Pha Makdouk,** about 2 km west of the radar station.

From Phu Kradung you can take Road 210 to Khon Kaen and rejoin the Friendship Highway for the return trip to Bangkok; or return to Loei and cut across country on a rough road to Phitsanulok for a trip to the North.

TOURING THE EASTERN GULF

A Burgeoning
Resort Area

A graceful, curving stretch of brilliant white sand, lapped by gentle waves; in the sea a few white sailboats, a lone water-skiier cutting like a knife through the sparkling water, and a tropical island surrounded by the darker blue of a coral reef; landward, all along the beach, luxurious modern hotels set in lush gardens, splendid private villas, and restaurants altogether serving a dozen or so different cuisines. This is the Eastern Gulf at Pattaya, arguably the greatest success story in the history of Southeast Asian resorts — at the very least one of the most remarkable. Barely more than two decades ago this lovely beach was a little-known retreat for a handful of rather adventurous foreigners and Thais from Bangkok, who braved the drive over poor roads to spend a weekend by the sea. There were no hotels then, luxury or otherwise, only a few collections of bungalows for rent, a rough clubhouse for a group of sailing enthusiasts, a couple of good seafood restaurants, and a small fishing village that gave the place its name. Apart from the beach, the main thing it had to recommend it was its greater proximity to the capital than the more traditional resort of Hua Hin on the other side of the gulf, where the royal family passed their summer holidays, and where most of the wealthier families had hot-season villas. Seafront property in Pattaya in those days could be had for a song, and few if any entrepreneurs ever thought of the place in terms of tourists. Then, in the early '60s, the boom came. Partly it was due to a general boom in trade and tourism at that time, partly to the new, low-cost package tours whose members were as interested in

At the port of Klong Dan (previous pages), just outside of Bangkok, the day's catch is unloaded onto the docks. Fishing is a major industry along the Eastern Gulf, which is dotted with such busy commercial centers.

finding sea and sun as in seeing the standard attractions in Bangkok. In addition, with the establishment of the vast U-Tapao air base and the deep-water port at Sattahip, just beyond Pattaya, a new superhighway was built linking the area with the capital, cutting the driving time from over three to under two hours. The first major hotel, the Nipa Lodge, went up; and in the astonishingly short space of only three or four years the whole place was transformed. Now there are a half dozen or so international-class hotels each of which has more than 200 rooms; a night life to rival Bangkok's when it comes to color and variety; restaurants that meet the standards of any in the capital; and facilities for such aquatic sports as waterskiing, scuba diving around the offshore islands, sailing, deep-sea fishing, parasailing, an exhilarating sport where you are towed up in the air behind a speed boat, and windsurfing.

The development of Pattaya as a resort opened up the whole Eastern Gulf Coast of Thailand, an almost unbroken stretch of beaches that goes down to Trat, the narrow finger of land that joins Cambodia. Other, less spectacular resorts than Pattaya have been built at Bang Saray and Rayong, farther down the coast than Pattaya. Close to Bangkok, about half an hour before Pattaya, Bang Saen has become the favorite seaside place for middle-class Thai families. According to dedicated skin divers, the waters of the gulf get clearer the farther down the coastline you go, the best of all being those off Chanthaburi Province, where the coast starts curving in toward Cambodia.

Some visionary developers now foresee the transformation of the whole region into a Thai Riviera, with hydrofoils as well as air-conditioned buses plying back and forth to Bangkok.

Although tourism has brought the Eastern Gulf Coast prosperity in a new form, it is far from being the

region's sole source of income. Other, older industries in the area have long played an important part in the Thai economy. Much of the seafood consumed or exported by Thailand comes from Eastern Gulf ports, and some of the largest fruit orchards are located between Rayong and Chanthaburi. The latter province is the country's major center for gem mining, especially of sapphires, both blue and black, which are probably Thailand's best bargain in precious stones. Some rubies are also mined there, though the best ones reputedly come from across the Cambodian border. Cities like Si Racha and Chon Buri, if somewhat lacking in visual charm, are nonetheless important commercial centers, with many plants for processing and canning the produce of the region. Si Racha, in particular, is noted as the home of a fiery hot chili sauce bearing its name that is a prominent feature of Thai dinner tables. Among the newer east coast industries, the growing of orchids for export in the form of cut flowers or plants prospers in dozens of huge nurseries, covering many hectares, some with more than half a million brilliantly blooming plants. The mushroom growth of this industry in recent years has pushed Thailand into the number-one spot among orchid exporters in Southeast Asia. The port at Sattahip, originally built as part of the American effort in the Vietnam War, is the biggest in the country and now handles a large part of Thailand's commercial shipping.

All this industry notwithstanding, the main lure of the Eastern Gulf for the average visitor to Thailand is its sun and sand and plentiful tourist facilities. Some of the older

A fishmonger at the morning market of Ban Amphur proudly displays some of the small fish that figure prominently in the Thai diet. In one form or another they find their way into almost every meal of all classes.

Leaving Bangkok

hands in Bangkok, resentful at having to share their once-private pleasures with so many strangers, grumble that Pattaya has been "ruined" and issue dire warnings about "uncontrolled" development. A controversy about the lack of proper planning has raged for several years, and a conservationist group has been leading the fight against indiscriminate building of shop houses and hotels in the resort. To the average tourist, however, the Eastern Gulf still seems a long way from the overcrowded resorts of America and Europe, and most visitors go home singing praise of the region just southeast of the capital.

* * *

The Eastern Gulf lies within easy reach of Bangkok. Buses leave from the Eastern Bus Terminal on Sukhumvit Road for the main cities on the Eastern Gulf: Chon Buri, Si Racha, Sattahip, Rayong, Chantha-buri, and Trat. Airconditioned tour buses leave several times daily for the resorts of Bang Saen and Pattaya, and seats can be booked through tour companies such as Ital-Thai, Raj-prasong Shopping Center, and Diethelm Travel, Ploenchit Road. Airplanes do not serve the Eastern Gulf, as it is only a few hours by road from the capital.

The main route for travel along the Eastern Gulf Coast is Sukhumvit Highway, which becomes Route 3 outside of Bangkok. Route 3 officially originates at the busy Bangkok intersection near the Erawan Hotel on Ploenchit Road; one kilometer to the east, over the railroad tracks, it becomes Sukhumvit. On Sukhumvit past the numbered *sois*, the home of Bangkok's western population, the traffic gradually thins out. Beyond

Fishermen offload their catch at the beach of Lam Mae Phim, typical of the many alluring beaches along the Eastern Gulf which now attract numerous visitors from everywhere.

the Phra Kanong Canal, the highway reaches the suburb of Bangna. From there a new shortcut to Bang Pakong cuts 20 km off the journey south by avoiding Pak Nam (or Samut Prakarn) at the wide mouth of the Chao Phya River.

Branching left and heading southeastward at Bangna, the fast shortcut offers fewer sights and less upcountry atmosphere than the old road, which arcs slightly seaward, passes the Ancient City, the Crocodile Farm (see "Bangkok Surroundings"), and Klong Dan, and beyond Pak Nam follows a scenic *klong* for 75 km.

Life along the old Sukhumvit *klong* seems resistant to most change, its traditional tranquillity shattered only by the occasional roar of a long-tailed boat and the silent sprouting of another television antenna. Framed by coconut trees, nipa palms, and bougainvillea, diamond-shaped fishing nets on the end of long counter-weighted poles perch over the canal's waters. Huge water jars sit at the feet of the stairways which climb up stilts to the thatched-roof huts above. Boys in tucked-up sarongs play *takraw*; girls shampoo in the *klong*. Old ladies sell fruit and the well-known chestnutlike *luk jak*. Along the right-hand side of the highway, stretch mangrove flats where villagers gather wood to make into charcoal, while their children catch crabs in the mud. As civilization steadily encroaches, factories compete with the quaint village *wat*s for space along the highway.

On the old Sukhumvit Road,

Young girls (opposite) enjoy an evening stroll along the beach at Pattaya. Once a sleepy fishing village visited by only a few sun-and-sea lovers from Bangkok, Pattaya has now developed into a Thai Riviera with dozens of luxury hotels overlooking the blue waters of the Gulf. The old Sukhumvit Klong (right), just outside Bangkok on the way to the Eastern Gulf, still offers views that have changed little over the years.

The numbers in the margin in this section refer to the map on page 212.

about 12 km past Pak Nam and 3½ km past the Crocodile Farm turn-off, a seafood restaurant beckons from a marshy bank. Years ago, when the single good road south from Bangkok went just this far, the restaurant's fresh breezes, tangy food, and seclusion drew the capital's high society for evening feasts or just relaxed conversation. Today you can share in the local nostalgia by ordering splendid dishes of shrimp *(gung),* crab *(poo),* and oyster *(hoy).*

At the 56-km-stone, Route 3 arrives at the busy fishing port of Klong Dan just a short way from the sea. The old highway then curves east to merge with the new road at Bang Pakong. The road swings south once more and heads for the distant hills of Chon Buri.

* * *

A pleasant and industrious town of about a quarter of a million people, mainly merchants, traders,

Along the Coast

and craftsmen, **CHON BURI** for most tourists is but a lunch-stop on the way south to Pattaya. Most of Thailand's oyster population breeds on the Chon Buri coast and farther south along the gulf. Outside the town, about 3 km to the north, sits a hilltop monastery known as **Wat Buddhabat Sam Yot**, "Buddha's Footprint Mountain of Three Summits." Built amid green trees by an Ayuthaya king and renovated during the reign of King Chulalongkorn, it was once used to conduct a royal "Water Oath of Allegiance."

Near the center of Chon Buri, sits a colossal gold-mosaic image of the Buddha, belonging to **Wat Dhamma Nimitr**. The largest in the Eastern Gulf region and the only one in the country depicting the Buddha in a boat, the 40-meter-high statue recalls the story of the Buddha's journey to the cholera-ridden town of Pai Salee. Through inspiration and compassion, the Buddha cured many of the afflicted. On the same hill is found the local Chinese Buddhist Society, surrounded by the burial shrines of prominent members.

Those interested in the historical arts will want to stop in the midst of Chon Buri near the old market at a temple gate flanked by fruit sellers. The oldest and most important *wat* in the province, **Wat Intharam** presents an antiquated front: several buildings feature up-turned curved bases typical of the Ayuthaya period. The original wooden pedestals and roof decorations have disintegrated; but the roof replacement, also of an older, interesting style, has *cho-fas* (upturned eaves characteristic of royal and religious Thai architecture) with angels in molded stucco. Patterns composed of antique porcelain decorate the window arches. Within the *bot,* murals portray *devas* ("gods") in the upper panels, and the

1. Chon Buri
ชลบุรี (ตัวเมือง, จังหวัด)

Wat Buddhabat
วัดพุทธบาทสามยอด

Wat Intharam
วัดอินทาราม

Wat Dhamma Nimitr
วัดธรรมนิมิตร

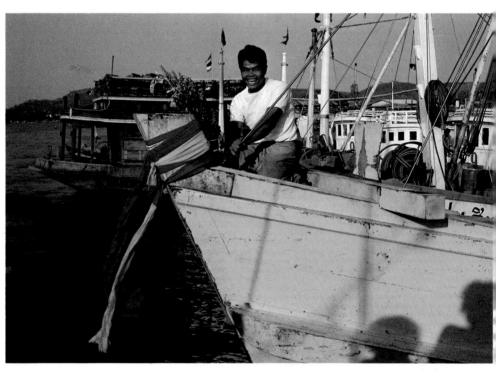

Vessantara legend of the Buddha's life in the lower panels. The vitality of the frescoes, rendered within strict scenic formulas, belongs solely to the 18th century. Prince Narís, one of the most renowned Thai artists in past decades, once visited the *bot* and told the abbot, "The workmanship is excellent. You must not allow anyone to restore it." His wish was kept.

South of Chon Buri 7 km is the town of **ANG SILA**. Once favored by Thai royalty as a sea resort, the town takes its name of "Stone Basin" from the chain of rocks that forms an oval protrusion into the sea. The din and clang of hammers fills the air at Ang Sila, which produces mortars and pestles for the Thai kitchen for pounding chilis, grinding spices, and mashing coconut. Wooden shop houses on the beachfront sell locally made beachwear, hats, and baskets.

Farther south on the Ang Sila road, sits an unobtrusive yet unusual monastery called **Ruh Sam Pao.** Facing seaward, its walls have the shape of a huge hull which some say points to a shipwreck in which emigrants from China were lost.

The more than 300 cells for the monastery's residents are also in the shape of hulls. Many of the residents will never leave, although they are free to do so, because they believe that to die at Ruh Sam Pao brings good fortune. The old women of Chinese descent, some of whom have lived in the monastery twenty years or more, believe that when they die their souls will be carried to sea, past the shipwreck of their fellows, back to China.

Within the monastery are two miniatures of the giant Nakhon Pathom *chedi.* A Thai monk heads the monastery, in which the Chinese dialect of Teochew is commonly heard. The residents *kin jeh*, "eat strictly vegetarian."

A sailor near Chon Buri (opposite) decorates the prow of his boat with colored cloths and flowers, following an old custom of placating the all-important goddess of the sea. Indispensable mortars and pestles for the Thai kitchen (above, left) are produced nearby at Ang Sila. South of the town, at the monastery of Luh Sam Pao, a nun's chamber has been built in the shape of a boat (above, right) ; sweet-smelling wreaths and joss sticks adorn the prow.

South of Chon Buri 18 km on the road past Ang Sila, the beach at **BANG SAEN** is a carnival each weekend and merry madness during the hot season. A profusion of multi-colored beach umbrellas, black inner tubes, and wrinkled watermelon rinds cover the sandy beach that is a favorite with Thai tourists. By Sunday night, Bang Saen is again a sleepy hollow of quiet beach bungalows and restaurants.

The T.O.T. runs the Bang Saen Beach Hotel which has a swimming pool and comfortable, if not plush, rooms. Near the beach there are also bungalows under coconut trees. **Bang Phra Golf Course** can be found nearby, on the left off Sukhumvit Highway, just past the Bang Saen market. The golf course has a motel, a lodge, a swimming pool, and a bar called the 19th Hole. The caddies by the way are all girls. Longest in Thailand at 7,249 yards, the 18-hole course lies in beautiful hills.

* * *

SI RACHA, 24 km south of Chon Buri, descends from the hills and extends into the sea on tentacle-like piers. Its famous hot sauce can be enjoyed overlooking the water at the Si Racha Restaurant, where fresh shrimp, crab, oyster, mussel, or abalone make fine dippings for the thick and tangy red liquid. An offshore rock supports a picturesque *wat* containing a lively mixture of Thai and Chinese Buddhist elements. Shrines honor a monk who spent many years atop the seaside hillock. An inevitable footprint of the Buddha, cast in alloy, graces the *wat,* and so do pictures of the beloved Chinese goddess of mercy, Kuan Yin, and the Monkey God, possessed of magical powers in Chinese lore. The *wat* overlooks arrow-shaped fish traps made of nipa palm — a construction so functional that it has endured for

3. Bang Saen
บางแสน (หาด)
4. Si Racha
ศรีราชา (ตัวเมือง, อำเภอ)

Bang Phra Golf Course
สนามกอล์ฟบางพระ

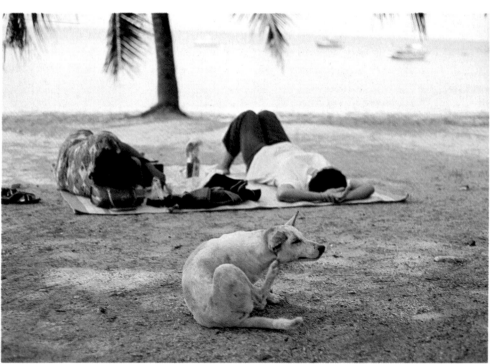

centuries in Southeast Asia. Large tankers carrying crude oil from the Persian Gulf stream past Si Racha to the TORC Petroleum Refinery, 8 km south of town, which fuels Bangkok's growth and development. From the longest pier at Si Racha, boats ferry passengers to the nearby island of Koh Sichang. The weatherbeaten diesel fishing boats rent for not less than 400 baht per roundtrip and take less than one hour to reach the island.

* * *

Before the Chao Phya River was dredged and a channel cut through the bar at the river's mouth, ocean-going vessels unloaded their cargo and passengers at **KOH SICHANG**. Today the island is quiet; there are no sailors' brawls at the merchant marine club; and the coffers of the customs house, once filled to the brim, gather dust. Koh Sichang's waters, clear from November through January, offer snorkelers

and scuba divers a glimpse of abundant sea life. The dilapidated piers at the old refueling station make an interesting dive, and so does the nearby rusty shipwreck, both best explored with experienced divers. On the northern side of the island a lovely beach stretches beneath the sky.

* * *

Just 5 km from Si Racha at the 120-km-stone on the Sukhumvit Highway, the road on the right leads to the sea and **RED CLIFF BEACH**. Here is a moderately priced Thai resort with bungalows of one, two, or three bedrooms. As Red Cliff Beach is popular with locals, it is less expensive and less pretentious than Pattaya farther down the road, but nevertheless has pleasant seaside scenery, an enclosed saltwater swimming area with sand beach, a Thai night club, a small golfing area, and a restaurant that serves European, Thai, and Chinese food.

A couple takes a siesta on the sandy beach at Bang Saen (opposite) shaded by coconut palms. Only an hour or so from Bangkok, Bang Saen is a favorite resort with Thai tourists, who come in crowds on weekends during the hot season. Spacious Red Cliff Beach (above), not far from Si Racha, is another popular holiday spot that offers moderately priced bungalows beside the sea. During the week, both resorts are relatively empty and accommodations are plentiful.

The Thai Riviera

PATTAYA, everybody's paradise, is the premier beach resort in Thailand. Strange, because Pattaya really does not have much of a beach. However, this is mitigated by beaches on several small offshore islands and some hotels boast their own beaches. Swinging singles of any sex, contented families and lovers of water sports all agree that Pattaya spells bliss. Everyone does his own thing and nobody is affronted. Air-conditioned coaches leave Bangkok daily and cover the 154 km to Pattaya in about three hours.

Basically, Pattaya consists of one straight 4 km road along the sea. The northern part of this is bordered, on one sided, by 96 hotels, bars and restaurants. On the other side is the beach backed by wattle, flame and palm trees. Both sides of the southern quarter of this road are jammed with shops, bars and restaurants. A parallel road gives access to several hotels. Numerous short *sois* joining these two thoroughfares have their share of nightclubs, shops, bars and restaurants. Transport up and down the beach is by "5-baht" busses — small open-sided trucks seating about a dozen persons.

Many bars are nothing more than open-air kiosks with about a dozen stools and two or three bargirls. From these bars you can keep an eye on the activity or temporarily leave your drink for some spontaneous shopping.

South Pattaya starts to swing when the sun sets. Traffic practically comes to a halt. Scores of food stalls and itinerant vendors selling Buddhas and leather belts, amulets and bracelets move in. Fruit and flower stalls further brighten the scene. Jewellers do a brisk trade in sapphires and rubies. Tailors cajole customers into having a dress or safari suit run-up in 24 hours. Music blares from bars and stores selling pirated cassettes. The biggest and best bars — best because they are the most raucous — are the Marine, Grace and Simons. They

Tourists enjoy the creature comforts of South Pattaya, Thailand's foremost luxury resort.

stretch out over the water and you can share your beer with mosquitoes and lovely Thai girls. And if Eros is shooting his arrows there is no saying what will happen.

Pattaya is paradise for the lover of water sports. Ski-boats and sail boats, snokelling and scuba-diving equipment, and water scooters can be rented. The adventurous will try parasailing. You are strapped into a parachute harness and then attached to one end of a tow rope, the other end of which is connected to a speedboat. The air current lifts your parachute and up, up you go to be granted a bird's-eye view of Pattaya. No training, no skills, are required and it is perfectly safe. Wind surfing is just as exciting but demands much skill. The keen angler can test his skills in landing groupers and red snapper, mackerel and bonito, sailfish and barracuda Nearly all the large hotels have immaculate tennis courts and 10 km east of

Pattaya is the Siam Country Club which boasts what is probably the best golf course in the Kingdom.

Those less athletically inclined and those who tire of sunbathing need not be bored. Excursions are organized to such places as sapphire mines, an orchid farm and an elephant kraal. Evenings can be spent at the movie house which shows English soundtrack films only and the top hotels all have discos featuring live music.

Accommodation ranges from deluxe international hotels — the Royal Cliff Beach is a resort in itself — to simple bungalow units where it is sea breezes rather than air-con and the opportunity to do your own cooking. Not that dining is a problem. Dozens of food stalls where the adventurous may dine al fresco for nearly nothing line the main drag in South Pattaya. At the up-end of the market many restaurants offer international cuisine.

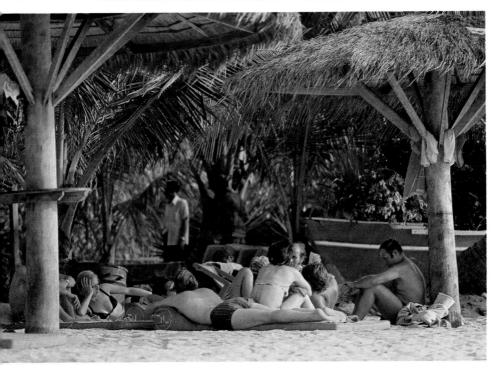

Island Hopping and Scuba Diving

One of Pattaya's prime virtues lies hidden underwater. Within a week, it is possible to arrive as a neophyte and depart as a certified scuba-diver. One of the best ways to achieve this status is to visit Steven's Dive Shop, at the north end of Pattaya Beach, where professional instructors provide a boat, equipment, and a skin diving course. The instructors belong to both the National Association of Underwater Instructors and the Professional Association of Diving Instructors. Their courses are least expensive per person for a group of at least four.

Although some of the islands off Pattaya can at times become "crowded" with divers in favorite spots, there are altogether enough interesting undersea areas to provide plenty of space for all adventure seekers. Boats may be rented for the day at a price depending on the size and facilities of the vessel and the visitor's bargaining prowess. Rates are generally better on weekdays and during tourist lulls, when a buyer's market prevails. Dive shop employees or owners can furnish tips on boat rental. Take along beverages kept chilled in an ice chest for sipping under the awning. The boats chug along at a leisurely pace just fast enough to reach the nearest group of islands in less than an hour. For the impatient there are speedboats.

Among the favorite nearby islands are the twins **KOH LARN** and **KOH SAK**. The first island is larger and more developed, though less spoiled, and now boasts several hotels and bungalows at Nuan Beach, and an 18-hole golf course as well. Be sure to sample some of the mouthwatering freshly caught crab and King Mackerel served at the simple little shops on Koh Larn. Good diving beckons in the whole area. Fifteen meters or so

13. Koh Larn
เกาะล้านและ
14. Koh Sak
เกาะสาก

down in the clear waters off the southern end of Koh Larn flourish beautiful coral formations and an abundance of colorful and exotic marine life. To the north of Koh Sak lies a shallow bay with both sandy and coral areas only 7 to 10 meters deep.

The tropical fish in these waters make one realize that an aquarium is only a peephole into a vast universe. Easily recognizable are the tube worms that sprout from the coral like tiny Christmas trees in fabulously varied colors. Eye-catching orange and white clownfish live in curious symbiotic rapport with the orange anemone, bringing food to the anemone in exchange for the protection of its stinging tentacles to which the clownfish are immune. Everywhere dances and shimmers a profusion of colors and shapes: soldierfish, damselfish, green parrot wrasse, polka dot grunts, batfish, and huge friendly groupers.

Diving naturally calls for precaution; and the wise diver takes care to look and photograph rather than to touch or step on, especially when meeting up with the spiny sea urchin or the well-camouflaged stonefish. A less obvious danger is the tropical sun, the strength of which is often underestimated by visitors from temperate lands; a T-shirt protecting one's tender back allows the day's snorkeling to be recollected in tranquillity that evening.

Southwest of Koh Larn, about another hour or so by boat, lies **KOH LIN**. Although quite small, this island has many good diving spots. On the sea bottom are a relatively recent wreck, good coral formations, and fascinating sea life. Due west of Koh Larn, at about the same distance away as Koh Lin, is **KOH PAI**. Here, in water as deep as 25 meters or more, are found strikingly beautiful fish, coral, and shells.

Several quiet areas lie just south of Pattaya towards Sattahip. These include a seaside retreat for the royal family (closed during visits by the king), and the Varuna Yacht Club where Thai helmsmen compete in a variety of classes of small sailboats. About 6 km south of Pattaya is the usually quiet **Y.M.C.A. BEACH**. The beach may be reached from Sukhumvit Highway by making a right turn at the 56-km-stone (measured from Chon Buri). Another tranquil spot, with a fine view of the sea and offshore islands, is a cliff that runs to the right of the highway up a track just beyond the 68-km-stone. One way to visit these places is to rent a motorcycle at Pattaya Beach. Resist the temptation to zoom through the changing of gears.

Boats with awnings (facing page) can be rented for excursions to offshore islands near Pattaya. There the clear waters (left) offer a new world of exploration for enthusiasts of spear fishing and scuba diving.

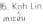

5. Koh Lin
เกาะลิน

6. Koh Pai
เกาะไผ่

Y.M.C.A. Beach
หาด วาย. เอ็ม. ซี. เอ.

South of Pattaya

Overlooking a scenic bay containing scattered islands, the little fishing town of **SATTAHIP** about 20 km south of Pattaya grew up overnight to become an attractive, busy deep-water port. In the heart of town a large, modern temple rests on turquoise pedestals, while in the commercial center, a boisterous market brims with fresh fish, fruit, and vegetables.

The shop signs Apollo Optical, Man Fashion, and Florida Shoemaker beam the prosperity reaped from nearby military bases. The economic influence of the American military, however, once considerable when B-52 bombers and their crews were stationed at nearby U-Tapao, quickly evaporated, and along with it many of the gaudy trappings designed for the off-duty serviceman.

The Royal Thai Navy with headquarters in Sattahip is in charge of much of the coast between Pattaya and Sattahip. Sukhumvit Highway passes the Thai Naval Academy at the 167-km-stone.

In Sattahip, stroll past the shops or drop in for an *o liang* (the great local version of sweet iced coffee that came from French colonial Cambodia), have a spicy curry near the market, or browse over teak elephants in the souvenir shops, where you may find the perfect keepsake.

* * *

Six km past Sattahip, a broad, modern road on the right leads to the large. Thai military base. When the base is reached, turn right again and then, after 1 km, turn left along the fence at the side of the base. The road, which again turns right after a couple of kms, deteriorates and 8 km further on ends at Samae San.

Jetties poke out from the hill-

Amulets and tattoos help protect this fisherman (right) when he is at work in the Gulf of Thailand. His catch is likely to include such delicacies as baby squid, which at Rayong ends up barbecued (facing page).

backed fishing town of **SAMAE SAN** into the translucent turquoise bay, rimmed by an immediate archipelago of five islands. White and purple squid dry in the sun near the long wooden piers which have nautical gasoline stations. Near the docked boats, fishermen spend their time repairing nets or catching up on their laundry. On the village's single road, husky women tend their kitchens and sundries stores, some with games machines and juke boxes.

Few out-of-towners ever reach the lovely white beaches of the nearby islands, and those who have want to shield them from publicity. Visitors may rent a boat for approximately 200 baht per day to explore the islands' tree-lined beaches and neighboring reefs. Boats of shallow draft enter the bay between the islands of **KOH AI RAET** and **KOH SAMAE SAN**, the latter mountainous with bright white beaches and a

238

small fishing hamlet surrounded with coconut trees. To the west is **KOH KHAM** and beyond **KOH CHUANG**, fringed with a tabletop coral reef, and **KOH CHAN**, where the beach has an itchy reputation for sand flies.

* * *

Situated 221 km from Bangkok **RAYONG** is split in two by an estuary, unseen from the Sukhumvit Highway which plows through the commercial district of sundries shops, coffee stalls, and a forest of high TV antennas. A right turn at the stop light just past the air-conditioned O-Tani Hotel leads across a dilapidated bridge to an older but just as industrious fishing village that is strung along a strip of land between the beach and the estuary.

Rayong is famed for its *nam pla*, or "fish sauce," the sine qua non of Thai condiments. Producing the sauce is a cottage industry in Rayong, and many homes have backyard factories. A small silver fish that abounds in the gulf is allowed to decompose for about seven months to produce the ruddy liquid that is filtered and bottled on the spot. Every Thai eating establishment, from the fancy restaurant to the humble noodle stall, serves the fish sauce, sometimes mixed with sliced chilies (called *prik nam pla*). Indeed, *nam pla* is a staple food throughout Southeast Asia: many poor farmers have raised their families in difficult times on a diet of plain rice flavoured only with fish sauce.

* * *

On busy days, about 20 km east of Rayong, the wharfs of **BAN PAE** are covered with quiltwork thrown up by Poseidon. Dressed in weathered black shirts, straw hats, and sarongs, women spread out square carpets of tangerine-colored shrimp to dry in the sun. Though the sight is compelling, the smell may overpower the newcomer, as the sun quickly decomposes the scraps and leftovers that will be used for chicken and crocodile feed.

This scenic fishing port is sheltered to the west by an outcrop of rocks, and by the island of **KOH KEO PISADAN** (also called Koh Samet) to the south. The island is remembered by students of Thai literature as the place where the poet Sunthorn Pu retired to compose some of his works. An undaunted romantic of the early 19th century, Sunthorn carried on love affairs that occasionally raised eyebrows at the Bangkok palace.

The coastal road leading directly south from Ban Pae, passing the local fish sellers and barber shops, is a lovely drive, bordered by palms and white beach. It enters the pine forest and national park of **BAN PHA PHRAE** which overlooks the rocky islets east of Koh Keo Pisadan.

Down the road 7 km lies **SUAN WANG KAEW** beach resort, where bucolic paths weave in and out among seaside gardens.

* * *

Past the Suan Wang Kaew Resort 10 km on the coastal road, the beach of **LAEM MAE PHIM** extends for kilometers against the low surf of the gulf. In front of the fishermen's shacks along the shore, women sell sugared treats and squid roasted on skewers. The dwellings are impermanent, with walls tacked together from scrapwood and hung with kitchen utensils. Housewives do their daily washing out of a water jar on the porch, while scruffy dogs scavenge in the sands, occasionally clashing in a storm of growls and toothy snarls, much to the amusement of the villagers.

240

Just offshore Laem Mae Phim are two jagged islands called **KI PLAEM,** "Fish Droppings." They serve as a backdrop for weathered fishermen unloading the small silver fish used to make *nam pla*. To the left of a small promontory lie another three islands that provide a natural perspective, decreasing in size with distance. The nearest and largest **KOH MAN NAI**, is privately owned and has a sheltered beach on its western side, coconut groves, and clumps of old mango trees. There are little bungalows for rent and seafood restaurants, catering to busloads of young Bangkok students on holiday trips to Chanthaburi.

To return inland to Route 3, the Sukhumvit Highway, you take the road branching to the left after Laem Mae Phim, passing through dense rubber plantations and clusters of bamboo. Three kilometers farther the small village of Ban Kram centers around a large old tree that is the object of animistic worship; cloth is wrapped around it and nearby stands a spirit house.

* * *

On Route 3 at the 288-km-stone, a turn north along a small town street leads to a rough dirt road (check conditions beforehand during the rainy season) and 13 km later to an inland adventure at Khao Wongse.

Villagers say that people have tried to take photographs from the mystic jagged peaks of **KHAO WONGSE**, but when they returned to Bangkok their film mysteriously was blank. The gray-streaked outcrop dominates the valley of red laterite dust and humble farmlands. To the left of the simple *wat* and Chinese shrine lying at its base, Buddhist monks recite scripture in their living quarters fashioned out of crevices in the cliff face.

Khao Wongse is full of caverns. One old woman, her face powdered white to cool her skin after bathing, has lived there since childhood, but claimed she has not yet seen all the caves. In Tam Plak, a hollow near the *wat*, water continues to drip on the brow of the stalagmite image of Lord Buddha. Worshipers visit the cave to offer prayers, light yellow candles, shake divining sticks, and read their fortunes.

Village children happily offer their services as guides to those who wish to climb to the top of Khao Wongse. The path jumps over tree roots and boulders, dried leaves, and brilliant red bugs and breaks out upon a succession of small, contemplative clearings, where the children ring temple bells to mark their ascent. Villagers claim that crocodiles live in underground streams, and that some of the cave walls gleam with diamonds.

A sailor climbs to the crow's nest (facing page) near one of the islands called Ki Plaem, just offshore. Villagers (left) enjoy Thai chess.

Chanthaburi and Surroundings

Farther south along the Eastern Gulf, about 330 km from Bangkok lies **CHANTHABURI**, a town with a raffish air of prosperity. Gem fever continually grips the place; local gossip buzzes with news of big finds — the proverbial 10,000- or 20,000-baht stones. Even the income from polishing small gems comes as an economic windfall by local standards.

Motorcycles clog the streets, another immediately noticeable sign of the town's wealth. It seems that everyone has a bike, and for good reason. Many of the youngsters who pick fruit in the nearby orchards where no buses go, afterwards zoom back into town for an afternoon of profitable gem polishing. Nearly every shop in Chanthaburi has a row or rows of wooden lathes. The gem mines, rubber plantations, and fruit orchards provide a livelihood for many residents, including a large

number of ethnic Chinese and Vietnamese. Chanthaburi now has several air-conditioned hotels, such as the Muang Chan, Chanburi, Kasemsarn, and Travel Lodge.

The nearest gem mining area, at **KHAO PLOI WAEN** ("Hill of the Sapphire Ring"), is reached by a slightly indirect route that leads out of the market and goes 11 km to the port, where the Chanthaburi River empties into the gulf. Back towards town 4 km a road on the left goes 4 km to Ban Kacha, with the sapphire-laden slopes of Ploi Waen on the left. Here, under jackfruit trees, miners and middlemen haggle over the price of gems. The open pits gouged out of the hillside are about 2 to 10 meters deep.

Organized tours are conducted of the Chanthaburi mining areas, including a find-it-yourself tour in which visitors can prospect on their own, keeping whatever gems they un-

31. Chanthaburi
จันทบุรี (ตัวเมือง, จังหวัด)

Gems are cut and polished (above) in small shops throughout Chanthaburi. At the open mines of Khao Ploi Waen, a gem dealer displays with pride polished blue sapphires, the most famous stone found in the area.

242

earth. Check with the local tour agencies.

About 5 km south of Chanthaburi stands Khai Nern Wong, "Camp on a Small Circular Hill," where King Taksin retreated after the fall of Ayuthaya in 1767, to regroup his forces, recruit new soldiers, and construct a fleet of warships. Afterwards he returned north to defeat the Burmese invaders. On the same hill are the remains of a fortress built by King Rama III. In spots around the hill derelict cannons point emptily at the now silent jungle. Several of the artillery pieces are of great size; locals claim they could protect the mouth of the Chanthaburi river about 11 km away. Today, spirits are believed to still keep watch in the ruined stronghold.

Also of interest in Chanthaburi is the French-style Church of the Immaculate Conception, the largest in Thailand, built around 1880. It is still active, and attended by the Thai-Vietnamese community of Chanthaburi, the members of which migrated to Thailand over the last two centuries. The descendants of these immigrants engage in a number of businesses, foremost of which is the making of reed products, such as mats, handbags, and tableware, which are woven in attractive shapes and patterns. Many are made in their homes and some of the best can be ordered from the nuns of the church. There is also a reed-ware factory in the city.

Chanthaburi residents are fortunate in having two good waterfalls relatively near. Directly opposite the Chanthaburi turnoff on the Sukhumvit Highway at the 324-km-stone, a dirt road leads inland and goes for 22km through orchards of rambutan, strong-smelling durian, oranges, and lichis; then the road turns right and goes another 3km to

An old cannon (left) still menaces intruders at the old fortifications outside Chanthaburi. The town's French-style cathedral (above), built around 1880, has an active congregation of Thai-Vietnamese Catholics.

reach **NAM TOK KRATING** ("Bull Waterfall") a cascading series of small falls tumbling over granite for some 400 meters. Trees dedicated by Thai officials, enclosed by white picket fences, decorate the area. A painted map hangs on a tree, pointing out hideaways up a rocky path that winds to the side of the falls. On weekends and holidays the falls attract many visitors, but on weekdays one can find repose next to the small pools and cascades.

Farther down Route 3, near the 347-km-stone, inland lies another popular waterfall, **NAM TOK PRAEW**. Beyond makeshift shacks in which women sell sticky rice and durian jam is a simple gray *chedi* overlooking the fall.

The *chedi* commemorates a consort of King Chulalongkorn who drowned while being rowed up the Chao Phya River to Bang Pa-In. Her death was particularly tragic, since her attendants could have saved her had they not been forbidden by custom to touch the body of a royal person.

Young people like to swim in the pools here, and the area is seldom deserted in daylight. While boys in shorts and sarongs do flips into the cool water, modest girls sit fully covered under the big splash. The fish are more daring and come nibbling at the feet dangling in the water. During the durian season, busloads of Thais from as far as Bangkok roar in to see the falls and bargain for the seductive fruit.

The province of Trat, just beyond Chanthaburi and centered about 400 km from Bangkok at the end of the Sukhumvit Highway, or Route 3, extends between the Gulf of Thailand and the Cambodian border like a mandarin's fingernail. The road from Chanthaburi sweeps through a green panorama of paddy, rubber trees, and marshland. For a

244

good view of the sea, take the turnoff at the 348-km-stone (just past the turnoff for Nam Tok Praew) for the 16-km trip to Laem Sing.

Named for a lion-shaped island offshore, **LAEM SING** is a small fishing town with two remnants of a brief French colonial presence at the turn of the century: a red brick Customs House and "Chicken Dung Prison."

Return to Route 3 for the remaining 75 km drive to the town of **TRAT**. The provincial capital itself is undistinguished, but trips to scenic islands begin 16 km down the road at **LAEM NGOP**. There you can rent a boat to **KOH CHANG**, Thailand's third largest island, famed for wild boar and the **MAIYOM WATERFALL**. Off the northern tip of Koh Chang some of the largest sharks in the gulf cruise near a rock outcrop. Your rented boat can sail on to **KOH MARK** and **KOH KUT** which offer clear-water lagoons for good diving. Stock up on provisions in Trat for the island trips. In the town itself, the Thai Rong Roj Hotel offers modest lodging if you wish to stay overnight while exloring the Eastern Gulf's most far-flung province.

Depending on conditions in the area, one may make a diversion toward Bangkok on Road 317, which leaves Route 3 northeast of Chantha-buri and hugs the Cambodian border all the way to Sa Kaeo, east of Bangkok. Many new settlers farm the jungled hills, but most activity is scarce and the countryside mostly wild and unpopulated. On the way, places of interest include the waterfall on Khao Soi Dao, "Mountain of the Harvest of Stars," about 66 km from Route 3; and Wat Tham Lek Khaw Chaka, a cave monastery about 140 km north of Route 3.

The waterfall of Nam Tok Praew (facing page) tumbles into a pool which is a popular place for bathing and picnicking. During the durian season, busloads of Thais from Bangkok come down on outings. Playing at being a skipper (above), a little boy enjoys the gentle surf at Koh Chang, one of Thailand's largest island, famed for its wild boar, and picturesque waterfall; nearby islands offer clear-water lagoons which are ideal for diving.

TOURING THE SOUTH

An Unheralded Region

A stretch of pure white sandy beach lies, this time, on an island off the west coast in far South Thailand. On one side of the island, steep rocky limestone cliffs rise sheer from the indigo waters of the Andaman Sea looking like strange seagoing prehistoric monsters. On the other side, a simple fishing village looks suspiciously like a postcard of an unreal tropical paradise. But it is very real and even mundane to the people who live on it and derive their livelihood there. Lithe young men, who have never heard of vertigo, scale to the top of the interior of enormous caves via rickety bamboo ladders to harvest tiny glutinous nests of a certain kind of swift. These are prized by Chinese all over the world as the principal ingredient of the delicacy known as bird's nest soup and South Thailand is reputed by connoisseurs to have the purest and tastiest of this delectable gourmet's delight. The fishermen from the village go out with their nets in the evening, return in the early morning with the dependable treasures of the sea, their lives as inexorably paced by the rhythms of nature as those of the farmers in the Central Plains, more than 1500 kms away.

There are countless large and small islands like this one scattered down the narrowing strip of land that leads to Malaysia, its eastern coast on the Gulf of Thailand, the other on the Indian Ocean. Except for some of the larger islands like Koh Samui (*koh* in Thai means "island") and Phuket which is now being developed as a major tourist center, few are ever seen by visitors, their tropical beauties known only to those who live and work around them.

Thailand's South, a long arm consisting of fourteen provinces, is a

The many spires of a venerated temple (previous pages) strain toward a scorching tropical sky at the southern town of Nakhon Si Thammarat, far down Thailand's gulf coast.

richly beautiful area of wild jungle and rocky mountains and broad beaches of powdery sand. It offers the visitor excellent recreation, seafood, skindiving, and spectacular scenery — it is the unheralded, untrammeled part of the country that can provide some of the 'most rewarding vacations.

In many ways the South is a different world from the rest of the country, especially the farther south you go: different in climate, religion, and industry. Shady plantations of rubber trees are more common than rice paddies. As the visitor enters the four most southern provinces — Betong, Pattani, Narathiwat and Yala — the gilded dome of a Muslim mosque becomes a more familiar sight than the sloping roof of a Buddhist temple. Especially in the provinces near the border where the people speak Malay as well as Thai, and throughout the region, there is a distinctive southern dialect, as well as a southern cuisine that resembles Malaysia's more than that of central Thailand. The southern rainy season — two of them, in fact — is wetter and longer than in the rest of the country, the wettest months of all being December and January.

Like the North, the South was for many years semiautonomous, governed by its own rulers, separated from the capital by both culture and distance. Only within the present century has the South become an integrated part of the Thai kingdom.

It has had its own problems, too. Many of its people have felt cut off from the mainstream of Thai culture, misunderstood by the rulers in far-off Bangkok. One result of this has been a small but worrying separatist movement composed of radical Moslems who would like to see the distant provinces joined to Malaysia. After long neglect of this problem, the government is now taking positive steps to relieve the sense of alienation: officials who are sent to the South from other parts of the country are

now encouraged to learn the local customs and dialect; a southern university has been established; and the royal family recently built a palace at Narathiwat, not far from the border, from where the time is spent traveling among the people of the region. In addition to the Southern Railway Line, modern superhighways now run from Bangkok to the Malaysian border, making the South more accessible than ever before.

The South is rich in natural resources and is, after Bangkok, Thailand's most prosperous region. Rubber, the country's second largest export product after rice, thrives in the humid climate, and there are thousands of hectares of coconut plantations. Tin is mined in the South and all Thailand's tin is refined in Phuket's huge smelter. Haadyai, the railway terminus of the South, is one of the fast-growing cities in Thailand, a brash, brassy, boom town, attracting not only businessmen seeking to cash in on local industry, but also thousands of Malaysian tourists lured by its free-swinging night life. (Malaysians constitute the largest single group of tourists coming to Thailand, incidentally, and the majority of them come for the pleasures of Haadyai.) Tourism is a fairly recent part of southern development, but if forecasts are correct, it will prove an important one in the near future. For many years, the principal means of getting to the area was the railway, and that was convenient to only a few of the most scenic spots along the peninsula; the only dependable way up until 1976 of getting to the lovely islands of the gulf was to take a freighter of the Thai Navigation Department — still a very pleasant trip if one has the time — and getting to Phuket, on the Andaman Sea, was a major journey. The

Turbaned against the sun, a boatman steers along the narrow peninsula of South Thailand; tourism is a recent development in this prosperous area.

new highways, regular flights by the domestic airline, and a causeway connecting Phuket with the mainland have changed all that, and the incredible natural beauty of the southern beaches are becoming known in the travel world. *Time* Magazine in a recent Asian travel story listed Phuket among a small number of destinations still unspoiled by package tours. Despite the apparent serenity, a number of important resort projects for that idyllic island are already under construction or on the drawing board. "The South is the coming place," says a travel agent in Bangkok. "A few years ago hardly anyone had heard of it. Now everybody wants to go there."

* * *

Thai Airways (not to be confused with Thai International) has daily flights from Bangkok to Phuket, Trang, Haadyai, Pattani and Narathiwat. Most of these provincial capitals are also linked by flights of Thai Airways.

Thailand's State Railway offers. daily express service leaving Bangkok's central Hua Lampong Station in the late afternoon for the South. Although designated "express," this is no scenery-blurring train; its leisurely pace affords a good view of green rice paddies, *klong*-side villages, abrupt mountains, and growing towns. Each stop provides a sampling of local food. Hawkers rush to the train's windows selling fresh fruits, *kanoms* (or "sweet") wrapped in banana leaves, barbecued meats, dried squid, and the ubiquitous iced drinks served in plastic bags.

Travelers in no particular hurry should break their journey in several provinces to see attractions otherwise passed after dark. However, the

The seascape at Phangnga Bay, filled with limestone outcrops which seem to spring out of the calm inland waters, has the haunting delicacy of a classic Chinese watercolor painting.

traveler must note that on a journey of 200 km he can break his journey once and once only and then for no longer than 48 hours. You can set off from railway towns on bus, taxi, or boat for a varied and thorough appreciation of the South. When booking seats do not overlook second-class passage, which on many trains equals the comfort of first-class. For those rushing on to Peninsular Malaysia, the express (Express 11) leaves Bangkok on Mondays, Wednesdays and Saturdays in the afternoon and arrives at Butterworth (the terminal for the Malaysian island of Penang) about 24 hours later. Connections can then be made with trains for Kuala Lumpur and Singapore.

The young and resolute might prefer to board one of the air-conditioned coaches of the many companies which make the run from Bangkok to the South. Bangkok to Phuket takes about fourteen hours; Bangkok to Haadyai about twenty hours.

Alternatively, South Thailand may be approached from Peninsular Malaysia. Thai Airways has five flights a week from Penang to Phuket: three of these are via Haadyai. Malaysian Airlines has flights from Penang to Haadyai on Fridays and Sundays. Trains depart Butterworth daily at 7:50 a.m. for the six-hour journey to Haadyai. Quicker by far are the busses from Butterworth to Haadyai and faster still are the "shared" taxis. The latter depart Butterworth when they have a full load of five persons; fares are very reasonable.

Those approaching the South from Malaysia's east coast (Kota Bharu) would cross the Thai-Malaysia border to the station of Sungai Kolok from where it is a two-hour journey to Yala.

During low tide, this broad secluded beach covered with shells extends to the offshore islands, at Hat Noparat Thara, near Krabi.

If you are leaving Bangkok by car, the main roads lead to the South's first attractions: Phetchaburi Province and the beaches and hills near Hua Hin. On the way South, you can include a visit to the Rose Garden and Nakhon Pathom (see "Bangkok Surroundings"), or take a shortcut and go directly to Phetchaburi.

The provincial capital of **PHET-CHABURI**, 165 km south of Bangkok, has several worthwhile sights. As you approach the town on Route 4, turn left at the T-junction just outside the town, continue past a rocky hill on the right, cross the railroad tracks, and stop under the shady trees for a visit to **Khao Luang Cave**. Here you will see huge stalactites and many Buddha images, illuminated around midday by a natural shaft of light, presenting an inspiring scene.

As Route 4 enters Phetchaburi town, *naga*-topped walls frame the ascent to a **Palace built by King Mongkut** in the last century. Several buildings surrounding the hillside palace afford a fine vista of the city, its river, rice fields, and the mountainous Burmese border to the west.

Farther south on Route 4, 17 km from Phetchaburi, a dirt road on the right leads to **Kang Krachan Dam** (also called Ubol Ratana Dam after King Bhumibol's eldest daughter). The road first follows a canal, then passes an older dam, and finally comes to the earthen walls of Kang Krachan. The Irrigation Department usually grants permission to tourists to stay at its bungalow overlooking the scenic reservoir and to take boats up the reservoir to the river.

South again on Route 4 about 50 km lies **HUA HIN**, the oldest beach resort of prominence in Thailand. Hua Hin, about 232 km from Bangkok, was majestically "discovered" in 1910 when Prince Chakrabongse, brother of Rama VI, led an

1. Phetchaburi
เพชรบุรี (ตัวเมือง, จังหวัด)
2. Kang Krachan Dam
เขื่อนดินแก่งกระจาน

Khao Luang Cave
ถ้ำเขาหลวง

3. Hua Hin
หัวหิน (ตัวเมือง, อำเภอ)

The numbers in the margin in this section refer to the map on page 248.

entourage of international princes and grand dukes down the coast to hunt game. King Prachadipok, Rama VII, built a palace in Hua Hin called *Klai Klangwan*, meaning "far from worries." Fittingly, the king was vacationing there on 24 June 1932 when a bloodless coup toppled him from an absolute to a constitutional monarch and launched Thailand's first experiment in democracy.

Yet Hua Hin lost none of its appeal. A 1932 *Guide to Bangkok* touted the resort as being "most popular with travelers, especially those longing for a game of golf." In those days, golf traps included tiger tracks, as wild game came down from the hills in a nocturnal search for water. Today Hua Hin's 18-hole course attracts many local and foreign golfers.

Remnants of the genteel '30s live on at the stately Railway Hotel. With high ceilings, pleasant gardens, a games room, and a slightly decadent air, the hotel faces a beach of fine white sand that runs for 3 km; the Stone Head (or *Hua Hin* in Thai) rock formation marks the beach's southern end. Boys offer ponies for hire in the beach area to the right of the hotel.

Hua Hin town lacks the charm of the Railway Hotel. Its shops sell plastic blow-up porpoises and ducky tubes, seashells artfully fitted into vases and ashtrays, beachware, and floppy hats. However for a bit of lively local color, stroll down to the pier in the morning or evening, order a drink in one of the coffee shops, and watch the fishermen unload their catches and women stoop to examine and bargain for a wide variety of fresh seafood, including an occasional shark or stingray.

Leave Hua Hin by heading south again on Route 4. About 22 km from the town, the highway crosses Pranburi River, then enters a town by the

Limestone hills (facing page) rise near Petchaburi, the first provincial capital as you enter South Thailand. Farther down, children (above) play in the placid water near Hua Hin, one of the country's oldest beach resorts and still popular with Bangkok residents who like the quiet, old-fashioned atmosphere of the place; a royal palace at the resort, built by King Rama VII, bears the evocative name Klai Klangwan, meaning "far from worries."

same name. A road to the left leads to Pak Nam Pranburi situated 8 km away at the river-mouth. Children play under stilt-houses while fishermen hang their nets to dry on wooden racks.

On Route 4 south of Pranburi you begin to glimpse the jagged outline of the **NATIONAL PARK OF KHAO SAM ROI YOT** (Mountain of 300 Peaks). Turn left down a dirt road and continue 14 km to the limestone outcrops. The gorges and caves here used to shelter highwaymen who robbed unwary travelers; their haunts were cleared out long ago. Now deer and monkeys roam the picturesque park.

The sky above Khao Sam Roi Yot is fondly remembered in the annals of the Chakri Dynasty. On 18 August 1868, King Mongkut, an astute mathematician and astronomer, brought the governor of Singapore and members of the Bangkok court to this place to view a total eclipse of the sun which he himself had foretold. The king's prediction, to the astonishment of local astrologers, was only four minutes off. News of this event helped to discredit the superstition that an eclipse happened when a giant swallowed the sun and disgorged it when impelled by gongs and general noisemaking.

Ninety-one kilometers south of Hua Hin, down a road that branches left just before the 323-km-stone, **PRACHUAP KHIRI KHAN** faces a scenic little harbor enclosed by knoblike hills. As you enter Prachuap, a hill rises to the left and seems, in certain light, to reflect a patch of sky. In fact, on **Khao Chong Krachok** ("Mirror Mountain") a natural arch lets you see through to the sky on the other side. Steps, 395 in all, lead up the hill to a small monastery surrounded by frangipani trees. Within the *chedi* are special Buddha relics

4. Khao Sam Roi Yot
เขาสามร้อยยอด

5. Prachuap Khiri Kha
ประจวบคีรีขันธ์ (ตัวเมือง, จ

Khao Chong Krachok
เขาช่องกระจก

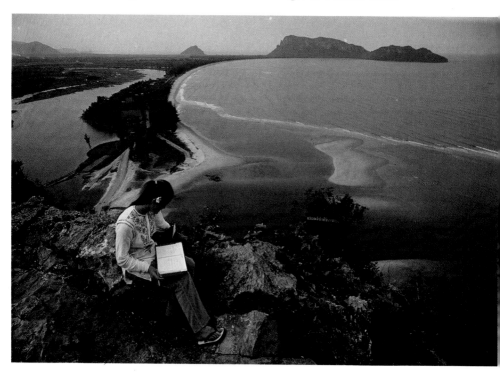

which were bequeathed to the state by Rama I and Rama IV and are used in the coronation of Chakri kings.

Continue on the road to town, pass the administrative offices, then turn left on to a road that leads to the northern end of the beach. Beach bungalows shaded by trees serve as a pleasant stopover if you wish to break your journey here. Near the end of the jetty that pokes far out into the bay, Pla Mong Restaurant serves delicious seafood — crab salad, deep-fried fish, lobster — to diners seated around a concrete patio overlooking the water.

From Prachuap, 27 km south on Route 4 at the 350-km-stone, turn right continuing for 7 km to reach **HUAY YANG WATERFALL.** The cascade spills over 120 meters of boulders in a jungle setting not far from the Burmese border. The waterfall is located in an area called Thap Sakae District which is famous for its infor-

mal trading. Burmese cross the mountainous frontier to swop animals or produce for manufactured goods that are scarce in their own country.

About 35 km beyond Thap Sakae District lies the town of **BANG SAPHAN** which is divided into two by the southbound railway tracks. As you enter the town, turn left and 12 km later the road ends at the edge of a wide, pretty bay rimmed by a 6-km-long beach. The green outcrop of Khao Mae Pamphung marks the northern end of the beach; Koh Thalu Island lies off its southern extremity. If you do not mind sand in your shoes, enjoy some seafood and drinks served on the wooden tables right on the beach.

Back on Route 4, south of Bang Saphan, the countryside becomes more lush, mountainous, and overgrown. In cleared spots, rubber plantations spread beneath limestone

The South offers a wide variety of scenic views over the ever-present sea. A hillock looks down upon a finger of land near Prachuap Khiri Khan (left), where bungalows line the white-sand beach. At a temple on the same hill (above, left) pilgrims have adorned a footprint of the Buddha with gold leaf. The strenuous fishing life along the southern coast produces handy people, such as this fisherwoman wearing a traditional hat at Bang Saphan (above, right).

Crossing the Isthmus

cliffs that appear sporadically down the Kra Isthmus and far into the Malay Peninsula.

Around 490 km south of Bangkok, Route 4 comes to an important junction where it branches right and goes to the Indian Ocean on the coast of South Thailand. The left branch leads to Chumphon provincial capital, while straight ahead 76 km away is the seaport of Lang Suan which lies at the beginning of a recently completed highway linking Bangkok to the towns of Surat Thani, Nakhon Si Thammarat, and Songkhla.

Left at this junction marked by signs and gas stations, a road goes 8 km to **CHUMPHON** which is noted for its cut-rate bird's nest soup. The city itself has little of scenic interest; but east of it lies **PAK NAM CHUMPHON** at the mouth of the Chumphon River, a fishing port that has boats for hire by the hour for trips to nearby islands where swallows build the nests so highly prized in Chinese cuisine. During the mating season from March through August authorized collectors climb high up the cliffs to fetch the delicacies. The island of Lanka Chio is especially famous. Merchants bid for concessions to take the nests, and even hire gunmen to guard their stake. It is fascinating to watch the gathering of nests, but be sure to let the guards know you are just looking. The island-dotted coastal waters here make for exciting sailing too.

From the provincial capital of Chumphon, Route 4 strikes out west across the narrowest neck of the Kra Isthmus, then veers south and follows the Pak Chan River through Kra Buri on the way to Ranong.

About 12 km beyond Kra Buri, turn left just before the 504-km-stone to reach **Tham Prakayang,** a temple in a cavern. If you have no flashlight, the monks will usually lend one for the dark ascent in the image-filled cave. One totally black Buddha gazes upon you through mother-of-pearl eyes. A limestone and wooden stair-case leads up and out of the cave to wellworn paths trodden by monks who meditate amid the isolated foliage atop the outcrop.

South of Tham Prakayang, the highway begins to cut briskly over jungled hills and crosses a wide river. Soon after the 597-km-stone, **PUNYABAN WATERFALL** lies just next to the road. Truck drivers stop, don their sarongs, and take a quick bath in the splashing water. This is a popular domestic tourist spot. A teahouse serves snacks near the falls. Climb a path to the left of the falls for a good view of the scenic countryside: the Pak Chan estuary; nearby islands; and the mountains of the southern tip of Burma.

At the 612-km-stone turn right near the Thara Hotel to enter the provincial capital of **RANONG**. The hotel itself has one of Ranong's main attractions: hot mineral water piped in from nearby thermal springs. To reach the springs, travel up the sideroad left of the river behind the hotel. The road follows a rocky riverbed bordered by thatch huts and banana trees. After 1 km, on the right stands a small shrine to the spirit of the springs. A well encloses the main outlet which pours forth 500 liters per minute of 70°C sparkling mineral water. You can cross a suspension bridge leading over the river to a little park. Or you can climb the hill behind the shrine to a small *wat* enclosed by a lovely, deep-shaded forest.

Continuing up the road past the hot springs, you reach the village of **HAT SUPIN** in tin-mining country: stark landscapes of white silt, bamboo scaffolding, deep pits, and gouged-out cliff faces. In open cast mining, gushing water carves holes in the earth. The mineral-laden water is filtered through a platform sieve supported by a.bamboo framework. The

10. Punyaban Waterf.
น้ำตกปัญญาพรรณ

8. Pak Nam Chumph
ปากน้ำชุมพร
11. Ranong
ระนอง (ตัวเมือง, จังหวัด)

12. Hat Supin
หาดสุพิน

9. Tham Prakayang
ถ้ำพระขาหย่ง

The evening market (right) bustles at the mouth of the Ranong River.

Wat Hat Supin
วัดหาดสุพิน

3. Pak Nam Ranong
ปากน้ำระนอง

tin ore is then sorted out of the mud and sand. In the morning you can watch sturdy women carrying wooden bowls to pan tin in the river, while their husbands work in the chalk quarry behind the village. One of Thailand's major exports (after rice, other crops, and natural rubber), tin is mined all along the Indian Ocean coast of the Kra Isthmus. Much of the production, which ranks second in the world, comes from private businesses like those around Hat Supin.

A small sign with fish painted on it points the way to **Wat Hat Supin** where children rush up to sell sweet popcorn. Visitors feed the popcorn to hundreds of carp that swarm in a pool by the side of the temple.

Drive back to Ranong, then take the 3-km-long road to **PAK NAM RANONG** on the sea. There boats unload fish at a modern wharf and trucks dump tonnes of crushed ice

on emptied decks. From this port some boats sail the Indian Ocean as far as Pakistan in search of fish.

Ranong Island, with its houses on stilts and fishing boat anchorage, lies directly opposite Pak Nam Ranong. You can rent boats on the mainland for island trips.

Return to Route 4 and continue south past Kapoe, Khuraburi, and the 776-km-stone, the last road marker showing the distance from Bangkok. About 4 km north of Takua Pa there is a junction with Road 401 leading east to Surat Thani and Chaiya.

A great drive full of ups, downs, and sharp corners, Road 401 zigzags over and around the cloud-cloaked limestone pinnacles of the Kra Isthmus. For the first 37 km, it traverses the wide valley of the Takua Pa River, passing tin mining camps flanked by mountains. Then the road enters the hills and plunges through a remarkable series of streaked limestone precipices and splintered rocks — some of the most breathtaking scenery in Thailand. Rarely do you see a another vehicle. The old dream of a canal across the Isthmus linking the Indian Ocean and the Gulf of Thailand seems unlikely to materialize in this wild setting.

For a midway rest, stop 59 km from the start of Road 401 at **Wat Thamwaran**, just to the left of a small river. The *wat* provides a simple shelter for monks who meditate near a cave that opens on the other side of the outcrop to a serene spot on the riverbank.

Approaching Surat, as the Thais call it, Road 401 leaves the hills and enters dense rubber plantations. About 120 km from the Route 4 turnoff, Road 401 bends right for the final 12 km into the town of **SURAT THANI**, a busy ship-building, fishing, and mining center lying on the

right bank of the Tapi River. Surat itself has little worth seeing, but is the point of departure for worthwhile sidetrips. The first sidetrip is for those interested in ancient history who should here board the northbound train for an hour's trip to Chaiya.

A small, sleepy town of unpainted wooden buildings, a 60-second pause for the Bangkok express, it could be any small town of South Thailand. But **CHAIYA** is the subject of a dispute claiming it to be the capital of a once great empire. A group of historians now believe that the capital of the Srivichaya empire, described by the wandering Chinese Monk, I Ching, in A.D. 671, was not Palembang in Sumatra, but. Chaiya. In fact, they claim, the date previously accepted as the founding of the empire in Palembang was actually the date it was conquered by Chaiya, and even the name Chaiya, they believe, is

Wat Thamwaran
วัดธรรมาวาส
15. Chaiya
ไชยา (ตัวเมือง, อำเภอ)

14. Surat Thani
สุราษฎร์ธานี (ตัวเมือง, จังา

Wat Mahathat
วัดมหาธาตุ

Suan Mok
สวนโมกข์

Wat Wieng
วัดเวียง

Wat Long
วัดลอง

Wat Kaeo
วัดแก้ว

a contraction of Srivichaya.

Only a few traces of this mighty empire, which once stretched from Java through Malaysia to Thailand, remain today. Less than 2 km out of town stands **Wat Mahathat**, one of the most revered temples in Thailand. Its central *chedi* is claimed to be over 1,300 years old and is a direct visual link between Chaiya and the Srivichaya period. A small museum adjoining the *wat* has some interesting relics from the vicinity.

Closer to town is **Wat Wieng**, where an inscription was found, dated A.D. 755 and erected by a King Vishnu. It was the erroneous attribution of this inscription, fifty years ago, to a different location that led to the hypothesis that Palembang was the Srivichaya capital. Two other *wat*s, **Wat Long** and **Wat Kaeo**, equidistantly spaced from Wat Wieng, mark the sites of the Srivichaya edifices. Today only Wat Kaeo holds

a dim reminder of a forgotten past with the crumbling wall of a once great stupa. All that is known is that it was built to commemorate a victory. Perhaps the shattered remains of a Buddha, peering through a mist of cobwebs from his lonely niche, knows the truth.

A few kilometers farther west from these historic remains, a small hillock rises from the flat countryside. Here stands a Buddhist retreat named **Suan Mok**, as new as Chaiya's past is old. The walls and columns inside the central building are covered with an eclectic series of paintings that span everything from the history of Buddhism to Aesop's fables. Suan Mok owes a surrealistic touch to a wandering Zen Buddhist, Emanuel Sherman, whose search for enlightenment led him from the United States to Japan and Thailand, eventually ending on the island of Phangan off the Thai coast. After his death

Crossing the Kra Isthmus, the narrowest point on the southern peninsula, the highway zigzags over and around impressive limestone pinnacles (facing page). A good place to make a cool stopover along the way is the cave temple of Wat Thamwaram (above, left), where a simple shelter is provided for monks who come to meditate. Children also enjoy playing in the cave and its serene surroundings, and one bold youngster poses au naturel (above, right).

Idyllic Islands

local artists covered one wall with illustrations to portray Sherman's epigrams.

Bas-reliefs telling the story of the Buddha decorate the outer walls. They were modeled locally from photos of the Indian originals. Suan Mok's quirky touch continues into its adjoining structures. In what could almost be a bilingual pun, the *bot* really is a boat. A large concrete ship serenely sails the sea of suffering to eventual nirvana. Suan Mok's abbot is a much respected man whose followers flock from all over Thailand, and his lay brother is one of the chief proponents of the Chaiya capital theory.

From Surat it is 20 km to **BAN DON,** a small fishing port from where boats depart for **KOH SAMUI,** the largest island in the western part of the Gulf of Thailand and the third largest in the country. Two kinds of boats make the crossing. The ferry leaves Ban Don at noon and at midnight and the voyage takes six hours: the speedboat leaves at noon and takes three hours. On the return trip the ferry leaves Koh Samui at 8:00 a.m. and midnight while the speedboat departs about 8:00 a.m. Deck space on the ferry costs 12 baht; a mattress indoors on the floor is 15 baht; a cabin for four is 50 baht per person. The tariff on the speedboat is 15 baht.

The first hour of the journey, whether on the speedboat or the ferry, offers glimpses of life on the Tapi River. Then the boat enters the Gulf and stays close to land until making the passage across open sea to **Ban Ang Thon** (also called Ban Hna Thon) the island's main town.

Koh Samui, one of a group of more than 80 smaller islands, six of which are settled, is still an idyllic tropical retreat. Plans however are being promoted to develop it as a

Regular ferries (above) ply the waters between Ban Don on the coast and the idyllic tropical island of Koh Samui (right), 32 km away. The largest island in the western Gulf of Thailand, Koh Samui is also one of the most beautiful and unspoiled; its economy is based on coconuts, reputedly the best in Thailand, and the aroma of roasting coconut flesh pervades the island. In addition to the six-hour ferry a speedboat makes the trip in only three hours.

tourist resort. About 250 sq km, or the size of Penang Island, Koh Samui has a mountain ridge lying east-west along its back while coconut plantations cover the rest of the land. Coconuts are food and fuel in Koh Samui, and with a reputation as the best in all Thailand they are the mainstay of the island's economy. The smell of roasting coconut flesh, rich and pleasant, pervades the island.

Accommodation is adequate but by no means luxurious. In Ban Ang Thon relatively comfortable, if not plush, accommodation can be found at Bungalow Chao Kho. Several Chinese hotels try to make up in hospitality for what they lack in comfort.

Simple food is cheap and delicious on Koh Samui. At the morning market you can breakfast on noodles and mild coconut curry for a few baht. Hawkers sell an endless variety of coconut and rice sweets. Try the coconut and date paste balls covered with sweet dough and deep fried. Fruits grown on the island — coconuts (the main export), papayas, bananas, mangoes (in season), pineapples, and jackfruit — are incredibly cheap.

The main activity for visitors on Koh Samui is "beaching." The beaches have it all: long stretches of dazzling white sand littered with cowries and crawling with harmless crabs; warm, clear water; and a sun that never quits, except in December when the rains claim that distinction.

The most private of visitors to Koh Samui will charter a small fishing boat for 350-400 baht per day, and explore some of the many smaller and uninhabited islands nearby. These have splendid untouched beaches, and one can be Robinson Crusoe for the price of a boat. The boatman will prepare a lunch of barbecued fish, glutinous rice with mangoes and pineapples, and serve it on the beach out of coconut bowls on a mat of palm fronds.

A fleet of *song tao*, small pick-up trucks converted to taxis with two parallel rows of seats in the back, serve Koh Samui. Cheap and fast, they never refuse a fare and load up until passengers are hanging off the tailgate and roof. Visitors can organize a "do-it-yourself" island tour. For about 50 baht a head half a dozen persons can pile into a *song tao* or, alternatively, make a similar round-the-island tour by boat for about the same price. Places worthy a visit are **Na Muang Falls** and the **Hin Ngu Temple** where a seated Buddha towers above a surf-swept rocky promontory and a tiny virgin beach with "grandmother" and "grandfather" rocks both of which are implicitly phallic.

An excursion worth making is a visit to the small villages that are dispersed throughout Koh Samui. Thirty-two thousand people live on the island and that is an enormous amount of hospitality. Near the mountains are coconut plantations and lush forests where the occasional path cuts through to a cluster of beautiful, yet simple, hardwood homes. Wrinkled old ladies sit in the shade of thatched porches and giggle to each other over the *farangs*, but they are delighted with each new visitor and adore attention. Children gawk unabashedly and dart about at the emergence of a camera.

There is a remarkable sense of peace on Koh Samui. The island and the sea produce an abundance of food and the forests provide bamboo and wood for shelter. Life seems easy. There are several schools on the island and the wealthier families send their bright children to universities on the mainland. And whoever decides not to aspire to an intellectual or commercial career in the modern cities of Thailand knows there are plenty of coconuts in the forests.

* * *

Route 4 continues down the peninsula along the Indian Ocean passing through the small district town of **TAKUA PA**. Over a thousand years ago, Takua Pa was a port for Indian traders who settled along the coasts of the Malayan Peninsula when the region was called Suvarabhumi, Land of Gold. Some scholars think the Indians sought shortcuts to the South China Sea. Unearthed statues have helped trace caravan routes across the Kra Isthmus to Surat Thani. Two 7th-century Davaravati statues, found on an island in the mouth of the yellowish Takua Pa River, add to the archaeological evidence. Today Takua Pa has little claim to fame except as the district center of a rich tin

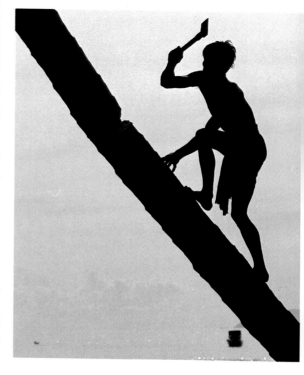

An islander on Koh Samui nimbly scales a coconut tree to cut it down; every part of the tree finds a use—the flesh of the nut for food, the fronds for thatching and matting, and the trunk for timber and fuel.

18. Bang Sak Beach
หาดบ้านสาก

21. Lam Pi Waterfall
น้ำตกลำปี

19. Khao Luk Beach
หาดเขาลูก

mining area. Travelers can stop here for a bite to eat on the way to Phuket.

About 13 km south of Takua Pa, tire tracks branching off Route 4 to the right under some casuarina trees lead to **BANG SAK BEACH** on a wide bay. Behind a refreshment stand, a thatched palm screen encloses a freshwater well for bathing and changing clothes. With its turquoise waters and white sand, isolated Bang Sak Beach lacks only Tahitian drums to complete an idyllic Polynesian setting.

Soon after Bang Sak, the road rises from sea level and meanders along jungled cliffs. In gaps between the trees, wide white beaches and small fishing fleets appear below. Farther out at sea, barges are engaged in small-scale mining.

About 36 km from Takua Pa, as the highway completes a twisting descent back to the sea, **KHAO LUK BEACH** lies immediately to the right.

Some thirty families live most of the year in the natural shelter of this cove. The men do not fish; with the aid of air pumps and goggles, they dive for tin. Like nautical prospectors, they stay under water one or two hours at a time, loading tin-bearing sand into buckets. Workers hoist the full buckets onto bamboo rafts and sieve their contents.

Every June the powerful monsoon churns up the ocean and halts the tin diving off Khao Luk. The mining families abandon their huts to the destructive lashing of wind and sea until the monsoon relents.

Returning to Route 4, south about 69 km from Takua Pa, a reddish dirt road to the left, just before a small school on the other side of the highway, marks the entrance to **LAM PI WATERFALL**. Follow the dirt road 2 km through a rubber plantation to the three-part fall and clear pool perfect for bathing.

The thirty-odd families who live on the sheltered beach of Khao Luk (above, left) do not earn their living by fishing, as one might expect, but by diving offshore for tin-bearing sand on the bottom of the sea: operations are halted in June each year by the powerful monsoon storms. About 30 kilometers away a drive through a rubber plantation takes you to the waterfall of Lam Pi (above, right), at the foot of which is a clear pool that is ideal for bathing.

Fifty km south of Takua Pa is the exiguous town of Khok Kloi. Another 30 km southwards on road 402 and the Sarasin Bridge is reached. This is a 1200-meter long concrete causeway which leads to a tropical paradise called **PHUKET.** This island, about the size of Singapore, cannot fail to delight the beach lover, the sun worshipper, the scuba diver — in a word, those who delight in a seaside vacation.

An interesting bronze statue is passed at the Tha Rua crossroad, about 38 km south of the causeway and 12 km north of Phuket town. It depicts two short haired girls, one of whom is leading the other by the hand. In the 18th century, during the reign of Rama I, the Burmese invaded Phuket. The governor of the Thalang region was unwell and died. Chan, his wife and Mook, her sister, continued the struggle and successfully repelled the invaders. Rama I, in honor of their bravery conferred the title of Tao (Lady) Tepsatri on Chan and Tao Srisuntorn on Mook.

Phuket, a town of about 43,000 persons which, at least until now, derives its enormous wealth from tin rather than tourism, is not very attractive. However, some glories of the past still remain in the shape of Sino-Portuguese shop-houses. The upper part of the facades of these buildings have arched windows set between foliated pilasters and are painted in pastel colors. The most impressive building in town is the Chartered Bank which, with its double-storey of arched loggias, would not be out of place in Bologna. Immediately facing it is a massive Romanesque clock tower. It tops a police station built to protect the bank, which was the first foreign bank built in Thailand outside of Bangkok. Yet, even long before this the British presence was known in Phuket. Captain Light of the British East India Company, who founded the colony of Penang, had his base in Phuket. In 1786, the Sultan of Kedah offered Light both

Penang and Phuket and the British, having dragged their feet for some dozen years, finally accepted Penang but, for lack of funds, spurned the suzerainty of Phuket.

The most historically important temple in Phuket is **Wat Chalong,** 6 km south of town on Vichit Road. Tattered gold leaf covers the statue of Luang Pho Chaem, abbot of Wat Chalong during the reign of King Chulalongkorn, remembered for his skill in setting broken limbs. This medical knowledge was drawn upon when local people battled gangs of Chinese who came from Malaysia to seize the town and its tin mines. The king eventually sent an army south to rout the invaders and Luang Pho received a special ecclesiastical title for his assistance to the injured.

Put Jaw Chinese Temple, past the market on Ranong Road, is the oldest and largest in Phuket. Its central altar, usually festooned with flowers, fruit, and incense, is dedicated to Kuan Yin, Goddess of Mercy.

For a leisurely evening, go north on Patipat Road and up **Phuket Hill** where local residents love to stroll. From here, you have a splendid view of the sight of Phuket town and nearby temples. Evenings need not be dull. In the center of town are half a dozen Ramwong parlors. In these you can dance, to the accompaniment of live music, with your choice of more than fifty dance hostesses. All are dressed alike in pretty mini-skirts and it's only 1 baht a dance. Then, there is the Pearl Bowling Alley where, under signs annoucing "No Gambling: Gambling Strictly Forbidden" literally thousands of baht change hands on the roll of a ball. Three of Phuket's innumerable cinemas have English sound rooms where, behind plate-glass, the *farang* can enjoy original sound tracks. And, finally, the Pearl

Chinese immigrants have played an important part in the development of many of the leading towns and cities of the South. On the wealthy, tin-mining island of Phuket, the Temple of Put Jaw (above, left), the oldest and largest, is dedicated to Kuan Yin, the Goddess of Mercy. Colorful and distinctive festivals, such as fire-walking rituals, are held annually at this gaudily-decorated temple, under the supervision of the resident priests (above, right).

Hotel has both a night club and massage parlor.

Phuket's principle attractions are its beaches and offshore islands. Do not be disappointed if the beach at **RAWAI,** 16 kms south of the town center fails to meet your expectations. It is on the east side of the island where silting and the indiscriminate removal of corals have resulted in much ecological damage. Make your way to the west coast bordering the Andaman Sea where there is what appears to be one long paradisiacal stretch of sand divided by short rocky promontories into nearly a dozen separate beaches.

One bonus provided by the rocky promontories — apart from the seclusion they afford — is the exquisite coral and fish life around them. No need to be a scuba diver or even a swimmer. Simply don a pair of goggles, protect your feet, bend your head into the water and explore a colorful new world. The only complaint that the underwater photographer might have is that the schools of powder-blue surgeon fish are so large and so common that they are in the way when he tries to photograph the clown triggerfish — claimed to be the most beautiful and the most expensive fish in the world — and the royal empress fish; the emperatur and the blue ring angel fish; the lion fish and the damsel fish, the ..... Incidentally, deep-sea fishing is excellent whether you are interested in a fish of one or two kg or forty to fifty kg tuna or groupers.

The names of the beaches roll off the tongue like a litany — Karon, Patong, Nai Yang, Mai Khao — and each beach has its own special characteristics.

PATONG, 8 km west of town, is large and gently sloping, making it ideal for children. **SURIN,** 23 km north of town, is relatively small

Rawai Village
หมู่บ้านราไว

Laem Ka Noi
แหลมขาน้อย

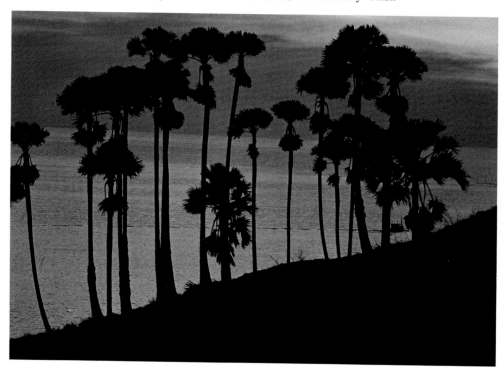

270

(about 2 km long) and slopes sharply, making it especially dangerous during the monsoon season from April through September. There is a 9-hole golf course at Surin and it is the best place to enjoy Phuket's sunsets. **NAI YANG** or **AIRPORT BEACH,** 3 km past the airport, is well shaded by casuarina trees and is ideal for picnics. It offers good snorkeling among sea anemones and fish traps. North of Nai Yang stretches **MAI KHAO (WHITE WOOD) BEACH,** Phuket's longest. Each year, from December to February, giant sea turtles lumber ashore at Mai Khao to lay eggs which are prized delicacies.

Each of these beaches has one or more clusters of small palm thatch huts providing simple, inexpensive accommodation, and all have one or several food stalls where — naturally — seafood abounds. If none of these beaches appeal, then hire a boat and visit one or other of the nearly two score small islands surrounding Phuket. Only half a dozen of these islands are inhabited. There is always a boatman to waft the visitor to the island of his choice, and the nearest is but twenty minutes away. Not only will the boatman transport you, but he will also catch fish, climb trees for coconuts and prepare a barbecue fit for the King of Siam.

All Phuket's beaches and, indeed, everywhere on the island, can be reached by buses which leave from the market and the Fountain Circle. *Tuktuks* will take you anywhere in town for 5 baht and everywhere on the island for a negotiable fare. It is claimed that Phuket was the first town in Thailand to boast paved roads and automobiles. As the visitor will soon note, there is also, in terms of population, the largest number of motor bicycles found in any town in Thailand. These may be rented.

Among the most interesting peoples of Phuket are the *Chao Lay* or "Sea Tribes." They live at **KOH SIREH** and also at Rawai. Nobody appears to know the origin of the

couple of thousand sea gypsies who compose these two communities. However, it is believed they are related to the dark-skinned, curly-haired fishing people of the Andaman islands.

From an early age, sea gypsy boys learn to dive, staying three minutes or longer underwater while spearing lobsters or gathering oysters. Girls learn that after marriage they must not touch the bedding of the husband who is away at sea. To do so, these animist folk believe, would cause him to drown.

Near the sea gypsy village, up 439-fitness-testing steps, **Wat Koh Sireh** affords a good view of Phuket town, Laem Nga Bay, Saphan Phra (where boats leave for nearby islands,) and most of the southeastern coast. A reclining Buddha helps create the peaceful atmosphere of the *wat*. The image is enhanced by deep-red lips, mother-of-pearl eyes, and gold leaf

Tribes of exotic sea gypsies preserve their own way of life on Koh Sireh near Phuket town. Anthropologists believe these independent people are related to the fisherfolk of the Andaman Islands.

attached by worshippers and fluttering from one elbow.

If time permits, set aside one day to see two sources of Phuket's wealth: tin mining and pearl farming. **Saphan Hin Park**, 1 km south of the town center was formerly sea and here, in 1907, dredging for tin first took place in SE Asia. This historic fact is marked by an attractive, abstract monument which resembles a bucket with a hole in it. All Phuket's tin and, indeed, all Thailand's tin, is smelted at the THAISARCO smelter at Laem Pan Wa, 8 km south of Phuket town. The three moving islands you see from the Thaisarco jetty and which are not on the chart are tin dredges. A couple of km beyond the smelter is the Thai-Danish Marine Biological Centre. It is well worth a visit, not only for its marine specimens, but also for the lovely views of the islands.

In the quiet, sheltered waters off Phuket's east coast are half a dozen pearl farms. All but one of these grow *mabe* or half pearls. This is child's work compared to growing full round pearls. No problem to visit the farms where half pearls are cultivated. However, if you approach idyllic **KOH NAKA NOI** without a permit you are liable to find a gun trained on you. South Sea pearls — and that is what they grow on Koh Naka Noi — can be worth thousands of dollars a piece.

Excursions by sea can be made from Phuket to the rocky islands of Phangnga Bay (see following pages) and Koh Phi Phi (p. 267). On excursions to Phangnga the boat can be taken across the bay and the return to Phuket made by land.

Returning to the mainland, about 30 km northeast from Khok Kloi, a dirt road on the left leads to **SUAN KU** where a limestone cave shelters dozens of Buddha images. Light streaming in through an opening gives the cave a my mystical aura.

Koh Naka Noi
เกาะนาคาน้อย

Island Interlude

Route 4 soon enters Phangnga's small provincial town where your choice of lodgings is limited to one of several lackluster Chinese hotels. If they seem below standard, remember that the sights in **PHANGNGA BAY** will more than make up for the dearth of good lodging in town. As there may be a number of tourists in town at the same time, it is always a good idea to arrange your boat rental the afternoon or evening before setting out for the bay. To do this, go 6 km back towards Khok Kloi and turn left for 4 km to the Phangnga Customs House and a small village where fishing and tourist boats are rented.

Enroute to Phangnga Bay, the boat glides along glassy, green riverways flanked by mangrove swamps. Old ladies under big hats paddle past in narrow boats piled with bananas. The boatman stops at green signs naming the islands after the shape of their silhouettes (such as Koh Ma Chu or "Puppy Island").

Just before the mouth of Phangnga River, the boat approaches the base of the mountain **KHAO KIEN** where a cavern contains primitive paintings depicting human and animal forms like the cave drawings of Lascaux. To the right lies a large rock island called **KOH PANNYI** where an entire Muslim fishing village stands on stilts over the water.

The boat proceeds into a maze of islands, one more astonishing than the next, where part of the James Bond movie *Man With The Golden Gun* was filmed. Highlights of this "lost world" setting include:

THAM LAWD: On a seeming collision course with a huge limestone outcrop, the boat slips into a barely discernible, overgrown entrance to a cave. For more than 50 meters you slide under giant stalactites. Rocks protruding from the water appear to

The clear waters around Phuket are good for pearl farming (facing page); a large pearl farm is maintained on Koh Naka Noi, an island just thirty minutes off the eastern coast of Phuket. Towering limestone outcrops (above left), carved by weathering and then flooded by a rise in the sea level, stand in Phangnga Bay, one of Thailand's most scenic spots. Primitive, ancient paintings (above, right) adorn the walls of the cave on the island of Khao Kien in the bay.

have been sliced by a machete-wielding god.

THAM NAK: A twisted stalagmite at the entrance resembles a *naga* serpent, giving this cave its name. Green stalactites burst from the ceiling like a frozen waterfall. The whole mountain-island seems from the outside to drip with streaked limestone. Scenes from numerous Thai movies have been filmed here.

KOH THALU: *Thalu* means to pass from one side to the other, in this case not over the mountain, but under it. The boat squeezes through a cave filled with stalactites.

KOH KHAO PING GUN: This is the spot to shut off the motor, to swim, and picnic. A small beach overlooks another island, **KOH TAPOO**, which looks like a thorny spike drilled into the sea. Behind the beach is a huge rock slide: the mountain seems to have split in two. The halves appear to lean against each other. Locals say they are two lovers. A small staircase leads to a cavern above the water where limestone formations look like a large mound of solidified spilled glue.

Several onshore caves in Phangnga are worth visiting. Approached from town, **THAM RUSSI** or "Hermit Cave" lies on the left 2 km before the Customs House turnoff. A stalagmite in the approximate shape of a hermit has been embellished by human hands with a long white beard, a saffron cloth around the shoulder, and a cane. Many believe the *russi* has power to cure the sick and predict winning lottery numbers.

Unusual labyrinthine grottoes weave through Tham Russi. In a parklike atmosphere, lovers stroll over bridges crossing pools within the cave that is well-appointed with neon lights and even toilet facilities.

Continuing 500 meters down the road, passing the governor's office on

Tham Nak
ตำหนัก

Tham Russi
ถ้ำฤาษี

Koh Thalu
เกาะตาลุ

Koh Khao Ping Gun
เกาะเขาพิงกัน

Koh Tapoo
เกาะตะปู

The Southwest Coast

The seascape at Phangnga Bay is filled with a fantastic array of weathered limestone outcrops and islands.

the left, you see a blue sign pointing out a trail towards **Wat Tham Pong Chang**, "Temple-Cave in the Elephant's Stomach." A claustrophobic tunnel to the left of a pool leads into a small shrine adorned with statues of three sacred elephants.

Just 2 km from Phangnga on Route 4 you reach a fork where a sign points right, 85 km to Krabi. Beyond the fork the road rises into a winding pass through giant limestone hills and fertile valleys. At the foot of the pass on the right, you are greeted by the humble visage of a Buddha statue at **Wat Kirirong**, at the entrance to a hollow under huge cliffs.

South of Wat Kirirong the horizon continues to defy gravity in places where huge rocks rise above the jungle in seemingly towering upheavals. About 45 km from Phangnga the road squeezes between two gargantuan rocks and glides into the town of **AO LUK**, 40 km before Krabi. Turn-

ing right at the main junction in town, you go 2 km to reach **THAN BOKKORONI NATIONAL PARK**, one of the most beautiful in Thailand. Like a scene from *Lost Horizon*, the park funnels through lofty cliffs. In one spot an underground stream rises amid lush vegetation at the base of a mountain. Gravel paths snake beneath cliff faces covered in green vines punctuated by red hibiscus. The bay of Ao Luk is fascinating with its huge limestone rocks towering majestically above calm, green waters.

Returning to Route 4 you can stop at **Ban Thong Agricultural Station** where botanists breed new strains of rubber, coffee, and tea. Continuing along Route 4, you wind through dense stands of rubber trees. Strips of white latex hang drying from bamboo poles in front of many houses. Unlike Malaysia with its vast plantations, Thailand has a multitude of small, privately owned groves.

About 25 km south of Ao Luk, still traveling beneath and around unpredictable limestone "eruptions," you pass **Naichong Rubber Experimental Station.**

By taking Route 4 all the way toward Krabi (the highway actually bypasses the provincial capital 5 km to the north of it), you miss a scenic sidetrip. If you have an extra few hours, turn right about 7 km beyond the Naichong Station. Continue for 6½ km, then left for 11½ km through small farming villages not far from the sea. A white sign points to Hat Noparat Thara Beach 7 km down a dirt road.

The usually deserted broad beach of **HAT NOPARAT THARA** faces rocky islands half a kilometer off-shore that can be reached on foot at low tide. Along the beach casuarina trees extend for kilometers, providing shade for occasional benches. The sand varies in texture from sugar-like fineness to a grainier composition of millions of tiny shells.

Drive back 7 km to the sideroad and go 3 km farther to another white sign, this one marking the 9 km road to **SUSARN HOI ("SHELL CEMETERY") BEACH.** This is not a sand beach; rock slabs, made of petrified shells 25 million years old, feel like irregular concrete slabs underfoot. Many of the nipa huts along the beach sell choice pieces of petrified cones.

Back on the sideroad to **KRABI,** you enter the town behind the province's administrative offices on a hill overlooking the port. From there you can drive to the Krabi River and the wharves. Old black junks with yin and yang talismans painted on their bows will often berth at Krabi after voyages from Singapore or Penang. From the docks you can catch boats to Koh Phi Phi, the island of high cliffs and curious cave drawings.

27. Susarn Hoi Beach
หาดสุสานหอย

28. Krabi
กระบี่ (ตัวเมือง, จังหวัด)

26. Hat Noparat Thara
หาดนพรัตน์ธารา

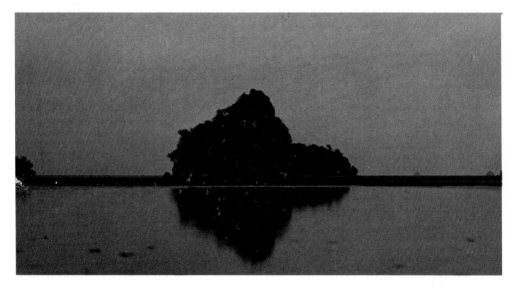

Scenic, unexplored beaches run for kilometers along the coast around Trang and Krabi, on the Andaman Sea. The sand varies in texture from sugarlike fineness to a grainy composition of shells, and the water is often limpidly blue. The beach at Noparat Thara (above) looks out on a line of rocky offshore islands that can be reached by foot at low tide. A bit farther down the coast past Trang stretches Pak Mong Beach (opposite), where the scenery is memorable.

Turquoise waves caress a beach so dazzlingly white it is almost painful to the eye. Colorful fishing boats bask in a wide, sheltered bay. Called **KOH PHI PHI**, this island paradise, fringed with secluded beaches and surrounded by clear, warm waters, lies south of the fishing town of Krabi.

From Krabi, the boat follows a seemingly aimless path to avoid the mud banks. Koh Phi Phi is visible ahead as soon as you hit the open sea, and gradually the morning mist clears to reveal an undulating island with a high, rocky, tree-covered headland at the southern tip. No regular boats make the four-hour trip out from Krabi, but if you ask at the wharves, there usually is someone planning on going. If you want to be sure of returning on a particular day, you will have to charter in advance.

The tiny population of Koh Phi Phi lives in a scattering of fishing huts; in one spot there are almost enough to warrant the word village. Should you want to stay for a few days, someone will offer to unroll an extra mat on the floor. But bring along your Thai phrase book as no one speaks a word of English.

When exploring the island, you will not fail to be impressed by the huge kilometer-long rock that rears out of the sea south of the island. The sea funnels down between the steep cliffs of this barren island and the equally formidable ramparts of Koh Phi Phi's headland, creating a choppy swell that can be frightening in the small boat that ferries you across. A flimsy jetty, suspended from overhanging rock by a tangle of ropes, projects out over the sea. Clamber along it and you find yourself in a huge, dripping cavern. A web of bamboo scaffolding reaches up, disappearing into the gloomy upper recesses. Men climb up these precarious ladders to collect swallow's nests which are sold as an expensive delicacy for the gourmet. One glance at the shaky supports reaching up in darkness to the ceiling of the cave is enough to explain why bird's nest soup is very expensive.

The cave's denizens provide a more mundane product in the guano that coats the cave floor and fills the air with its distinctive odor. On the cave wall close to the entrance are a mysterious series of paintings depicting a variety of sailing ships.

* * *

For kilometers around Krabi on the mainland, eerie limestone outcrops erupt from the earth trailing a green canopy of vegetation behind them. They are the land-based kin of the islands that dot the sea around Phi Phi. To soften the blow of returning to "civilization," Krabi has an excellent and inexpensive little hotel with a downstairs restaurant that has that small town rarity, an English menu. It promises such unusual delicacies as "four things soup in a firepan" or "assorted duck's feet."

As you head southeast from Krabi on Route 4, the land gradually flattens. Dike-enclosed rice fields appear on both sides of the road. Seemingly abandoned suitcases and boxes on the roadside designate bus stops; would-be passengers wait patiently under banana trees nearby.

Only a fanatical spelunker would venture off Route 4 to investigate the minor caves at **KHAO PINA**. All fanatics should turn left 92 km from the Krabi junction down a dirt road leading 1½ km to a small temple at the base of a tall staircase climbing up to two caves. Bring your own flashlight. An unexpected statue of a Thai official dressed in a white, medalfestooned jacket and blue pants stands stiffly before a chapel.

Back on Route 4, you pass

Folk art decorates the southern countryside everywhere you go along the road. There is a simple and playful artistry about many of the statues, such as this pastel Buddha just north of Krabi (above, left). An unexpected statue of a Thai official (above, right) stands stiffly before the chapel at Khao Pina. Trang's Chinese heritage is revealed at the elaborately decorated Teochew shrine at Ban Bangrok (facing page), dedicated to a red-faced god of war.

30. Trang
ตรัง (ตัวเมือง, จังหวัด)

Pak Mong Beach
หาดผาเมอง

Ban Bangrok
บ้านบางรก

Surin Park
สวนสุรินทร์

through Huai Yot 108 km from Krabi and go another 28 km to **TRANG** provincial capital. Everyone gets down to business in Trang, one of the smaller but prosperous links in the chain of largely Chinese southern towns. Many of the Teochew-speaking immigrants sought work here panning tin but wound up running the rubber trade.

Trang's Chinese heritage is reflected in monuments at the northern approach to the city. In **BAN BANG ROK**, 3 km north on Route 4, a Teochew shrine honors Kwan Tee Hun, a red-faced, bearded god believed to have the power to prevent or start war. Tortoises, symbolic of longevity, sun themselves around the pool in the main hall. Farther south on Route 4 a dragon gate guards the city.

The provincial town itself is drab. Trang Hotel offers air-conditioned rooms, but its dining room downstairs appears dark and dreary. The town does boast one celebrated restaurant, however, just to the right of the post office one block north of the railway station. Its owner proudly serves hot Chinese plum wine, roasted cashews, thick spring rolls and excellent fried fish. Eel imported from Kwangtung, prepared with pork in heavy gravy, called *pla thua na*, is the specialty of the house.

When in Trang you can take a number of interesting sidetrips. **PAK MONG BEACH** lies on the Indian Ocean off Road 4046 (the Sikao Road) just after the 28-km-stone from Trang. It is a long bumpy trip but the scenery and sunsets are memorable. **SURIN PARK**, which lies a short distance west of Trang on Route 4, has a beatiful large pond surrounded by well-kept gardens. Going northeast from Trang through Huai Yot will take you through a beautiful winding valley and to Nakhon Si Thammarat.

The Deep South

A long main street runs through the ancient city of **NAKHON SI THAMMARAT**, or Nakhon, as the Thais call it for short. Painted wooden shop houses, a new museum, Thai-style administrative buildings, a store selling shadow-play puppets, and several temples line this street. The Thai Hotel near the market has air-conditioned rooms.

Nakhon was an important city in the Davaravati and Srivichaya empires. A few Davaravati sculptures remain in **Wat Mahathat**, one of the oldest temples in Thailand, on the southern outskirts of town. The *wat* features a 77-meter-high *chedi* with a top covered by 270 kilograms of gold. To the right of the *chedi*, a temple museum houses a great assortment of delicate gold and silver offerings. Next to the *wat*, the Viharn Luang, with its inward-leaning columns, presents a fine example of Ayuthaya period design.

Thailand's nielloware industry began in Nakhon. You can observe some of the craftsmen who started it all about fifty years ago at the original Nakhon shop on Chakrapetch Road. Niello looks like enamel, but in fact is a black alloy that fills spaces between lines of silver or gold in objects ranging from ashtrays to royally commissioned jewelry.

When the road north from town is improved, the trip to Sichon on the Gulf of Thailand will reward visitors with scenic views and Srivichaya artifacts. Until then, visit the cave that once sheltered King Taksin when he fled from the Burmese. Take the road across the railroad tracks to Lan Saka Village, turn right at the first fork, and go 9 km to the cave where the view of the countryside is magnificent.

* * *

31. Nakhon Si Thamma
นครศรีธรรมราช (ตัวเมือง, จั

Wat Mahathat
วัดมหาธาตุ

An all-weather highway linking Nakhon Sri Thammarat to Songkhla recently has been completed. It runs through numerous lemon orchards and past several dusty arenas where fighting bulls are trained. But an alternative to the new road is the older Route 4 which leads to Phatthalung by going through the provincial capital of Trang.

Enroute to Phatthalung on Route 4, about 20 km east of Trang, the **KHAO CHONG NATURE RESERVE** encompasses slightly tamed jungle, a rocky creek, and a waterfall. Drive into the reserve but do not panic if you encounter soldiers brandishing weapons. The reserve also hosts a military camp. Khao Chong represents part of Thailand's nascent conservation and ecology movement. Students at the Nature Education Center here can study southern animals in a natural rain forest environment. The small zoo houses a sam-

pling of local fauna, like the Binturong civet, Prevost squirrel, Bramani kite, hog badger, and some endangered species including the white-handed gibbon which is usually captured by killing a mother with young.

The hog badger has an interesting connection with southern bull fighting, which is the regional entertainment and occasion for gambling that involves no matador, but just two bulls in a locked-horns pushing contest. The hog badger's meat does not taste good, but the unfortunate long-clawed mammal is occasionally shot for the fat on its nose. A bull with this wild-smelling fat rubbed on its horns, it is claimed, can intimidate and defeat any opponent. Naturally, the use of this fat is regarded as cheating.

From the Khao Chong Nature Reserve, drive 34 km to **PHATTHA-LUNG**. Along this stretch of Route 4, a few motorists have been relieved of their cash and valuables by bandits

Adorned with gold leaf, a Buddha image gazes out serenely at Wat Mahathat one of the oldest and most revered temples in Thailand, just outside the ancient city of Nakhon Si Thammarat (facing page). Old cannons (above, left), now playthings, line the front of the administrative buildings of the city. A white-faced gibbon (above, right) is one of the many native animals of the South that can be seen at the Khao Chong Nature Reserve, not far from Trang.

but such occasions are rare. You will likely only see Thai Army soldiers camped in tents between rows of rubber trees.

Route 4 to Phatthalung zigzags under towering jungle trees, past pink earthen rock, up and down the mountainous watershed along the center of the isthmus. About 3 km before Phatthalung, the highway branches south to Haadyai. You continue straight, past the provincial administrative offices, then bear left on the road to Khuan Khanun ("Jackfruit Hill") and **Wat Ku Ha Sawan**. This temple was recently renovated, but behind its yellow buildings a staircase climbs up to a large grotto lighted by a natural arch. A delightful obese, laughing Buddha marks the entrance. Around a copper-leafed Bodhi tree are gathered dozens of Buddha images. Light from the arch glints off the gold leaf on the statues. To the right of the *wat* lies another cave formerly inhabited by a hermit monk. His personal collection of images remains there.

To visit another temple and the northern end of the inland sea, take the road leading east from town. **Wat Wang** ("Palace Temple") is 8 km from the city on the left side of the road. An attractive *chedi* graces the front of the temple courtyard. Inside the temple proper are unrestored frescoes dating back about 200 years.

Continue down the road another 7 km to Ban Lampam where the water of the inland sea, 70 km from its entrance to the Gulf of Thailand, is fresh.

A short boat trip from Phatthalung town leads to **THAM MALAI**, a cave lying between the province's two famous peaks: Broken-Hearted Mountain and Broken-Headed Mountain. Legend says these represent two women turned to stone in punishment for jealousy. Catch the

Wat Wang
วัดวัง

Wat Ku Ha Suwan
วัดคูหาสวรรค์

Tham Malai
ถ้ำมาลัย

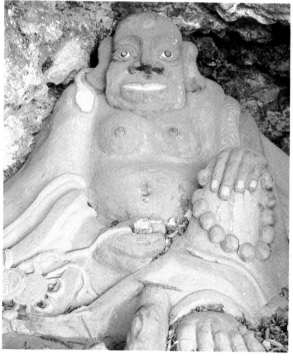

Behind a building at Wat Ku Ha Sawan (above) sits a delightful laughing Buddha (right). At Haadyai, a bull fight (facing page) means that the beasts compete against each other, in locked-horn wrestling.

boat behind the train station for the 15-minute ride to Tham Malai. A monk caretaker will turn on a generator to light up the cave that features some good stalactites.

As Phatthalung offers no really good hotels, head back to Route 4 and turn south for Haadyai.

* * *

HAADYAI, the commercial capital of south Thailand, is a growing city, frontier in style, with rubber and tin in its surrounding areas and a thriving night life. Because prices of many items (including night life) are lower in Thailand than in Malaysia, Haadyai has become a shopping and sybaritic haven for Malaysians who pour across the border on buying sprees.

Few hotels can have more musical outlets than the Sukhontha. Three big bands, each with a galaxy of singers, swing every night in the hotel's clubs and discos and, in addition, a

group performs in the coffee shop. The hotel also has a Pink Lady — a massage parlor. Other massage parlors, branches of Bangkok organizations, are the Atami and Chao Phya.

Haadyai has several points of interest for those recovered sufficiently from their revels of the previous night. In the town at Wat Haadyai Nai is the third largest reclining Buddha in the world. Do not just admire the exterior of this giant who sits atop a 3 meter high base. Ascend this pedestal and enter into the Buddha's innards where lungs and shrines sit side by side.

On the outskirts of the town, en route to Songkhla, is the **Rubber Research Center**, serving all the Thailand, where graft and tapping methods are tested, and then experimental studies for their high yield are made on rubber trees. Small-holding farmers come to study at the center where there is a rubber processing laboratory. (Telephone one day in advance to request a tour.)

Next to the research center is the **Songkhla Nakharin University,** set on 120 hectares and spectacular in its architectural style. A pumpkin-shaped building containing the auditorium and laboratories is surrounded by a moat. Arched windows in the pumpkin catch breezes from all directions and channel them through the building to provide natural air conditioning. An exhaust pump in the center sucks the warm air out.

Sunday is the day for bullfights. However, do not envisage a *corrida* with *matadors* and *picadors:* bull fighting Thai style is a contest which pits one humpbacked bull against another. Two animals are brought face to face. They lower their heads, practically interlock their horns and paw the ground. Each pushes against the other. The fight may last minutes or a couple of hours. It ends when one bull gains the ascendancy by pushing the other back, back, back or when one simply turns and takes flight. He, sensible fellow, has heard that "the bull who fought and ran away lived to fight another day." Betting on "Yellow Baby" and "Elvis" is heavy.

For food try the Haivathene at 69 Themanoonvithi Road. People come all the way from Bangkok to salivate over the shark's fin soup and reservations are needed. Other specialities are poached duck and fried pigeon. Several large open-air restaurants serve superb seafood to the accompaniment of raucous live music and go-go girls. Try the Ton-Nga Chang with its imaginative decor.

Other than to Songkhla, Haadyai has no taxis, but buses will take you anywhere in town — a door to door service — for 5 baht. The railway station has a bath and changing room and an attractive swimming pool can be found behind City Hall.

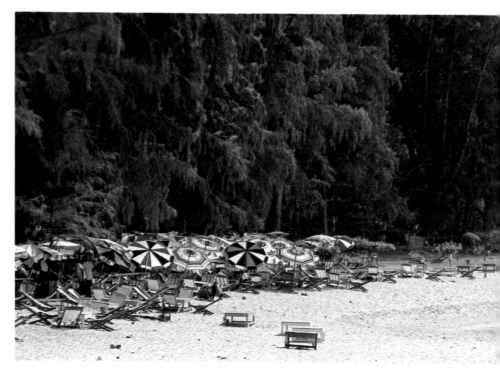

Songkhla and to Malaysia

If Haadyai is brash then **SONGKHLA** is discreet, like the inexpensive restaurant in Paris (now, alas no more) that one passes on to a friend with the promise not to tell anyone lest it be spoiled. Indeed, Songkhla is the main reason for the international traveler visiting Haadyai. Trains, buses and taxis cover the 25 km between the two towns. The really adventurous can make arrangements to make the journey by water.

Built on a peninsula, Songkhla is an old Chinese city peacefully surrounded on three sides by water. However, only the seaward (eastern) side is suitable for sunning and swimming. The north part of the beach is backed with lush casuarina trees and here one finds such unlikely traffic as monks is saffron robes and humpbacked bulls being prepared for the bullfights. The focal point of the beach is a bronze statue of a mermaid immediately opposite the Samila

Hotel, the only hotel of distinction in Songkhla. The hotel also serves as the clubhouse for the *Thongyai Golf Course.* Immediately northwest of the mermaid, and on the sandy beach, are a score of seafood restaurants. Select your meal from uncooked displays including 35-cm-long tiger prawns and then, while waiting for it to be cooked, relax in colorful deck chairs alongside low tables.

Three km south of the Samila Hotel is a small, extremely active fishing village inhabited mainly by Muslims. But it is the fishing boats rather than the fisher people who fascinate. It would be difficult to beat these *gorlae* for sheer pizzaz and imagination: captivating folk art in a riot of color and a multitude of visual themes cover them stem to stern.

Beyond the fishing village lies the rock beach of **Kao Seng** whose fame rests on a precariously poised giant boulder called **Nai Bang's Head.** If

Jammed with visitors, popular Samila Beach (left) faces the gentle inlet at Songkhla and boasts more than twenty seafood restaurants where one can select one's meal from the day's catch. Over on the Gulf, another stretch of beach is lined with graceful casuarina trees and is generally more deserted (above, left). At a Muslim village about 3 km down the coast, fishing boats with finely decorated sterns (above, right) wait on the sand to head out to sea.

you manage to push it over then you might be fortunate enough to uncover the millionaire's treasure reputedly hidden below. Inland from the beach is the **Banloa Coconut Plantation** where one can watch trained monkeys who, on demand, climb trees and bring down selected coconuts.

Then visit **Wat Kho Tum,** built among enormous boulders on a nearby hilltop and see Buddha's footprint in a cave and a sleeping Buddha reclining underneath an overhanging rock. Around the corner from this is **Wat Maeche,** a charming sandy spot where Buddhist nuns reside. The nuns, often young, with white robes and shaven heads, grow flowers, rise at 4:00 a.m. to meditate, and read philosophy before setting out for alms.

Across the road from the entrance to the Samila Hotel is **Khao-Noi** — a topiary garden — with realistic fighting bulls, birds in flight and

an elephant that is elephantine in size, sculpted out of yew. Around the corner from this, on Sukhum Road, in the late afternoon, you will find gatherings of monkeys. They have come down from the hilltop to sit, hands on knees, scratching or blinking, seeming to philosophize like old men. Continue towards the lake to Viehienchom Road from where a steep path and steps lead in 20 minutes to the top of **Mount Tangkuan** where stand the ruins of an ancient *chedi.* The panorama is spectacular and the amazing activity at the wharves along the lake give credence to Songkhla's claim to being the busiest fishing port in all Asia.

A pleasant excursion is to **Kho Yor** (Yor Island) situated in **Thale Sap** or **Songkhla Lake**, one of the largest lakes in SE Asia. Actually, it is a deep inlet rather than a lake, being connected to the sea, and its waters are brackish. En route to Yor Island a

Banloa Coconut Plan
สวนมะพร้าวบ้านเลา
Wat Kho Tum
วัดเขาทุ่ม

Wat Maeche
วัดแม่เจ

stop may be made at the Fisheries Station where enormous white *pla kapong* are bred. Kho Yor is renowned for its locally woven cotton and has a number of ancient Buddhist monuments. But the real joy is the tranquillity of the idyllic landscape in comparison to which gentle Songkhla becomes a bustling frenetic metropolis.

Another excursion by boat is to the offshore islands of **Maew** and **Nu** (Cat and Rat). No is the larger and has some pleasant picnic spots and bathing beaches.

Songkhla boasts two museums. The chock-a-block museum in the **Majimawat Temple** (popularly called **Wat Klant**) is in marked contrast to the spic and span recently renovated **Old Governor's Palace**, a beautifully proportioned Chinese mansion of 1878. The latter contains an excellent collection of ceramics and documented remains, recovered by scuba divers from an ancient wreck in the Gulf of Thailand. The Majimawat museum collection ranges from early Thai five-color pottery and 200-year-old shell boxes of the Buket style to a pre-electric fan that operates on gas. You are on your own, though, because there are no labels and the monk in charge speaks only Thai. The 200-year-old marble Buddha gracing the altar inside the temple of the same complex lacks the pure gold lotus that it once wore on its head, as the lotus crown is now safely stored in a vault. Chinese lions, a gift of some rich Chinese in the early days, guard the doorway opening on to the interesting murals within. Some show scenes of Songkhla while others depict European sailors and a steam boat.

Lift your eyes as you walk along Nakorn Noak Road and Nakorn Nai Street: old Chinese families living in the lovely Sino-Portuguese shop-houses are reputed to be extremely rich and conservative.

From Songkhla there are two basic routes to Malaysia. The shorter and most frequently traveled road follows approximately the railway line to the western Malaysian cities of Alor Star and Butterworth. From Haadyai, Route 4 leads directly south to the border, or if you wish to visit every provincial capital, head west of Route 4 towards Ratphum District. This side trip leads to the remote and unspoiled provincial town of Satun.

The adventurous traveler with time to spare might wish to make his way towards Malaysia's east coast. En route the provincial Thai capitals of Pattani, Yala and Narathiwat may be visited. Many residents of these towns are Chinese but the majority of the people are Malay. Mosques can be seen and the Malay language is commonly spoken. Of interest near Yala are the Silpa caves. The large cave of **Tham Koo Ha Pimak** contains a 25-meter-high Buddha, considered a holy pilgrimage site by southern Thais. It is surely an apt place to conclude your Thai adventure.

Almost every accessible cave in Thailand is believed to be the dwelling place of spirits and provides a setting for a grotto temple. An example is Silpa Cave near Yala which contains interesting Buddha images.

GUIDE IN BRIEF

TRAVEL FORMALITIES

PASSPORTS. All foreign nationals entering Thailand must be in possession of a valid passport.

VISAS. All foreign nationals before traveling to Thailand must apply for and obtain visas from Thai Embassies or Consulates abroad. Exceptions are:
1) Citizens of the U.S.A., West Germany, Sweden, Denmark, and Norway who can stay up to 15 days without a visa.
2) Transit passengers with tickets for onward passage on an airplane or a ship over 500 tonnes who can stay without a visa up to 15 days.
3) Persons travelling from countries that do not have a Thai Embassy or Consulate.
4) ASEAN citizens who can stay without a visa up to 15 days.
5) Hong Kong nationals with British passports who can stay without a visa up to 15 days.
6) Holders of Official or Diplomatic passports from Benelux, Israel, Italy, Denmark, South Korea, West Germany, Malaysia, Singapore, the Philippines, and Tunisia who can stay without a visa up to 15 days.

Tourist Visa. All Tourist Visas are granted for a period of sixty days. An extension of one or two months is sometimes granted if a resident sponsor posts a guarantee-bond of US$250. However, this red-tape requirement can be side-stepped by leaving the country upon expiry of the visa and then reentering on a new Tourist Visa. This can be done *twice*. The cost of a Tourist Visa is US$5.00 (100 baht). Applications must be accompanied by three passport-size photos.

Re-entry Visa. A person who wishes to leave Thailand and return before expiry of his or her Tourist or Nonimmigrant Visa must first obtain a Re-entry Visa. This can be done Monday to Friday between 8:30 a.m. and 3.30 p.m. at the Immigration Division of the Police Department, Soi Suan Plu, South Sathorn Road (286-9222). Saturday, Sunday and government holidays between 8:30 a.m. and 3.30 p.m. at the Tourism Authority of Thailand, Rajadamnern Avenue.

Exit Visa. An Exit Visa normally is not required.

Validity of Visas. A visa is valid for use for a period of sixty days from the date of issue. Should the holder of the visa be unable to enter Thailand within this period, Thai Embassies or Consulates generally will extend the visa for a period not exceeding the period of validity of the applicant's passport, nor exceeding a period of six months.

HEALTH REGULATIONS. Incoming visitors need an International Certificate of Health, showing a smallpox vaccination within the last three years. Yellow fever inoculations are required by persons coming from or going to contaminated areas; children less than a year old are excepted.

CUSTOMS. As with most countries, Thailand prohibits visitors bringing in illicit narcotic drugs and explicit pornography. Firearms require a permit from the Police Department. Goods that visitors may bring in duty free include 200 cigarettes, one liter of wine or spirits, a camera with 5 rolls of film and a reasonable amount of personal effects. Persons taking up residence in Thailand can bring in used household wares duty free. Used cars cannot be imported. Pet animals can usually be cleared through customs upon arrival at the airport. Visitors arriving by sea must apply to the Disease Control Division, Livestock Department, Ministry of Agriculture, Phaya Thai Road, Bangkok. Veterinary vaccination certificates are necessary.

Visitors are permitted to bring in any amount of foreign currency for personal use, but must fill in the currency declaration form. No one can take out foreign currency in excess of the amount shown on the customs declaration filed upon entry. As for Thai currency, no one can bring in or take out of Thailand more than 500 baht. Holders of family passports are permitted to export 1,000 baht.

GETTING THERE. The million visitors each year prove that Thailand is a focal point for Asian travel. Part of this popularity is due to the expanding transportation network which brings ever-greater ease of entry and exit.

By air. The great majority of visitors arrive and depart by air on no fewer than 35 international airlines, which have scheduled flights and chartered tours to Thailand. Bangkok's improved airport at Don Muang has done away with much of the ground lag that used to test one's patience. It is an hour's taxi ride to most areas in Bangkok, the fare of which costs 200 baht if you hire a private taxi outside the arrival lounge, or 150 baht if you walk out to the main road and flag one down yourself. A minibus will take you to your hotel for about 80 baht. Remember that the airport tax is 50 baht for outgoing passengers on international flights.

Although nearly all air passengers arrive and depart from Bangkok, there are at least two recommended alternative ways of entering the country by air. You can fly to Haadyai in South Thailand on Malaysian Airlines System (MAS) from Kuala Lumpur via Penang Island. Thai flies from Penang to the South Thailand island resort of Phuket and Hat Yai. Thai Airways, the domestic airline, then links Phuket and Haadyai to Bangkok and the major cities in the country, by using Boeing 737 aircrafts.

By road. Thailand is currently experiencing an automotive boom. Roads are being improved and extended into the more remote provinces; but aside from the southern road-links with Malaysia, Thailand is virtually road-locked.

At present there is no road access from or to Burma. The Burmese section is the only missing link in the Asian Highway stretching from Turkey to Singapore. If and when Burma opens its land frontiers, the point of entry will be at Mae Sot in the province of Tak.

There are three main roads crossing the Thai-Malaysian border in the South; inexpensive taxis and minibuses ply the routes between the major towns. Keep in mind when fixing your itinerary that the Malaysian border closes each day at 6.00 p.m.

By rail. If trains are your mode of travel, there are reliable rail ties between Singapore, Malaysia, and Thailand. For example, there is the two-day rail odyssey originating in Singapore, offering third-class sit-ups, second-class sleepers, and first-class air-conditioned compartments. Magic Arrow Express leaves Singapore Sunday, Tuesday, Thursday at 8:10 a.m. and arrives at Kuala Lumpur at 3:35 p.m. that afternoon. North Star Night Express then leaves Kuala Lumpur Sunday, Tuesday, and Thursday at 9:30 p.m. and arrives at Butterworth (on the mainland opposite Penang) at 6:47 a.m. the next morning. The International Express leaves Butterworth for Bangkok at 7:40 a.m. on Monday, Wednesday, and Friday and arrives in Bangkok within 24 hours.

There is a dayliner service between Butterworth and Haadyai in Thailand. There is no seat number on the ticket, however, so you may find yourself riding "second-class standing" for the four-hour trip. For the same price take a shared taxi instead.

On the east side of Malaysia you can take a train to Kota Bharu, do the short distance to the border by road, and meet the Thai railhead at Sungai Kolok.

By sea. In this day of hurried leisure, passenger liners are finding themselves in dire straits. Currently the only way to reach Bangkok by sea is by freighters, which generally make a point of providing excellent accommodation and food at a fare rather less than cruise ships. From Europe such companies as Ben Line Steamers, Polish Ocean Lines, and Nedloyd ship out to Bangkok. From the United States, Pacific Far East Line, American President Lines, and State Lines go to Bangkok. There are also many ships regularly sailing from Japan, Hong Kong, and Singapore. Inquire with local travel agents for schedules and fares.

WHEN YOU ARRIVE

WEATHER. Although Thailand is situated well within the tropics, there is a wide climatic range, depending on the time of the year and the part of the country. The Central Plains (which includes Bangkok), the hilly North, and the arid, flat Northeast share the same seasonal patterns. The hot season spans March, April, and May, although many foreign residents dispute that, because it is always hot throughout the year when it is not raining. Daytime temperatures in the hot season are in the 30°C (86°F) range and can reach 40 °C (104° F) especially in the North. In June the southwest monsoon ushers in the rainy season with slightly lower temperatures, but higher humidity. Many travelers unfamiliar with Asia have a misconception of the monsoon and expect months of unbroken cloudy, rainy weather. In Thailand the monsoon season amounts to five months of unpredictable weather — some days bring erratic rainstorms while other days are clear and sunny. November ushers in the cool season, particularly in the North where night temperatures can drop to 8°C (46°F). Bring a sweater or jacket if traveling there between November and February.

The long isthmus in South Thailand which straddles the Gulf of Thailand and the Indian Ocean has a climate similar to that of Malaysia — subtle seasonal variations with the weather generally warm, humid, and sunny all-year round; and rain is possible almost any time.

CLOTHING. Light and loose clothes are best suited to Thailand's climate most of the year. For the hot season, pack clothes that provide adequate protection from the direct sun; for the rainy season, clothes that dry quickly after a sudden downpour. For four months, from November to February, warmer clothes (at least a sweater and warm socks for the chilly nights) are necessary in the North and other hilly regions, as there is no central heating or even household fireplaces.

Bangkok is highly westernized in its business and social dress, with provincial centers following suit. At traditional ceremonies and formal gatherings, however, Thai women often prefer to don their ethnic silk costumes.

HYGIENE. In a country where people are as personally neat and cleanliness-conscious as the Thais, there are relatively few health hazards stemming directly from poor sanitation. In Bangkok most visitors will spend most of their time in air-conditioned hotel rooms, restaurants, stores, bars, and tour buses that are usually quite sanitary. For the more ambitious sightseer, Bangkok has certain little hazards (like most any other city of more than 5 million) which prove to be more unpleasant than unhealthy, such as the pungent smell of some stagnant canals and the noxious exhaust of cars and buses. Also, walking in Bangkok can often be dangerous, but you can greatly minimize the risk by staying on the sidewalks and crosswalks.

Tap water in Bangkok is considered relatively safe, but to be doubly-sure drink purified bottled water. Small shops and mobile vendors abound selling all sorts of cool drinks to quench your curiosity and thirst. Try them without worrying if the ice has been boiled; they are all *relatively* safe to drink.

Travelers who have never reckoned with the tropical sun should keep in mind that noon is not the wisest time to sunbathe as you will earn a burn in just fifteen minutes. Also, if you are out touring exposed to the elements, wear a straw hat or, if in the Chiang Mai area, carry a paper parasol. If you spend much time moving around in the sun (sweating a lot in the process) and start feeling a little weak and dizzy, you probably need more salt. Either carry salt tablets with you or do as the Thais do and mix salt in your lemonade or Coke. Visitors traveling upcountry (out of the Bangkok/Thonburi area) may encounter another minor malady. Since there is no familiar Western food in most provincial capitals and in any of the villages, the traveler may have to eat native Thai food which can have as many chili peppers in it as a salad has cucumbers. The result could be what the Thais call "walking stomach" (diarrhea).

Prevention: Eat Chinese food instead, more bland but less volatile, or ask for food without peppers. Cure: Take one or two Lomotil pills.

ELECTRICITY. Thailand operates on 220-volt, 50-cycle AC power. Most modern hotels will provide transformers for guests with 110-volt appliances. Upcountry, electrical outlets of any voltage are sometimes hard to come by, so travelers would be wise not to rely on electric shavers and hair dryers, but rather stay well stocked on razor blades and thick hair-drying towels.

CURRENCY. The unit of currency in Thailand is the *baht,* which is worth slightly more than four US cents (23 baht = US$1.00). The baht is divided into one hundred *satang;* coins are valued at 25 and 50 satang, and 1 and 5 baht. The 25-satang coin is called a *salehng* in small market dealings (6 salehngs = 1½ baht). Paper notes are valued at 10, 20, 100 and 500 baht.

If you have traveler's checks in American dollars, they can be cashed at banks in all provincial capitals. So there is no need to carry unmanageable amounts of baht notes with you when you travel outside of Bangkok. Traveler's checks in other currencies, however, are best cashed in Bangkok. As a rule, hotel exchange rates are lower than those offered by banks and authorized money changers.

The baht is pegged to a basket of currencies with the American dollar predominant. During the Vietnam war when thousands of American servicemen were stationed in Thailand U.S. coins and currency often were used around the large air force bases, but today Thai merchants are reluctant to accept anything but baht.

BUSINESS HOURS. As in most Asian countries, people like to begin the day early. In this way, they can beat the midday heat, having attended to important matters first thing in the day.

Government Offices. Most government offices are open Monday through Friday from 8:30 a.m. to 4:30 p.m. with a noon-to-one break for lunch. The best time to do business is generally as early as possible; the worst time is after 3.00 p.m.

Tourism Authority of Thailand (T.A.T.). The T.A.T. (near Boxing Stadium) is a government agency, and therefore its staff keeps government hours, with the exception of the Information Service which aids tourists Saturdays, Sundays, and holidays as well. The T.A.T. has branch offices in Pattaya, Phuket, Korat, Chiang Mai, Kanchanaburi, and Haadyai, and overseas in New York, Los Angeles, Tokyo, Sydney, Frankfurt, London, Paris and Singapore.

Banks. Monday through Friday, from 8:30 a.m. to 3:30 p.m.

Post Offices. The General Post Office or G.P.O. (*Prisanee glang*) on New Road and its branch facilities around Bangkok are open from 8:00 a.m. to 6:00 p.m. Monday through Friday, and 9:00 a.m. to 1:00 p.m. on Saturday, Sunday, and holidays. Telegrams and telephone calls can be arranged at the G.P.O. any time of the day or night. Upcountry post offices close at 4:30 p.m.

Retail Stores. Most stores stay open 12 hours a day seven days a week, but to be sure of a particular store's hours check first by phone. The only time of the year when shops close en masse for three or four days is during Chinese New Year.

COMMUNICATIONS. Thailand's postal system is reliable. All major hotels provide basic mail services on their premises. The General Post Office on New Road is open daily for mail (see "Business Hours" above), and the telecommunications section of the G.P.O. on the third floor is open round the clock every day.

THE MEDIA. Thailand is a modern country with a thriving press, radio, television, and film industry.

Press. Numerous dailies in Thai and Chinese serve Bangkok, and many more provincial newspapers are published every 10 days, to coincide with the results of the National Lottery. The main English dailies in Bangkok are the *Bangkok Post* and *The Nation*. The *Post* provides the best coverage of international events, while *The Nation* is best for Thai politics and syndicated columns.

Radio. The pace of Thai AM radio, to unattuned Western ears, is even more nerve-racking than that of most Western pop-radio. In some upcountry towns the single station broadcasts at four different frequencies; even hilltribe people of the North tote portable radios. The FM fare is generally better, with classical music, interviews, features, and the BBC news. Certainly the most program variety is found on the shortwave bands, where you can pick up Indian music, Vietnamese polemics, or the Voice of America, which also broadcasts world news in simplified English.

Television. Thailand was the first country in Southeast Asia to begin regular TV transmission, and since that epic day in 1955, the Thais have become no less hooked on this medium than citizens of more developed nations. The Thais produce their own soap operas, and broadcast as well Japanese, British, and American series, usually with the Thai soundtrack dubbed in. However, the English is often there for the listening on the FM radio, particularly for feature movies. Undoubtedly, sports draw the largest Thai viewing audience; the flickering cathode-ray tube becomes the community focal point every Saturday or Sunday afternoon. Those shops with TV's display them prominently and most anyone is welcome to come and watch.

Cinema. Thailand has a prosperous film industry supported by throngs of admiring fans. Most movies go to great lengths (2 hours plus) to include all variety of entertainment at one sitting: musical comedy, violent action, and romance. The same faces keep turning up, bigger than life, with familiar scripts and familiar roles. For example, when a certain popular actor was injured while filming a scene, production was halted on fourteen different movies he was making simultaneously. Although Thai feature films are generally slap-dash and slapstick, there have been several notable exceptions, which were well-received by resident foreigners and shown at international film festivals. In Bangkok, many American and European movies draw bigger crowds than Thai features. To comfortably accommodate the ever-burgeoning crowds of escapists, Thailand can rightly boast having some of the best cinemas anywhere, and at the best prices. Most foreign films are left with the original soundtrack, with Thai and Chinese subtitles added. Upcountry provincial capitals often have an English sound-room, at a distance that rarely lends enchantment — beyond the plate-glass window, the Thai audience is treated to a live Thai translation, done by a versatile fellow (and woman) sitting in the projection booth who can impersonate four or more different voices. For those who relish Chinese or Japanese "inner power" flicks, they abound throughout Thailand's movie world. Some theaters exclusively feature martial-arts epics on their marquees. Most have English subtitles.

COURTESY AND CUSTOM

Some customs are important to keep in mind during a visit to Thailand. The Thais are far too genial and easygoing to expect a *farang* ("foreigner") to observe all their ways, but here, as anywhere, it helps to have a few general ideas about the *dos and don'ts* of polite society.

Temples. Perhaps the one area (besides showing proper respect for the monarchy) where they *can* be sticky is regarding behavior in a temple. Visitors are required to remove their shoes before entering the building containing the principal Buddha image, which is the one where people will be sitting about the floor paying homage to the Buddha. Women are not allowed in the monks' quarters, nor should they hand anything directly to a monk. (Should the occasion arise when a woman *has* to give something to a monk and no man is around to perform the service, she places the object on a table or on the ground and then the monk is free to pick it up for himself.) What few unpleasant incidents there have been involving foreigners in *wats* have arisen because the Thais felt some deliberate insult had been given to their religion. One, a few years ago, came about when some visitors to the ruins of Sukhothai were photographed sitting on the head of a huge Buddha image — a double insult actually, since the head is considered the most sacred part of the body. Another resulted from a singularly insensitive team of fashion models who not only posed provocatively but even changed their clothes in the compound of Wat Phra Keo.

Greetings. When Thais meet one another, they do not usually shake hands. The customary greeting is the *wai*, with the hands raised as if in prayer. Traditionally, the higher the hands are held the more respectful is the *wai*, so that by observing two people you can tell theoretically their respective ranks. But rank is a complicated matter in Thailand, involving, as it does, such things as age, occupation, and social position. For an outsider, it is enough to make the gesture.

As the feet are the lowest part of the body, it is considered rude in Thailand to point your feet at anybody, especially if the gesture is deliberate. Most Thais strive mightily to avoid doing so even accidentally, and as a result you seldom see people with their legs crossed, or if they are, they tend to keep the toes pointed carefully toward the floor.

Dress. Thais are extremely neat in their appearance, and even in a slum it is rare to see anyone who is really dirty or unkempt; mechanics, covered with grease and grime at the end of the day, emerge from their evening bath as spotless as if they had never come within reach of an engine. (All Thais bathe at least once a day and usually twice.) To say that someone is *mai rieb-roi* ("not neat") is almost as serious as saying that he is *mai suparb* ("not polite"), and very often it is the same thing; disorderliness can be regarded as rude in certain circumstances. Although among some younger, westernized Thais — the kind you see roaming about Bangkok shopping centers — it is considered smart (*sa-mart*) to dress in the loose, semi-hippie garb of Western teenagers, to the great majority of the population it is simply *mai rieb-roi*. Similarly, to conservative Thais, there are polite and impolite colors — a brightly colored dress is acceptable on a young girl but not on an older woman, who ought to wear somber shades or pastels. (There are even certain colors for certain days; Sunday, for example, is the only day on which almost anyone can wear red without being considered *mai-suparb* in the extreme.) As a general rule, of course, foreign visitors are not included in all these strictures, and as long as you look reasonably presentable (even in a *mai-suparb* color) you are not likely to get a second look on the street. It *is* frowned upon, however, for a woman to wear shorts in public particularly in a temple, or to show too much of the rest of her body either for that matter.

In Public. It is common to see two Thai men holding hands as they walk along the street — a sign, incidentally, of simple friendship; nothing else — but very rare to see a man and woman doing it, for public displays of affection between the sexes is an old and strong taboo. During the Vietnam war, when Bangkok was a major rest and recreation center for thousands of American servicemen, one of the most frequent criticisms leveled at them was their public behavior with bar girls, innocent though most of it was by American standards. The experience has left many well-bred Thai girls wary about even being seen with a *farang*, for fear she will be held in contempt by others.

Names. Surnames are a relatively recent innovation in Thailand, having been introduced only fifty-odd years ago during the reign of King Rama VI. Before that, people were called simply by a single name, followed by an explanation, if necessary, such as "son of . . ." or "from the town of . . ." Even today the average Thai last name is usually so long and complex that it is seldom used; thus Mr.

Kraisri Nimmanahsominda is called, simply, Mr. Kraisri. *Khun*, in Thai, is the equivalent of either Mr. or Miss or Mrs., and is used for both men and women. You may encounter titles of Thai royalty, which in descending order are Mom Chao (M.C.), Mom Rajawong (M.R.), Mom Luang (M.L.).

Expressions: Three Thai expressions, Thai soul talk in fact, to remember: *mai pen rai*, *pai-tio*, *sanuk*. None of them can be translated into English with great precision, but all of them are important to understanding the Thai heart and character.

Mai pen rai is usually rendered into English as "never mind," and in many cases this seems a fair enough translation. You forget something you said you would do for a friend and he responds to your apologies with *mai pen rai*, meaning, "Don't worry about it; it doesn't matter; stay cool." But *mai pen rai*, as more than one writer on Thailand has pointed out, suggests a state of mind as well as a specific reaction to a situation. In that sense, it can be seen as an extension of the Buddhist philosophy — a shrugging off of the unimportant, the merely transient. To a certain, rigid kind of Western mind it can be an exasperating attitude, particularly when applied to matters he regards as important. But to others it is an essential part of the relaxed atmosphere of Thailand — the reluctance to get overexcited about things (certainly things one cannot do anything about, such as making a late train hurry or a canceled flight airborne), the tendency to accept difficulties casually, the preference for laughter over tears.

Sanuk means "fun," but as in the case of *mai pen rai* this literal translation gives only a shadow of its real extended meaning and the role it plays in Thai life. The Thai love of *sanuk*, their *joie de vivre*, is deep-rooted and irrepressible and pervades almost every aspect of their daily existence. Without really thinking, they tend automatically to divide the experiences of life into those that are *sanuk* and those that are not, or *mai sanuk*; and to classify something in the latter category is a very grave criticism indeed. Going *pai-tio* is *sanuk*. So is going to a movie, to a festival, to a wedding, to visit an old friend, to have a bowl of noodles at a good restaurant, almost any kind of trip. Work, on the other hand, is not *sanuk*, at least not if it is totally unrelieved and — most damning criticism of all — "serious." A highly qualified lecturer arrived a few years ago to take up a post at one of Thailand's leading universities. On paper, and in fact, he was an acknowledged authority on his subject, which

he had taught successfully in several famous institutions abroad. He bombed in Thailand almost from the start because his students, with pitiless accuracy, labeled him as *mai sanuk*. "He just *taught*," one of them said later, after the professor had left in total bewilderment. "He didn't even smile." A Japanese manufacturing company ran into the same opposition when it tried to duplicate the efficient, production-line techniques that worked so well back home; the Thai workers became "bored" (another devastating term of criticism) with the unrelieved routine, and since boredom is very definitely *mai sanuk* the plant came perilously close to disaster. It was only when they injected a little *sanuk* into the process — piped-in music, snack breaks, games between various departments — that things began to take a turn for the better.

The Thai fondness for *sanuk* does not, as some outsiders may mistakenly conclude, indicate a frivolous mentality, a refusal to face up to the less palatable realities of life; rather, it reveals an ingrained sense of joy, without which life for the Thais would be a drab and meaningless affair. They are willing to work hard when it is necessary (look at the labor gangs along the roads, where women are carrying the same loads as men under the sweltering sun), and to fight bravely, too, in emergencies (visit one of the military hospitals and see the soldiers wounded in battles against Communist insurgents in the South); but they see no point in either work or fighting that is devoid of joy — those road workers, as likely as not, will be cracking jokes and devising small but vital ways to make the labor a little less of a routine.

Pai-tio reflects another aspect of Thai life, one much less readily translatable. Generally speaking, to *pai-tio* means to go for a stroll, to wander about with no particular aim, to go see what's up, to take the evening air, to stand around a movie theater and watch people — but already the possibilities, the variations, stretch into infinity. It may be best to put it this way: whenever you see Thais on foot outside their homes or places of work, unless they are walking *very* purposefully the chances are that they are going *pai-tio*. Outside of a monastery, the desire for solitude mystifies Thais, who delight in putting on their best clothes and going to some public place to observe the activity. A foreigner who expressed surprise at the crowded movie theaters in Thailand despite the television antennas that loom over almost every house was told, "But you can't *see* people at home." To see people, you have to go *pai-tio*. Places to *pai-tio* vary in quality.

The most traditional are the marketplaces, where almost everybody goes to buy or just to look; in Bangkok, on Saturday and Sunday (the most popular *pai-tio* days), the great Weekend Market in the oval field across from the Temple of the Emerald Buddha is crowded with people, the great majority of whom are simply there to *pai-tio*.

Conversation. Finally, a word should be said about the avid curiosity of Thais concerning subjects that are not normally regarded as suitable topics of conversation in most Western countries. Not long after meeting you, for instance, a Thai friend might suddenly inquire, "How much did that shirt cost?" Or how large your salary is; or how old you are; or whether you are married and, if not, why. Such questions, personal as they may sound, are not regarded as rude but as simply a way of showing interest; they would ask the same questions of another Thai. You are not necessarily required to give correct answers, or any answer at all as long as you accompany your refusal with a friendly smile to show that you have not been offended. One *farang* resident of Bangkok has worked out a standard reply to questions about his salary. He simply smiles and says, "Not enough."

FESTIVALS & FAIRS

The ceaseless pursuit of *sanuk* in Thailand guarantees a plenitude of festivals, fairs, seasonal sports, and similar pleasures, as well as a number of more solemn religious ceremonies. The greatest concentration of these comes in the cool season, from November through February, but something or other is going on most months of the year.

Most of Thailand's annual events, especially religious holidays, are determined by the Thai lunar calendar. Therefore it is impossible to provide exact dates for these happenings well in advance. (The Tourist Organization of Thailand does publish each year a revised calendar of festivals.) Thailand has adopted the Western calendar for official purposes, but the years are still numbered as well according to the Buddhist Era, which began in 543 B.C. So A.D. 1977 is the year B.E. 2520. The following is a list of some of the annual highlights to look for on your visit.

JANUARY

New Year's Eve and Day are official holidays; as in the West the night of the 31st is a time for celebration. In Bangkok, all the leading hotels stage some sort of festivity, usually of the paper-hat-and-noisemaker variety. But if you want to join celebrating Thais go either to Khao Din (Dusit) Zoo or to Sanam Luang, the big field across from the Temple of the Emerald Buddha. A word of caution about the latter: the pushing, squeezing, and general high spirits can get fairly enthusiastic if you go into the middle of the crowd and it may not appeal to the sedate and fainthearted.

Outside Bangkok, Chiang Mai is the best place for New Year's, for there is a three-day **Winter Fair** with gala parades, beauty contests, and all sorts of northern amusements.

Usually held in January — though sometimes in February, depending on the organizing committee — is the **Red Cross Fair**, normally opened by the king and queen, in Amporn Gardens near the old Parliament building. There are stalls operated by foreign embassies, Thai film stars, government departments, and various universities, as well as performances of folk and classical dancing and other nightly entertainment. All proceeds go to the Thai Red Cross, whose honorary president is the queen.

FEBRUARY

Maka Puja, an important Buddhist holiday, is celebrated toward the end of this month, depending on the moon. It commemorates the miraculous occasion when 1,250 of the Buddha's disciples gathered without prior arrangement to hear him preach. On this day Thai temples are crowded, and the faithful gain merit by such acts as releasing caged birds. The day's ceremonies culminate in a candlelight procession around the *bot*, the main temple building.

Chinese New Year falls on the first day of the first Chinese lunar month, usually in February. No gay celebrations fill the streets as in other countries. For Thailand's several million Chinese the occasion calls for family reunions, feasts, gift giving, and the only time-out all year from the paramount matters of business. Most Chinese shops close for three or four days. Chinese Buddhist temples, near Yaowaraj Road in Bangkok and in Thonburi, are crowded with devotees, offering prayers for good fortune.

Phra Buddhabaht Festival finds Budhist devotees flocking to the Shrine of the Holy Footprint near Saraburi, 136 km north of Bangkok. Originally built in the 16th century, the famed shrine annually attracts pilgrims who flock to honor what is believed to be a genuine footprint of the Buddha. According to legend, a hunter discovered the footprint filled with water which had miraculous curative power.

apa**photo**agency

The photographs in the "Insight Guides" series are available from the Apa Photo Agency library for travel promotion, calendars, display prints, advertising and editorial illustration.

Call, write or telex us.

From Bangkok, fly Kuwait Airways and enjoy real Arabian hospitality, Western style.

On board our luxury flights from Bangkok to Kuwait you'll enjoy international standards of comfort, cuisine and considerate service — with friendly hospitality that is part of our tradition.

Enjoy such hospitality wherever your business takes you. Our fast, frequent connections from our magnificent new terminal in Kuwait fly you to the major centres of the Gulf and Middle East, and on to Europe and New York.

Kuwait Airways now serves 43 destinations on 4 continents. Plan your next trip with us. You owe it to yourself.

KUWAIT AIRWAYS

You owe it to yourself to try us

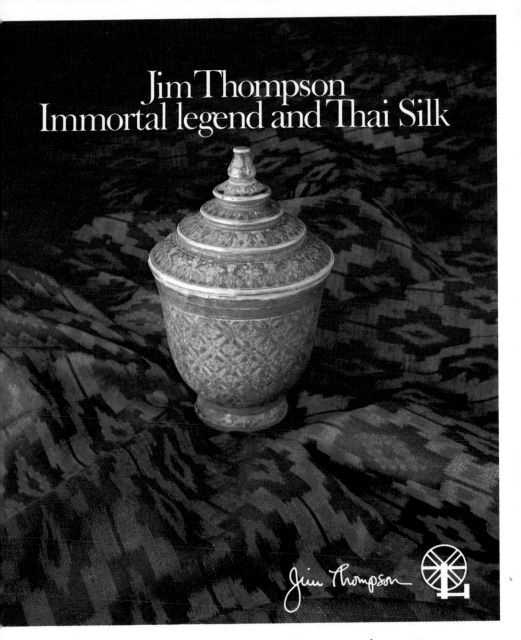

Jim Thompson
Immortal legend and Thai Silk

Bencharong, or "five colors", are Thai pentachromatic
porcelains, first hand produced in the 17th century, like this exhibit
at Jim Thompson's House on the Klong.
The art of making silk is as old as Thailand. It takes hours and
many talented hands to produce one yard of this precious fabric
at Jim Thompson's. The immortal legend lives on.

Jim Thompson Thai Silk Company
9 Surawong Road, Bangkok, Thailand. Tel. 234-4900

MARCH

There is no official holiday in March, but this month (and April, too) happens to be the best time for **Kite Flying** because of the breezes that spring up nearly every afternoon on even the hottest days. In Bangkok there are official kite-fights every weekday afternoon from 4:30 until dusk at Sanam Luang. Restaurants are set up on the Thammasat University side of the field, and for the price of a beer or a soft drink you can relax in deck chairs and watch the overhead activity.

APRIL

Chakri Day on 6 April is a national holiday which commemorates the founding of the Chakri dynasty of which the current ruling monarch is the ninth king. People take flowers and incense to the Temple of the Emerald Buddha to pay respect to former kings of the dynasty. The Pantheon, a building on the temple grounds adjoining the Grand Palace, housing the statues of each king, is open to the public only on this day of the year.

The highlight of this month is **Songkran**, the old Thai New Year, which takes place between the 13th and the 15th. Songkran is essentially a religious holiday, marking the beginning of the Buddhist year. Traditional Thais observe it by going to temple, sprinkling water on Buddha images, and giving their houses a thorough cleaning. However, over the years decidedly secular manifestations have been added to the holiday, the principal one being the freedom to throw water on anyone who happens to be passing by — not altogether unwelcome, if you are prepared for it, since April is the hottest month of the Thai year. Everyone is fair game for a sudden drenching, especially in Chiang Mai, where many of the old traditions are still observed. Such carefree water throwing is uncommon in Bangkok, but a popular place near the capital is at Phra Pradaeng, down near the mouth of the Chao Phya River. It is best to go to Phra Pradaeng by boat, since the road traffic gets congested; once there, you will see parades, boat races, and folk dances — and also probably come back soaking wet.

MAY

Coronation Day on the 5th is a national holiday marking the anniversary of the coronation of His Majesty King Bhumibol Adulyadej. Inside the Royal Chapel of the Grand Palace, high-ranking government officials pay their respects to the king.

The Ploughing Ceremony takes place around the middle of this month in Sanam Luang in Bangkok. As previously noted, this is a basically Hindu ceremony celebrating the beginning of the rice-planting season; seeds that have been blessed are ritualistically sown, and the coming harvest is predicted by Brahman priests.

Visakha Puja, another important Buddhist holiday, comes on the full moon day of the sixth lunar month, which usually falls in May. Perhaps the most sacred of all Buddhist days, this celebrates the birth, death, and enlightenment of the Buddha. In the evening at nearly every temple, there are processions of people carrying candles; one of the loveliest of all Thai festivals.

JULY

Asalaha Puja marks the beginning of **Buddhist Lent** *(Khao Pansa)* — three months during which monks must remain in their temples and strictly observe their religious duties. It is also the time that most young Thai men choose to enter a monastery for a temporary stay that may last anywhere from a week to the full three months; and almost anywhere you go in Thailand you will come across a *buat naag*, or "ordination ceremony." As with so many Thai ceremonies, this is a combination of the high-spirited (on the eve of his ordination the novice customarily gives a festive party for all his friends) and the deeply religious (he exchanges his white supplicant's robes for the priest's saffron ones, thereby bidding symbolic farewell to the world which can be deeply moving).

The Buddhist Lent period also marks a temporary halt to most festivals in Thailand, for these are the rainiest months and it is risky to schedule outdoor events until the cool season starts and the rains stop.

AUGUST

The **Queen's Birthday** on the 12th is a public holiday throughout Thailand, when Her Majesty Queen Sirikit makes offerings to monks at Chitralada Palace and attends various religious ceremonies.

OCTOBER

Ok Pansa, during this month, is the end of Buddhist Lent and the beginning of the *kathin* season. *Kathin*s are ceremonies in which groups of people go to various temples to present robes and other gifts to the resident monks. All over the country you see supplicants along the roads, either in buses or on foot, usually accompanied by music and dancing. The most spectacular of all *kathin*s in the past was when the king went by river in the gilded royal barges to Wat Arun, but this has not been held for years due to the condition of the barges; plans have been announced, however, to revive it in the near future, and if this comes about visitors will be able to see one of the world's truly great spectacles.

The 23rd of this month is **Chulalongkorn Day**, commemorating the death of King Rama V. Thousands of people go on this day to his statue in front of the old Parliament building to lay wreaths in homage to his memory.

NOVEMBER

This is the best of all festival months in Thailand with various fairs, large and small, going on all over the country. One of the most beautiful is **Loy Krathong**, which takes place on the night of the full moon of the twelfth lunar month, the exact date of which varies each year. A *krathong*, traditionally, is a small, lotus-shaped boat containing a candle, incense sticks, and often a coin; both adults and children place them in the rivers and canals to honor the water spirits and, some believe, carry away their sins. The best places in Bangkok to enjoy this charming celebration are on the river, along Klong Saen Sap (the one that runs behind the British Embassy), or around the lakes at Khao Din Zoo and Lumpini Park. Thousands of people from all over the country also go to Chiang Mai for Loy Krathong, where it is a city-wide festival; the Ping River that runs through the middle of Chiang Mai is a magical sight as countless *krathong*s, some of them huge, elaborate affairs, drift downstream twinkling along the dark waters.

The **Golden Mount Fair** is another major November event in Bangkok. Around Wat Sakhet are dozens of little food stalls, open-air theaters, and shops; and the Golden Mount is alive with light as people carry candles in a procession to the top.

Close to the time of Loy Krathong is the Hindu celebration called **Deepavali**, or the Festival of Lights. At this time most of the Hindus in Bangkok, and many from the countryside, come to the ornate little Indian temple on Silom Road in Bangkok to watch various entertainments, including feats of self-mutilation performed by pious zealots.

Also around Loy Krathong time is the large, six-day **Phra Pathom Chedi Fair** in Nakhon Pathom, west of Bangkok (less than an hour's drive). This takes place at the largest *chedi*, or pagoda, in Thailand, and people come from all over to this fair, regarded as one of the best of the year.

Some time in November is the **Elephant Roundup**, staged by the Tourist Organization of Thailand and the local government of Surin Province, at which hundreds of elephants put on a spectacular show that has become a great favorite with tourists. Special air-conditioned trains make the overnight trip from Bangkok to Surin, and sheltered viewing stands and an English commentary are provided for ticket-holders.

Also of possible interest is the **Trooping of the Colors** on the 8th, when contingents of the army, navy, and air force parade in review at Bangkok's Royal Plaza often before the king.

DECEMBER

The King's Birthday on 5 December is a national holiday, and most of Bangkok is decorated with colored lights, flags, and portraits of the king in honor of the occasion. The best places to enjoy the decorations are along Rajadamnern Avenue and around the Grand Palace.

Christmas is not celebrated in Thailand, except by the tourist hotels, the few Thai Christians, and of course many members of the foreign community.

SHOPPING TIPS

Shopping is a pleasure, not only because of the variety of things to buy but also, nowadays, because of the ubiquity of Bangkok's air-conditioned shopping centers where it is possible to get a good deal of your buying done without being laid out by the heat. The following are some of the things Thailand is noted for, both the quality and the price, in most cases, being superior to anywhere else.

Thai fabrics. Thai silk is too well known to need any introduction; suffice to say that it is here, in quantity, in assorted weights, in meters, or made up into clothes and other items. It may, however, be useful to note that the quality of silk is not always uniform, and in some shops that offer suspiciously good bargains, the cloth may have been cleverly interwoven with rayon or some other synthetic; stick to the better-known shops unless you are good at telling. Handwoven Thai cotton is less famous and unjustly so, for it is a soft but durable material that is wonderful for dresses, upholstery, and other uses. In many shops you can get the cotton in the same colors and prints as the silk, at around 40 to 50 baht a meter.

Jewelry. Gold in Thailand is considerably cheaper than in Europe or the United States, and the craft of making modern jewelry — as distinct from the traditional Thai designs — has progressed to the point where many tourists now rank Bangkok ahead of Hong Kong. Best buy among native stones is the sapphire, blue or black, star or plain; also you can sometimes find good rubies from Cambodia and Burma. Most stones are less expensive than in the West. For something different, look at the Thai princess ring, which has nine tiers set with nine different precious and semi-precious stones.

Handicrafts. If you are going to Chiang Mai, where most of the Thai handicrafts come from, wait and buy them there. Otherwise, look for the hilltribe embroidery, lacquerware, painted umbrellas, wood carvings, basketwork, and delightful fish mobiles made of woven bamboo which Thai mothers hang over cribs as pacifiers. The government-sponsored Narayana Phand, on Larn Luang Road in Bangkok is a good place to buy most of these.

Celadon. This was originally made in Thailand during the Sukhothai period, died out, and was revived about 20 years ago, Vases and lamp bases are a good buy; complete dinner sets are also available as well as a variety of souvenir pieces.

Dolls. For collectors, there is a wide selection in classical dance costumes or depicting the various hilltribes of the North.

Bronzeware. Long one of the most popular buys with tourists, bronzeware now comes in plain, modern designs as well as the traditional Thai ones. You can get everything in it from complete cutlery sets to salad bowls; look also for bronze temple bells to hang on a terrace or patio. At several shops you can get bronzeware that has been siliconized so that it will not tarnish.

Spirit Houses. There are some charming ones in the shape of little Thai-style houses which are not too bulky to send or carry.

Antiques. Read the section on Bangkok's Nakorn Kasem in Chinatown for added information on these. Best buys are Chinese porcelains and furniture, carvings from Thai temples, Sawankhalok (a porcelain made near Sukhothai in the 14th century), old Thai paintings, silver betel-nut boxes, Burmese tapestries and wooden figures. Fakes abound, especially in Buddha images, so know what you are doing or go to the best shops. For most Buddhist art of Thailand, a permit is required from the Fine Arts Department before the pieces can be taken out of the country. The good shops will take care of this complicated job for you.

RECOMMENDED READING

1. *A History of Siam*, by W.A.R. Wood (Chalermnit Press; Bangkok). The first complete history of the country and still the best, especially for the early periods up until the 1932 revolution.
2. *Lords of Life*, by Prince Chula Chakrabongse (Alvin Redman; London). A study of the Chakris by Chulalongkorn's grandson.
3. *Essay on Thai Folklore,* by Phya Anuman Rajadhon (DK Books, Bangkok). A study of Thai culture, language and religious festivals.
4. *The Culture of South-East Asia*, by Reginald le May (George Allen & Unwin; London). Good general introduction to the Buddhist art of Thailand and Cambodia.
5. *1688: Revolution in Siam,* by E.W. Hutchinson (Hong Kong University Press). An account of a critical period in the history of Ayuthaya, with a good account of the Greek adventurer Constantine Phaulkon.
6. *Everyday Life in Thailand,* by Niels Mulder (DK Books, Bangkok). Excellent analysis of Thai values as reflected in daily social life.
7. *King Mongkut of Siam*, by John Blofeld (Asia Pacific Press; Singapore). Biography of one of Thailand's most remarkable kings, the original of *The King and I.*
8. *Ten Lives of the Buddha*, by Elizabeth Wray, Clare Rosenfield, Dorothy Baily, and Joe Wray (Weatherhill; Tokyo). Handsome picture book on traditional Thai paintings that tell the Jataka stories; the only real book available on Thai painting so far.
9. *Nine Temples of Bangkok*, by Helen Bruce (Chalermnit; Bangkok). An examination of some of Bangkok's leading temples, including Wat Phra Keo and Wat Po.
10. *Mai Pen Rai*, by Carol Hollinger (Houghton Mifflin; Boston). What it was like to live in Bangkok as an American wife in the late 1950s. Don't be put off by the subject matter; it is both funny and informative.
11. *The Legendary American*, by William Warren (Houghton Mifflin; Boston). An account of the career and strange disappearance of Jim Thompson, the man who made Thai silk into an industry.
12. *The House on the Klong*, text by William Warren, pictures by Brian Brake (Weatherhill; Tokyo). The Jim Thompson House and art collection, in color,
13. *Gardening in Bangkok*, by Pimsai Amranand (Siam Society; Bangkok). What the title says, plus many pictures of exotic plants.
14. *Bird Guide of Thailand*, by Boonsong Lekagul and Edward Cronin (Kuruspha; Bangkok). Hundreds of color drawings.

THAI FOODS

"Thai foods," an expert on the subject writes, without mincing words, "are very, very hot." If you find a Thai cook pondering over a simmering pot of *gaeng pet*, "hot curry," chances are you will catch her resolutely adding another handful of tiny green chilies, called in Thai *prik kee nu*, a single one of which would be enough to blast the average *farang* out of his chair.

Not all Thai foods are so hot, of course. There is a wide range of native sweets, including delicate custards in ripe coconut and sugary confections wrapped in banana leaves, as well as a number of only moderately seasoned noodle dishes; but the fundamental fact remains that the Thais like their food highly spiced, especially the curries. A half dozen or so different kinds of chilies are used with what may appear to the uninitiated as abandonment, the hottest of all being a deceptively pretty little orange one called *prik kee nu luang*. Restaurants catering to foreign tourists have learned their lesson and produce a kind of watered-down version that Thais regard with undisguised amusement.

Actually, curry is only one small part of Thai cuisine, which, on closer acquaintance, reveals itself as immensely varied and complex — so complex, indeed, in its proper preparations that you rarely get it in restaurants, which generally offer only basic dishes and Thai-Chinese concoctions. Aside from chilies, the basic seasoning of Thai food are coriander (fresh and sprinkled on nearly everything), garlic, basil, cardamom, and a small, round, pealike vegetable that is a form of eggplant. There are also a number of basic sauces that appear at every dinner, the most essential being *nam pla*, or fish sauce,

Since the majority of Thai dishes are either soft or soupy, chopsticks are not used at a Thai dinner; a large spoon and a fork are usually the only utensils provided, the fork being used to push the food onto the spoon. A large platter of rice is the mainstay of the meal, with five or six smaller bowls of curry, vegetables, fish, soup, and the like set around it. You put a pile of rice in the middle of your plate and then add a little of each dish to it.

The different regions of Thailand have their own distinctive cuisines, and while certain basic dishes are similar there are many variations. Chiang Mai food, for example, is milder than that of the Central Plains where glutinous rice (eaten by hand) is usually included. In the South, curries predominate. Northeasterners enjoy a number of

specialties that may give fastidious *farang* eaters cause for thought, like pig's head and frog curry, but many Thais insist that cooking in the Northeast is the best in the country.

Eating in Bangkok. The problem of eating in Bangkok, as one gourmet has observed, is not so much where as what. The city probably has a more diversified selection of restaurants than any other capital in Asia, with the possible exception of Tokyo, with a range running from cheeseburgers to sukiyaki and almost everything in between. Within a relatively small area you can eat Mexican, French, German, Italian, Scandinavian, Hungarian, Japanese, Vietnamese, Korean, English, American, Laotian, Filipino, Indian, Indonesian, Swiss, Burmese, and Austrian — and not, in most cases, vague approximations but the real thing, prepared by cooks from the country in question. Half a dozen provinces of China are represented, from bland Cantonese to spicy Szechuanese, offering not only such splendors as Peking Duck but esoteric oddities like duck tongues and chicken breast stuffed with bird's nest.

You can dine on Central, Northern, Southern, and Northeastern Thai food, either in fairly basic surroundings or in lavish, air-conditioned comfort while watching a show of folk and classical dancing. Your hotel bookshop will probably have a number of restaurant guides to help you make a choice; one that is recommended is *Eating Out In Bangkok* by Harry Rolnick, a highly personal but dependable compilation by a long-time resident of Bangkok.

Except for weekends, reservations are usually unnecessary, even at the fanciest restaurants; only one hotel restaurant requires a jacket and tie.

Roadside Kitchens. Inveterate snackers, Thais like to eat when the mood strikes them, at almost any hour of the day or night. Their philosophy regarding food is, quite simply, "Eat when you are hungry." Wherever you go in Thailand you will see them around a noodle vendor's bicycle or at one of the temporary sidewalk stalls that spring up as if by magic wherever people are likely to be working or passing by — eating a bowl of rice noodles garnished with a bit of fried meat and coriander, a delicate little pancake folded around a sugary sweet, or a deep-fried banana fritter.

These portable kitchens, using only the basics in equipment — usually only a brazier of charcoal and a few pots and pans — turn out culinary delights remarkably complex by any standards.

A THAI MENU

Appetizers

peanuts	*tua*
cashews	*met mamuang himmapan*
salty dried beef	*nua sawan*
crispy pork skin	*kaab muu*
crispy noodles	*mee krob*
deep-fried shrimp	*gung tawt krob*
shrimp chips	*khao kriep gung*
barbecued pork	*muu satay*
spring rolls	*poh pia*

Soups and Noodles

rice soup (with chicken pork, shrimp, or egg)	*kow tom*
rice porridge (with chicken and shredded ginger—egg optional)	*jok*
clear soup (with celery and bean curd)	*tom juut*
lemon shrimp soup	*tom yaam gung*
wanton soup	*geo nam*
white-noodle soup (with fish balls, pork, chicken, or duck)	*kwit-teo nam* (*luuk chin, muu, gy, pet*)
yellow-noodle soup	*bami nam*
hot white noodles	*kwit-teo hehng*
dry yellow noodles	*bami hehng*
crispy yellow noodles	*mii grawp*
fried wanton with greens	*geo raat naa*
fried white noodles	*kwit-teo raat naa*
fried yellow noodles	*bami raat naa*
fried noodles (with egg and bean sprouts)	*kwit-teo pat ty*

Rice

dry white rice	*kow plow*
Chinese rice soup	*kow tom plow*
sticky rice	*kow neo*
fried rice with shrimp and vegetables	*kow pat gung*
fried rice with pork	*kow pat mu*
fried rice with egg	*kow pat ky dow raat naa*

Main Dishes

omelette with pork	*ky yat sy*
sweet and sour (chicken, pork, fish, shrimp)	*preo waan* (*gy, muu, pla, gung*)
barbecued chicken	*gy yaang*
deep-fried chicken	*gy tawt*
sliced chicken and rice	*kow man gy*
fried chicken and cashews	*gy pat met mamuang*
fried chicken with mint and cloves	*gy pat by gaprow*
Thai chicken curry	*gaeng gy*
Indian chicken curry	*gaeng garii*
beef in oyster sauce	*nua pat namman hoy*
ginger beef	*nua pat king*
partly boiled egg with seasoning	*kai luak*

Sauces and Spices

fish sauce (substitute for salt)	*nam pla*
light soy sauce	*nam sii iw kow*
dark soy sauce	*nam sii iw dam*
red spicy sauce	*nam prik*
sweet plum sauce	*nam buay wan*
vinegar with chilies	*nam som*
dried chili flakes	*prik kee nu bon*
salt	*glua*
black pepper	*prik ty*
ginger	*king*
garlic	*gratiam*
curry	*gaeng*

Sweets (*Kanom*)

sticky rice baked in bamboo	*kow laam*
mango and sticky rice with coconut sauce	*kow neo mamuang*
brown sticky rice	*kow neo deng*
banana fritters	*gluay tawt*
bananas in sweet coconut milk	*gluay buad chee*
egg custard	*kanom maw gang*
Chinese tarts	*kanom pia*
peanut brittle	*tua dut*
fruit, beans, or jelly with sweet juice and shaved ice	*tubtim krab*

Drinks.

to take out	*sy tung*
ice water	*nam yen*
cold Chinese tea	*nam keng plow*
hot Chinese tea	*nam cha rawn*
iced tea with sugar	*cha dam yen*
iced tea with lemon	*cha manow*
hot tea with sweet milk	*cha rawn*
hot pekoe tea with lemon	*cha rawn kab manow*
iced black sweet coffee (Chinese)	*o-liang*
iced Thai coffee with sweet milk	*gafeh yen*
hot Thai coffee with sweet milk	*gafeh rawn*
instant coffee	*nesgafeh*
hot ovaltine with sweet milk	*owaltin rawn*
iced ovaltine	*owaltin yen*
bottled soybean milk	*wytamilk*
fresh milk	*nom sot*
iced lemonade with salt	*nam manow*
iced lemonade without salt	*nam manow* (*my sy glua*)
fresh orange	*nam som sot*
coconut milk	*nammaprow*

THE THAI LANGUAGE

History. When the first Thais began emigrating from southern China to North Thailand, they naturally brought language with them. Akin to Chinese, their words were tonal and monosyllabic. However, as the Thais moved south into the Central Plains they conquered and merged with the Mons and Khmers thereby absorbing certain words of their languages. Perhaps the most radical changes occurred when the Thai language borrowed elements from Sanskrit and Pali, ancient languages of India that Buddhist monks had introduced to the Mons and Khmers. These languages of the scriptures are nontonal and polysyllabic and their influences are today most evident in the complicated grammar of literary Thai. Sanskrit, Pali, and Khmer are the primary sources of a special vocabulary called *rachasap* — the Thai court language used in the presence of royalty. Interestingly, those royal words which are of Khmer origin are at present in common use in Cambodia. Thai language has also been influenced to a lesser extent by the Malays and immigrant Chinese.

The Thais have had an alphabet since A.D. 1283, when Ramkamhaeng of the Sukhothai dynasty instituted a writing system modeled by an Indian one with Khmer characters. The modern Thai alphabet has 44 consonants, 24 vowels, and four diacritical tone marks. Thai is written from left to right.

Dialects. Each of Thailand's four main regions has its own dialect: Northern Thai, Northeastern Thai (Lao), Central Thai (with several subdialects), and Southern Thai. They are almost as different from each other as are the Romance languages, Spanish, Portuguese, and Italian. However, standard Thai, a synthesis of central dialects, is the one language taught in schools throughout the country and recognized as the official government medium.

Grammar. Spoken Thai in all regions is grammatically simple in comparison with European languages. Each word is complete in itself — there are no prefixes or suffixes, no genders for nouns, no articles, no plurals, and no verb conjugations of any kind. There are no set rules making Thai words belong to a particular part of speech, so a word may be used as a noun, verb, adjective, or adverb, depending upon its position in the sentence.

Verb tenses are indicated (if at all) by several fixed auxiliaries before the verb: *ja* for the future, and *gamlang* (meaning "energy") for the present continuous. The past tense is usually indicated by a time phrase.

The basic word order of a sentence is subject-verb-object, with modifiers following each appropriate word. For instance: "He (*kow*) eats (*gin*) rice (*kow*) fried (*pat*)."

In the case of question tags, such as "There isn't much time, is there?" a Thai will often respond to the form with "Yes," while an English speaker would respond to the *meaning* with "No." So double-check such answers, if you are not sure.

Lyrics. Many common Thai words when translated literally bespeak a muse or a minstrel. Some examples:

spirit's clothes = butterfly
slow forest = cemetery
sky cries out = thunder
sky fire = electricity
walking stomach = diarrhea
rice scarce and fruit dear = famine

Tones. Tones were originally adopted to differentiate between identical monosyllabic words. Without tones, the meaning of *my my my my*? could be little more than emotive; but giving each word a separate tone, and thus a meaning of its own, makes the sentence clearly ask: "Does new silk burn?" "Clearly" to a native speaker, that is. Central Thai has five tones that are relatively easy to distinguish, compared with the tones of other regions. (Northern Thai has seven tones that vary greatly from province to province.) For simplicity, the guide below does not indicate the five tones of Central Thai. The visitor who seriously desires to learn the Thai language needs to befriend and win the heart of a sympathetic bilingual native to help give voice to the proper cues.

Consonants. There are 20 consonant sounds in Thai, all of which are close to English sounds though several fall somewhere in between two English consonant sounds, as indicated below.

p	This sound falls between *b* and *p*. It occurs in English only after *s*, as in the word *space*. Say *space* three times then drop the *s*.
t	This sound falls between *d* and *t*. It occurs in English only after *s*, as in the word *stay*. To practice *t*, say *stay* several times, then drop the *s*.
j	This sound falls between *j* as in *jet* and *ch* as in *chop*.
ng	Unlike in English this sound can begin a word in Thai. To practice it, say *singer* several times, then drop the *si—er*.

g   a hard sound as in *go*, but sometimes falls closer to *k*.

All other consonant sounds are pronounced as they would be in English.

Note: When the three sounds *t*, *p*, and *k*, appear at the end of a word, there is no follow-through of breath as there often is in English. These consonants are sometimes aspirated, as in *phai,* "to paddle," in contrast to a hard *p* in *pai-tio,* "to stroll."

It is common to hear *l* substituted for *r* in Thai, especially in Bangkok.

Vowels. Thai vowel sounds are rather more difficult than the consonants; for some sounds there is no equivalent in English, nonetheless a rough guide is presented below.

i	as in *sip*
ii	as in *seep*
e	as in *bet*
eh	as in *bat*
uh	as in *earn* (without the *r*)
a	as in *pun*
aa	as in *pal*
u	*uu* as in *pool*
o	as in *so*
ai,y	as in *pie*
ʉ	no equivalent; approximated by a guttural *u*.
ow	as in *cow*
aw	as in *paw*
iw	as in *you*
ew	as in Elmer Fudd's pronunciation of Merry (*mewy*)
eo	as in *Leo*
oy	as in *toy*
uy	as in *we*

Politeness. In the Thai language there are a number of words used to convey mood rather than meaning. Two such essential words in polite speech are the particles *krap* (used by men) and *ka* (used by women) for statements and questions. For extreme politeness, you would say them after every request and reply. To attract someone's attention a man would say *kun krap* and a lady *kun ka*.. Thais in addition often omit the pronouns *poom/chan* (*I*) and *kun* (*you*) for an added touch of discreetness.

USEFUL EXPRESSIONS

Note: Alternative pronunciations are given within parentheses.

NUMBERS

1.	one	*nung*
2.	two	*sawng (sorng)*
3.	three	*sam (sarm)*
4.	four	*sii*
5.	five	*ha*
6.	six	*hok*
7.	seven	*jet (chet)*
8.	eight	*beht (paet)*
9	nine	*kow*
10.	ten	*sip*
11.	eleven	*sip-et*
12.	twelve	*sip-sawng (-sorng)*
15.	fifteen	*sip-ha*
20.	twenty	*yii-sip*
21.	twenty-one	*yii-sip-et*
25.	twenty-five	*yii-sip-ha*
30.	thirty	*sam (sarm)-sip*
31.	thirty-one	*sam (sarm)-sip-et*
40.	forty	*sii-sip*
50.	fifty	*ha-sip*
100.	one hundred	*nung roi (roy)*
200.	two hundred	*sawng (sorng) roi (roy)*
1,000.	one thousand	*pan (ban)*
10,000.	ten thousand	*muun*

DAYS OF THE WEEK

Sunday	*wan athit*
Monday	*wan jan (chan)*
Tuesday	*wan angkaan*
Wednesday	*wan put (bhut)*
Thursday	*wan paruhat*
Friday	*wan suk*
Saturday	*wan saw (sao)*
today	*wan ni*
tomorrow	*phrang (brung) ni*
everyday	*thuk wan*
when?	*mua rai?*

GREETINGS AND CIVILITIES

hello, good morning, goodbye	*sawatii (sawadee) krap/ka*
excuse me, pardon me	*kaw toot (khor thot)*
never mind	*mai pen rai*
Please come in.	*Chuhn (choen) kow.*
Please sit down.	*Chuhn (choen) nang.*
May I come in?	*Kow dai mai?*
How are you?	*Sabai di rue?*
Well, thank you	*Sabai di, kawpkun (khorpkhoon)*
thank you	*kawpkun (khorpkhoon)*
I cannot speak Thai.	*Puut (phoot) thai mai dai.*
Please speak slowly	*Proht(d) puut cha-cha.*
May I take a photo?	*Tai ruup dai mai?*

What do you call this in Thai?	*Phasa thai ii riak waa arai?*	Where is the lavatory?	*Suam tii nai?*
Where do you live?	*Yoo tii nai?*	Where is the bathroom?	*Hawng (horng) naam tii nai?*
no	*mai*		
not, not good	*mai dai*		
very good	*dee mark*		

ORDERING & BARGAINING

		Do you have . . .?	*Mii . . . nai?*
		yes	*mii*
		no	*mai mii*
		I want . . . please	*Ow . . . krap/ka.*
		I want more . . .	*Ow iik . . .*

DIRECTIONS AND TRAVEL

where	*tii nai*	How much is this?	*Nii raka towry (thao-rai)?*
left	*sai*	How much per meter?	*Met la towry (thao-rai)?*
right	*khwa*	I want to buy 4 meters.	*Tawng-gan (torng-kan) sii met.*
straight ahead	*trong pai*		
slow down	*cha-cha*	How much of a discount?	*Ja lot towry?*
stop here	*yud (yut) tii nai*	Do you have something cheaper?	*Mii tuuk gwaa (kaa) tii mai?*
drive	*khab (khap)*		
be careful	*ra wang*	Do you have another color?	*Mii sii uhn mai?*
fast	*rew*		
What street is this?	*Nii thanon arai?*	Do you have a smaller size?	*Mii kanaat lek gwaa (kwa) nii mai?*
What town is this?	*Nii muang arai?*		
How many kilometers to . . .?	*Gii kiilo by (pai) . . .?*	O.k. I'll take it.	*Toklong.*
Wait a few minutes	*Khoi deo.*	Wrap it for me.	*Haw hai duai.*
I want to go to . . .	*Yaak ja (cha) by (pai) . . . .*	Bill please.	*Gep taang, krap/ka.*
entrance	*khao*	No chilies please.	*Yaa sai prik na.*
exit	*ork*		
bus station	*sathani rot meh*		

OTHER HANDY WORDS

railway station	*sathani rot fai*	enough	*paw*
airport	*sanam bin*	a lot	*maak-maak*
gas (petrol) station	*pam namman*	too much	*maak kuhn pai*
hotel	*rongrem*	who	*krii*
police station	*sathani tamruat*	what	*arai*
embassy	*kongsun*	when	*muarai*
taxi	*thaksii*	where	*tii nai*
pedicab	*samlor*	how old?	*aayuu towrai?*
motorized pedicab	*thuk-thuk*	yes, right	*chai*
long-tailed boat	*hang-yao*	no, not right	*mai chai*
river ferry (fast boat)	*rua rew*	comfortable, well	*sabai*
canal	*klong*	not well, sick	*mai sabai*
bridge	*saphan*	cold weather	*now*
lane	*soi*	cold temperature	*yen*
street	*thanon*	hot	*rawn (rorn)*
village	*ban*	water	*nam*
town	*muang*	spicy hot	*pet (phet)*
city	*nakhon*	delicious	*aroy*
island	*koh*	sweet	*waan*
beach	*hat*	sour	*preo*
hill	*khao*	hungry	*hiw how*
mountain	*phukkhao (doi)*	thirsty	*hiw nam*
		fresh	*sot*

AT THE HOTEL

hotel	*rongrem*	ripe	*suuk*
Do you have a double room?	*Mii hawng (horng) kuu mai?*	sleepy	*nguang nawn*
		young	*awn*
I want air conditioning.	*Ow hawng (horng) air.*	old (age)	*geh*
I want to see it first.	*Yaak ja duu hawng (horng) gawn.*	new/old	*my/gow*
		big	*yy*
Do you have a cheaper room	*Mii hawng (horng) tuuk gwaa (kwa) nii mai?*	small	*lek*
		to like	*chawp*
Wake us at 7 a.m.	*Pluuk row ton jet mong chow.*		

ACCOMMODATION

The following is an attempt to guide the visitor to the accommodation available in Bangkok and the provinces. Whilst all the hotels in Bangkok listed below are air conditioned, some in the provinces are not. Most of them have swimming pools, shopping facilities and travel agencies.

Fluctuations in exchange rates and rampant inflation make it virtually impossible to pin-point hotel rates, especially in US dollars. Therefore a rough guide to the cost of accommodation is given below in Thai currency, using this approximate scale:

Class		Rates (in baht)
A (De-luxe)	Single	1,400 — 1,700
	Double	1,700 — 2,000
	Suite	4,000 — 12,000
B (International)	Single	1,100 — 1,400
	Double	1,300 — 1,600
	Suite	2,500 — 6,000
C (Average)	Single	700 — 1,000
	Double	900 — 1,400
	Suite	1,500 — 3,500
D (Budget)	Single	300 — 700
	Double	400 — 800

In Bangkok, Chiang Mai, and Pattaya where Thailand's luxury hotels are concentrated rates are the highest in the country, so it is advisable to call ahead or check with a travel agent about the latest price.

In the list below, hotels are presented alphabetically within each category.

BANGKOK

Amarin, 526 Ploenchit Road, Tel: 2529810, Class B. Conveniently situated in the center of town with splendid Chinese and Japanese restaurants.

Ambassador, Soi 11 Sukhumvit Road. Tel: 2515141. Class B. Has Western, Japanese, Chinese, Thai and Seafood restaurants, 3 bars and 2 coffee houses; a 24-hour room service and basement nightclub. In the center of the commercial and entertainment districts.

Asia, 296 Phya Thai Road, Tel: 2811433. Class B. Easy access to town, poolside snacks. European-Chinese-Japanese cuisines.

Bangkok Trocadero, 343 Suriwongse Road, Tel: 2348920. Class D. Dining room, bar, coffee shop. Has all the usual amenities. 2 min. to General Post office.

Century, 9 Rajprarob Road, Tel: 2529755. Class D. European-Chinese-Japanese cuisines. Friendly atmosphere.

Chavalit, 171 Sukhumvit Road (Soi 13), Tel: 2526161. Class C. Continental, Chinese, Japanese and Thai cuisines in separate restaurants. Western grill. Coffee shop with 24-hour service.

Continental, 971 Phaholyothin Road, Tel: 2781596. Class D. European, Oriental and Thai cuisines and all the usual amenities.

Dorchester, 21 Soi Kotoey, Pratipat, Tel: 2792641. Class D. Restaurant, coffee shop, swimming pool and shopping arcade.

Dusit Thani, 946 Rama IV Road, Saladang Circle, Tel: 2331130. Class A. One of Bangkok's top hotels. Several restaurants and varied cuisines. Has discotheque, sauna in addition to all the standard amenities. Located in business and entertainment area.

Erawan, 494 Rajdamri Road, Tel: 2529100. Class A. One of Thailand's distinguished hotels, it has a tropical garden and Continental restaurant, post and travel offices and the full range of other services.

Federal, 27 Sukhumvit Road (Soi 11), Tel: 2525143. Class D. Centrally situated in the residential area with all facilities.

First, 2 Petchburi Road, Tel: 2813322. Class C. European, Chinese and Thai cuisines and round-the-clock coffee shop. Features a nightclub and "sightseeing" counter. Conveniently situated in center of movie district.

Florida, 43 Phya Thai Square, Tel: 2524141. Class D. Undistinguished but pleasant and homely. Features all the usual amenities in addition to being close to a delightful Laotian nightclub.

Fortuna, 19 Sukhumvit Road (Soi 5), Tel: 2515121. Class D. Situated in the center of the bar district and somewhat unprepossessing but boasts of all the standard amenities.

Grace, 12 Sukhumvit Road (Soi 3), Nana North, Tel: 2529170. Class D. In the center of the bar district and known for its exotic coffee shop. Provides all facilities.

Honey, 31 Soi 19 (Soi Wattana), Sukumvit Road, Tel: 2527111. Class D. Restaurant, coffee shop, swimming pool.

Hyatt Rama, 981 Silom Road, Tel: 2341010. Class B. An international-standard hotel. Features European, Japanese, Chinese and Thai cuisines. Cocktail lounge and nightclub with excellent luncheon buffet.

Impala (Luxury), 9 Soi Kasem (Soi 24), Sukumvit Road, Tel: 3910038. Class D. Restaurant and coffee shop. Conference rooms, car rentals and the usual amenities.

Indra Regent, Rajprarob Road, Tel: 2511111. Class B. One of the larger international-type hotels with European, Chinese, Thai cuisines and a splendid coffee shop. Should satisfy the most demanding tourist.

Liberty, 215 Sapan Kwai, Pratipat Road, Tel: 2790606. Class D. Dining room, bar, coffee shop, swimming pool, travel agency and shopping arcade.

Majestic, 97 Rajadamnern Avenue, Tel: 2815000. Class D. Garden, nightclub and garage. Pleasant and close to government ministries and UN offices.

305

Malaysia, 54 Ngam-du-plee Road, Rama IV Road, Tel: 2863582. Class D. Dining room, bar, swimming pool. Has the usual amenities.

Mandarin, 662 Rama IV Road, Tel: 2334980. Class B. Conveniently located near railway station has all the standard amenities including European, Chinese, Japanese and Thai cuisines.

Manhattan, Soi 15, Sukhumvit Road, Tel: 2527141. Class C. European, Chinese, Japanese, Korean and Thai cuisines. Round the clock coffee service, beer-garden and a very friendly atmosphere.

Manohra, 412 Suriwongse Road, Tel: 2345070. Class B. European and Thai cuisines. Quiet and friendly. Near the Post Office and souvenir shops.

Miami, 2 Sukumvit Road (Soi 13), Tel: 2525140. Class D. Bar, coffee shop, swimming pool, travel agency and money changer.

Metro, 1902 New Petchburi Road, Tel: 3911736. Class D. All the usual facilities plus a 24-hour bar and restaurant service.

Miramar, 777 Mahachai Road (Samyod Road), Tel: 2221711. Class D. Bar, restaurant and coffee shop, 2 conference rooms, travel agency and money changer. Located in Chinatown and business center of Bangkok.

Montien, 54 Suriwongse Road, Tel: 2348060. Class A. High class hotel with luxury appointments; situated in the center of the entertainment district.

Morakot, 2802, New Petchburi Road, Tel: 3910341. Class D. Dining room, bar, coffee shop, swimming pool, travel agency and shopping arcade.

Narai, 222 Silom Road, Tel: 2333350. Class B. Top international standard hotel. Boasts a revolving roof-restaurant, European and Asian cuisines, German beer-cellar, Italian coffee shop, etc.

New Amarin, 477 Sri Ayuthaya Road, Tel: 2526110. Class C. European, Chinese and Japanese cuisines and all the standard facilities. Has a money-changer, travel agent and gift shops.

New Empire, 572 Yawaraj Road, Tel: 2346990. Class D. Chinese restaurant, European and Thai food. Free transportation from hotel to airport.

New Fuji, 299-301 Suriwongse Road, Tel: 2345364. Class D. One of the smaller hotels with no swimming pool; catering somewhat to the middle-class Japanese and provides one of the nicest and cheapest meals in the city.

New Imperial, 6 Soi Ruamrudee, Ploenchit Road, Tel: 2528071. Class B. Pleasant and luxuriously appointed, has shopping arcade and spacious garden.

New Nana, 4 Soi Nana Tai, Sukumvit Road. Class D. Restaurant, 24-hour service coffee shops, bar, conference rooms, swimming pool, money changer, taxi service.

Oriental, 48 Oriental Avenue, New Road, Tel: 2348620. Class A. Picturesque top class hotel with a historic past associated with personages like Joseph Conrad and Somerset Maugham. Special appeal is its site overlooking the Chao Phya river.

Park, 6 Sukumvit Road (Soi 7), Tel: 2525110. Class

D. Restaurant serving European and Chinese food, bar, money changer and the usual amenities.

Peninsula, 295/3 Suriwongse Road, Tel: 2343910. Class C. Medium type hotel with all the standard facilities.

President, 135/26 Gaysorn Road, Tel: 2529880. Class B. International standard hotel. Conveniently situated in the center of town. Has all facilities with European and Thai cuisines.

Prince, 1537/1 New Petchburi Road, Tel: 2513318. Class D. Somewhat far from town but has all facilities and reasonable rates.

Princess, Charoen Krung Road, Tel: 2342951. Class D. Medium type hotel with standard facilities.

Rajah, Sukhumvit Road (Soi 4), Tel: 2525102. Class C. All facilities with European, Chinese, Thai cuisines.

Rajsubhamitra, (R.S.) 269 Larn Luang Road, Tel: 2813644. Class D. An unassuming place with attractive monthly rates. Besides standard services has a roof garden. European, Chinese, Thai cuisines.

Ramada, 1169 New Road, Tel: 2348971. Class D. Dining room, nightclub, cocktail lounge, coffee shop and tea lounge.

Reno, 40 Soi Kasemsan 1, Rama 1 Road, Tel: 2526121. Class D. Restaurant, swimming pool.

Rex, 762/1 Sukhumvit Road, Tel: 3910100. Class D. Very reasonable rates for the services offered, which is about everything.

Rich, 136/14 Sukhumvit Road, Tel: 2529174. Class D. Small in size but easy on the purse. Has all the basic amenities plus a swimming pool.

Rose, 118 Suriwongse Road, Tel: 2337695. Class D. Favored for brief stays of short duration.

Royal, 2 Rajadamnern Avenue, Tel: 2229111. Class D. One of Bangkok's oldest hotels conveniently close to Government Ministries, UN Offices and temples. All facilities available.

Sakol, Soi 2, Phya Thai Road, Tel: 2528161. Class D. All the standard facilities at reasonable rates.

Sheraton, 80 Suriwongse Road, Tel: 2335160. Class B. Located in the center of the entertainment district, it provides excellent service with all facilities.

Siam, 1777 New Petchburi Road, Tel: 2525081. Class D. Medium class hotel with all the standard facilities.

Siam Inter-Continental, Srapatum Palace Property, Rama I Road, Tel: 2529040. Class A. International standard hotel set in pleasant garden surroundings which includes a miniature zoo, tennis courts, mini golf range. Liable to be confused with Siam Hotel (see preceding entry).

Thai, 78 Prachatipat Road, Tel: 2813633. Class D. Medium class hotel with most of the standard facilities. European and Chinese cuisines. Close to government ministries and UN offices.

Viengtai, 42 Tani Road, Banglampu, Tel: 2815788. Class D. Close to UN and government ministries.

Victory, 322 Silom Road, Tel: 2339060. Class C.

Restaurant, coffee shop, swimming pool, money changer and the usual amenities.

Windsor, Soi 20, Sukhumvit Road, Tel: 3915300. Class C. All facilities plus car-rentals and tennis court.

World, 1996 New Petchburi Road, Tel: 3924340. Class D. Dining room, bar, swimming pool, conference room.

YMCA, 27 Sathorn Tai Road, Tel: 2865134. Class D. All facilities including sports. Some cottages also available. Variety of European, Chinese and Thai food.

CENTRAL THAILAND

ANG THONG

Bua Luang, Tambol Posa, 16 rooms.

Suvapan, Amphoe Muang, 35 rooms, air-conditioned.

KANCHANABURI

Luxury, Tambol Ban Nua, 17 rooms.

Muang Thong, Tambol Ban Nua, 36 rooms.

Prasobsuk Bungalow, Tambol Ban Nua, 33 rooms.

River Kwai Jungle, Tambol Sai Yok Yai, (Bangkok reservation, Tel: 2516525). 18 rooms.

River Kwai Village, 284/3-16 Sang-Chooto Road, Tambol Ban Nua, Tel: 511565, (Bangkok reservation, Tel: 2346840). 60 rooms, air-conditioned. Conference room.

River Kawi Rafts, Tambol Sai Yok Yai, (Bangkok reservation, Tel: 2510178). 15 rooms.

Wang Thong, 60/3 Sang Chooto Road, Tel: 511739. 20 rooms.

LOPBURI

Asia Lopburi, 1/7-8 Surasak Road, Tel: 411892. 111 rooms, air-conditioned.

Muang Thong, Surasongkram Road. 48 rooms, air-conditioned.

Nett, 17/1-2 Rajdamnoen, Tel: 411738. 41 rooms, air-conditioned.

Taipei, 24/6-7 Surasongkram Road, Tel: 411524. 105 rooms, air-conditioned.

Vidoonsi, 388 Naraimaharaj Road, Tel: 411009. 50 rooms, air-conditioned.

NAKHON PATHOM

Mit Phaisarn, Phra Pathom Chedi. 59 rooms.

Mitsumpan, Lungphra Road, 23 rooms, air-conditioned.

Rose Garden, Km 32 Petchkasem, (Bangkok reservation, 4/8 Sukhumvit Soi 3, Tel: 2515735). 106 rooms, air-conditioned. 25 bungalows.

Sirichai, 37-41 Saiphra Road, Tel: 241800. 25 rooms.

NONTHABURI

Golden Dragon, 20/21 Ngamwongsvarn. 114 rooms, air-conditioned.

Hotel 73, Tambol Suan Yai. 19 rooms.

Mitr Sukchai, Tambol Suan Yai. 18 rooms.

PATHUM THANI

Chom Krao, 1/3 Tambol Ta Ram. 36 rooms.

Mit Phaisarn, 146/12 Tambol Bang-Proke. 20 rooms.

Pattamarom, 145-155 Tambol Bang-Proke. 22 rooms.

Teke Heng Chong, 74-76 Tambol Ta Ram. 32 rooms.

PETCHABURI

Khao Wang, 36 Tambol Klong Kra-Sang. 49 rooms.

Petchkasem, 14 Tambol Rai Som. 50 rooms.

Salee Villa Bungalow, 285 Ruamchit Road, Cha-am Beach, (Bangkok reservation, Tel: 2818308). 40 rooms.

Santi Suk Bungalow, Km 206 Nang Ramperk, Cha-am Beach, (Bangkok reservation, Tel: 2511847 Ext. 13, 17). 43 rooms.

PHRA NAKHON SI AYUTHAYA

Cathay, Tambol Hor Rattana Chai, 26 rooms.

Thai Sena, 286 Senanawin 2 Road, 17 rooms.

Thai Thai, 13/1 Naresuan Road, Tel: 251505. 25 rooms, air-conditioned.

U-Thong, 86 U-Thong Road, Tel: 251136. 65 rooms.

Vieng Fah, Tambol Pratu-chai. 22 rooms.

RATCHABURI

Araya, Tambol Na Muang, Amphoe Muang. 80 rooms, air-conditioned.

Kasem Suk, Tambol Ban Pong, Amphoe Ban Pong, 24 rooms.

Lucky, Tambol Ban Pong, Amphoe Ban Pong, 51 rooms.

Namsin, 2-16 Krai Petch Road, Tel: 337551. 75 rooms, air-conditioned.

Sala Thai, Tambol Na Muang, Amphoe Muang, 44 rooms, air-conditioned.

Si Ban Pong, 8 Sangchooto Road, Amphoe Ban Pong. 30 rooms, air-conditioned.

Siri Sumpan, Tambol Ban Pong, Amphoe Ban Pong. 47 rooms.

Siroj, 139-141 Amarin road, Tel: 337021. 24 rooms, air-conditioned.

Zin Zin, 32/4-7 Railway Road, Tel: 337474. 50 rooms, air-conditioned.

RIVER KWAI see KANCHANANBURI

SAMUT PRAKAN

Bunthomtip, Tambol Sam Rong Nua, Amphoe Muang, 20 rooms.

Charoen Suk, Tambol Pak Nam, Amphoe Muang, 24 rooms.

Hom Huan, Tambol Sam Rong Nua, Amphoe Muang, 20 rooms.

Kwanchai, Amphoe Phra Pradaeng, 32 rooms.

New Sisawat, Amphoe Phra Pradaeng, 42 rooms.

Phra Pradaeng, Amphoe Phra Pradaeng, 30 rooms.

Sukumvit, Tambol Pak Nam, Amphoe Muang, 36 rooms.

SAMUT SAKHON

Kasem, Sethakit Road. 46 rooms.

Viengtai, Tambol Mahachai, Amphoe Muang. 19 rooms, no air conditioning.

Wiangthai, Sukhontip Road. 19 rooms.

SAMUT SONGKHRAM

Mae Klong, 526/10-13 Petchsamut Road. 20 rooms.

SARABURI

Keo Un, 1741/7-8 Paholyothin Road, Tel: 211222. 169 rooms, air-conditioned.

Saen Suk, 209/1 Tambol Pak Preaw. 89 rooms.

Saraburi, 497 Tambol Pak Preaw. 81 rooms.

Supsin, Amphoe Muang, 46 rooms.

Thanin, Amphoe Phra Phutthabat, Tel: 266088. 45 rooms, air-conditioned.

SINGBURI

Chaophya, Tambol Bangbhutsa. 44 rooms, air-conditioned.

Singburi, 882/18-21 Khunsan Road, Tel: 511752. 110 rooms, air-conditioned.

Thavorn Panich, Amphoe Muang. 23 rooms.

SUPHAN BURI

K.A.T., 433 Near Police Station, Prapanvasa Road, 51 rooms.

Kalaket, Tambol Tha Piliang. 32 rooms.

Petch, Tambol Tha Piliang. 40 rooms.

Si Muang, 531-536 Prapanvasa Road. 39 rooms.

Si Suphan, Tambol Tha Piliang, 47 rooms.

Suksan, Tombol Tha Piliang. 60 rooms.

UTHAI THANI

Hua Thai, Tambol Uthai Hong. 13 rooms.

Phiboon Sook, Tambol Uthai Hong. 40 rooms.

Prasertsri, Tambol Ban Rai. 12 rooms.

NORTHERN THAILAND

CHAI NAT

Arunothai, Tambol Nai Muang. 30 rooms.

Nam Chai, 63/22 Tambol Nai Muang, Tel: 411725. 57 rooms, air-conditioned.

Suk Sawasdi, Tambon Nai Muang. 41 rooms, air-conditioned.

Thepchoom Boonma, Tambol Nai Muang. 35 rooms.

CHIANG MAI

Anodad, 57-59 Rajmaraka Road, Tel: 235353, 150 rooms, air-conditioned .

Chiang Inn, 100 Changklan Road, Tel: 235655, (Bangkok Reservation, Tel: 2516883). 175 rooms, air-conditioned.

Chiang Mai President, 226 Vitchayanon Road, Tel: 235116, (Bangkok reservation, Tel: 3147776). 150 rooms, air-conditioned.

Diamond, 33/10 Charoen Prated Road, Tel: 234155. 145 rooms, air-conditioned.

Muang Mai, 502 Huey Kaew Road, Tel: 221392. 155 rooms, air-conditioned.

New Asia, 55 Rajawongse Road, Tel: 235288. 204 rooms, air-conditioned.

Porn Ping, 46-48 Charoen Prated Road. 152 rooms, air-conditioned.

Poy Luang, 146 Super Highway Road, Tel: 234633, (Bangkok reservation, Tel: 2520200. 225 rooms, air-conditioned.)

Prince, 3 Tai Wang Road, Tel: 236396. 112 rooms, air-conditioned.

Railway, 471 Charoen Muang Road, Tel: 236463, (Bangkok reservation, Tel: 2230341). 76 rooms, air-conditioned, 8 bungalows.

Rincome, 301 Huay Kaew Road, Tel: 221044, (Bangkok reservation, Tel: 2526118). 158 rooms, air-conditioned.

Sri Tokyo, 63 Chang Klan Road. 144 rooms, air-conditioned.

Sumit, 198 Rajpakinai Road, Tel: 235996, (Bangkok reservation, Tel: 2794525). 165 rooms, air-conditioned.

Surawongs, 110 Changklan Road, Tel: 236789. 168 rooms, air-conditioned.

CHIANG RAI

Krung Thong, 412 Sanambin Road, Tel: 311033. 112 rooms, air-conditioned.

Rama, 331/4 Trairat Road, Tel: 311344. 43 rooms, air-conditioned.

Ruang Nakhon, 25 Ruang Nakhon Road, Tel: 344566. 61 rooms, air-conditioned.

Siam, Amphoe Muang. 54 rooms.

Suknirun, 424/1 Bunpakarn Road, Tel: 311055. 105 rooms, air-conditioned.

Wiang Inn, 893 Pholyothin Road, Tel: 311551. 112 rooms, air-conditioned.

KAMPHAENG PHET

Chakunglao, Near Ping River. 120 rooms.

Chong Sawasdi, 180 Tesa Vicihit Road. 29 rooms.

Naowarat, Near Ping River. 100 rooms.

Nittayaprapa, 118/1 Tesa Road, Amphoe Muang. 32 rooms.

Phet, 99 Vichit Road Soi 3, Amphoe Muang, Tel: 711283, (Bangkok reservation, Tel: 2516512). 234 rooms.

Rajdamnoen, 892 Rajdamnoen Road, Tel: 217029. 74 rooms.

LAMPANG

Asia Lampang, 229 Boonyawat Road, Tel: 217844. 64 rooms, air-conditioned.

Siam, 260/29 Chatchai Road. 84 rooms, air-conditioned.

Sri Sgna, Tambol Suandong, Amphoe Muang. 35 rooms, air-conditioned.

LAMPHUN

Chamchantr, Tambol Viangthong, Amphoe Muang. 17 rooms.

Notanon, 51/2 Tambol Nai Muang. 15 rooms.

MAE HONG SON

Meitee, 55 Khunrum Prapas Road, Tambol Chomkham. 38 rooms, air-conditioned.

Mit Aree, Tambol Mae Sariang, Amphoe Mae Sariang. 18 rooms.

Mitniyom, 90/1 Khunrum Prapas Road. 44 rooms, air-conditioned.

Sguan Sin, 35 Singhanat Road. 28 rooms.

Singhanat, Singhanat Road, Amphoe Muang. 25 rooms, no air conditioning.

Suk Somchai, Singhanat Road. 16 rooms, air-conditioned.

NAKHON SAWAN

Anodad, 479-483 Kosi Road, Tel: 212856, 153 rooms, air-conditioned.

Irawan, 1-5 Matulee Road, Tel: 212070. 43 rooms, air-conditioned.

New White House, 2 Matulee Road, Tel: 212157. 48 rooms.

Sala Thai, 221-225 Tambol Pak Nam Pho. 40 rooms.

Toek Lueng, 24-44 Tambol Pak Nam Pho. 50 rooms.

Visanu 2, 30 Uttakavee Road, Tel: 212932. 117 rooms, air-conditioned.

NAN

Amornsri, Tambol Nai Wiang. 26 rooms.

Nan Fah, 436-438-440 Sumon Thevaraj. 24 rooms.

Suk Kasem, Anantaworaritdej Road. 60 rooms, air-conditioned.

Thevaraj, 466 Sumon Thevaraj Road, Tel: 710095. 115 rooms, air-conditioned.

PHAYAO

Chai Kwan, 53 Tah Kwan Road. 10 rooms.

Chiang Kham, 643 Tambol Yuan, Amphoe Chiang Kham. 32 rooms.

Siriphan Bungalow, 648/2 Kwan Phayao, Tel: 431314. 20 rooms.

Tharn Thong, 55-57-59 Donsnam Road, Tel: 431302. 94 rooms.

Wattana, 69 Donsnam Road, Tel: 431086. 34 rooms.

PHETCHABUN

19 Hotel, Tambol Chi-smor-tod. 42 rooms.

Pen Silpa 1, 333/8 Wajee Road, Amphoe Lomsak. 28 rooms.

Pen Silpa 2, Wajee Road. 16 rooms.

Phetch Siam, Tambol Chi-smor-tod. 72 rooms.

Srichai, Tambol Lom Sak, Amphoe Lom Sak. 70 rooms.

Wilawan, Kotchaseni Road, Tambol Kong Thoon. 17 rooms.

PHITSANULOK

Amarin Nakhon, 3/1 ChaoPhya Phitsanulok, Tel: 258588. 124 rooms, air-conditioned.

Hor Fah, 73/1-5 Phya-Lithai Road, Tel: 258484. 70 rooms.

Phitsanulok, 82 Naresuan Road, Tel: 258425. 60 rooms.

Samai Niyom, Tambol Nai Muang. 33 rooms.

Unhachak, 66-67 Phya-Lithai Road, Tel: 258387. 34 rooms.

PHRAE

Nakhon Phrae, Tambol Nai Wiang. 100 rooms, air-conditioned.

Paradorn, 177 Yantrakijkosol Road. 25 rooms, air-conditioned.

Sawasdikarn, 76—78 Yantrakijkosol Road. 30 rooms.

Tang Sri Paiboon, 84 Yantrakitkoson Road. 49 rooms, air-conditioned.

Thepwimarn, Tambol Nai Wiang. 51 rooms, air-conditioned.

PICHIT

Buraparat, Amphoe Taphan Hin. 23 rooms.

New Hua Hin, Amphoe Taphan Hin. 51 rooms, air-conditioned.

Phaisarn, 522-526 Busaba Road. 19 rooms.

Taphan Hin, 7/17 Daeng Thong Di Road. 21 rooms, air-conditioned.

SUKHOTHAI

Chinwat, 1, 2, 3 Nikornkasem Road. 46 rooms.

Phong Prasert, 92/6 Nilornkasem Road. 30 rooms, air-conditioned.

Roong Fah, 8 Singhawat Road. 14 rooms.

Sawasdipong, 56/2-56/15 Singhawat Road. 28 rooms.

Sukhothai, 15/5 Singhawat Road. 40 rooms.

TAK

Bhumiphol Guest House, Bhumiphol Dam, (Bangkok reservation, Tel: 4243805). 31 rooms.

First, Tambol Mae Sot. 38 rooms.

Mae Ping, 321 Tambol Nong Luang. 46 rooms.

Sgnuan Thai, 619 Tak Sin Road, Tel: 511265. 37 rooms.

Siam, 185 Tambol Mae Sot. 70 rooms.

Tak, 8/9 Tambol Nong Luang, Tel: 511234. 29 rooms.

Thavisak, 561/8 Mahatthai Bamrung, Tel: 20235. 32 rooms, no air conditioning.

UTTARADIT

Chai Fah, Tambol Thasao, Amphoe Muang. 14 rooms, air-conditioned.

Thanothai, 149-153 Kasemras Road. 27 rooms, air-conditioned.

Uttaradit, 24-28 Rasanarn Road. 28 rooms.

Vanich, 1 Sri-Uttara Road. 74 rooms, air-conditioned.

NORTHEASTERN THAILAND

BURI RAM
Grand, 137 Niwat Road. 71 rooms, air-conditioned.

Krung Rome, Amphoe Muang. 75 rooms, air-conditioned.

Maitrichitr, 169/2-169/4 Soonthornthep Road. 18 rooms, air-conditioned.

CHAIYAPHUM

Charoen, Yutti Dham Road. 18 rooms, no air conditioning.

Lert Nimit, 336 Harurthai Road. Tel: 811053. 38 rooms, 15 bungalows.

Lert Nimit Co., Ltd, 447 Niversrat Road, Tel: 811522. 80 rooms, air-conditioned.

Phaiboon, Yutti-Dham Road. 20 rooms.

Saeng Petch, Tambol Nai Muang, Amphoe Muang. 25 rooms.

KALASIN

Mit Wattana, Tambol Kalasin, Amphoe Muang, 36 rooms.

Sang Thong, Kalasin Road. 31 rooms, air-conditioned.

Saeng Chai, Amphoe Kushinarai. 12 rooms, air-conditioned.

Saeng Fah, Amphoe Muang. 20 rooms.

Thai Thong, 107/7-8 Phirom, Tel: 811661. 28 rooms.

KHON KAEN

Chatchai, Tambol Nai Muang, Amphoe Ban Phai. 27 rooms.

Choo Charoen, Tambol Nai Muang, Amphoe Ban Phai, 54 rooms.

Grand, 39 Soi Samaki-Utid. 70 rooms, air-conditioned.

King's, Tambol Nai Muang, Amphoe Muang. 99 rooms.

Kosa, 250-252 Srichan Road, Tel: 236772. 115 rooms, air-conditioned.

Lilla, Tambol Nai Muang, Amphoe Muang. 46 rooms, air-conditioned.

Mung Korn Thong, 41/1-6 Na Muang Road, Tel: 236411. 40 rooms, air-conditioned.

Queen's, 207-9 Maliwan Road, Chumpare. 120 rooms.

Roma, 50/2 Klang Muang Road, Tel: 236276. 97 rooms, air-conditioned. Conference room for 500-800 persons.

Royal, Tambol Nai Muang, Amphoe Muang. 20 rooms, air-conditioned.

Sawasdi, Na Muang Road, Tambol Nai Muang. 68 rooms, air-conditioned.

Thani Bungalow, Tambol Nai Muang, Amphoe Muang. 113 rooms.

Vanchai 2, Tambol Nai Muang, Amphoe Ban Phai. 44 rooms.

LOEI

Porn Sin, 93 Kaew Asa Road. 15 rooms.

Sarai-thong, Ruamchitr Road. 43 rooms.

Thai Deam, 122/1 Charoen Rat Road, Tel: 811763. 55 rooms, air-cconditioned.

MAHASAKHAM

Pattana, Tambol Talad, Amphoe Muang. 70 rooms.

NAKHON PHANOM

Chai Pattana, 550 Fuang Nakhon Road. 42 rooms, air-conditioned.

First, 370 Sithep Road, Tel: 511253. 63 rooms, air-conditioned.

Nakhon Phanom, 528/39 Abhibarn Buncha Road, Tel: 511253. 57 Rooms, air-conditioned.

Sithep, 708/11 Sithep Road, Tambol Nai Muang, Tel: 511036. 56 rooms, air-conditioned.

Windsor, 692/19 Bamroang Muang Road, Tel: 511538. 60 rooms, air-conditioned.

NAKHON RATCHASIMA

Chumphol, Tambol Nai Muang, Amphoe Muang. 69 rooms.

Chomsurang, 2701/2 Mahad-Thai Road. 119 rooms, air-conditioned.

Fah Sang, 112-114 Mookhamontri Road, Tel: 242143. 77 rooms, air-conditioned.

Fah Thai, 849-851 Pho Klang Road, Tel: 242533. 90 rooms, air-conditioned.

Korat, 4014 Asdang Road, Tel: 242444. 121 rooms, air-conditioned.

Lak Muang, Tambol Nai Muang, Amphoe Muang. 83 rooms, air-conditioned.

Sakol, Tambol Nai Muang, Amphoe Muang. 82 rooms.

Siri, Tambol Nai Muang, Amphoe Muang. 60 rooms.

Sri Pattana, 3571/5 Suranari Road, Tel: 242944. 183 rooms, air-conditioned.

Thai Hotel, Tambol Nai Muang, Amphoe Muang. 69 rooms.

Thai Hotel 2, Tambol Nai Muang, Amphoe Muang. 60 rooms.

Thai Pokphan, 104-106 Asadang Road, Tel: 242454. 66 rooms.

NONG KHAI

Banterngchitr, 626 Banterngchit Road. 27 rooms.

Phantawee, 1241 Haisoke Road. 39 rooms, 6 bungalows.

Phoonsap, Meechai Road. 20 rooms.

Prachak Bungalow, 1178 Prachak Road. 28 rooms, air-conditioned.

Thong Wichit, 1244 Banterngchit Road. 32 rooms.

ROI ET

Bua Luang, Talad Roi Et. 36 rooms.

Bungalow 99, Tambol Nai Muang. 32 rooms, air-conditioned.

Niyom, Tambol Nai Muang, Amphoe Muang. 50 rooms.

Suriya, Tambol Nai Muang. 41 rooms.

Thiende, Tambol Nai Muang. 42 rooms.

Tokyo, Phoenchit Road. 58 rooms.

SAKON NAKHON

Araya. 1432 Prem Preeda Road. 49 rooms, air-conditioned.

Charoen Sook, 636 Charoen Muang Road. 40 rooms, air-conditioned.

Krong Thong, 645/2 Charoen Muang Road. 38 rooms, air-conditioned.

New Hotel, 22 Thanasarn Road, Tel: 511341. 56 rooms, air-conditioned.

Saeng Charoen, Tambol Nai Muang. 46 rooms.

SI SA KET

Nittrakarn, 370 Si Sa Ket Road, Amphoe Muang. 44 rooms.

Phothong, 1055/11 Railways Road, Tambol Muang Tai, Amphoe Muang. 20 rooms.

Prom Phimarn, Amphoe Muang. 80 rooms, air-conditioned.

Santisook, 370 Si Sa Ket Road, Amphoe Muang. 68 rooms, air-conditioned.

Thai Serm Thai, 370 Si Sa Ket Road, Amphoe Muang. 34 rooms.

SURIN

Angsupan, 155-161 Tanasarn Road, Amphoe Muang, Tel: 511302. 59 rooms, air-conditioned.

Erawan, 37 Kroong Sri Road, Tel: 511328. 24 rooms.

Krung Sri, Kroong Sri Road. 65 rooms.

Memorial, 186 Lak Muang Road, Tel: 511288. 56 rooms, air-conditioned.

New Hotel, 22 Thanasarn Road, Tel: 511341. 56 rooms, air-conditioned.

Saeng Charoen, Tambol Nai Muang. 46 rooms.

Saeng Thong, 155-161 Thanasarn Road, Tel: 511302. 62 rooms, air-conditioned.

UBON RATCHATHANI

Bordin, 14 Phalochai Road, Tel: 254209. 117 rooms, air-conditioned.

Pathumrat, 173 Chayang-kul Road. Tel: 254417. 145 rooms, air-conditioned.

Rajthani, 229 Khuan Thani Road, Tel: 254599. 107 rooms, air-conditioned.

Siam, 94 Phalochai Road, Tel: 254771. 62 rooms, air-conditioned.

Thong Poonpan, Upparaj Road. 67 rooms, air-conditioned.

Ubon Pattana, 333 Ubonkit Road, Tel: 254333. 126 rooms, air-conditioned.

UDON THANI

Chaiyaporn, 209-211 Mak Khang Road, Amphoe Muang, Tel: 220913. 77 rooms, air-conditioned.

Charoen, 549 Phosri Road, Amphoe Muang, Tel: 221332. 120 rooms, air-conditioned.

King's, Tambol Mak Khaeng, Amphoe Muang. 135 rooms.

Krung Thong, 195-199 Phosi Road, Amphoe Muang, Tel: 221161. 85 rooms.

Mapakdi, Tambol Mak Khaeng. 45 rooms.

Pracha Pakdi, 156/8 Prachak Road, Amphoe Muang, Tel: 221805. 45 rooms.

Siri Udon, 79-91 Amphoe Muang Road, Tel: 221816. 130 rooms, air-conditioned.

Sri Chai, Tambol Mak Khaeng. 29 rooms.

Subhamitr, Tambol Mak Khaeng. 60 rooms.

Udon, 81-85 Mak Khaeng Road, Tel: 221628. 80 rooms, air-conditioned.

Victory, 60 Phosi Road, Amphoe Muang, Tel: 221462. 49 rooms, air-conditioned.

YASOTHORN

Arun Pattana, Amphoe Muang, 18 rooms, no air conditioning.

Surawej Wattana, 128/1 Changsanit Road. 30 rooms, air-conditioned.

Udom Pharn, Uthai Rermmit Road. 35 rooms.

Yos Nakhon, Uthai-Ramaritti Road. 64 rooms, air-conditioned.

EASTERN THAILAND

CHACHOENGSAO

Chachoengsao, Tambol Na Muang. 45 rooms.

Mitsampan, Tambol Na Muang. 37 rooms.

Yenchitr, Tambol Na Muang. 29 rooms.

CHANTHABURI

Chai Li, Tambol Wat Mai, Amphoe Muang. 60 rooms.

Chanthaburi, Amphoe Muang. 70 rooms, air-conditioned.

Eastern, Tambol Bangkaja, Amphoe Muang. 142 rooms, air-conditioned.

Kasemsan 1, 98/1 Benjamarachuthid Road, Tel: 311100. 36 rooms, air-conditioned.

Kasemsan 2, Tambol Wat Mai. 120 rooms.

Kiatkajohn, Tambol Wat Mai, Amphoe Muang. 63 rooms.

Muangchan, 257-259 Srichan Road, Tel: 311116. 120 rooms, air-conditioned.

NAKHON NAYOK

Khao Yai, Tambol Hintang, (Bangkok reservation, Tel: 2825209). 30 bungalows, 18 motels, 9 guest houses.

Panjai, 352/1 Suwanansorn Road, Opp. Nakhon Nayok Hospital. 48 rooms, air-conditioned.

Tansamai, Tambol Nakhon Nayok. 30 rooms.

Tansamai, Tambol Ta Chang. 35 rooms.

PATTAYA

Amnueythip Villas, (i) Chomthein Beach, Banglamung (ii) Soi Chya Prux, 151 km Sukhumvit Road (Bangkok reservation, Tel: 4650270 Monday to Friday mornings and evenings between 7 and 9 only). 25 bungalows each with 2 to 3 bedrooms, sitting room upstairs, kitchen, dining and maid's rooms downstairs. Fully furnished with crockery. Fans but no air conditioning.

Arbur and Development, Pattaya Tal, Tel. 68 rooms, no air conditioning.

Asia Pattaya, Pattaya Beach, Tel: 418577, (Bangkok reservation, Tel: 2820121). 270 rooms, air-conditioned.

Bangphra Motel, Tambol Bangphra, Amphoe Si Racha. 20 rooms.

Bangsaen Beach Hotel, 55-150 Tambol Saensook, (Bangkok reservation, Tel: 2813041). 29 rooms, 138 bungalows, air-conditioned.

Bang Saray, 17/1 Na Chomtean (Bangkok reservation, Tel: 2863407). 52 rooms, air-conditioned, garden beach, swimming pool and fishing and skiing facilities.

Golden Sand, Pattaya Beach, Tel: 418114 (Bangkok reservation, Tel: 2528594). Motel and 11 bungalows each with 2 to 3 bedrooms. Motel is air-conditioned but has no kitchen. The bungalows are not air-conditioned but have fans, kitchen, gas stove and crockery.

Merlin Hotel, Pattaya Beach, Tel: 418755, (Bangkok reservation, Tel: 2330802). 360 rooms, air-conditioned.

Pattaya Palace, Pattaya Beach, Tel: 418319, (Bangkok reservation, Tel: 2341010) 220 rooms, air-conditioned.

Koh Larn Vac, Larn Island, (Bangkok reservation, Tel: 2453221 Ext. Koh Larn Vac). 78 rooms.

Manhattan, Pattaya Beach, Tel: 418580. 50 rooms, air-conditioned.

Nipa Lodge, Pattaya Beach, Tel: 418321, (Bangkok reservation, Tel: 2526118). 138 rooms, air-conditioned.

Ocean View, 382 Pattaya Beach, Tel: 418084, (Bangkok reservation, Tel: 2529590). 115 rooms.

Orchid Lodge, Pattaya Beach, Tel: 418175, (Bangkok reservation, Tel: 2526045). 172 rooms, air-conditioned.

Palm Lodge, Pattaya Beach, Tel: 418779. 72 rooms.

Regent Pattaya, Pattaya Beach, Tel: 418311, (Bangkok reservation, 2522083). 299 rooms, air-conditioned.

Royal Cliff, Pattaya Beach, Tel: 418344, (Bangkok reservation, Tel: 2453037). 520 rooms, air-conditioned.

Royal Garden, 218 Pattaya Beach, Tel: 418126, (Bangkok reservation, Tel: 3928885). 115 rooms.

Siam Bayshore, Pattaya Beach, Tel: 418677, (Bangkok reservation, Tel: 2512458). 274 rooms, air-conditioned.

Tropicana, 98-9 Pattaya Beach, Tel: 518566, (Bangkok reservation, Tel: 2529187 Ext. 216). 116 rooms, air-conditioned.

Chiang Inn, Pattaya 380 Sukhabhibarn Road, Tel: 418400, (Bangkok reservation, Tel: 2513844). 120 rooms.

Wongse Amatya, Pattaya Beach, Tel: 418118, (Bangkok reservation, Tel: 2224551). 108 rooms.

PRACHIN BURI

Ammuey Suk, 110/1 Rat Utit Road, Amphoe Aranyaprathet. 53 rooms, air-conditioned.

Kasem Suk, 4-5-6 Chitasuwan Road. 14 rooms.

Kavee, Tambol Sa Kaew, Amphoe Sa Kawe. 36 rooms.

King's, 65/7, 65/8 Rajdamri Road, Amphoe Muang. 61 rooms, air-conditioned.

Prom Charoen, Tambol Kabin Buri, Amphoe Kabin Buri. 22 rooms.

Sirimonkol, Tambol Kabin Buri, Amphoe Kabin Buri.

RAYONG

Asia Mai, Tambol Tha — Pradu. 65 rooms.

Rayong, Tambol Tha — Pradu. 46 rooms.

Rayong O-Tani, 169 Sukumvit Road, Tel: 611161. 117 rooms, air-conditioned.

Sahayon, Tambol Cherng Noen. 36 rooms.

Tawan Ok, Tambol Tha — Pradu. 34 rooms.

Wang Kaew, Km. 248. Bangna-trat, Amphoe Klaeng, (Bangkok reservation, 153/2 Soi Mahad Lek Luang 1, Rajdamri Road, Tel: 2510836). 62 rooms. Conference room for 150 persons.

TRAT

Muang Trat, 11/1-11/2 Sukumvit Road, Tel: 511191. 80 rooms, air-conditioned.

Tang Nguan Seng, Amphoe Muang. 52 rooms.

Thai Roong Roj, 296 Viwattana, Tel: 511141. 76 rooms, air-conditioned.

SOUTHERN THAILAND

CHUMPHON

Sri Chumphon, 127/22-24 Saladaeng Road. 100 rooms, air-conditioned.

Suriya, 125/24-26 Saladaeng Road. 26 rooms.

Thai Prasert, 202-204 Saladaeng Road. 47 rooms.

HAT YAI

Asian Hotel, Niphat Uthit 3 Road, Hat Yai, Songkhla, Thailand, Tel: 245938/245271/245455.

Cathay, 93/1 Niphat Utit 2 Road, Tel: 243106. 28 rooms.

Emperor Hotel, 1 Tanrattanakorn Road, Hat Yai, Tel: 245698/245709.

Grand, 443/1 Phetchkasem Road, Tel: 243286. 15 rooms.

Hat Yai Motel, 58/4 Sangsi Road, Tel: 244207. 144 rooms air-conditioned.

Hor Fah, 124/8 Damnoen Witi Road, Tel: 243444. 33 rooms.

King's, 126-134 Niphat Utit 1 Road, Tel: 243966. 66 rooms.

Kosit, Niphat Utit 2 Road, Tel: 244576. 182 rooms, air-conditioned.

Lam Thong, 42 Damnoen Witi Road, Tel: 244433. 100 rooms, air-conditioned.

Metro, 86 Niphat Utit 2, Tel: 244422. 151 rooms, air-conditioned.

Nora, 4 Niphat Utit 2 Road, Tel: 244944. 192 rooms, air-conditioned, restaurant, shops, travel agency.

President, The Rama of Hat Yai Hotel, 420 Pratharn Utit Road, Tel: 244477. 110 rooms, air-conditioned, located in residential area, close to airport and railway terminal, dining room, cocktail lounge, swimming pool.

Sukhontha, 26 Saneha-Nuson Road, Tel: 243999. 204 rooms, air-conditioned, restaurant, bar, nightclub.

Yong Dee, 99 Niphat Utit 3 Road, Tel: 244499. 101 rooms, air-conditioned.

KRABI

Kittisak, 9 Sri Phangnga Road. 18 rooms.

Thai, 2/1 Adisorn Road. 27 rooms, air-conditioned.

Viengthong, 22 Uttarakit Road, Tel: 611188. 80 rooms, air-conditioned. Conference room for 100 persons.

NAKHON SRI THAMMARAT

Burapha, Tambol Klung. 33 rooms.

Muang Thong, 1459/7-9 Charoen Wattana Road, Tel: 356177. 52 rooms.

Nakhon, 1477/5 Yommaraj Road, Tel: 356318. 42 rooms.

Nakhon Tak Sin, Sri Praj Road, Amphoe Muang. 150 rooms, air-conditioned. Conference room for 500 persons.

Neramit, 1629-1631 Neramit Road, Tel: 356514. 75 rooms, air-conditioned.

New Sir Thong, Tambol Tha-wang. 41 rooms.

Seri, Amphoe Muang. 52 rooms, air-conditioned.

Siam, 1407/17 Chumroen Vithi Road. 67 rooms, air-conditioned.

Soon Thorn, Tambol Sichol. 40 rooms.

Suntisook, Tambol Sichol. 80 rooms.

Taksin Hotel, Sriprach Road. 120 rooms, Tel: 356121.

Thai Hotel, 1369-1375 Rajdamnoen Road, Tel: 356451. 115 rooms, air-conditioned.

Thai Wattana, Tambol Pak Prak. 15 rooms.

Thiem Fah, Tambol Sichol. 41 rooms.

Yaowaraj, Tambol Klung. 53 rooms.

NARATHIWAT

Lilla, 28-32 Saritwongse Road, Amphoe Sungai Kolok, Tel: 611188. 72 rooms, air-conditioned.

Merlin, 40 Charoenket Road, Amphoe Sungai Kolok, Tel: 611003. 96 rooms, air-conditioned.

Merry (Madee), 19/4 Chuenmanka Road, Amphoe Sungai Kolok, Tel: 611122. 31 rooms, air-conditioned.

Rex, 6/1-2 Chumroon Nara Road, Amphoe Muang. Tel: 511134. 40 rooms, air-conditioned.

Tak Sin 1, 3 Pracha Samrarn Road, Amphoe Sungai Kolok, Tel: 611083. 39 rooms, air-conditioned.

Tak Sin 2, 4 Pracha Samrarn Road, Amphoe Sungai Kolok, Tel: 611085. 49 rooms, air-conditioned.

Tanyong, 20-28 Sopapisai Road, Amphoe Muang, Tel: 511477. 92 rooms, air-conditioned.

Thai Eak, 43 Wongse Witee Road, Amphoe Sungai Kolok, Tel: 611052. 37 rooms, air-conditioned.

Thani, 4/1 Chuenmanka Road, Amphoe Sungai Kolok, Tel: 611046. 72 rooms, air-conditioned.

Un Un, 183/1-2 Pracha Viwat Road, Amphoe Sungai Kolok, Tel: 611058. 48 rooms, air-conditioned.

PHANGNGA

Lak Muang, 1/2 Petchkasem Road, Tel: 411125. 26 rooms, air-conditioned.

Padoang, 22-24 Tambol Takua-Pa. 32 rooms.

Rak Phangnga, Petchkasem Road. 36 rooms.

Rattanapong, Petchkasem Road. 30 rooms.

Takua-Pa, 178/6-8 Tambol Takua-Pa. 27 rooms.

Tan Prasert, 23/1-2 Tambol Takua-Pa. 30 rooms.

PHATTHALUNG

Hoh Fah, 56-58 Posa-ard Road, Tel: 611045. 42 rooms, air-conditioned.

Kink Fah, 210/1-2 Rames Road. 27 rooms.

Phatthalung 2, Tambol Khoohasawan. 26 rooms.

PHUKET

Bungalow Nai Harn, Had Nai Narn. 100 rooms.

Domrong, 52 Luang Poh Wat Chalong Road, Tel: 211704. 85 rooms, air-conditioned.

Imperial, 52 Phuket Road, Tambon Talat Yai, Tel: 212311. 41 rooms, air-conditioned.

Kata Tropicana (Bungalow), Had Kata, (Phuket Office; 64/11 Krung Thep Road, Tel: 211606). 63 rooms.

Kata Villa, Had Kata. (Phuket Office, 2 Krabi Road, Tel: 211014). 20 rooms.

Patong Beach, 96/1 Pisit Road, Had Patong, (Phuket Office, 55 Phuket Road, Tel: 211426). 104 rooms, air-conditioned.

Pearl, 42 Montri Road, Tel: 211091, (Bangkok reservation, 1035/4 Pleonchit Road, Tel: 2516527).

Phuket Cabana (Bungalow), Had Patong, (Phuket Office, 63 Phuket Road, Tel: 211932. 29 rooms.

Phuket Island, 73/1 Rasada Road, Tel: 211421, (Bangkok reservation, Tel: 2515989. 194 rooms, air-conditioned. Conference from for 300 persons.)

Phuket Merlin Hotel, 158/1 Jawaraj Road, 220 rooms, air-conditioned, Tel: 211618.

Phuket Sin Thavee, 89 Phang-nga Road Tel: 211186. 139 rooms.

Rawai Bungalows, Wiset Road, Tambon Rawai, Tel: 211205 (Bangkok reservation, Tel: 5855860). 30 rooms.

Roong Roje Resort, 14 Vesed Road, Tel: 211066, (Phuket Office, 129 Phang-nga Road, Tel: 211848) (Bangkok reservation, 96/9 Chakapadipong Square, Larn Luang, Tel: 2814345). 40 rooms.

Sampam Inn, Ban Sapam, (Phuket Office, 96 Yaowaraj Road, Tel: 211440). 22 rooms.

Sea View (Bungalow), 3 Had Patong, (Phuket Offices 351/1 Yaowaraj Road, Tel: 211346). 27 rooms.

Thavorn, 74 Rasada Road, Tel: 211333. 200 rooms, air-conditioned.

PRACHUAP KHIRI KHAN
AND HUA HIN BEACH RESORT

Chatchai, 59/1-3 Petchkasem Road, Amphoe Hua Hin. 35 rooms, air-conditioned.

Damrong, 46 Petchkasem Road, Talat Chatchai, Hua Hin, Tel: 511574. 30 rooms, air-conditioned.

HUA HIN Railways, 1 Damnoenkasem Road, Hua Hin, Tel: 511012, (Bangkok reservation, Tel: 2230341 Ext. 223). 85 rooms, air-conditioned.

Namsin, 40/8-10 Petchkasem Road, Hua Hin, Tel: 511051. 20 rooms.

Prakarn Siri, Amphoe Pranburi. 84 rooms.

Saflom, Hua Hin Beach, Tel: 511890, (Bangkok reservation, Tel: 2515735). 46 rooms, air-conditioned.

Suksun, 131 Soosuek Road, Amphoe Muang, Tel: 510131. 92 rooms.

Supamit, 19 Amnuaysin Road. Tel: 511208. 36 rooms.

Tessaban Bungalow, Chaitalay Road, Tel: 510157. 36 rooms.

RANONG

Asia, Ruangraj Road. 51 rooms.

Charoen Sook, Ruangraj Road. 51 rooms.

Rattanasin, Ruangraj Road, 44 rooms.

Sin Ranong, Ruangraj Road. 104 rooms, air-conditioned.

Sook Somboon, Tambol Bangrin. 36 rooms.

Suriyanant, Ruangraj Road. 31 rooms.

Thara, 2/2 Petchkasem Road, Tel: 811510. 65 rooms, air-conditioned.

SONGKHLA

Rado, 59 Sanehanusorn Road, Hat Yai, Tel: 245266. 96 rooms, air-conditioned. Conference room for 40 persons.

Railways, 1 Dhamnoon Witee Road, Hat Yai, Tel: 244766. 46 rooms, air-conditioned. Conference for 200 persons.

Sakol, 47-8 Sanehanusorn Road, Hat Yai, Tel: 245256. 91 rooms, air-conditioned.

Samila, 1/11 Rajdamnoen Road, Samila beach, Tel: 311289. 75 rooms, air-conditioned.

SATUN

Rian Thong, 124/1 Samantapradit Road. 25 rooms.

Satun Thani, Tambol Piman. 50 rooms.

Udom Sook, Tambol Piman. 33 rooms.

SURAT THANI

Chao Koh, Koh Samui, (Bangkok reservation, Tel: 2512305. 12 motels, 10 bungalows.)

Kong Meng, Tambol Talad. 40 rooms.

Muang Thong, 282/6-10 Na Muang Road, Tel: 272960. 180 rooms, air-conditioned. Conference room for 50 persons.

Phanfah, 247/5 Na Muang, Tel: 272287. 57 rooms.

Surat, Tambol Talad. 40 rooms.

Tapee, 100 Chonkasem Road, Tel: 272575. 120 rooms, air-conditioned.

TRANG

Bungalow Caesar, Amphoe Muang. 27 rooms.

Koteng, Rama 6 Road, Tel: 218148. 56 rooms, air-conditioned.

Nara, Amphoe Muang. 34 rooms.

Queen's, 85-89 Visetkul Road, Tel: 218522. 150 rooms, air-conditioned.

Sahathai, Amphoe Muang. 30 rooms.

Trang, 134/2-5 Visetkul Road, Tel: 218229. 64 rooms, air-conditioned.

YALA

Fah Un Roong, 130 Chantarothai Road, Amphoe Betong. 38 rooms.

Hua Un, 352/1 Siriroj Road, Tambol Satang, Tel: 212771. 47 rooms, air-conditioned.

Keng Thai, 33 Chaya chavalit Road, Amphoe Betong. 32 rooms.

Sri Yala, 20 Chai Charas Road, Tel: 212170. 91 rooms, air-conditioned.

Tepvimarn, 31-37 Sri Bamroong Road, Tel: 212796. 84 rooms, air-conditioned.

Un Un, 352/1 Siriroj Road, Tambol Satang. 47 rooms.

EMBASSIES IN BANGKOK

Argentine Embassy, 5th Floor, Thaniya Bldg., 62 Silom Road, Tel: 2346911-3. Office Hours: 8.30 a.m.-1.00 p.m.

Austrian Embassy, 14 Soi Nandha off Soi Attakarnprasit, Sathorn Tai Road, Tel: 286-3011, 286-3037.

Austrian Embassy, 3rd Floor, Maneeya Bldg., 518/2 Ploenchit Road, Tel: 2528327, 2529781. Office Hours: 8.00 a.m.-2.00 p.m. (Mon to Fri) 8.00 a.m.-1.00 p.m. (Thurs) 3.00 p.m.-5.30 p.m.

Belgium Embassy, 44 Soi Phya Pipat, Silom Road, Tel: 2330840, 2330841. Office Hours: 8.30 a.m.-1.00 p.m.

Bangladesh Embassy, 28 Soi 43, Sukhumvit Road, Tel: 391-2804, 391-8070.

Brazilian Embassy, PIM Bldg., 8/1 Sukumvit Soi 15, Bangkok 11. (Ruamchai) Office Hours: 8.30 a.m.-4.00 p.m. Tel: 2526043.

British Embassy, 1031 Ploenchit Road, Tel: 2527161-9. Office Hours: 8.00 a.m.-4.30 p.m.

The Embassy of the People's Republic of Bulgaria, Rm. 609, 6th Flr. Summit Bldg., 197/1 Silom Road, Tel: 2330087. Office Hours: 8.30 a.m.-3.00 p.m.

Burmese Embassy, 132 Sathorn Nua Road, Tel: 2332237, 2342258. Office Hours: 8.30 a.m.-12.30 p.m., 1.00 p.m.-4.30 p.m. (Mon to Thurs), 8.30 a.m.-12.00 noon, 1.00 p.m.-5.00 p.m. (Fri).

Canadian Embassy, 11th Floor, Boonmitr Bldg., 138 Silom Road, Tel: 2341561-8. Office Hours: 8.00 a.m.-4.30 p.m. (Mon to Fri).

Chinese Embassy, Capital Mansion, 1371, Phaholyothin Road, Tel: 2797075. Office Hours: 8.00 a.m.-12.00 p.m., 1.00 p.m.-4.30 p.m.

Czechoslovakian Embassy, 7th Floor, Silom Bldg., R. 705. 197/1 Silom Road, Tel: 2341922, 2334535. Office Hours: 8.00 a.m.-3.00 p.m.

Danish Embassy, 10 Soi Attakarn Prasit, Sathorn Tai Road, Tel: 2863930, 2863932, 2863936. Office Hours: 8.00 a.m.-1.00 p.m. (Mon to Fri).

Egyptian Embassy, 49 Soi Ruam Rudee, Ploenchit Road, Tel: 2526139, 2527767. Office Hours: 9.00 a.m.-2.30 p.m.

Finnish Embassy, 3rd floor, Vithayu Place, 89/17 Wireless Road, Tel: 252-3636, 252-3637.

French Embassy, Customs House Lane, Tel: 2340950-56. Office Hours: 8.00 a.m.-1.30 p.m.

German Embassy, 9 Sathorn Tai Road, Tel: 2864223-27. Office Hours: 8.00 a.m.-1.00 p.m.

Indian Embassy, 46 Soi Prasarnmit, Sukhumvit 23, Tel: 2335065. Office Hours: 8.30 a.m.-12.30 p.m., 1.00 p.m.-4.00 p.m.

Indonesian Embassy, 600-602 Petchburi Road, Tel: 2523135-9. Office Hours: 7.30 a.m.-12.00 noon, 1.00 p.m.-4.00 p.m.

Iranian Embassy, 9th Floor, Shell House, 140 Wireless Road, Tel: 2514925, 2510205. Office Hours: 8.30 a.m.-4.00 p.m.

Israeli Embassy, 31 Soi Lang Suang, Ploenchit Road, Tel: 2523131-4. Office Hours: 8.00 a.m.-3.30 p.m. (Mon to Thurs) 8.00 a.m.-3.00 p.m. (Fri).

Italian Embassy, 92 Sathorn Nua Road, Tel: 2349718, 2349230. Office Hours: 8.30 a.m.-1.30 p.m.

Japanese Embassy, 1674 New Petchburi Road, Tel: 2526151-9. Office Hours: 8.30 a.m.-12.00 noon.

Korean Embassy, 28/1 6th Floor, Phraphavit Bldg., Surasak Road, Tel: 2340723-6. Office Hours: 8.30 a.m.-12.00 a.m., 2.00 p.m.-5.00 p.m.

Embassy of the (Lao) People's Democratic Republic, 193 Sathorn Tai Road, Tel: 2860010, 2863362. Office Hours: 8.00 a.m.-12.00 noon, 2.00 p.m.-4.30 p.m.

Malaysian Embassy, 35 Sathorn Tai Road, Tel: 2861390-2, 2867769. Office Hours: 8.30 a.m.-12.30 p.m., 2.00 p.m.-4.30 p.m.

The Consulate of Monaco, 3rd Flr. Nailert Bldg., 888 Petchburi Road, Tel: 2528106 Ext. 46. Office Hours: 9.00 a.m.-12.00 noon, 2.00 p.m.-4.00 p.m.

Nepalese Embassy, 189 Soi Puengsuk, Sukhumvit Soi 71, Tel: 3917240. Office Hours: 8.00 a.m.-12.00 noon, 1.30 p.m.-4.30 p.m.

Netherlands Embassy, 106 Wireless Road, Tel: 2526103-5. Office Hours: 8.00 a.m.-2.30 p.m. (Mon, Wed, Thurs, Fri), 8.00 a.m.-12.30 p.m. (Tues), 2.00 p.m.-5.00 p.m.

New Zealand Embassy, 93 Wireless Rd. Tel: 251-8165.

Norwegian Embassy, 20 Floor, Chockchai Bldg., Sukhumvit Road, Tel: 3921164, 3921160. Office Hours: 9.00 a.m.-2.45 p.m.

Pakistan Embassy, 31 Soi Nana Nua (3), Sukhumvit Road, Tel: 2527036-8. Office Hours: 8.00 a.m.-3.30 p.m.

Peru Consulate, Louis T. Leonowens Bldg., 723 Siphya Road, Tel: 2335910-7, 2345840. Office Hours: 8.30 a.m.-12.00 noon.

Philippines Embassy, 760 Sukhumvit Road, opposite Soi 47, Tel: 3910008, 3910211. Office Hours: 8.00 a.m.-12.00 noon, 1.00 p.m.-5.00 p.m.

Polish Embassy, 61 Soi Prasanmit Soi 23, Sukhumvit Road, Tel: 3910668, 3912356. Office Hours: 8.00 a.m.-2.00 p.m.

Portuguese Embassy, 26 Bush Lane, Tel: 2340372, 2342123. Office Hours: 8.30 a.m.-1.30 p.m.

The Embassy of the Socialist Republic of Romania, 39 Soi 10 Sukhumvit Road, Tel: 2528515. Office Hours: 8.30 a.m.-2.30 p.m. (Mon to Fri) 8.30 a.m.-12.00 noon (Sat).

Saudi Arabia Embassy, 138 Silom Road, 10th Floor, Boonmitr Bldg., Tel: 2337941-2. Office Hours: 8.30 a.m.-2.00 p.m. (Mon to Fri)

Singapore Embassy, 129 Sathorn Tai Road, Tel: 2862111, 2861433. Office Hours: 8.30 a.m.-12.00 noon, 1.00 p.m.-4.30 p.m.

Spanish Embassy, 104 Wireless Road, Tel: 2526112, 2528368. Office Hours: 8.30 a.m.-1.30 p.m.

Sri Lanka Embassy, 7th Nai Lert Bldg., 87 Sukhumvit Road, Soi 5, Tel: 2518534, 2524164. Office Hours: 8.30 a.m.-12.00 noon, 1.00 p.m.-4.45 p.m.

Swedish Embassy, 11th floor, Boonmitr Bldg. 138 Silom Road, Tel: 234-3891-2, 233-0295.

Switzerland Embassy, 35 North Wireless Road, Off Ploenchit Road, Tel: 2528992-4, Office Hours: 8.00 a.m.-4.00 p.m.

Turkish Embassy, 153/2 Soi Mahadlek Luang 1, Rajdamri Road, Tel: 251-2987-8.

Union of Soviet Socialist Republic Embassy, 108 Sathorn Nua Road, Tel: 2349824, 2342012. Office Hours: 7.30 a.m.-4.15 p.m. (Mon), 7.30 a.m.-3.13 p.m. (Tues to Fri).

United States of America Embassy, 95 Wireless Road, Tel: 2525040-9. Office Hours: 7.30 a.m.-12.00 noon, 1.00 p.m.-4.30 p.m.

Yugoslavia Embassy, 15 Soi 61, Sukhumvit Road, Tel: 3914858, Office Hours: 8.30 a.m.-2.30 p.m.

Vatican Holy See. Apostolic Nunciature, 217 Sathorn Tai Road, Tel: 2339109, 2357269. Office Hours: 8.30 a.m.-1.30 p.m. (Mon to Fri).

Bangladesh Embassy, 4th Floor, Pata Tanakit Bldg., 183 Sukhumvit Road, Soi 43, Tel: 2524058-9, 2511131, 2525160 Ext. 145, 149. Office Hours: 8.30 a.m.-12.30 p.m., 1.00 p.m.-4.30 p.m.

Dominican Consulate, 92/6 Changwattana Road, Laksee, Bangkaen, Tel: 5793537, 5791130. Office Hours: 9.00 a.m.-1.00 p.m.

The Consulate General of Hellenic Republic (Greece), 3rd Floor, President Travel Service Bldg., 412/8-9 Siam Square, Rama I Road, Tel: 2521681-6. Office Hours: 9.00 a.m.-12.00 noon, 1.30 p.m.-3.00 p.m.

The Consulate of the Republic of Iraq, 27-29 Anuwong Road, Tel: 2229353, 2220753. Office Hours: 8.30 a.m.-2.00 p.m.

Vietnamese Embassy, 83/1 Wireless Road, Tel: 2517203, 2515836-7. Office Hours: 8.30 a.m.-4.30 p.m. (Mon to Sat).

AIRLINE OFFICES IN BANGKOK

Aeroflot Soviet Airlines, 7 Silom Rd. Reservation & Ticketing: Tel. 2336965-7. Airport: Tel. 2860190 Ext. 111.

Air France, 3 Patpong Rd. Ticketing: Tel. 2337100-19 Ext. 248, 258, 268. Reservation: Tel. 2347901. Airport: Tel. 2860190 Ext. 113, 114.

Air India, 287 Silom Rd. Ticketing: Tel: 2338950-4 Ext. 156-8. Reservation: Tel. 2347558, 2334525. Airport: Tel: 2860090 Ext. 121, 122.

Air Canada, 1053 New Road, Tel: 234-5593. Airport Tel. **286-0190 Ext. 293, 294.**

Air Lanka, 62/1-4 Silom Road, Tel. 2349850-5. Airport: 2860190 Ext. 332.

Air New Zealand, Rajaprasong Corner, 133/19 Rajaprasong, Tel. 2529871. Airport: 2860090 Ext. 145

Alia Royal Jordanian Airlines, Yada Building, 56 Silom Road, Ticketing Tel. 235-3970-9.

Alitalia, 138 Silom Rd. Tel. 2334000-4. Reservation: Tel. 2345253, 2345257. Airport: Tel. 2860190 Ext. 132.

Bangladesh Biman, Ground & 6th Floor Chongkolnee Bldg., 56 Surawong Rd. Tel. 2336178 Airport: Tel. 2860190 Ext. 25

British Airways, 133/19 Rajaprasong Tel. 2529871-9. Airport: Tel. 2860190 Ext. 144, 145.

Burma Airways, 208-208/1 Surawong Rd. Tel. 2349692, 2333052. Airport: Tel. 2860190 Ext. 266.

Canadian Pacific Airways Ltd, c/o Thai Airways International, Boonmitr Bldg., 138 Silom Rd. Tel. 2343110-9. Reservation: Tel. 2343111-9 ext CP AIR 168, 169.

Cathay Pacific Airways, 1 Silom Road, Tel. 233-1544-8, 233-6105-9, Airport Tel. 286-0190 Ext. 156.

China Airlines, Siam Center Rama I Rd. Ticketing: Tel. 2519656-9. Reservation: Tel. 2521748-9. Visa Section: Tel. 25179780. Airport: Tel. 2860190 Ext. 160, 5237300.

Delta Airlines G.S.A. Getz Corp., 1/2 Convent Road, Tel. 2334500-3.

Egyptair, 120 Silom Road, Ticketing & Reservation: Tel. 233-7601-3. Airport Tel. 286-0190 Ext. 274.

Look closer at what Thailand has to offer you with an insider.

*T*hailand has so many places off-the-beaten-track. To enjoy travelling in this country you need an insider—someone who knows all the right connections to the best places.

When you don't have much time, he makes sure you get the most out of your trip by taking you to all the best places on the "Around Thailand Trip" that includes Chiang Mai, the charming 13th century capital city of the North.

And if, like many travellers who are charmed into extending their stay in the North, you will love the special " Chiang Mai Trip" and the surrounding areas.

For those who enjoy nature, the jungle setting of the "River Kwai Village" with adventurous excursions into areas of caves and waterfalls is an exhilarating trip.

If you're working your way south towards Malaysia and beyond, don't miss the opportunity of taking the " Bangkok-Singapore Overland Trip" that takes you through the scenic wonders of Southern Thailand.

These trips are offered with guaranteed departures by Diethelm Travel.

Diethelm Travel — a knowledgeable insider on the unusual places to visit in Thailand.

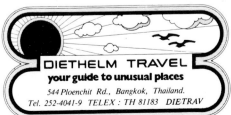

Above Bangkok

The 27-storey tower is a promise of the best
of Bangkok. The Ambassador style of living that is
reflected in spacious guest rooms and lavish suites.
Where the efficiency of service and the warmth of
hospitality is as sweeping as the view from every
window. And where eleven specialty restaurants
and a fine collection of bars and nightspots put
a lot of pleasure into every food and fun occasion.
800 guest rooms and suites □ Spanish- Continental,
Thai, Japanese, Chinese and Seafood restaurants, plus
coffee shops and snack bars. □ Three cosy bars and a
lively nightclub. □ Conference rooms for 20 to 2,000
delegates. Full support facilities including simultaneous
translation. □ Arcades of 50 shops and service stores.
□ Health club, sauna and 25-metre swimming pool.

The Ambassador

Hotel and Convention Centre

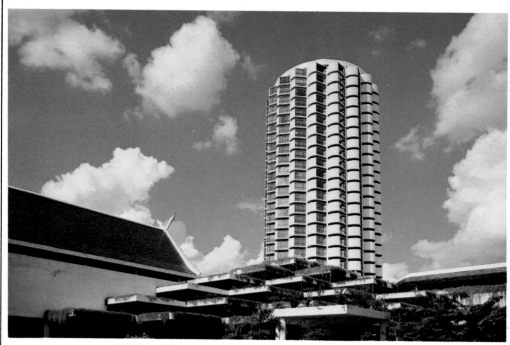

Soi 11, Sukhumvit Road, Bangkok, Thailand. Tel : 251-0404
Cables : AMTEL BANGKOK. TH 82910

For reservations : Loews Representation Inc, world wide.

Finnair, 2nd Floor, Panunee Bldg., 518/3 Ploenchit Rd. Tel. 2510393 Ext. 242, 243, 244. Airport: Tel. 2860190 Ext. 273, 274.

Garuda Indonesian Airways, 944/10 Rama 4 Rd. Reservation: Tel. 2330981-2. Airport: Tel. 2860190 Ext. 170, 171.

Gulf Air, 134/1-2 Silom Road, Tel: 235-6510-3.

Iraqi Airways, 981 Silom Road, (Hyatt Rama Hotel) Tel. 2341010 Ext. 1128. Airport: Tel. 2860190 Ext. 273.

Japan Airlines, Patpong Rd. Tel. 2349105-19. Reservation Ext. 125, 153. Ticketing Ext. 134, 135, 136. Airport: Tel. 2860190 Ext. 135, 136, 137.

KLM Royal Dutch Airlines, 2 Patpong Rd. Tel. 2335150-60. Reservation Ext. 36-38. Ticketing Ext. 31-33. Airport: Tel. 2860090 Ext. 191.

Korean Airlines, Rama IV Rd. (Dusit Thani Bldg.,) Tel. 2349283-9. Reservation Ext. 21-25. Ticketing Ext. 31-33. Airport: Tel. 2860190 Ext. 222, 233.

Kuwait Airways Corp., c/o Inter-Mart Co., Ltd (GSA) 4th Flr., IBM Tower, 1 Silom Rd. Tel. 2336657-8. Airport: Tel. 2860190 Ext. 388, 339.

Lot Polish Airlines, 5th Floor Dusit Thani Bldg., Rama IV Rd. Tel. 2331765. Airport: Tel. 2860190 Ext. 274.

Lufthansa German Airlines, 981 Silom Rd. Ticketing & Reservation (Hyatt Rama Hotel) Tel. 2341350-9. Airport: Tel. 2860190 Ext. 211, 213.

Malaysian Airlines System, c/o M.A.F. Bldg., 42/1 Suriwong Rd. Ticketing: Tel. 2349795-9. Reservation: Tel. 2349790-4. Airport: Tel. 2860190 Ext. 288, 5237270.

Pakistan International Airlines, Thai Style Bldg., Surawong Rd. Ticketing & Reservation: Tel. 2342961-4. Airport: Tel. 2860190 Ext. 129.

Pan American World Airways, Siam Center, 965 Rama I Rd. Reservation: Tel. 2522121-9. Ticketing: Tel. 2522131-40. Airport: Tel. 2860190 Ext. 231, 234.

Philippine Airlines, 1st-3rd Floor Chongkolnee Bldg., Reservation: Tel. 2332350-2 (1st Floor) Airport: Tel. 2860190 Ext. 190, 191.

Northwest Orient Airlines, 1st Floor of Siam Center, 965 Rama I Rd. Tel. 2519652-4. Reservation Ext. 3. Ticketing Ext. 1, 8. Airport: Tel. 2860190 Ext. 273, 274.

Qantas Airways, 14-8 Patpong Rd. Tel. 2344951-5, 2336114. Reservation: Tel. 2338701-5. Airport: Tel. 2860190 Ext. 220.

Royal Brunei Airlines, c/o Thai Airways International, Silom Rd. Ticketing: Tel. 2343111-9 c/o Thai Airways International, 89 Vipavadee Rangsit Rd. Reservation: Tel. 5110821. Ticketing: Tel. 5110121 Ext. 168, 169. Airport: Tel. 2860190 Ext. 273, 274, 150.

Royal Nepal Airlines, 8-8/1-2 Thai House Bldg., Silom Rd. Reservation: Tel. 2333921-4. Airport: Tel. 2860190 Ext. 152.

Sabena Belgian World Airlines, Ground Floor of Narai Hotel, 222 Silom Rd. Tel. 2335940-1. Airport: Tel. 2860190 Ext. 273, 274.

SAS Scandinavian Airlines System, 412 Rama I Rd. Tel. 2524181. Airport: Tel. 5236121 Ext. 134.

Saudi Arabian Airlines, Grd. Flr., Peninsula Hotel, 295/8 Surawong Rd. Tel. 2343910-9, 2338479.

Singapore Airlines, 62/1-4 Silom Rd. Ticketing: Tel. 235-1580-9. Reservation: Tel: 235-1570-9.

Swiss Air Transport, 1 Silom Rd. Tel. 2332930-4. Reservation: Tel. 2332935-8. Airport: Tel. 2860090 Ext. 225.

Tarom Remarian Air Transport, c/o Market Holdings Co. (GSA), 380 Wanner Bldg., 119 Mahaesak Road, Tel. 2343641-2.

Thai Airways, 6 Larn Luang Rd. Tel. 2811633, 2827151. Reservation: Tel. 2811626, 2811093. Weekends and Holidays: Tel. 2811737, 2811989, 2811626, 2811633. Airport: Tel. 5236201 Ext. 290.

Thai Airways International, 89 Vipavadee Rangsit Rd. Tel. 5110121. Ticketing: Tel. 5110121, Ext. 168, 169. Reservation: Tel. 5110821, 5112340. Airport: Tel. 2860190 Ext. 273, 274.

Trans Mediterranean Airways, 8th Flr., Wanglee Bldg., 297 Suranongse Road, Tel. 2341700, 2332408, Airport: Tel. 2860090 Ext. 169, 177.

Trans World Airlines, 64 Silom Rd. c/o Anglo Thai Bldg. Tel. 2331900, 2331910. Ticketing & Reservation Ext. 193, 194, 195. Airport: Tel. 2860190 Ext. 191, 195.

Union De Transports Aeriens, 3 Patpong Rd. Tel. 2337100-19. Ticketing Ext. 18, 28, 38. Reservation Ext. 22, 33, 44. Airport: Tel. 2860090 Ext. 262.

United Airlines, World Travel Service, Siam Center, 965 Rama I Rd. Tel. 2514928-32, 2513581.

BANKS IN BANGKOK

Banking Hours: Monday to Friday 8:30 a.m. to 3:30 p.m.

Asia Trust Bank, 80–82 Anuwong Rd. Tel: 2222171.

Bangkok Bank Ltd., 9 Suapa Rd. Tel: 2222111.

Bangkok Bank of Commerce, 171 Suriwong Rd. Tel: 2342930.

Bank for Agriculture, Mansion 1 Rajadamnoen Klang Ave. Tel. 281-3622.

Bank of America NT B SA, Wanglee Bldg., 297 Surawong Rd. Tel: 2330930.

Bank Of Asia For Industry & Commerce Ltd., Samyek Charoen Krung, 601 New Rd. Tel: 2225111.

Bank Of Canton Ltd., 197/1 Silom Rd. Tel: 2347030.

Bank Of Korea, 16 Soi 20 Sukhumvit Rd. Tel: 3918605.

Bank of Tokyo, Thaniya Bldg. 62 Silom Road. Tel: 233-0790-8.

Bank of Ayudhua, Ltd., 550 Ploenchit Rd. Tel: 2528171, 252-8391.

Banque de l'Indochine Et de Suez, 142 Wireless Rd. Tel: 252-2111-9.

Bharat Overseas Bank Ltd., 221 Rajawong Rd. Tel: 2218181.

Bangkok Metropolitan Bank Ltd., Yukol 2 Rd. Tel: 2823281.

Chartered Bank, Saladaeng Circle. Rama IV Rd. Tel: 2340821.

Chase Manhattan Bank, 965 Rama I Rd. Siam Center Tel: 252-1141-9.

Four Seas Communications Bank Ltd., 231 Rajawong Rd. Tel: 2222161.

Government Housing Bank, 77 Rajadamnern Ave. Tel: 2815155.

Hong Kong and Shanghai Banking Corp., Siam Center, 965 Rama I Rd. Tel: 2513252.

International Commerical Bank Of China, 95 Suapa Rd. Tel: 2218121.

Krung Thai Bank, 250 Yawaraj Rd. Tel: 2220131.

Laem Thong Bank Ltd., Opp. Phitphan Phanich Bldg., 289 Surawong Rd. Tel: 2339730.

Mercantile Bank Ltd., 63 Silom Rd. Tel: 2335996.

Mitsui Bank Ltd., Boon-Mit Bldg., 138 Silom Rd. Tel: 2343841

Siam City Bank Ltd., 13 Anuwong Rd. Tel: 2220161.

Siam Commercial Bank Ltd., 1060 New Petchburi Rd. Tel: 251-9111-30.

Thai Danu Bank Ltd., 393 Silom Rd. Tel: 2339160.

Thai Development Bank Ltd., 20 Yukol 2 Rd. Tel: 2813533.

Thai Farmers Bank, 142 Silom Rd. Tel: 2347050.

Thai Military Bank Ltd., 34 Phayathai Rd. Tel: 282-2727.

Union Bank Of Bangkok Ltd., 624 Yawaraj Rd. Tel: 2334740.

United Malayan Banking Corp., 3rd Floor of Hua Kee Bldg., 107–9 Suapa Rd. Tel: 2219191.

Wanglee Bank, Cathay Trust Bldg., 1st Floor, 1016 Rama IV Rd. Tel: 2332111.

Index/Glossary

A

Air travel to Thailand 290-91
    See also Thai Airways
Aisawan Thi Paya: Thai-style
    pavilion on the lake at Bang
    Pa-in 116
Akha: hilltribe of North Thailand
    44, 168, 185, *186*, 186
Amarin Vinichai Hall: audience
    hall in Grand Palace of
    Bangkok used for coronations
    65
Amnat Charoen: agricultural
    village in the Northeast 211
Amporn Gardens of Bangkok 80
Amulets 35, *79*, 79, *142*, *238*
Ancient City: billed as the "world's
    largest outdoor museum" 107-
    108, *107*
Ang Sila ("Stone Basin"): town on
    the Eastern Gulf close to Chon
    Buri *231*, 231
Angkor: ruins of ancient Khmer
    temple complex in northwest
    Cambodia, center of Ancient
    Khmer kingdom flourishing
    from around the 10th to 13th
    centuries A.D.
        Angkor Wat: 17, 199
            replica of 68
        Angkor Thom 206
Anna Leonowens: Englishwoman
    at the 19th-century court of
    King Mongkut who wrote *An
    English Governess in the Court
    of Siam* 24, 25
Antiques *84*, 299
    at Chiang Mai 171
Ao Luk: town in South Thailand
    275
Apsara (divinity) 139
Arboretum:
    at Chiang Mai 165
    in Muak Lek Valley 203
Archaeology:
    Ayuthaya ruins and restoration
        21, 110-115
    Ban Chiang, diggings at 16, 91,
        198, *214*, 214-215
    Museum, Silapakorn
        University 73
    Neolithic remains and museum
        in Kanchanaburi 124
    Northern kingdoms 177
    Phayao: remains from Bronze
        Age 184
Architecture:
    of the Ayuthaya period 230,
        280
    ancient Thai religions 145
    Buddhist 137
    cho-fa (upturned eave) 230
    classical Thai, examples of
        Aisawan Thi Paya *116*, 116
        Dusit Maha Prasad 64
    Khmer *22-23*, *140*, *205*, *206*,
        207, *209*
    modernizing influences on 268
    of the Central Plains 132
    Sukhothai 17, 139
Area of Thailand (514,000 square
    kilometers) 12, 13
Arporn Phimok Prasad: "disrobing
    pavilion" of the king 64
Art
    Davaravati (6th-11th centuries)
        16

in Jim Thompson's Asian
    collection 94
main periods, *see* "National
    Museum" 74
Sukhothai 17, 137, 139
Asalaha Puja: ceremony marking
    beginning of Buddhist Lent
    (*Khao Pansa*) 297
Asoka: first Buddhist Indian
    emperor, (274-236 B.C.) 16
Astrologers 35
Ayuthaya: early Thai kingdom
    founded in 1350; modern town
    just north of Bangkok 110-115,
    113, *114*, *115*
        art of 74, 280
        history of 20-21, 110, 163
        map of *110*

B

Bamboo: floating to market *122*
Bamrung Muang Road 77
Ban Amphur 225
Ban Ang Thong (or Ban Hna
    Thon): main town in the island
    of Koh Samui 235
Ban Bang Rok (South) 279
Ban Chiang: village and site of
    prehistoric burial ground in the
    Northeast, believed to be oldest
    remains yet discovered of
    agrarian, Bronze Age
    civilization 16, 91, *198*, 199,
    214, 214-215
Ban Don: small fishing port in the
    South
Ban Houei Sai: Laotian town
    opposite Chiang Khong
    (North) 189-190, *189*
Ban Keo: town near Neolithic
    diggings and museum in
    Kanchanaburi Province 124
Ban Pae: port on Eastern Gulf
    engaged in shrimp fishing 239-
    240
Ban Pha Phrae: national park near
    Ban Pae (Eastern Gulf) 240
Ban Renu: a small weaving village
    in the Northeast 212
Ban Tak (North) 159
Ban Thong Agricultural Station
    (South) 275
Bang Pa-In: summer retreat of the
    royal family (Bangkok
    Surroundings) 116, *116*
Bang Saen: seaside resort (Eastern
    Gulf) 223, *232*, 232
Bang Sak Beach (South) 267
Bang Saphan (South) 259
Bangkok: Thailand's capital city
    with a population over 4
    million 54-105
        beginnings 21
        divisions of 59
        early city 24
        map of *60-61*
        northeast of 108-109
        north of 110
        southeast of 106-107
        surroundings, map of *106*
        west of 119-125
Bangrak Market, Bangkok *86*, 86-
    87
Banks:
    business hours 293
Baphuon: early Khmer style of art
    207
Bats at Tham Pha Thai Cave
    (North) 184
Beaches: (*See also* Cottages)

Bang Saen (Eastern Gulf *232*,
    232
Bang Sak (South) 267
Bang Saphan (South) 259
Hat Noparat Thara (South)
    234, *276*, 276
Hua Hin resort (South) 256,
    257
Khao Luk (South) *267*, 267
    on Koh Mau Nai (Eastern
        Gulf) 241
    on Koh Phi Phi (South) 277-
        278
    on Koh Samui (South) 265
    on Koh Sichang (Eastern Gulf)
        227, 240
Nuan Beach on Koh Larn
    (Eastern Gulf) 236
Pak Mong near Trang (South)
    277, 276
Palm Beach (Eastern Gulf) 234
Pattaya (Eastern Gulf) 234, *235*
    at Pranchuap Khiri Khan *258*
Phuket Island (South) 268-272,
    270
Red Cliff (Eastern Gulf) *233*
    on islands off Samae San
        (Eastern Gulf) 238
Songkhla *284*, *285*
Suan Wang Kaew resort
    (South) 240
Susarn Hoi (South) 276
YMCA, near Pattaya (Eastern
    Gulf) 237
Behavior in public 294
Beliefs: *See* Spirits and beliefs
Benchurong: five-color porcelain
    originally made in old China for
    the Thailand trade 118
Bhubing Palace: summer palace of
    King Bhumibol near Chiang
    Mai 166
Bhumibol Adulyadej: *See* King
    Rama IX
Bhumibol Dam (Yanhee Dam),
    North *159*, 159
Bibliography: Recommended
    Reading 299
Bird's nest soup: a culinary delicacy
    prized by the Chinese world
    over 249
        collection of bird's nests
            Pak Nam Chumphon
                260
            Koh Phi Phi 278
Boat rides: (*See also* Waterways
    and tours)
    to Koh Chang (Eastern Gulf)
        245
    Koh Samui (South) *264*, 265
    Kuang Kud Ku rapids on the
        Mekong 219
    Mae Kok from Tha Thon to
        Chiang Rai *181*, 182
    Mekong from Chiang Saen to
        Chiang Rai 189
    across the Mekong to Laos
        216, 216
    off Pak Nam Chumphon
        (South) 260
    Pattaya (Eastern Gulf) *236*, 236
    to Ranong islands (South) 261
    Samae San (Eastern Gulf) 238
    Songkhla islands (South) 286
Bodhi tree (also *Bo tree*): sacred
    tree of enlightenment in
    Buddhist teachings 282
Books on Thailand, recommended
    299
Boon: Laotian fair 217
Borompiman Hall at the Grand

Palace 65
Bot: chapel or main building in a
temple (wat) 145, 230
Botan: Thai writer 49
Boxing, Thai 100-101, 100, 101
Brahman: Hindu sect of the highest
caste, traditionally assigned to
priesthood 35, 36
god, Phra Isuan 77
Swinging Ceremony 77
Bridge on the River Kwai 122-124
124-125
British Council 87
Bronzeware 299
Buat naag: ordination ceremony for
a novitiate entering the
Buddhist monkhood
Buddha footprint: 259
Shrine of the Holy Footprint,
Saraburi 296
at Wat Kho Tum, Songkhla
(South) 286
Buddha images: See also National
Museum, 33, 73, 75, 107, 108,
126-127, 134, 136, 137, 138,
144, 180, 189, 203, 278, 280,
282, 286
Bronze Buddha, Viharn Phra
Mongkol Bopitr, Ayuthaya
112
bronze seated Buddha (500
years old), Wat Suan Tan,
Nan 192
bronze walking Buddha,
Sukhothai 139
Davaravati, Wat Na Phra
Meru, Ayuthaya 114
Emerald Buddha, Bangkok 21-
22, 66
in four postures (standing,
sitting, walking, reclining):
Wat Chetupon, Sukhothai
142
Wat Phra Si Iriyaboth,
Ayuthaya 137
gilded Buddha, Prasat
Phranomwan 205
gold mosaic Buddha depicted
in a boat, Wat Dhamma
Nimitr, Chon Buri 230
Golden Buddha, Wat Trimitr,
Bangkok 85
largest Buddha image in
Thailand: Reclining
Buddha, Wat Po, Bangkok
70
largest seated Buddha (Phra
Achana) Wat Si Chum,
Sukhothai 126-127, 142
Phra:
Achana 142
Buddha Chakyamuni 77
Buddha Chinaraj 145
Buddha Sihing 75
Buddhamon 159
Khew Thong Thip 192
Sae Tang Tamani 163
Sila 163
reclining Buddha:
Wat Koh Sireh, Phuket 271
Wat Lokaya, Sutha,
Ayuthaya 114
Wat Po, Bangkok 70
sleeping Buddha, Wat Kho
Tum, Songkhla 286
stucco Buddha, Wat Chedi
Chet Thaew, Si Satchanalai
144
standing Buddha, Wat Saphan
Hin, Ayuthaya 142-143
walking Buddha, Sukhothai 138

Buddhaisawan Chapel: See
National Museum
Buddhism 16, 33-34, 192
Hinayana 17, 33, 35
Lent 33, 297
monks 33, 174, 260, 262
nuns 231, 286
in Northeast 214
school:
Wat Narai Cheng Weng
(Northeast) 214
Wat Prathat Haripoonchai
(North) 174
Theravada 139
Buddhist Era (b.e.): begins with the
birth of Buddha in 543 b.c.;
1980 is 2522 b.e.
Buddhist sects in Thailand:
Dharmayuti (or Dhammayuti):
the minority in Thailand,
following a stricter
regimen, having over a
1,000 temples and about
10,000 monks
Mahanikhaya (Majority
School): majority sect having
about 25,000 temples and
200,000 monks
Bull fighting 281, 283, 283
Bung Borapet: seasonal lake
(Central Plains) 135
Burmese 13, 110, 112, 115, 120,
124, 151, 144, 160, 165, 179,
188, 233
border 158
temple 158
Business hours 292

C

Catholicism:
Church of the Immaculate
Conception, Chanthaburi
(South) 243, 243
The Rae (Northeast) 213
Caves:
Cave drawings, Khao Kien
(South) 273, 273
Chiang Dao Cave (North) 180,
181
Khao Luang Cave 256
Khao Pina (South) 278
Khao Wongse (Eastern Gulf)
241
on Koh Thalu (South) 274
on Koh Phi Phi 277-278
Phra Ngam Cave (North) 203
Silpa Caves, Yala (South) 286,
287
Tham Koo Ha Pimak 287
Suan Ku (South) 272
Tham Kung 125
Tham Lawd island (South) 273
Tham Nak island (South) 274
Tham Pha Thai (North) 183,
183
Tham Prakayang and temple
(South) 260
Tham Russi, Phangnga (South)
274
Wat Tham Lek Khaw Chaka,
cave monastery (Eastern
Gulf) 245
Wat Tham Pong Chang,
Phangnga (South) 275
Wat Thamwaram (South) 263
Celadon pottery: See Sawankhalok
pottery
Central Department Store,
Bangkok 89
Central Plain 127-145

history, agriculture and people
of 129-135
map of 128
monsoons 13
transport in 135
Ceremonies
funeral 36
ploughing 35, 70, 297
wedding 36
Chaiya: historical town in the
South, known also as a center
for Buddhist studies 262-263
Chakangrao: old town of Central
Plains 135-136
Chakri Day (6 April): holiday
commemorating the founding
of the Chakri dynasty 68, 297
Chakri dynasty: present dynasty
of Thailand ruling since the
1700s 21
See also Kings Rama I-IX
Chakri Maha Prasad: former royal
residence at the Grand Palace,
Bangkok 63, 64
Chama Dewi: princess believed to
have founded Lampang 160
Chandrakasem Palace: defensive
palace in Ayuthaya, built by
King Naresuan in the 16th
Century 111, 112
Chanthaburi: a gem-mining town
on the Eastern Gulf 242, 243,
242-243
Chantra Paisan Pavilion 118
Chao Lay (or "Sea Tribe"): a tribe
of sea gypsies not ethnically
related to Thais 271, 271
Chao Pau Khun Dan Temple 108
Chao Phya: Thailand's main river
13, 96, 99, 112, 113, 209, 233
Chao Phya Museum, Ayuthaya 115
Charoen Krung: New Road,
Bangkok 86, 87
Chedi: tiered, pointed, spirelike
pagoda 246-247
Golden Mount Chedi, Bangkok
115
Phra Pathom Chedi 120, 120
Wat Chedi Luang, Chiang Saen
189
Wat Chedi Sao Phra 161
Chess, Thai 241
Chiang Dao Cave (North) 181
Chiang Khan: a northeastern town
near the Thai-Lao border 219

Chiang Khong: district town in the
North 189
Chiang Mai: principal city of the
North, and Thailand's second
largest metropolis with a
population over one million
162-172
arboretum 165
first Thai settlers in 17
founding of 151
history to the present day
162-163
hotels and restaurants 172
map 162
museum 177
university 165
zoo 165
Chiang Rai: provincial capital of
the North 182, 184-188
Chiang Saen (North)
ancient town 188
art 74
bronze images 141
first Thai settlers 17
King Mengrai 151

327

DISTRIBUTORS

AUSTRALIA: Lonely Planet Publications, P.O. Box 88 South Yarra, Victoria 3141.

BENELUX: Elsevier Focus, Gebouw Rivierstaete, Amsteldijk 166, Amsterdam, Netherlands.

CANADA: See USA

DENMARK: Medicinsk Forlag ApS, Tranevej 2, 3650 Olstykke.

FRANCE: Librairie Armand Colin, 103 Boulevard Saint Michel, 75005 Paris.

HAWAII: APA Productions Hawaii Inc., 339 Saratoga Road, Suite 21, Honolulu 96815.

HONGKONG: Far East Media Ltd, 1102A–1104A, Watson's Estate, Block B, 11th Floor, Watson Road, Hong Kong.

INDIA: India Book Distributors, 107/108, Arcadia Building, 195, Nariman Point.

INDONESIA: N.V. Indoprom Co. (Indonesia) Ltd, SGV Building, 2nd Floor, JI Letjend S. Parman Kav. 56, Slipi, Jakarta Barat.

JAPAN: Charles E. Tuttle Co. Inc., 2–6, Suido I-chrome, Bunkyo-ku, Tokyo 112.

KOREA: Korea Britannica Corp., C.P.O. Box 690, Seoul 100.

MALAYSIA: MPH Distributors Sdn Bhd, 13, Jalan 13/6, Petaling Jaya, Selangor.

NEPAL: Saraswati Distributors P.O. Box 242, Kathmandu.

NEW ZEALAND: David Bateman Ltd. P.O. Box 65062, Mairangi Bay, Auckland 10.

PHILIPPINES: Print Diffusion Pacific Inc., Ground Floor, Bancom III Building, Corner Rada & Legazpi Sts., Legaspi Village, Makati, Metro Manila.

SINGAPORE: MPH Distributors (S) Pte Ltd., 116-D JTC Factory Building, Lorong 3, Geylang Square, Singapore 1438.

SRI LANKA: K.V.G. De Silva, 415 Galle Road, Colombo 4.

SWEDEN: Esselte Kartcentrum AB, Vasagatan 16, S 111 20 Stockholm.

SWITZERLAND: EMA-Handel AG, 4410 Liestal, Burghade 34, Basel 40–13 308.

UNITED KINGDOM: Roger Lascelles, 3 Holland Park Mansions; 16 Holland Park Gardens, London W14 8DY.

USA (Mainland); Sino Publishing Co., 745 Fifth Ave., New York, NY 10151.

WEST GERMANY & AUSTRIA: Geo Center, Honigwiesenstrasse 25, D7 Stuttgart 80, Postface 800830, West Germany.

THE NEW APPROACH
TO THE ART OF TRAVEL

Published by Apa Productions
No: 5, Lengkong Satu,
Singapore 1441
Telex: Apasin RS 36201

Available at leading book outlets
and hotel drugstores